GOD, GRACE
AND THE GOSPEL

A Study in St. Thomas, Calvin and McLeod Campbell

D1399974

DANIEL P. THIMELL

Aventine Press

Published by Aventine Press
55 E. Emerson St
Chula Vista CA 91911

ISBN: 978-1-59330-829-2

Printed in the United States of America.

Acknowledgments

This book represents a substantial revision of my doctoral thesis completed in 1992 at the University of Aberdeen, Scotland. As a tribute to those who contributed so much to my theological pilgrimage, what follows is a reproduction of my original acknowledgments of indebtedness to three very special persons. Although all three have since (alas!) passed from this earth into the nearer presence of God, their influence lives on and continues to bear fruit. I must also mention my gratitude for the expert editorial assistance of a former student, Vanessa Platek.

It has been a singular gift of God that I have not been permitted the luxury of devoting all my time to the study or library. Always, whether in Scotland or America, I have been given to share in Christ's ministry of Word and Sacrament. As I have stood in the pulpit, I have seen written upon the faces of the congregation a thousand tales, with one theme: for their brokenness, their hunger, their thirst are all the same yearning--a yearning that only the Spirit of God can name and only the Gospel can address. It has been my hope to discover afresh the astonishing news of the Gospel amid the ponderings of St. Thomas, the expostulations of Calvin, and the preaching of McLeod Campbell.

Thankfully, I have had guides far wiser than I. It was Professor Ray Anderson, my mentor at Westmont College, Santa Barbara, California and then Fuller Theological Seminary, who first stirred my soul with the conviction that the living God has taken our weakness, our condemnation, our godlessness into his own being and the life and death of his Son, so to heal us in the ontological depths of our being. At Aberdeen University, Scotland, Professor James Torrance's comprehensiveness of theological vision and persistent underscoring of the wonders of God's grace in the humanity of his Son have prodded me on to finish this thesis no matter how tempted I may have been to put it aside in favor of the more "practical" concerns of everyday parish life.

No words could articulate the happiness it has been to have a wife like Adrian at my side, whose unconditional love has taught me more than all else on earth about the living God and whose extravagant confidence in me has at last seen itself justified in the completion of this project.

Naturally, any and all imperfections and errors in this document are wholly my own.

CONTENTS

INTRODUCTION

Martin Buber recounts how a friend remonstrated with him about his use of the name of God. The friend said,

> How can you bring yourself to say 'God' time after time?...
> What you mean by the name of God is something above
> all human grasp and comprehension, but in speaking
> about it you have lowered it to human conceptualization.
> What word of human speech is so misused, so defiled, so
> desecrated as this! All of the innocent blood that has been
> shed for it has robbed it of its radiance. All the injustice
> that it has been used to cover has effaced its features.
> When I hear the highest called 'God', it sometimes
> seems almost blasphemous.

In reply Buber acknowledged the sorry record of human abuse of the divine name and yet wanted to know,

> When all madness and delusion fall to dust, when they
> stand over against Him in the loneliest darkness and no
> longer say 'He, He' but rather sigh 'Thou,' shout 'Thou,'
> all of them the one word, and when they add 'God', is it
> not the real God whom they all implore, the One Living
> God, the God of the children of man?"[1]

Despite the incredible audacity of daring to speak the name of God, speak it I must as one who is convinced that in the midst of my brokenness God has come to me in Jesus Christ preaching peace. I cannot say that one of God's holy seraphim has cleansed my speech of all theological impurities, but I undertake this investigation in the hope that it may shed some light on who this God is, who has opened his holy heart to us in

---

1 *The Eclipse of God*, Harper, New York, 1952, pp. 16f, cited in Ronald Gregor Smith, *The Doctrine of God*, Collins, Glasgow, 1970, pp. 22-23.

the suffering of Jesus Christ. What I want to know, more than anything, is what conception of God ought to underlie our theological systems.

Does the Godness of God lie in his absolute will, as St. Thomas Aquinas and John Calvin sometimes suppose, or is his inmost heart laid bare in his loving self-sacrifice in Christ? Thomas and Calvin, although in disparate ways and to varying degrees, separate the thought of the will of God from the self-revelation of God in and through the Son, and consequently find difficulty in maintaining that God is love in his inmost life.

In the course of this comparative study, we will seek to demonstrate that the great mistake has been to detach the concept of the will of God from the self-disclosure of God in Christ. Examination of two great thinkers of the Christian tradition shows how such an approach can jeopardize the freeness of God's grace in the following ways: (1) the freedom of God's grace in that it is *unrestricted* is lost in the respective doctrines of predestination framed by Aquinas and Calvin; (2) the freedom of God's grace in that it is *unmerited* is lost in Thomas' soteriology.

It is to McLeod Campbell's credit that he recognized that *there is no will in God that is not the will of the Father*. Our knowledge of God must be controlled by his self-disclosure in his Son. The major thesis of this study is that McLeod Campbell's insistence that the revelation of God in Christ determine our understanding of God's nature and will serves as an important corrective. When the Father is known through the Son, the character of God as gracious towards all people irrespective of merit or achievement is upheld. Moreover for Campbell, the will of God is nothing other than the expression of the fatherly heart of God in his longing for the restoration of his estranged children.

Our intention is not to interact with the history of interpretation of these theologians in the secondary literature, for two reasons: (1) it would distract us from our central aim, which is to compare them with each other and (2) the primary literature required in order to fulfill this task is already vast enough. Pursuant to our investigation, we will compare and contrast the various doctrines of God which lie behind differing understandings of grace and law in the theologies of St. Thomas, Calvin and McLeod Campbell in order to highlight the significance of Campbell's concern to interpret the nature of God in the light of revelation, viz., in terms of the centrality of the Father-Son relationship.

Particular attention will be devoted to the ways in which Aquinas and Calvin ground their doctrines of election in a will of God known outside of Christ, leading, it is argued, to a kind of "soteriological voluntarism" in which God is free to decree the redemption of some and the damnation of others from all eternity. Our use of the term "voluntarism" in connection with Aquinian theology is qualified by the recognition that Thomas is a realist who locates the eternal ideas in the divine nature. What is more, in the simplicity of the divine being, God's will never acts independently of his intellect which contemplates these ideas. God's will can only will the good.[2]

Nevertheless, he tells us, God's will is not determined to one good only.[3] And it is precisely here, we argue, that the rub comes. For all the wonderful things which Thomas can and does say about the love of God, when he turns his thoughts to the crucial arena of eternal destiny, the divine will seems to assume a certain primacy. God loves all people insofar as he wills some good to all. But, "he does not will every sort of good to each."[4] God can manifest his goodness as he sees fit among humanity. He wills to show his goodness to the predestined by mercifully sparing them, and to those whom he reprobates by justly punishing them. This, declares Thomas, "provides a key to the problem of why God chooses some and rejects others...His so willing is the sole ground."[5] Thus the freedom of grace in the sense of its *unrestrictedness* is absent from Thomas' theology.

Significantly, Jesus Christ is absent from the discussion of predestination thus far. The plans and intentions of God for the human race are derived by the Angelic Doctor, not from reflection upon God's self-unveiling in his Word-made-flesh, but from deductions based upon

---

2 Thomas Aquinas, *Summa Theologiae*, la.19,1 ad 3. We have relied upon the Blackfriars' edition of the *Summa Theologiae*, sixty volumes, London, Eyre and Spottiswoode, 1963-1976, henceforth. Future references to this work will eliminate the title, *Summa Theologiae*, and simply indicate part, question, article, and (if applicable) objection or reply. Other translations specified where used.

3 St. Thomas Aquinas, *On the Power of God*, trans. English Dominican Fathers, Burns, Oates and Washbourne, 1932, III, 15.

4 la.23, 3 ad 1.

5 la.23, 5 ad 3.

the metaphysic of final causality.[6] On this basis, he constructs a doctrine of providence wherein God directs all things toward an end.[7]

Predestination follows for Aquinas, as a corollary of providence.[8] Not until much later, in the *Tertia Pars*, does the predestination of Christ receive consideration, when Christ comes to carry out God's eternal decree of salvation.[9] But God could have decreed the redemption of the elect by other means.[10]

For Thomas, the purposes of God are not known in Christ; they are known in general terms by deductions derived from certain postulates about the Unmoved Mover, which doctrine itself has been constructed by extrapolation from the world of effects to the Uncaused First Cause. This presents a problem, we think, not only for his doctrines of election and of revelation, but also for his concept of God.

Although, thanks to his loyalty to Scripture and the Christian tradition, he never fully pursues this line of thinking, he occasionally comes precariously close to the notion that God is fundamentally a God of Power, of self-determined will[11] whose will reigns supreme over his intellect.

If the freeness of divine grace, in that it is *unrestricted*, is lost in Thomas' theology, so too is it lost in the fullest sense of grace being *unmerited*. While he wants to say that all is of grace, his concessions to notions of cooperative grace and merit would seem to deprive grace of its unconditional nature.

Here again, the will of God appears to assume a certain primacy. Finite humankind could not perform any work which put God in debt. No human act per se bears an inherent claim to merit from God. But God is free to ordain by his own will that a person "obtains from God, as a reward of his operation, what God gave him the power of operation for."[12]

So it is that for Aquinas, "co-operating grace" comes into action, enabling the soul to do good works as God wills and thereby to acquire

6 la.19; la.22.
7 la.23.
8 la.23, 3.
9 3a.24, 4.
10 3a.24, 4 ad 3.
11 la.19, 4.
12 la2ae.114, 1.

merit. "God does not justify us without us,"[13] and therefore a motion of free will on our part is required to produce meritorious works."[14] By means of such merits, one is able to obtain an increase of grace and in that way acquire more merit so that he increasingly qualifies for the merit of everlasting life.[15]

Yet, at the same time and somewhat inconsistently, everything depends on God's predestination. Thomas injects confusion into the concept of grace by expounding it in the language of merit. On the one hand, he wants to affirm that the whole of our justification belongs to grace,[16] while also, as we shall see, maintaining that humans must do their part, by preparing themselves, trying to rise up from sin, and exercising free will to accept grace.

Grace is a gift God chooses to grant in varying quantities, depending in part on the use a person makes of the "first grace." In this manner, grace becomes a means of acquiring merit and justification the process whereby, through human cooperation with grace, a person is moved to a state of justice. Law, grounded in the eternal law within the divine essence, stipulates the conditions under which grace may be received and the life the *viator* must lead if he wishes to remain in the state of grace.

Indeed, law, found in its various forms as divine law, natural law, ceremonial law, moral law, positive law, and so on, has as its proper effect to "make men good,"[17] so as to be ready to receive the beatific vision. This, law accomplishes in us with the help of grace, since God "builds us up by law and supports us by grace."[18] While the Old Law was able to carry humans a long way towards that goal, it could not make them perfectly fit to share in the *felicitatis aeternae*. For this, the grace conferred by Christ through the New Law is needed. Christ merits grace through his passion which is then bestowed upon us, at first freely, and then in cooperation with human action.

For Aquinas, grace is conditional upon fulfilling the requirements of the law, albeit with the help of grace. He was so concerned that

13 la2ae.111, 2 ad 2.
14 la2ae.111, 2; 114, 1 et 2.
15 la2ae.114, 4; 114, 5; 114, 8.
16 la2ae.111, 2 ad 2.
17 la2ae.92, 1.
18 la2ae.90, intro.

humankind experience a justification that really makes just that he directs our attention to human acts essential to the process of appropriating and actualizing this justification. But in this way our gaze is averted from the self-revelation of God in Christ and onto a product of his will grounded, not in Christ, but in his eternal law.

It appears to us that the mistake has been to detach the thought of the will of God from the self-disclosure of God in Christ, such that God can will a semi-pelagian system of salvation in which grace is separated from Christ and becomes a quasi-material, causal energy which can be merited through human acts in cooperation with an earlier bestowal of grace. But in this way it would seem that the very graciousness of grace, as God's unconditional self-giving, is called into question.

For Calvin and McLeod Campbell, salvation is by Christ *alone*, which is to say by grace alone, not by grace plus merit or even by grace producing merit. Grace is God's love in redemptive action, his self-giving in Christ. Calvin saw clearly that the nature of God was at stake in the reformation's dispute with Rome. Was God the God of conditional grace, who prescribed long penances prior to the bestowal of forgiveness? No, said Calvin, God in Christ is disclosed as unconditionally gracious in his self-giving in the humanity of his Son for the salvation of the world.

But this means that in framing a true doctrine of God, a right understanding of revelation is required. Thus, Calvin offers a vital corrective to medieval theology in his insistence on the Incarnation as the only possibility of the knowledge of God for fallen humanity. True, the hidden and incomprehensible God[19] "daily discloses himself in the whole workmanship of the universe."[20] Indeed, "he manifested himself to us through his works and in them he is to be sought by us."[21] But now, the sinfulness of human nature blinds our minds to this display of God's glory, "not because the revelation is obscure, but because we are

---

19 John Calvin, *Institutes of the Christian Religion*, two vols, (hereafter *Institutes*), ed. John T. McNeill, trans. Ford Lewis Battles, Philadelphia, Westminster Press, 1960, III.ii.1.

20 *Institutes*, I.v.1.

21 Calvin, *The Catechism of the Church of Geneva, that is, a Plan for Instructing Children in the Doctrine of Christ*, in *Calvin: Theological Treatises*, ed. J. K. S. Reid, Philadelphia, Westminster 1954, p. 93.

mente alienati."[22] This side of the Fall, natural revelation continues, but because of the darkness in our minds, there can be no natural theology. Nevertheless, God has given himself to be known in the flesh of the God-man.

> For Christ descended to us and first was humbled. Therefore, that our faith may arrive at the eternal divinity of Christ, we must start off from that knowledge which is nearer and easier. Thus some have justly said that by Christ-man we are led to Christ-God....[23]

It is the presupposition of this study that the *assumptio carnis* provides the proper starting point for framing a true doctrine of God and his will. In Christ alone, Calvin tells us, the otherwise invisible God is revealed to us. If we seek God elsewhere, we can only replace this true knowledge with an idol. In Jesus Christ God "shows us His righteousness, goodness, wisdom, power--in short, *His entire self.*"[24]

And when the will of God is interpreted in light of the self-revelation of God, grace is disclosed as nothing other than the *self-giving* of God. In this way, the freedom of grace in all its *unmeritedness* is grounded in the very being of God as unconditionally gracious.

Nonetheless, at times Calvin speaks as if he has forgotten his Christological hermeneutic, when he says that God cannot be known as he is in himself, but only as he has chosen to act toward us. It is not for mere mortals to question the secret will of God. In his maintenance of the double decree doctrine, Calvin departs from his basic insights regarding God's nature and will.

We find a fundamental ambiguity in his doctrine of God, for on the one hand, Calvin's God reigns in absolute sovereignty and the consignment

---

22 Commentary on I Corinthians 1:21, *The First Epistle of Paul the Apostle to the Corinthians*, trans. John W. Fraser, ed. David W. Torrance, Thomas F. Torrance, Grand Rapids, Michigan, 1960.

23 Commentary on John 20:28, *The Gospel According to St. John 11-21 and the First Epistle of John*, trans. T.H.L. Parker, Grand Rapids, Eerdmans, 1961.

24 Commentary on Colossians 1:15, (emphasis mine), *The Epistles of Paul The Apostle to the Galatians, Ephesians, Philippians and Colossians*, trans. T. H. L. Parker, ed. David W. Torrance and Thomas F. Torrance, Grand Rapids, Eerdmans, 1965. The Latin reads *se denique totum nobis exhibet (Ioannis Calvini in Novum Testamentum Commentarii*, vol. vi., ed. A. Tholuck, Berlin, 1834, *in loc.)*

of masses to damnation from eternity past is his perfect prerogative. Yet, however inconsistently, the Genevan reformer earnestly expounds the nature of God as loving and unconditionally gracious as well. In this way he is able to say that the death of Christ was for the entire race of humankind. This tension in Calvin S thought is later resolved by Calvinists in favor of a particular redemption only. Nevertheless, we must ask Calvin whether it is helpful to defend a selectivity in God's love on the basis of some "secret will" which finds no correspondence in God's self-disclosure in and through his Son.

Paul Tillich suggests that such an approach assumes that God is 'hidden behind his revelation in Christ, as abysmal, ineffable, as the 'naked God" before whom no man can stand."[25] That there remains a hiddenness to God even in the light of the Word-made-flesh is not in dispute. God's essence is not exhausted by his self-disclosure in Jesus. But what is rejected is the notion that there might lurk behind the God and Father of our Lord Jesus Christ a dark side, looming in contradiction to the unconditional love manifested in Jesus. His declaration that "He who has seen me has seen the Father" stands as a powerful reminder that God tabernacled among us to illuminate and not to deceive regarding his innermost nature. His glory never shines more brightly than in the suffering of the One who was despised and rejected of men.

Is Calvin to be reckoned among the voluntarists? When charged with propounding a "pure and mere will in God," he rejoined that God never does anything that is not "wise, holy and just," although the cause may lie hidden from mortals.[26] His opponents found Calvin's God to be unjust, and tyrannical, a God of the *potentia absoluta*. But he termed the notion of "absolute might" a "hateful fiction," and further declared that "We fancy no lawless God who is a law unto himself...the will of God is not only free of all fault but is the highest rule of perfection and even the law of all laws."[27] This unity of reason and will in his doctrine of God protects him from a full-blown voluntarism.

The problem for Calvin, it seems to us, is not that of a separation between justice and power in the divine being, but between justice and

25 Foreword to John Dillenberger, *God Hidden and Revealed*, Philadelphia: Muhlenberg Press, 1953, p. vii.
26 Calvin, "The Secret Providence of God," *Calvin's Calvinism*, trans. Henry Coles, London, Sovereign Grace Union, 1927, p. 266.
27 *Institutes*, III.xxiii.2.

love. We wonder whether he has taken with full seriousness his own claim that God is loving and merciful in his innermost being. We are surprised to read that God, before he made the human race, decreed the future of every single human being, electing some while reprobating others, when all were equally undeserving of grace.[28]

But on this basis, Calvin appears open to the charge leveled against Aquinas, of "soteriological voluntarism." It seems clear that his motivation is to defend the doctrine of *sola qratia*, which gives his doctrine of election a different cast from that of St. Thomas, whose mixture of grace and merit amounts to a kind of semi-pelagianism. Nevertheless, Calvin's positing of a will in God unbounded by his own love constitutes an abstraction untrue to the self-revelation of God in Christ.

The freeness of grace in all its "unmeritedness," while lacking in Thomas' theology of law, is very much in evidence in the thought of John Calvin. And while his medieval predecessor lodged his conception of law in a will of God grounded in the eternal law apart from Christ, Calvin is strongly Christocentric here. In his prolegomena to his discussion of law, he says that the sacrifices of Old Testament law "openly and plainly taught believers to seek salvation nowhere else than in the atonement that Christ alone carries out. I am only saying that the blessed and happy state of the church always had its foundation in the person of Christ."[29] Clearly for Calvin, the law is grounded in grace, since it is anchored in Christ. Yet it is not through keeping the law, but through seeing our failure to keep the law and thus fleeing to grace, that we are saved.[30]

Exploration of strengths and weaknesses in Aquinas and Calvin opens the way for a consideration of that obscure nineteenth-century preacher, John McLeod Campbell. It cannot be pretended that his work is fairly compared with theirs, for in sheer scope and breadth of treatment they range far beyond him. He has not left us any *magna opera* on the scale of a *Summa Theologiae* or the *Institutio Christianae Religionis*.

And yet, his vigorous emphasis on the centrality of the revelation of God in Christ provides both an illuminating critique of the soteriological

---

28 *Institutes*, III.xxi.5.
29 *Institutes*, II.vi.2.
30 *Institutes*, II.vii.2-4.

voluntarism of St. Thomas and Calvin, as well as solid grounds for expounding the Gospel as unconditionally and sincerely held out to every sinner. In this way the freedom of grace, in that it is *unrestricted* as well as *unmerited*, are solidly anchored in Jesus Christ.

It was Campbell's conviction that the Father-Son relationship provides the interpretive key for the whole of theology. When his parishioners were troubled by a perceived inadequacy in their faith[31] or doubts as to whether the love of God in Christ was directed to them personally,[32] his response was to direct their attention away from their capabilities and feelings to the mind of God disclosed in Christ.[33] This was the burden of his entire theological work, as a pastor to draw his flock back to Calvary, back to the God-man in order to learn God's true feelings toward them. If their assurance was to be secure, it must be grounded in who God is.

To this end he focuses a great deal of his attention upon the will of God. Perhaps this is due in large measure to the central place which the "secret will" of God, providentially determining the eternal destinies of every individual human being, occupies in the Scottish Calvinism of his day.[34] In response, he argues that an atonement restricted to certain elect ones, with no other explanation than that God "wills it because he wills it," would fail to "reveal that God is love." Even the elect could not logically reason from their election to an essential love in God, because "an arbitrary act cannot reveal character."[35]

But McLeod Campbell is convinced that the atonement is not an arbitrary act of raw will. In fact, it occupies its place as the very climax of a life of revelation embodied by the Son of God in all his words and deeds. Revelation is at the heart of Christ's mission, although it is too

---

31 John McLeod Campbell, *Reminiscences and Reflections*, ed. Donald Campbell, London, Macmillan, 1873, pp. 132, 133, 146, 148, 151.

32 *Ibid.*, pp. 144, 150, 151, 154, 155.

33 Ibid., p. 133.

34 See George M. Tuttle, *John McLeod Campbell on Christian Atonement: So Rich a Soil*, Edinburgh, Handsel Press, 1986, pp. 21-32.

35 John McLeod Campbell, *The Nature of the Atonement and its Relation to Remission of Sins and Eternal Life*, fourth edition, London, James Clarke, 1959, pp. 64-65. Henceforth this work will be referred to as *Nature*.

much to say that Jesus comes to reveal that we are already forgiven.[36] He comes to work out a costly at-one-ment in his life and more especially in his death, but throughout all that he comes to disclose the heart and mind of the Father.

Far from detaching the thought of the will of God from the self-revelation of God in Christ, Campbell is sure that Jesus Christ, in all his teaching and action, leads us straight as an arrow to the will of God which always expresses the loving heart of God. In the Son's revealing the Father, "we have to do directly with the will of God; that is to say, His will as His mind and character,---that in respect of which we say, God is love."[37]

The reciprocity and constitutive identity of the Father-Son relation are fundamental for our apprehension of God: "We see the Father when we see the Son, not merely because of an identity of will and character in the Father and Son, but because a father as such is known only in relation to a son."[38] What do we see concerning the Father through the Son? We have said that we see that God is love. Indeed, when God is disclosed in and through the Son as love, God appears "as He is in Himself, as He eternally is.[39] But Campbell does not dilute the character of God to be nothing more than love. He recognizes the presence of a range of "divine attributes" in God, including "justice, righteousness and holiness." But all the attributes are unified in their "craving" for the salvation of sinners.[40]

We have said that for McLeod Campbell, Jesus Christ, in all his teaching and action, leads us straight as an arrow to the will of God which always expresses the loving heart of God. But the singular disclosure of God's nature is found in the atonement. According to Hebrews 10, argues Campbell,

The will of God, which the Son of God came to do and did, this was the essence and substance of the atonement, being that in the offering

---

36 An interpretation of McLeod Campbell espoused by Michael Jinkins in his PhD thesis, *Atonement and the Character of God: A Comparative Study in the Theology of Atonement in Jonathan Edwards and John McLeod Campbell*, University of Aberdeen, 1990, pp. 219, 231, 289.
37 *Nature*, pp. xxxvi, xxxvii.
38 *Ibid.*, p. lii.
39 *Ibid.*, pp. 41,42.
40 *Ibid.*, p. 29; cf. p. 63.

of the body of Christ once for all which made it acceptable to Him who in burnt offerings and sacrifices for sin had no pleasure....Let us then receive these words, 'Lo, I come to do thy will, 0 God,' as the great key-word on the subject of the atonement.. . the *will* of God contemplated is that WILL which immediately connects our thoughts with what *God is*, that will, the nature and character of which we express when we say, 'God is good,'---or, explaining what we mean by good, say, 'God is holy, God is true, God is just, God is love.'[41]

The sustained emphasis upon the will of God found in McLeod Campbell's theology serves to make three points crucial to his interpretation of the atonement: First, the unity of will highlights the ontological oneness of the Father and the Son. On this basis, grace is nothing other than God's self-giving. Over against the kind of penal theory which depicts God the Father as wrathful, while the Son is loving and therefore seeking to change the heart of the Father towards sinners by suffering, Campbell argues that since "Christ is God," the love of the Father is actually displayed in the love of the Son. When God commended his love toward us in that while we were yet sinners Christ died for us, he did not sacrifice one creature for another." The point of the verse is rather that "*God* takes credit to *Himself* for the love that *Christ* manifests in dying for us."[42]

Moreover, the ontological oneness of Father and Son precludes notions of conditional grace. The atonement reveals that gracious will of God which motivated his self-giving in the Son, not a decision of God which declared that only if sin was punished could he be gracious.

Second, the unity of will between Father and Son means that the atonement reveals the very heart of God as unconditionally loving. If the loving self-sacrifice of Christ is not anchored in the very heart of God as love, but only in an arbitrary decision to elect some, then the atonement sheds no light at all upon the inmost nature of God.

Third, the oneness of will between Father and Son serves to stress the faithful obedience of Christ in both its active and passive aspects. Actively, his entire life is an obedient 'Amen' to the Father's will expressed in his law. Passively, he fulfills the law right to the bitter end, on the cross accepting the verdict of guilty upon the sin of humanity.

---

41 *Nature*, pp. 124-25.
42 *Ibid.*, pp. 26,27.

Law thus represents the loving will of God for all people, but it is upheld by God's enfleshment, his taking our place in the saving deeds of Jesus Christ. For the Scottish theologian, the commandments are God's heart coming out in the shape of law, while Jesus Christ is his heart manifested in the fulfillment of law in the flesh of, and on behalf of, all people.

In his death Jesus says Amen to the divine judgment upon sin, removing the barrier for all to return. Yet, for Campbell, despite all the misunderstandings his oblique style has engendered, this was not a way of dispensing with the atonement. It was not a denigration of the wrath of God toward sinners or of the awful price that must be paid in order to reconcile God and the human race. But it constituted a ringing declaration of the forgiving love of God as existing prior to and motivating the atonement. Indeed, McLeod Campbell's insistence on the Son's vicarious Amen in humanity to the judgment of God on sin was not a denial of the shed blood of the Son as the means of reconciliation. Rather, it was a way of underscoring the *oneness of Father and Son in the entire movement of atonement.*

In this study, therefore, we will seek to show that the great mistake has been to divide the will of God from the self-revelation of God in and through Christ. When it is so divided, as we find at times in the thought of St. Thomas and Calvin, the freeness of grace, in that it is *unrestricted,* can be lost in a kind of 'soteriological voluntarism' (Thomas and Calvin), and the freeness of grace, in that it is unmerited, can also be wanting in a sort of 'semi-pelagianism' (Thomas).

McLeod Campbell's conviction that our knowledge of God is anchored in the self-disclosure of God in Christ opens the way for a recovery of the conviction that God is a gracious and loving Father in his inmost life, whose will is undivided in his desire that all people be reconciled to himself in the humanity of his Son. In his death Jesus says Amen to the divine judgment upon sin, removing the barrier for all to return. In this way, the freedom of grace, in all its *unrestrictedness* and *unmeritedness* is upheld.

CHAPTER 1

THE SEMI-PELAGIANISM OF ST. THOMAS

Introduction

In December of 1273, Thomas Aquinas had an experience of God while saying Mass which so moved him that he immediately stopped working on his *Summa Theologiae*. He told his secretary that he could not write any more, because "all I have written seems to me like so much straw compared with what I have seen and with what has been revealed to me."[43] Thus ended the writing career of one of the clearest thinkers and boldest innovators scholasticism ever saw. His achievements in synthesizing Christianity and philosophy, faith and science, Aristotelianism and Augustinianism are nothing short of magisterial. And yet for all his sheer intellectual brilliance, he remained a humble man of deep piety, and the reader of his works catches regular glimpses of each.

Nonetheless this is not the time to survey the magnificent architectonics of the Thomist system, nor to sample the plethora of illuminating insights into orthodox theology offered by the Angelic Doctor. Of particular interest for this study is his grounding of the doctrine of election in a will of God known outside of Christ. It would appear that his dependence upon the metaphysic of final causality proves to shape his concept of God in fundamental ways, so that natural theology provides the framework into which the revelation through Christ must be fitted.

But once a will of God is posited without reference to Christ, the freeness of grace would seem to be endangered. Aquinas has his doctrine of grace, and he is very concerned to expound human salvation as due solely to the grace and mercy of God. Yet we will seek to demonstrate that his separation of grace and election, his detachment of grace from Christ, and his concentration on human merit together serve to qualify grace to the point that it becomes adapted and subordinated to a synergistic scheme of divine-human cooperation in order to make a

43 F. C. Copleston, *Aquinas*, (Middlesex, Penguin, 1955), 10.

person eligible for the grace of justification. Thus the freedom of grace in that it is *unmerited* would seem wanting in Aquinian theology.

Moreover, St. Thomas' stress on the legal intentions of God for the human race, coupled with his stipulating the penance a sinner must undertake in order once again to place himself into the state of grace, tends to obscure the personal relationship God has sought to re-establish with the human race through Christ.

Indeed, the more one probes these twin issues of grace and law in Aquinas' thought, the more one begins to wonder whether or not the very nature of God is at stake. Is God truly gracious and merciful in his inner life, or has he only willed to be gracious provided certain prior conditions be complied with? Is he "pure, unbounded love," as Charles Wesley would later phrase it, or does he only decide to be loving?

It has often been observed that John Calvin propounded a relentless doctrine of predestination, but Aquinas, too, has his doctrine of foreordination. For all the emphasis on the intellectualism of Thomas Aquinas, his God, we shall argue, demonstrates a kind of "soteriological voluntarism" whereby the will of God before time decrees the reprobation of certain human beings to damnation while predestinating the other, equally undeserving persons, to glory. It would be too much to say that he was a thoroughgoing voluntarist[44] in the tradition of William of Ockham.[45] Yet already in Aquinas[46] we find a God who in terms of his *potentia absoluta* can do anything that does not involve a contradiction in terms. He is free, without respect to desserts, to elect some and reject others from all eternity; he could have wrought salvation without the Cross; he can and does dispense with Natural Law.

While his constant emphasis on the unity of reason and will in the divine essence and actions protects him from technical voluntarism in the sense of a true primacy of the will in God such that he can decree

---

44 Hans Meyer, *The Philosophy of St. Thomas Aquinas*, trans. Rev. Frederic Eckhoff, (St. Louis and London: Herder, 1946), 467-68.

45 Etienne Gilson, *History of Christian Philosophy in the Middle Ages*, (London: Sheed and Ward), 408ff, 498.

46 Heiko Oberman traces the notion of the omnipotence of God as being limited only by the law of non-contradiction as far back as Hugh of St. Victor, in "Some Notes on the Theology of Nominalism with Attention to its Relation to the Renaissance," *Harvard Theological Review*, vol. liii, 1960, 47-76.

anything without reference to his own being,[47] there are aspects of his thought which, while undeveloped, would seem to open the door a crack to a kind of voluntarism. The Divine Ideas, exemplars according to which he fashions creatures, comprehend finite participations in his being, but do not appear to comprehend the totality of who he is. Perhaps this leaves room for the kind of "soteriological voluntarism" which we find in Aquinas' doctrine of predestination, although he does not explicitly correlate the two doctrines in this manner. Nonetheless, his concept of election, based as it is in the will of God without reference to Christ, calls into question the freeness of grace in the sense of its *unrestrictedness*.

Aristotelian Orientation

St. Thomas Aquinas was quite enamored with the newly discovered metaphysical writings of Aristotle. He often speaks, in respectful tones, of "the Philosopher." It is of course true that "St. Thomas was never rigidly bound by the *dicta* of Aristotle."[48] There are elements in his thought which are traceable to Neoplatonic,[49] or Islamic or Jewish philosophy.[50] Nevertheless, much of the shape and contours of his philosophy are determined by the influence of the one who for him was "the Philosopher" par excellence.[51] Yet Peter S. Eardley and Carl N. Still aptly observe that, "[B]y the time Aquinas is finished interpreting him, the Philosopher's thought has been transformed into a new synthesis."[52]

For our purposes, it is particularly the *Summa Theologiae*[53] which will occupy our investigations, since it expresses his mature thought,

---

47 See Francis Oakley, "The Theology of Nominalism," in his *Natural Law. Conciliarism and Consent in the Late Middle Ages*, (London: Valorum Reprints, 1984), 59-73.
48 F. L. Cross and E. A. Livingstone, eds., *The Oxford Dictionary of the Christian Church*, Second Edition, (Oxford: Oxford University Press, 1974), reprinted in 1983, 1371.
49 Cf. Gerald Vann, *Saint Thomas Aquinas*, (London: Hague and Gill, 1940), 150.
50 Copleston, *A History of Medieval Philosophy*, (London: Methuen, 1972), 180-81.
51 Jacques Maritain suggests that "the reason why Aristotle could be baptized by Saint Thomas is that his metaphysical principles were based upon objective reality" *St. Thomas Aquinas: Angel of the Schools*, (London: Sheed and Ward, 1946), 47; cf. T. F. Tout, "The Place of Thomas in History," *Saint Thomas Aquinas*, Alfred Whitacre, O. P., Vincent McNabb, O. P., et. al., (Oxford: Basil Blackwell, 1925), 18.
52 Peter S. Eardley and Carl N. Still, *Aquinas: A Guide for the Perplexed*, (London and New York: Continuum, 2010), 8.
53 Henceforth, *Summa*.

and contains, as he tells us, a systematic and summary exposition of theology.[54]

Theology, properly termed a science,[55] receives clarification of its message from other sciences. In this way they guide our understanding through the "world of natural reason" and into the "world above reason," expounded in divine revelation. In so doing, however, their role is "subsidiary and ancillary," to assist our understanding.[56] In one sense, divine revelation, accepted in faith, only adds to natural knowledge: "The truths about God which St Paul says we can know by our natural powers of reasoning--that God exists, for example--are not numbered among the articles of faith, but are presupposed to them. For faith presupposes natural knowledge, just as grace does nature . . . ."[57]

But if there had been no divine revelation, only a few wise persons with great effort would have arrived at certain rational truths about God. And even this natural knowledge would have been "mixed with many mistakes." Since our entire welfare depends on knowing God, there was provided divine revelation not only as a supplement, but also as a corrective.[58] Some revealed truths may thus be objects of faith or knowledge, depending on the capability of the subject. A person may accept on faith that which he is unable to demonstrate, "even if that truth in itself is such that demonstration could make it evident."[59] Faith is therefore not the sole access to theological truth from the side of humanity. Nor is God's self-revelation in and through Christ the only way to know God. Indeed, Thomas thinks he can demonstrate certain truths about God; hence he will bring to divine revelation an *a priori* understanding constructed by his philosophical and empirical investigations.[60]

54 1a.1, Foreword.
55 1a.1, 2.
56 1a.1, 5 ad 2.
57 1a.2, 2 ad 1.
58 1a.l, 1.
59 1a. 2, 2 ad 1.
60 Ralph McInerny contends that for Thomas, theology begins with faith rather than reason, and that "revealed truths" and "common truths" (i.e., those known by reason reflecting on experience) overlap. But, as we will demonstrate, Thomas is arguing for much more than an overlap. He believes that grace perfects nature, and that in our knowledge of God we can begin with nature and derive true knowledge of God which is then added to by grace (or revelation). See *A First Glance at St. Thomas Aquinas*, (Notre Dame: University of Notre Dame, 1990), 59-62.

How then does a person come to know God? From the perspective of Aquinas' adaptation of Aristotelian teleology, the blessed reach the *summum bonum* of existence in seeing God in his essence. This comprises the culmination of the metaphysic of final causality, for "each thing achieves its perfection by rising as high as its source."[61] Even then the divine essence surpasses description since it contains to a transcendent degree "every perfection that can be described or understood by the created mind."[62] This is not to say that the beatific vision can be experienced by natural powers, for no created mind can see God's essence "unless he by grace joins himself to that mind as something intelligible to it."[63] But such a gift of grace is only bestowed on the good.[64]

What is more, there is a capacity in the human mind for being raised by grace beyond its nature.[65] True, created minds vary in their ability to see God, but that ability itself comes from "the light of glory." Yet those receive the light of glory who have more charity, because those who have more charity have more desire, which predisposes a person to receive what he desires.[66] It will be shown that this presents a marked contrast with the doctrine of *sola gratia* so prominent in John Calvin. There is a great concern here with prior conditions which must be present in a person, be they capacities or dispositions or virtues, before grace may come.

Thomas' moderate realism follows that of Aristotle, with certain modifications.[67] He follows Augustine and the Neoplatonists in understanding the forms to be divine ideas or "exemplars" used by God to create the world.[68] But while Augustine thinks the soul can only apprehend these forms with the assistance of divine illumination, Aquinas' soul, as the form of the body, knows forms by its natural power,

61 1a.12, 1.
62 1a.12, 2.
63 1a.12, 5; cf. Leo J. Elders, *The Philosophical Theology of St. Thomas Aquinas*, (Leiden: E. J. Brill, 1990), 192-93.
64 1a.12, 12 ad 3.
65 1a.5 ad 3.
66 1a.12, 7.
67 1a.85, 1 ad 1; cf. Copleston, *Aquinas*, 90; M. C. D'Arcy, *St. Thomas Aquinas*, (Westminster, Maryland: Newman Press, 1955), 60-64.
68 Elders, *Ibid.*, 242-45; Gilson, *The Christian Philosophy of St. Thomas Aquinas*, (London: Victor Gollancz, 1957), 125-27.

though solely in connection with sense perception. Knowledge that is natural to us originates in the senses and thereby we can be led from effects to God as the First Cause of all things.[69] We can thus know that God exists, that he caused all his creatures, that he is wholly uncreated, and that he is transcendent.[70]

There is no intrinsic moral problem for natural knowledge of God: "Knowledge of God in his essence is a gift of grace and belongs only to the good, yet the knowledge we have by natural reason belongs to both good and bad."[71] The Fall does not affect humankind's rational ability to abstract from sense data some knowledge of God. True, the first human's sin passes to his posterity. All who are born of Adam share in the one nature they inherit from him, "even as in political matters all belonging to one community are reckoned to be like one body."[72]

But in what does original sin consist? God bestowed upon all human nature in the first parent as a supernatural gift, *originalis iustitia*.[73] Original justice was the ordering of a human's nature such that his will was subject to God.[74] In the rectitude of his pristine state, his reason (i.e., his mind and will) was in submission to God, his lower powers (sense appetites) to his reason, and his body to his soul.[75] But "sin takes away grace"[76] and hence the Fall brought in its train the loss of original justice.

Original sin, then, is a *way* of talking about the privation[77] of *originalis iustitia*.[78] No longer is human nature perfected by the ordering of all its powers in subjection to God. Its powers are now left to themselves, lacking the harmony they once had.[79] But as a *privatio*, it begets no evil orientation, no direct inclination toward created goods rather than

69 *Summa Contra Gentiles*, five vols, various trans, (Garden City: Doubleday, 1954-1956), I, 3; cf. Elders, op. cit., 186-195; Copleston, op. cit., 44-46.
70 1a.12, 12.
71 1a.12, 12 ad 3.
72 1a2ae.81, 1.
73 1a2ae.81, 2.
74 1a2ae.82, 3.
75 1a.95, 1.
76 1a2ae.87, 3.
77 1a2ae 82, 2.
78 1a2ae.82, 1 ad 1.
79 Cf. Brian Davies, *The Thought of Thomas Aquinas*, (Oxford: Clarendon Press, 1992), 254-57.

the supreme good. It is not a turning of the will against God. It only means the removal of the restraint of original justice. Thomas' doctrine of original sin differs strikingly from that of Calvin.

It must be stressed that for Thomas the nature of humanity *qua* humanity is not changed by the Fall: "the principles constitutive of [human] nature together with the properties derived from them [such as] the powers of the soul . . . [are] neither destroyed nor lessened through sin."[80] Indeed, "human nature itself is not lessened by sin."[81] Such a distortion of nature would simply not cohere with the presupposed metaphysic. The Aristotelian human is a rational being with certain natural abilities and inclinations. Nothing he can do can alter the basic principles of his nature.

The loss of original justice is significant, to be sure. "After the fall Adam remained a human being, but what he had lost was the ability, by God's grace, to preserve in the actual exercise of his life the right order between the different parts of human nature."[82] Now, a postlapsarian human can lessen his "connatural inclination to virtue" by sinning. As he exercises an act in the direction of vice (a morally bad habit) he diminishes that inclination towards virtue.[83]

Nevertheless, to be human is to be rational, and as such one naturally acts in accord with reason, which is to act virtuously. For sin to cause a person to cease being rational is impossible, since he would then no longer be capable of sinning. Therefore a human's natural bent to virtue could not be totally taken away. When he sins, that inclination is diminished "in that an obstacle is placed between it and its term . . . . For as a person can add sin to sin, he can raise countless obstacles; yet the inclination itself cannot be totally destroyed, since its root always remains."[84] A person's natural awareness of God may be "obscured" by sinning, since "habitual sin" darkens the light of natural law and thus

---

80 1a2ae.85, 1. In light of this, we are surprised at Gilson's claim that for Thomas "original sin obscured this knowledge [of God] and weakened man in the power of knowing". *The Elements of Christian Philosophy*, (New York: Doubleday, 1963), 52.
81 1a2ae.85, 2.
82 Rudi A. Te Velde, "Evil, Sin and Death: Aquinas on Original Sin," in Rik Van Nieuwenhove and Joseph Wawrykow, eds., *The Theology of Thomas Aquinas*, (Notre Dame: University of Notre Dame Press), 2005, 158.
83 1a2ae.85, 1.
84 1a2ae.85, 2.

prevents its reason from its proper function.[85] Yet he cannot wholly lose his innate rational capacity to know something about God apart from divine revelation, and the precise measure of that capacity will vary from person to person, relative to each one's goodness.

All of this is of course in line with the well-known Thomist dictum that "grace does not destroy nature, but perfects it."[86] Grace's gifts are added only to enhance those of nature, not to take them away. Hence the "native light of reason" is only completed by the "light of faith." This indicates how philosophy relates to theology. Since "nature is a prelude to grace", Christian theology calls upon philosophy to demonstrate the groundwork of faith including the existence of God, and that he is one, to discover analogies common to nature and grace, and to defend the faith.[87]

> F. C. Copleston argues that for Thomas Aquinas, the theologian starts with God, presupposing his existence as a matter of faith and dealing with God's self-revelation and redemptive activity, whereas the philosopher starts with the objects of sense perception . . . and comes to knowledge of God only in so far as inference will take him."[88]

We can agree with this up to a point. Thomas' theological science is concerned with truth that comes through revelation rather than through discursive reason.[89] It begins with the disclosure of the one who alone knows himself and considers all else in light of this First Cause.[90] Holy teaching proceeds, then, from premises held as articles of faith, and "advances from them to make something known." (This would correspond with Aristotle's deductive science).[91]

---

85 1a2ae.98, 6.
86 1a.1, 8 ad 2.
87 *Exposition de Trinitate*, ii.3, cited in Thomas Gilby, ed. and tr., St. Thomas Aquinas, *Theological Texts*, (London: Oxford University Press, 1955), 7.
88 F. C. Copleston, *A History of Medieval Philosophy*, (Notre Dame: University of Notre Dame Press, 1972), 182.
89 1a.1, 6 ad 2.
90 1a.1, 6.
91 1a.1, 8.

But as we have seen, Aquinas sees grace as perfecting rather than displacing nature. The truths about God knowable by a human's natural powers of reasoning (such as his existence) "are not numbered among the articles of faith but are presupposed to them. For faith presupposes natural knowledge, just as grace does nature."[92] Now, how can that which is known by natural reason and presupposed by faith be itself an object of faith? It is not logically impossible that some may believe what others know; Thomas is well aware of that. But one cannot, he also reminds us, simultaneously know it and believe it.[93]

But the Angelic Doctor is not always consistent. In discussing the relation between natural law and the divine law, he says that because human reason was in some cases prevented from its proper perception by habitual sin, divine law promulgates as truths which we are required to believe, including "not only those unattainable by reason such as that there are three Persons in God, but also those attainable by right reason such as that God is one."[94] In any case, the results of Thomas' philosophical and empirical inquiries into the existence God are not altogether laid aside when he gets to divine revelation. His continued use of Aristotelian categories in his language about God proves to be decisive.

For divine revelation, the "light of grace" or "light of prophecy" supplements nature, thereby enabling the human intellect to know more profound intelligible realities than those accessible to the senses.[95] How does knowing God take place? Since all knowledge begins in the senses, we first derive images from the sensible world and then by the "natural intellectual light" we abstract intelligible concepts from these images. But grace can perfect this knowledge on both counts. The "light of grace" increases the intellectual light, and "prophetic visions" provide

---

92 1a.2, 2 ad 1. Moreover, in Thomas' thought, says Martin Grabmann, there are "two ways leading to God, the way of natural reason proceeding from the works of God in nature and the way of faith, which reaches higher" *Thomas Aquinas: His Personality and Thought*, trans. Virgil Michel, (New York: Russell and Russell, 1963), 82-83, cf. 88.

93 *de Veritate*, 14, 9, ad Resp et ad 6, cited in Gilson, *The Christian Philosophy of St. Thomas Aquinas*, cf. D. J. O'Connor, *Aquinas and Natural Law*, (London: Macmillan, 1967), 8-9.

94 1a2ae.99, 2 ad 2.

95 1a2ae.109, 1.

"God-given images which are better suited to express things than those we receive naturally from the sensible world." Such images include the sensible signs and spoken words given at Christ's baptism.[96]

This indicates how divine revelation in Scripture fits into the knowing process, and also how the Sacraments function noetically. St. Thomas asserts that human nature comes to know spiritual and intelligible realities through the process of deducing from its experience of sensible realities. Since divine providence works in accordance with each being's natural way of functioning, "it is appropriate that in bestowing certain aids to salvation upon man the divine wisdom should make use of certain physical and sensible signs called the sacraments." Even in an epistemic sense, therefore, the "sacraments are necessary for man's salvation."[97]

Thomas avers that we do not come to know God through Scripture. Only in the beatific vision will we see divine truth in itself. In the meantime, rays from divine truth "illumine us under certain sensible figures . . . in various ways, corresponding to the various states of human knowledge." Thus in the Old Testament, under the Old Law, divine truth was not manifest in itself, but the system of external worship prefigured the divine truth which would one day be revealed in the heavenly country, and also "Christ, the way leading to it." Hence we are given no direct knowledge of God this side of heaven.[98]

How then do we know God at all? Since we have no direct knowledge of any existence apart from sense perception, our knowledge of non-sensible reality must be discursive and attained inferentially. God, the Supreme Cause, cannot be known to us directly or *per se* but only *per suos effectus*, through his effects.[99] Thus Aquinas embarks on his Five

---

96 1a.12, 3.
97 3a.61, 1.
98 1a2ae.101, 2.
99 Cf. Francis John Selman, *St. Thomas Aquinas: Teacher of Truth* (Edinburgh: T & T Clark, 1994), 7.

Ways of proving the existence of God.[100] He begins by citing Romans 1:20, "the hidden things of God can be clearly understood from the things that he has made."[101] If that is the case, "one must be able to demonstrate that God exists from the things that he has made. He finds in this text full warrant for his inductive, empirical epistemology. That his Five Ways serve a noetic and not merely illustrative purpose seems clear, for he goes on to assert that this approach follows the order in which we know things, arguing from effect to cause: "for when an effect is more apparent to us than its cause, *we come to know the cause through the effect.*"[102]

Doctrine of Analogy

This draws our attention to the notion of analogy in St. Thomas, for his conception of the relation between the language of creatures and the being of God exposes fundamental assumptions underlying his epistemology. He treats the nature and division of analogy especially in Question 13 of the *Prima Pars*. The previous Question, under Article 12, had asked "can we know God by our natural reason in this life?"

100 "All of Aquinas' five ways depend on a notion of causality . . . the empirical facts he adduces are seen as dependent on a transcendent cause . . . a supreme unmoved mover" (Copleston, *Aquinas*, 113-14). Rudi te Velde contends, to the contrary, that "what Thomas is looking for is not so much rational certainty, but intelligibility, to wit the intelligibility of the truth expressed and asserted by the proposition 'God exists.' He notes that just prior to the exploration of the five ways, Thomas quotes a Scripture "in which God, in person, declares himself to exist." Therefore, te Velde avers, Thomas appeals to the authority of Scripture as the basis for his assertion that God exists and is only trying to demonstrate the intelligibility of the existence of God by the five ways (Rudi te Velde, *Aquinas on God: The Divine Science of the Summa Theologiae* (Hants, England: Ashgate Publishing, 2006), 38-39, cf. Ia 2, 3 sed contra. Certainly Thomas has great confidence in biblical authority. However, we are seeking to demonstrate by tracing the logic of Thomas' argument, that he claims to prove God's existence by these five ways.

101 Ia.2, 2.

102 Ia. 2, 2 (italics mine). Elders, op. cit., observes that "the *overall order* of the *Summa Theologiae* is dependent upon revelation . . . [while] the *inner* arrangement of the treatises on God, on creation, on man, etc. appears to obey the requirements of ordering reason and is not immediately derived from revelation" (viii). In fact, in some cases "a particular theme can be demonstrated by reason alone. If so, it can be taken out of its theological context and presented as a philosophical argument. What we are saying applies to the existence of God, divine attributes, God's knowledge and will, the analogy between created things and God, creation" (ix).

In response he acknowledged that since *cognitio naturalis* begins in the senses, it cannot reach the divine essence. But the sensory data we apprehend are effects from which we can trace back through a chain of causation to the "First Cause of all things." Sensible creatures, of course, cannot compare to the excellence of this Cause, and so we cannot perceive God's essence. But we can at least be led from them to know that God exists and also to know those attributes which must belong to such a Cause transcending all that which is caused.[103]

Herbert McCabe maintains that too much has been made of Thomas' teaching on analogy, since the latter only means it to be a "comment on our use of certain words", not a "way of getting to know about God."[104] On the other hand, Norbert Mtega demonstrates through a careful study of the *Summa Contra Gentiles* that the Angelic Doctor was convinced that "man can come to know God through creatures," because of an intrinsic likeness between God and creatures "due to the fact of causality."[105]

Furthermore, in the *Summa* we find the doctrines of the knowledge of God and of analogy to be interdependent. For instance, in Question 13, the first problem Aquinas has to face is how we can use words to refer to God when they are derived from creatures. He argues that our language parallels our way of knowing. We do not know God as he is in himself; we only know him inferentially, from creatures.

Therefore, we inductively reason back to him as the uncreated Source of sensible things. "It is the knowledge we have of creatures that enables us to use words to refer to God." Our words, which normally signify creaturely realities, can refer to him. Thomas seeks to obtain knowledge of divine attributes by analogical reasoning from the attributes of humans.[106] To be sure, names thus derived "do not express the divine essence as it is in itself," for God surpasses all creatures.[107]

---

103 *Summa* 1a.12, 12.

104 "Analogy", Appendix 4 to Thomas Aquinas, vol. 3, (Ia. 12-14), ed. and tr. by Herbert McCabe, (London: Eyre and Spottiswoode, 1964), 106.

105 *Analogy and Theological Language in the Summa Contra Gentiles*, Frankfurt am Main, Peter Lang, 1984, 49ff.

106 Cf. Elders, *op. cit.*, 206-212; D'Arcy, *op. cit.*, 88-100; Gilson, *The Christian Philosophy of St. Thomas Aquinas*, 360-61.

107 1a.13, 1.

Hence our way of signifying him is appropriate to material creatures, rather than God.[108]

If our words do not capture the essence of God, then in what sense do they refer to him at all? What do we mean, for example, when we say that God is "good"? This is not a case of extrinsic denomination,[109] by which we would mean no more than that God is the cause of goodness in things. There is a closer correspondence between Creator and creature than that: "Any creature, in so far as it possesses any perfection, represents God and is like to him, for he, being simply arid universally perfect, has pre-existing in himself the perfections of all his creatures."[110] Yet this correlation is not so intimate as to subsume both God and sensible things under the same species or genus, for it is one in which effects imperfectly resemble transcendent causes.

In this way, Aquinas firmly rejects any notion of an *analogia entis*[111] in which one deduces the nature of God from some prior concept of "being." There is a vast ontological gulf between God and creation. If we manage to speak at all about divine realities, and our words do "signify something that God really is," we must confess that they only signify it imperfectly because the "creatures represent God imperfectly." Nevertheless they do represent him. The goodness pre-existing in God is found in creatures, albeit in a lower way.[112] Thus we do not say that God is good in the sense that he causes goodness; "rather, goodness flows from him because he is good."[113]

But how can we qualify our names for God in such a way that we acknowledge the difference between the way in which the perfections we predicate belong to God and the mode in which they are found among creatures? Here we must distinguish between two aspects: (1) the perfection signified, and (2) the way of signifying.

> So far as the perfections signified are concerned the words
> are used literally of God, and in fact more appropriately
> than they are used of creatures, for these perfections

---

108 1a.13, 1 ad 2.
109 Cf. Mtega, *op. cit.*, 81-85.
110 1a.13, 2.
111 Cf. Gilson, "The Spirit of Thomism," *A Gilson Reader*, ed. Anton C. Pegis, (Garden City: Image Books, 1957), 151-52; Mtega, op. cit., 76.
112 Cf. Gilson, *The Christian Philosophy of St. Thomas Aquinas*, 104ff.
113 *Ibid.*

belong primarily to God and only secondarily to others. But so far as the way of signifying these perfections is concerned the words are used inappropriately, for they have a way of signifying that is appropriate to creatures.[114]

Even when we are attributing perfections to God, our words for these perfections are necessarily derived from creatures and in that sense are inappropriate to God. Their normal usage falls far short of signifying the divine reality. Our words, so far as the mode of signification is concerned, must be denied. But so far as the perfection signified is concerned, such words may be affirmed.

In Article Five St. Thomas treats the question whether names for God are used univocally or equivocally. He reasons that effects which fall short of the excellence of their cause can only represent it inadequately, so that what exists in a simple and undivided way in the cause exists in a divided and varied way in its effects. This applies to God as the supreme Cause and creatures as its effects: when we signify, for example, wisdom as possessed by man, we are naming something which is distinct from other things about him--his essence, his powers, or existence. Not so with God. "What ['wise'] signifies in God is not confined by the meaning of our word but goes beyond it." Wisdom in God is not distinct from his essence, power, or existence. Thus we cannot predicate anything univocally of God and creatures.

On the other hand, we are not falling into sheer equivocation either, for then we could never, proceeding from the creature, know or demonstrate anything about the Creator. Instead, Thomas suggests that names are attributed to God analogously.

> But names can be thus used in different ways: either according as many things are proportioned to one, thus, for example 'healthy' is predicated of medicine and urine in relation and in proportion to health of body, of which the latter is the sign and the former is the cause, or according as one thing is proportioned to another (thus, 'healthy' is said of medicine and an animal, since medicine is the cause of health in the animal body). And in this way some things are said of God and creatures

---

114 1a.13, 3.

analogically, and not in a purely equivocal nor in a purely univocal sense. For we can name God only from creatures. Hence, whatever is said of God and creatures is said according as there is some relation of the creature to God as to its principle and cause, wherein all the perfections of things pre-exist excellently. Now this mode of community is a mean between pure equivocation and simple univocation. For in analogies the idea is not, as it is in univocals, one and the same; yet it is not totally diverse as it is in equivocals; but the name which is thus used in a multiple sense signifies various proportions to some one thing: e.g., 'healthy,' applied to urine, signifies the sign of animal health; but applied to medicine, it signifies the cause of the same health.[115]

Divine names are predicated of God according to the analogy of one to another. Thomas presents the example of the predication of 'healthy' with respect to medicine and an animal. The ground for the analogy between healthy medicine and animal lies in the causal relation: medicine causes health in a healthy animal.

Now, Battista Mondin has shown that it is a fundamental principle for Aquinas that "effects are always precontained in some way in their causes."[116] This similarity between effects and their causes forms the basis for analogical discourse. Just as we can be led from sensible creatures (effects) to God as their "first cause" and through discursive reasoning to know that which logically must be attributed to him as the first cause of all things,[117] so the perfections we perceive in creatures provide a certain analogy to perfections in God.

Indeed, "whatever is said of God and creatures is said according as there is some relation of the creature to God as to its principle and

---

115 1a.13, 5, *Basic Writings of Saint Thomas Aquinas*, ed. A. C. Pegis, (New York: Random House, 1945). Pegis translation is used here since it is a more literal one.
116 Battista Mondin, *The Principle of Analogy in Protestant and Catholic Theology*, The Hague, Martinus Nijhoff, 1963, 32, citing *In Libros Sententiarum Petri Lombardi* I, 35, 4 ad 1; II, 1, 2, 2; IV, 4, 3; *Summa Contra Gentiles* I, 29; *De Potentia* 7, 1 ad 8; *De Malo* 4, 3; *Summa* I, 4, 3; I, 13, 5, cf. 1a2ae.107, 3.
117 1a.12, 12.

cause.[118] Therefore, explains Mondin, it is the likeness between terms united by a relation of efficient causality which enables us to predicate analogously attributes derived from the creature, with reference to the Creator.[119]

In Article Six Thomas argues that analogous names are predicated of God primarily rather than of creatures. For they are expressing more than the fact that God is the cause of certain perfections in creatures: "words of this sort do not only say how God is a cause, they also say what he is. When we say he is good or wise we do not simply mean that he causes wisdom or goodness, but that he possesses these perfections transcendently." The perfections signified, as we saw in Article Two, pre-exist in God in a higher way. Nevertheless these perfections do "flow from God to the creature." The perfections found in things made by God are also found in him, although far more excellently.[120] But since our knowledge of the creatures is prior, we use words to apply to them first and then to God.

Certainly analogy serves a noetic function in Thomas' theology. He is confident that the intellect can by abstraction from sensible particulars reach a certain analogical knowledge of God.[121] But the clear point that emerges here is that our speaking about God is rooted in the likeness between God and the creature which is grounded in the principle that effects are intrinsically like their causes.[122] This assumption continues to serve as the ground for Aquinas' use of the analogy *unius ad alterum* to make predications of God throughout the *Summa Theologiae*.

How are we to respond to this conviction that knowledge of God is reached *via analogiae* from our experience of creaturely realities? Certainly we are given a profound analysis of theological language, one which was to provide a primary source for much Christian discussion of the problem. And Thomas contributes an important insight with his reminder that our words for God are words which are normally used for creatures and thus must take on an analogical sense when predicated

---

118 1a.13, 5.
119 Mondin, *op. cit.*, 31-32.
120 Cf. Mtega, *op. cit.*, 76.
121 Cf. Hans Meyer, *The Philosophy of St. Thomas Aquinas*, (St. Louis: B. Herder, 1946), 188.
122 So also, Mtega, *op. cit.*, 83-86; cf. Oliva Blanchette, *The Perfection of the Universe According to Aquinas*, (University Park: Penn State Press, 1992), 167-73.

of God. But when this notion of analogy is fused to the axiom that there is an intrinsic likeness between effect and cause, the result is a postulated way of knowing God out of a center in humankind, in which we abstract certain concepts from data gained by sense-observation from the corporeal world. But might not this tend to result in a God of our own projection, rather than true knowledge of One who graciously discloses himself in Christ?

The Five Ways

The first of his Ways illustrates his constructing a definition of God on the basis of empirical induction. Things that are in the process of change are moving towards a perfection not yet possessed, although they are capable of possessing it. That which causes the change, he reasons, has that perfection already. Thus Thomas introduces into his theological vocabulary the concepts of *actus* and *potentia*. Things in the process of change are moving from potentiality to actuality. Moreover they are being changed by something else, which itself is also being changed by something else. We cannot posit an infinite series, for if there were no first cause of the change there could be no subsequent causes. "Hence one is bound to arrive at some first cause of change not itself being changed by anything, and this is what everybody understands by God."[123]

What does this demonstration tell Aquinas about God? "In the first existent everything must be actual; there can be no potentiality whatsoever . . . the first existent is God. In God then there can be no potentiality."[124] Indeed, *Deus est purus actus*. The conclusion that God's essence is identical with his existence follows the same logic.[125]

Clearly the Thomist mind does not come to divine revelation as a *tabula rasa*. Much about God is already defined by Aristotelian induction. Although Aristotle's ideal science was deductive, in which entities are arranged in order of being and their natures are determined by syllogistic logic, he also affirmed that we come to know things inductively, abstracting from the particular to the general or universal.

---

123 Ia.2, 3; cf. D'Arcy, *op. cit.*, 119-121; Gilson, *The Christian Philosophy of St. Thomas Aquinas*, 59-66.
124 Ia.3, 1.
125 Ia.3, 4.

If he vacillated at times between the ontological and epistemological orders,[126] so did his thirteenth century counterpart. And certainly in connection with his demonstrations of the existence of God, Aquinas proceeds from sense experience to arrive at a conceptual understanding of the being of God before ever he consults divine revelation.[127]

Thus, in considering Question 2, Whether There is a God, it is objected that God's existence cannot be demonstrated since (in Aristotelian logic) the middle term of a demonstration is a definition and we cannot know what God is. Thomas replies that "when demonstrating from effects that God exists, we are able to start from what the word 'God' means, for, as we shall see, *the names of God are derived from these effects*."[128] Thus he will induce that God is pure actuality, with no potentiality;[129] that he is essentially form and thus does not experience dispositions such as anger or joy (such emotions are only "ascribed to God by a metaphor drawn from their effects");[130] and so on.

If the Aristotelian influence is prominent in Thomas' epistemology, it is even more pronounced in his metaphysics. Final causality is presuppositional to his entire theology.[131] He accepts Aristotle's teleological approach as his foundation. Before discussing "the Goodness of God" (Question 6), he first considers "the general notion of good" (Question 5). He begins by telling us that

> The goodness of a thing consists in its being desirable;
> hence Aristotle's dictum that good is what all things

---

126 Diogenes Allen, *Philosophy for Understanding Theology*, (London: SCM, 1985), 118, Pierre Rousselot, S. J., *The Intellectualism of Saint Thomas*, trans. James E. O'Mahony, (New York: Sheed and Ward, 1935), 139-40.

127 Elders, *op. cit.*, suggests that Thomas' identification of the Being whose existence has been demonstrated in each of the Five Ways with God is not meant to constitute "our Christian idea of God, but rather the pre-Christian notion of the divine." Yet we do recognize the God of revelation, avers Elders, in these conclusions. In this way, he suggests, "philosophy serves as a preparation for the faith" (131). Nevertheless we wonder whether or not such philosophically derived preconceptions about God might distort our understanding of what revelation tells us about God.

128 Ia.2, 2 ad 2 (emphasis mine).

129 Ia.3, 1.

130 Ia.3, 2; cf. Blanchette, 24.

131 Cf. the comment by D'Arcy, *op. cit.* "There are few subjects which interest [St. Thomas] more than that of final cause. I suspect that his thoughts grouped themselves and defiled before him under that standard" (108).

> desire. Now clearly desirability is consequent upon perfection, for things always desire their perfection. And the perfection of a thing depends on how far it has achieved actuality. It is clear then that a thing is good inasmuch as it exists, for . . . it is by existing that everything achieves actuality.[132]

Thus, the good is the end of the existence of all things. All things by their very nature desire the good, their perfection, and further actuality. What is more, there is a notion of causality implicit in this conception of goodness: "we have the words of Aristotle: that for the sake of which things exist is their good and their goal. Being good therefore involves being an end or goal."[133] Aquinas thinks that the idea of good presupposes "notions of operative cause and form": "in the act of causation we begin with the good end which influences the agent to act, then follows the action of the agent eliciting the form, and finally there arises the form."[134]

How this relates things to God is now apparent. Things, which are effects, desire their perfection, and an effect's perfection and form is found in resembling its cause. Therefore, the cause itself is desirable. Since goodness is consequent on desirability, the cause is also good. "Clearly, then, since God is the primary operative cause of everything, goodness and desirability fittingly belong to him."[135] Aquinas is thus able to say that each thing in desiring its own perfection is actually desiring God himself.[136]

This may lead one to conclude that wrong choices cannot be made, since the good is naturally desired and chosen. But there are many goods, not all of which are desired by every thing.[137] Moreover, a human differs from non-intelligent creatures in that "he is master of what he does." Thomas differentiates between "acts of a man" and "human acts," the latter being those subject to his control. This control is exercised freely

---

132 Ia.5, 1.
133 Ia.5, 4 sed contra.
134 Ia.5, 4.
135 Ia.6, 1.
136 Ia.6, 1 ad 2.
137 Ia.6, 2 ad 2; cf. O'Connor, *op. cit.*, 49-56 for a critique of this analysis of the freedom of the will.

by his mind and will.[138] How then are decisions made? Again final causality is determinative. He cites Aristotle as finding the motivation for human deeds always to be derived from a *finis*.[139] Hence, "an end comes first in respect to the agent's intention: it is thus that it has the force of a cause."[140]

Now, the object of the will is the *universale bonum*, which is found in God alone.[141] From that "ultimate end" which is the "first good", there issues "derivative goods."[142] "Complete happiness requires the mind to come through to the essence itself of the first cause."[143] If we were presented with the supreme perfection, we would cleave to it at once, for to gaze on God and yet "to will not to see him is impossible." We may set aside other, lesser goods, for they may be found wanting or tiresome. But "by seeing God just as he is, the soul is filled with every good."[144]

But we do not see the universal good, and hence we are reduced to trying to determine which among the particular,[145] derivative[146] goods are grounded in God himself. "And therein," says Etienne Gilson, "consists our very liberty."[147] Indeed, while all seek their complete fulfillment in God, their final end, not all do so consciously. Hence they differ as to that in which their perfection is to be realized, for "some want riches, others a life of pleasure, others something else.[148] But such lesser goods are "incomplete" and fall "far short of our *summum bonum*."[149] To choose them is to sin. And in so doing, people "turn away from that in which the idea of the ultimate end is realized, not from the intention of reaching it, which mistakenly they seek elsewhere."[150]

Thomas has taken over much of Aristotle's teleological ethic, in which the *causa finalis* plays a central role. In both philosophies,

---

138 1a2ae.1, 1.
139 1a2ae.1, 1 sed contra.
140 1a2ae.1, 1 ad 1.
141 1a2ae.2, 8.
142 1a2ae.1, 4 ad 1.
143 1a2ae.3, 8.
144 1a2ae.5, 5.
145 1a2ae.2, 7.
146 1a2ae.1, 4 ad 1.
147 *History of Christian Philosophy in the Middle Ages*, 379.
148 1a2ae.1, 8.
149 1a2ae.2, 1 ad 3.
150 1a2ae.1, 8 ad 1.

the good serves as the principle of attraction, and human acts derive their moral quality from their relation to humankind's final end. And in both, humans by nature are seeking the good, and thus cannot do otherwise. This concept of final causality will be decisive, not only for his understanding of the nature of law and ethics, but of God, humanity, creation, redemption; indeed, the whole of the theological enterprise.

In considering the relationship between Thomas and his philosophical mentor, Copleston finds supplementation and completion. Hence, Aquinas begins his discussion of humankind's final end with the Aristotelian conception of happiness and ends with the Christian doctrine of the beatific vision. And to the Aristotelian natural virtues he adds the infused theological virtues of faith, hope and charity.[151] Aristotle was concerned with an imperfect and transient happiness attainable on earth by human effort. But, says Copleston, Aquinas "was convinced that Aristotle's outlook on the world and on human life was incomplete and inadequate rather than simply wrong . . . . Grace perfects nature but does not annul it: revelation sheds further light."[152]

Thomas' great debt to Aristotle is evident. But it would be a mistake to conclude that he has accepted the latter's philosophy *ex toto*. As Gilson observes, the Greek philosopher's positing his Unmoved Mover as a thinking thought safeguards his ontological separateness from everything else, but at the cost of banishing God from experience. Thus humans are reduced to experiencing the desire of experiencing God.[153] Such a deity cannot be much concerned with the details of our acts, or demand our accounting of them. He remains in his eternal beatitude, leaving humans to themselves and their own efforts to imitate this beatitude. But for Thomas, avers Gilson, a human is one created by a God "who remains intimately present in his being, in his faculties, in their operations, and in every act proceeding from them . . . man can do nothing save through Him."[154]

Nevertheless, there are fundamental tendencies in Thomas' theology which are quite reminiscent of the abovementioned Aristotelian flaws. Thomas' God is basically unknowable in this life. And if grace is

---

151 *Aquinas*, 193.
152 *Ibid*, 198.
153 *The Christian Philosophy of St. Thomas Aquinas*, 83.
154 *Ibid.*, 304-305.

required for every act of humans, so too, decision and exertion on their part become (as we shall see) the *sine qua non*, if not for their initiation into the life of grace, certainly for their perseverance and perfection therein. And both these problems--the unknowability of God and the conditional nature of grace---seem to stem from the same separation of the will of God from the self-revelation of God in and through Christ.

Thomas' entire epistemology is grounded in the axiom that all knowledge begins in the senses, and thus in the case of God proceeds from effect to cause. The names of God are derived *via analogiae* from these effects. Thus knowledge of God is only inferential. It is also negative. We are not given to know God in his essence, but rather what he is not.[155] The knowing mind can come to know God as the uncaused First Cause and as one,[156] but little else. Hence even scriptural revelation fails to bridge this gulf. It discloses more information about him, such as his Trinitarian nature and some of his greater works. Faith, which is directed to this data, is a sort of *cognitio* "in that it makes the mind assent to something . . . . In that it lacks the element of seeing, faith fails to be genuine knowledge . . . ."[157] It would seem then that Aquinas is left with a God about whom he knows little, and whom he knows not at all. And in fact that is his conclusion: "in this life revelation does not tell us what God is, and thus joins us to him as to an unknown."[158]

T. F. Torrance observes that Thomas' dependence on Aristotelian modes of thought had the result that "the doctrine of the One God was cut off sharply from the doctrine of the Triune God, the former only being related to the epistemological structure of the knowing mind."[159] But to know God at all is to know him in the *homoousion*, in his self-disclosure in his Son. If we begin with the God who has given himself to be known in the God-Man, we shall know Him, and not only about him. But Aquinas begins in the traditional manner by considering *utrum Deus sit* before *quid Deus sit*. His Aristotelian presuppositions then determine the kind of God he will find.

---

155 See Thomas' introduction to 1a.3 in his *Summa*.

156 1a2ae.99, 2 ad 2.

157 1a.12, 13 ad 3.

158 1a.12, 13 ad 1.

159 T. F. Torrance, *Theology in Reconciliation*, (London: Geoffrey Chapman, 1975), 285.

In Thomas' thought, God has not even given himself to be known in Christ. Christ is only the means, the way, but not the content of the divine self-revelation. Only in the Beatific Vision shall we see and know God in Himself.

But it might be argued that if our concepts are to be ontologically derived from God's own nature, we must begin with his self-disclosure rather than inferential logic. In other words, the doctrine of revelation is at stake. To begin with the creature and reason backwards is to make humanity the measure of things and impose a prior conception of certain abstract "attributes" (derived, no doubt, from painstaking discursive reflection) onto God. But this is to lay a presuppositional foundation for our doctrine of God which becomes the light in which we examine his self-revelation. And in this way our prior philosophical formulation may easily become a self-confirming hypothesis.

The Nature of God

Given his Aristotelian teleology, we are not surprised to find Thomas espousing a God who is spirit (a body possesses the potential of division but God has no potentialities),[160] perfect (as the First Cause, he must contain within himself all perfections),[161] good (all things desire God as being the source of their perfection),[162] infinite (only that which is pure form is not potentially other forms, and only that form which is identical with its own existence as pure form is not contained or restricted by anything),[163] omnipresent ("he is in every place giving it existence and power to be a place"),[164] immutable (he is sheer act, with no potentiality),[165] eternal (since he is unchangeable),[166] and supremely one (he alone is his existence and undivided both actually and potentially).[167]

It is true of course that he cites Scripture in support of many of the above positions, but read through the lenses of Aristotelian metaphysics. For example, Thomas appeals to Malachi 3:6, "I am God, I change not",

---

160 1a.3.
161 1a.4.
162 1a.5, 6.
163 1a.7.
164 1a.8.
165 1a.9.
166 1a.10.
167 1a.11.

in support of the *immutabilitate Dei*. But what sort of unchangeableness is meant? He explains: "we have proved that there must be some first existent, called God, sheerly actual and unalloyed with potentiality . . . . Now any changing thing, whatsoever the change, is potential. So it clearly follows that God cannot change in any way."[168] It is doubtful that the text can bear such ontological weight. Where in context the passage seems to be stressing the faithfulness of God, who is moved by the plight of his wayward people, Thomas finds an Unmoved Mover.

When he comes to the doctrine of Providence (located, significantly, prior to his discussion of the Trinity and long before he comes to Grace at the end of the *Prima Secundae*), he begins by considering the will of God. He breaks with the philosophical necessitarianism of Aristotle, Avicenna and Averroes, in which the world flows as a necessary consequence from a god who is self-thinking thought:[169] "We cannot but hold that God's will is the cause of things, and that he works through will and not . . . through necessity of his nature." How does Thomas know this? He finds it in his demonstration for God's existence: "Since God is first in the order of efficient causes, the conclusion that he acts from intelligence and will follows strictly." God's being, containing all perfections, is self-determinate, and therefore he does not act from necessity of being but from his perfection by the decision of his intelligence and will.[170]

---

168 1a. 9.

169 Cf. Gilson, *The Elements of Christian Philosophy*, (New York: New American Library, 1963), 179ff.

170 1a.19, 4; cf. Thomas Aquinas, *On the Power of God*, trans. English Dominican Fathers, (London: Burns, Oates and Washbourne, 1932), 111, 15.

If this carries hints of voluntarism,[171] evidence is to be found elsewhere as well. Thomas consistently affirms that in the simplicity[172] of the divine being, God is a unity of intellect and will. But are the two aspects given equal weight, or is not the will in some sense dominant, at least at times? The natural order is created by God's free will, and determines the purpose and end of the universe.[173] Yet God could have ordained another order.[174] Indeed, as the First Cause, he is able to produce effects above a given order, as in the case of miracles. However, God cannot act against his own "foreknowledge, or His will, or His goodness."[175]

And yet, God is not subject to a given order: "On the contrary, this order is subject to Him, not by a natural necessity, but by the choice of His own will; for He could have created another order of things."[176] Therefore, "since the order of nature is given to things by God, if He does anything outside this order, it is not against nature."[177] Examples cited elsewhere in this connection include the preservation of the faithful

---

171 Cf. Roland H. Bainton, "The Immoralities of the Patriarchs According to the Exegesis of the Late Middle Ages and of the Reformation," *Harvard Theological Review*, vol. xxiii, 1930, 39-49; William J. Courtenay, "Covenant and Causality in Pierre D'Ailly," *Speculum*, vol. 46, 1971, 94-119; Courtenay, "The King and the Leaden Coin: The Economic Background of 'Sine Qua Non' Causality," *Traditio*, vol. 28, 1972, 185-209; George Lindbeck, "Nominalism and the Problems of Meaning as Illustrated by Pierre D'Ailly on Predestination and Justification," *Harvard Theological Review*, vol. 1ii, January 1959, 43-60; Heiko Oberman, "Some Notes on the Theology of Nominalism With Attention to its Relation to the Renaissance," *Harvard Theological Review*, vol. 1iii, 1960, 47-76; Oberman, "Facientibus Quod in Se Est Deus Non Denegat Gratiam," *Harvard Theological Review*, vol. 1v, 1962, 317-342; Oberman, "Fourteenth-Century Religious Thought: A Premature Profile," *Speculum*, vol. 53, 1978, 80-93; Oberman, *The Dawn of the Reformation*, (Edinburgh: T & T Clark, 1986); *Forerunners of the Reformation*, (Philadelphia: Fortress Press, 1981); *The Harvest of Medieval Theology. Gabriel Biel and Late Medieval Nominalism*, (Durham: Labyrinth Press, 1983); Charles Trinkhaus, "Erasmus and the Nominalists," *Archiv Fur Reformationsgeschicte*, vol. 67, 1976, 5-32.
172 St. Thomas Aquinas, *On Being and Essence*, trans. Armand Maurer, (Toronto: Pontifical Institute of Medieval Studies, 1983), ch. 5.
173 *Summa Contra Gentiles*, 1, 78, 85, 86.
174 *Ibid.*, 11, 28; Ia.26, 6 ad 3.
175 1a. 25, 6; cf. Meyer, *op. cit.*, 307-312.
176 *Ibid.*
177 Ia.105, 6 ad 1; cf. Walter Farrell, *A Companion to the Summa* vol. 1, (New York: Sheed and Ward, 1941), 381-82.

Israelites in the fiery furnace, the stoppage of the Jordan River's flow, and the virgin birth.[178]

It is clear that Thomas is not a true voluntarist, for God does nothing without reference to his goodness.[179] But there does seem to be a remarkable degree of divine freedom in reference to any order which God has established.

Thus he declares that God could have forgiven humankind without the satisfaction made by the passion of Christ. True, God's justice requires satisfaction for human sin, "but even this justice depends upon the divine will." That is to say, God alone decides the meaning of justice. If he chose to free humanity from sin without any satisfaction, he would not be acting unjustly. "God has no one above him, for he is himself the supreme and common good of the entire universe."[180] In the actual course of things God knew and willed the passion of Christ in advance. But "simply and absolutely speaking. God could have freed man otherwise . . . for nothing is impossible with God."[181]

Oliver O'Donovan finds an "astonishing insistence on the freedom of God" not only in the oft-cited late-medieval voluntarism of Duns Scotus and William of Ockham, but in the "whole scholastic tradition from Peter Lombard."[182] Thomas is thereby able to insure the freedom of God, but at the risk of opening at least a certain gap between the divine act and being, between the revelation and nature of God. For if there is no perceivable connection between who God is and how he wills to act in a given order, then he would be unknowable on the basis of his actions. Calvin and, more consistently, McLeod Campbell, would later argue that God is known only in his self-revelation in his Son, but that God is identical with himself in that disclosure such that we do know him.

At any rate, the Thomistic God is free. His willing is in no way caused.[183] Moreover, because it is the universal first cause, it must

---

178 *On the Power of God, vi., 1 ad 3.*

179 Cf. Pierre Rousselot, S. J., *The Intellectualism of Saint Thomas*, trans. James E. O'Mahony, (New York: Sheed and Ward, 1935), 50-56.

180 3a.46, 2 ad 3.

181 3a.46, 2.

182 *Resurrection and the Moral Order*, (Leicester: InterVarsity and Grand Rapids: Eerdmans, 1986), 40-41.

183 1a.19, 5.

always achieve its effect. This may appear difficult to maintain in the light of evil, but "whatever seems to depart from his will from one point of view returns to it from another." Thus a person who sins "re-enters" the divine plan when "by divine justice he is punished."[184]

How are we to understand I Timothy 2:4, "God wills all men to be saved" in light of the manifest fact that all are not saved? The text can be understood in three senses: (1) "God wills those to be saved who are saved;" (2) "God wills some to be saved of every condition, men and women, Jews and Gentiles, humble and great, but not all of every condition;" (3) "It refers to an antecedent, not a consequent will." Thus justice may be said antecedently to wish every man to live, but consequently to pronounce the capital sentence. This is willing in a qualified sense, Thomas concedes, more akin to "wishing than a sheer willing." We may therefore conclude that "whatever God wills simply speaking comes about, though what he wills antecedently does not."[185]

This is no limitation on God, we are assured. As the universal first cause embracing within itself all causality, his will has a plan from which "no effect can stray in any way at all."[186] But his plan is not that he alone will possess efficacy, while the rest of the universe remains inert. When he creates things, he confers upon them at the same time their efficacy. In a sense, then, a double causality lies behind each effect. All secondary causes receive their efficacy from the First Cause, and yet once they are given this efficacy it is theirs and so it is they who perform their operations.[187]

But this is not to say creatures are granted total freedom. God moves each thing in conformity to the principles of its nature. On some things his will does impose necessity. Certain things will "become real necessarily", but others will do so contingently. For the latter, he has "prepared contingent causes,"[188] which are, as he elsewhere explains, "causes able to act otherwise."[189] In the case of evils, he neither wills

---

184 1a.19, 6.
185 1a.19, 6 ad 1.
186 1a.19, 6 ad 3.
187 Gilson, *The Christian Philosophy of St. Thomas Aquinas*, 182-83.
188 1a.19, 8.
189 Exposition, *Perihermenias*, i, lect. 14, cited in *St. Thomas Aquinas. Theological Texts*, ed., tr. Thomas Gilby, (London: Oxford University Press, 1955), 99.

them to be nor not to be. He "wills to allow them to happen." And this, declares Aquinas, "is good."[190]

One cannot talk about the will of God without referring to his love, "for the first motion of will . . . is love." Love is always directed toward what is good and thus of its very nature lies at the root of all activity of will.[191] Being impassible, God cannot be said to "feel" love toward his creatures. His love is not a passion or emotion.[192] But since every existing thing insofar as it is real is good, God may be said to love everything.[193] Thus God loves sinners "as being real things of nature." Notwithstanding, to the extent they are sinners they are "unreal and deficient", and as such "he holds them in hatred."[194]

St. Thomas takes predestination as a chapter in the workings of Providence. This strikes him as perfectly logical, since divine providence governs everything and arranges them to an end.[195] What precisely is predestination? It is "the plan, existing in God's mind, for the ordering of some persons to salvation. The carrying out of this is passively as it were in the persons predestined, though actively in God."[196] But lest it drive the non-predestined to despair and the predestined to negligence, it is kept secret.[197]

In light of this, it is surprising that Thomas F. O'Meara, O.P., contends that for St. Thomas, God predestines all to the graced life:

> God has predestined every human being to live in a higher order of life called "graced" or "supernatural." Yet this original predestination, antecedent to the course of each life in freedom, does permit human wills to turn against nature and grace, to choose to fall away from the journey to God (I, 23, 3). Predestination is neither an arbitrary choice of some for heaven nor a force fixing freedom. For Aquinas predestination is a plan effecting

190 1a.19, 9 ad 3.
191 1a.20, 1.
192 1a.20, 1 ad 1.
193 1a.20, 2.
194 1a.20, 2 ad 4.
195 1a.23, 1.
196 1a.23, 2.
197 1a.23, 1 ad 4.

an order of grace offered to all who in their lives affirm
its gift.[198]

Yet St. Thomas seems to present a very different understanding of
predestination. As we have seen, he describes predestination as
God's plan for the ordering of "some" (not all) persons to salvation,
which is carried out "passively" in individuals who are predestined
and "actively" in God. He affirms that divine providence works
in all cases, ordaining some human beings to eternal life, while
allowing some to fall short of this goal. Reprobation therefore
exceeds foreknowledge, for it expresses the will to permit this falling
and indeed, to inflict the penalty of damnation in consequence.[199]

Does this call into question the universal love of God? Not at all: God
loves all people insofar as he wills some good to all. But "he does not
will every sort of good to each." Indeed, "in that he does not will to
some the blessing of eternal life he is said to hold them in hate or to
reprobate them."[200]

Despite his emphasis on the universal love of God, one cannot escape
the notion that we are here given a quite different picture of God, of one
who, in an important sense, may not be love in his innermost being. This
God is one who, by an act of will, determines to grant more goodness,
indeed eternal life to some, while withholding these from others and
then hates them for failing to have what he did not give them. And
such a point of view flows naturally from the doctrine of the Unmoved
Mover, the First Cause, albeit modified by the conception of an active
will in God[201] which determines the fate of his creatures.

The problem is not overcome by positing an active will as a means
of personalizing this Deity, for the divine will is still permitted quite a

198   Thomas F. O'Meara, O.P., *Thomas Aquinas: Theologian* (Notre Dame: University of Notre Dame Press, 1997), 104.
199   1a.23, 3.
200   1a.23, 3 ad 1; cf. *Summa Contra Gentiles*, I, 91.
201   Cf. Meyer, *op. cit.*, 272. Meyer also observes that Platonism as mediated through St. Augustine and the Pseudo-Areopagite modified Aristotle's Unmoved Mover with the concept that "Working as the supreme cause, the divine artisan by the free causality of His will brought into existence the universe modeled after the eternal ideas in His intellect." Yet as we shall see, the additional concept of the divine omnipotence tends to call into question the consistency of the relation between the divine ideas and divine action.

latitude in its relation to love and mercy. Gilson argues that goodness, and not power, is God's principal attribute, since God has willed to communicate "productive fecundity and efficacy" to the beings he has created. Power would have the right to retain these, but Goodness would wish to give them away.[202] But the question presses itself as to what Goodness it is that bestows itself stintingly on some of its creatures and then damns them for its absence?

St. Thomas argues that divine goodness lies behind both predestination and reprobation, since everything God does is "so that his goodness may be represented in things." But here a problem arises, for the simplicity of the divine being means that his goodness is also "single and simple", yet its outside expression must take form among creatures who are not. "Thus for the completeness of the universe diverse grades are required, some of high degree and some of humble." The "humble grades" are needed for the sake of those higher: many goods would be hindered were not evils allowed by God.[203]

In connection with the previous Question, he had observed that God, as the "universal guardian" exercises his providence so as to "allow defects in some particular things" for the "complete good" of the universe. Were all evils disallowed, many goods would be lacking: there would be no lions for want of prey, and no patience in martyrs for lack of persecution.[204]

If God in his goodness can allow evil where he chooses for the greater good of the universe, then he can certainly manifest his goodness as he sees fit among humanity. He wills to show his goodness to the predestined by mercifully sparing them, and to those whom he reprobates by justly punishing them. This, declares Thomas, "provides a key to the problem of why God chooses some and rejects others . . . His so willing is the sole ground." Therefore we have no grounds for questioning God's fairness in preparing "unequal lots for equals." No one is owed predestination: "He who grants by grace can give freely as he wills, be it more or less, without prejudice to justice."[205]

---

202 Op. cit., 183-84.
203 1a.23, 5.
204 1a.22, 2 ad 2; cf. Blanchette, *op. cit.*, 126-127; Grabmann, *op. cit.*, 120.
205 1a.23, 5 ad 3.

Aquinas affirms the unity of intellect and will in God and the inherent goodness of God in his being and actions.[206] Thus he cannot be charged with thoroughgoing voluntarism. But a kind of "soteriological voluntarism" emerges in his insistence that God's will has decreed "unequal lots for equals." Not only does the divine will here assume preeminence, but the very status and significance of the love of God is called into question.

Grace can be given "freely, as he wills, be it more or less" in a context wherein more means eternal bliss and 'less' means eternal misery. God can will whatever good he chooses--even the 'good' of reprobation and still display his love. One wonders whether the concept of love has in this instance been emptied of meaningful content. So again we find that behind the goodness, the grace of God, lies a will which can withhold eternal life from some and bestow it upon others equally undeserving.

For Thomas Aquinas, grace is not the first word in the divine plan. God only determines to be gracious to certain ones. In a telling comment on Peter Lombard's definition of predestination as "a preparation for grace in the present, and for glory in the future,"[207] he says

> Grace is not included in the definition of predestination as though it were an essential element, but because predestination implies a relationship to grace, namely a relationship of cause to effect, and of act to objective.[208]

Predestination precedes grace, as cause to effect. In other words, God is not gracious within his innermost being. He is Will, Power. And by his will he determines that some shall be brought through a process that will result in grace. For Aquinas, it seems evident, law precedes grace.

But God is not the author of evil, and so Aquinas posits an asymmetry between reprobation and predestination. The latter is the cause both of glory in the future and grace in the present. Yet reprobation does not cause that which is in the present, namely, moral fault. And moral fault is the cause of someone being left without God now, while reprobation is the cause for his receiving eternal punishment in the future.

---

206 Cf. W. J. Hankey, *God in Himself. Aquinas' Doctrine of God as expounded in the Summa Theologiae*, (Oxford: Oxford University Press, 1987), 106-110.
207 *Sentences* 1, 40, 2, cited *in loc.*
208 Ia.23, 2 ad 4.

In this way Thomas can preserve free will: "The fault starts from the free decision of the one who abandons grace and is rejected, so bringing the prophecy to pass, Your loss is from yourself, O Israel."[209] Therefore reprobation does not qualify the rejected one's freedom. That he cannot "acquire grace" is a "hypothetical" rather than an "absolute impossibility." That is, if he abandons grace, God's judgment will be that he cannot acquire it; he is rejected. "Likewise . . . one predestined must needs be saved, namely on a conditional necessity, which does not impair freewill."[210]

At the same time, he does not want to give ground to the Pelagians, whom he understands to have held that predestination is based on foreknowledge of merit. They thought, he explains, that a person merits the first grace. Hence predestination is an effect given only to those who "make a good start" and "prepare themselves for it." No, says Thomas, St. Paul declares, "We are not sufficient of ourselves to think of anything as of ourselves" (2 Cor. 3:5). Therefore "it is not tenable . . . that we can initiate anything in ourselves that can be the reason for predestination as an effect."

Others suggest that God grants grace to a person and, knowing he will use it well, predestines him. This is not to be rejected outright. The fallacy here lies in distinguishing between what is an effect of grace and what is an effect of free will. In fact, the two cannot be separated any more than what is due to a "secondary cause" can be from what is due to the "first cause": "God's Providence procures its effects through the operation of secondary causes. Hence what is through freewill is also from predestination."

Now, if we analyze predestination in terms of its parts, we find that one effect of it may logically be the motive and reason of another. In that case, one effect may be the cause of another when considered in terms of final causality, but the reverse may be true in terms of "meritorious causality." Thus we may say that "God pre-ordains that he will give glory because of merit, and also pre-ordains that he will give grace to a person in order to merit glory."

On the other hand, if we look at predestination as a whole, the effect of predestination "in its completeness" has no cause in man. Even his

---

209 1a.23, 3 ad 2.
210 1a.23, 3 ad 3.

"preparing himself for grace" is comprehended in predestination as a total effect, for this is only done with God's help. Here he cites Lamentations 5:21: "Turn thou us to thee, O Lord, and we shall be turned."[211]

Thomas thinks that by resisting the separation between grace and merit which he finds in Pelagianism he can attribute all to grace and yet retain free will. At the same time he rejects a passive role for humans in salvation: They are freely choosing even as God is freely electing. At the end of the day, it would seem that there is too much emphasis on humankind's role, and salvation becomes in some sense anthropocentric and subjective.

Aquinas clearly emphasizes that human freedom is not bound by divine Providence. Indeed, Providence grants humans power to choose freely among a range of choices. He comments on Ecclesiasticus 15:14 where it is said that when God made man he left him *in manu consilii sui*, in the hands of his own counsel. The text is not denying Providence, rather:

> it means that their active power, unlike that of physical things, is not set to follow one narrow track . . . self-determining agents . . . shape themselves to a purpose, in the manner of rational creatures who deliberate and choose by free judgement. Hence the pointed expression, of their being in the hand of their own devices (*in manu consilii sui*). Yet because the very act of freewill goes back to God as its cause, we strictly infer that whatever men freely do on their own falls under God's Providence.[212]

He wants, it would appear, to have it both ways. While Providence's plan is "unfailing" and predestination is "certain", "freedom of choice" remains. To explain this conundrum, Thomas appeals to the language of causality. Under Providence, some things happen "necessarily" and others "contingently", the latter being, as we have seen "causes able to act otherwise." Indeed, predestination, though certain, depends on human decision: " . . . the plan of predestination is certain, though the

211 1a.23, 5.
212 1a.22, 2 ad 4.

47

freedom of choice, from which predestination as an effect contingently issues is not abolished."[213]

Nevertheless the number and even names of the predestined are fixed. It would seem the only way to resolve the paradox would be to appeal to foreknowledge of human decision, but no, predestination is also "by reason of [God's] own defining decision and choice." The number of the reprobate is not predetermined in the same way, but only "in light of what is good for the elect." Again Thomas resorts to the notion that the elect somehow benefit from the damnation of others.[214]

This fundamental equivocation in his conception of grace forms the Achilles heel in the entire attempt to synthesize freedom and grace, reason and revelation, nature and grace. Aristotelian logic, with its categories of primary and proximate causality, when amalgamated into theological discourse, can lead to an overemphasis on the efforts of the creature at the expense of the grace of the Creator.

Thus Thomas will tell us that predestination is "helped" by the prayers of the saints and "good works", because predestination works through secondary causes. We may even speak of such deeds as those "without which he will not reach" salvation. The shift away from God as the sole source of grace and onto secondary causes has implications for the spiritual life: "Those predestined must strive in prayer and good works, for through them the effect of predestination will surely be fulfilled. This is why Peter says, Give diligence to make your calling and election sure.[215] According to Thomism, it would seem, our salvation is not complete in God. It is begun in Him and completed by humankind. Our calling and election are not sure in Christ, but in our deeds.

Elsewhere the question is raised whether a person can know he has grace. In a manner characteristic of his epistemology, Thomas replies that we can know something in three ways. The first, by direct revelation, is only granted to a few. In the second way we know it "in and of itself." But God is "beyond the reach of our knowledge", and so we cannot be assured we have grace by looking to God. However, there is a third way in which we know things "inferentially, by perceptible signs." He proceeds with a method bearing a pronounced resemblance

213 1a.23, 6.
214 1a.22, 2 ad 4.
215 1a.23, 8.

to later Federal Calvinism's *syllogismus practicus*.[216] "In this sense someone can know that he has grace, for example, by perceiving that he takes delight in God and despises worldly things, and by not being conscious of any mortal sin in himself . . . ." Thomas concedes that such knowledge is "imperfect", but he can offer nothing better to replace it.[217]

Yet there is a profound consistency here with the rest of his teaching, for in line with his conviction that all knowledge begins with sensory experience, he reasons from effect to cause, from signs of election to election, from works in a person to grace in God. But this appeal to *experentia* as an independent source of knowledge provides an illuminating contrast to Calvin's conviction that certainty of election is to be found in Christ alone.[218]

It would seem that the graciousness of grace is at stake here. Grace is not always the alpha and omega of the Christian life. For some, the non-elect, it may serve as the alpha only. This momentous separation between grace and election means that a person may walk for a time in the "life of grace," heading toward the "life of glory" and yet fail to arrive. Grace is something which may be possessed at one moment and lost the next.[219] Only if one has, in addition to grace, predestination, will he assuredly reach eternal life. Those who have only grace can "lapse through grave sin." They are entered "provisionally" in the Book of Life; their names can be "struck off."[220] By contrast, the predestined, "though they should fall many times, eventually rise again."[221]

All of this is in line with the Thomist conviction that God is not gracious in his innermost being; he only decides to be gracious to certain ones. And this is so because fundamentally, this God who is the pure Act of Being and hence utterly self-determining, possesses a will which is in some sense prior to his love. When we refer to his own *voluntatem*, we are speaking of his "very essence." It is true that in terms of the

---

216 R T. Kendall, *Calvin and English Calvinism to 1649*, (Oxford: Oxford University Press, 1981), 8-9, 29, 33-34, 40- 41, 56-57, 63, 69-74, 179-81; M. Charles Bell, *Calvin and Scottish Theology. The Doctrine of Assurance*, (Edinburgh: Handsel Press, 1985), 50, 82, 84-85, 136.
217 vol. 30 (1a2ae.106-114), tr., ed. Cornelius Ernst O. P., 112, 5.
218 Calvin, *Institutes*, III.xxiv.4f.
219 1a.24, 2 ad 3.
220 1a.24, 3.
221 3a.9, 2 ad 1.

ratione horum by which God made the creatures, his will can be spoken of as intelligence (ratio) itself.[222] But as O'Donovan observes, Thomas demonstrates that this identification of will and reason in God "can be put to the service of a fundamentally voluntarist perception of divine omnipotence."[223]

Law

We are not surprised to learn that Aquinas' exposition of law flows directly from his conception of the nature of God. If will is a primary category for God's essence, and grace only his occasional determination, law would logically require treatment before grace. Thus Thomas reasons that "From outside the principle of our going towards good is God, who builds us up by law and supports us by grace. So we shall speak about law in the first place and grace afterwards."[224] Law is first because by our conformity to it we arrive at the goal of life, (the "good"). In this sense it may be said that the proper effect of law is to "make men good."[225] But in order that we might keep the law, God assists us by grace. Grace helps persons bear the "yoke of the law."[226] Is not this tantamount to suggesting that humankind was created with primarily legal intentions, for obedience, while grace only enters afterward to serve the ends of law?

Now, that from which all true laws descend is the "Eternal Law",[227] which *lex aeterna* is "the rational order of divine wisdom inasmuch as it directs the acts and motions of everything."[228] But we must ask: what is the relation between this law and the being of God? No sovereign can be compelled to obey the law, "Yet of his own will a sovereign is subject to the directive power of the law", for a person should practice a law he establishes for another. Consequently he is above the law; he only binds himself to fulfill it. So his keeping within the law is a matter of will, not of any necessity of his being. However, he ought to will this, because he

222 vol. 28, (1a2ae.90-97), tr., ed. Thomas Gilby O.P. (London: Eyre and Spottis-woode, 1966), 93, 4 ad 2.
223 *Op. cit.*, 41, cf. 1a.25, 3 ad 5.
224 1a2ae.90 intro.
225 1a2ae.92, 1.
226 1a2ae.98, 1 ad 3.
227 93, 3 sed contra.
228 93, 1, cited in O'Donovan, *op. cit.*, 133.

has already willed to establish this order. At the same time "he is above the law in that he can change it if expedient . . . ."[229]

To be sure, God is the "sovereign of the universe",[230] and the Eternal Law, as we have seen, is the rational order by which the divine wisdom directs all acts and motions. "Consequently all laws in so far as they share in right reason to that extent derive from the Eternal Law."[231] This would seem to suggest that Thomas grounds true law in the being of God himself as rational. And indeed, Copleston argues that the knowability of natural law (natural law being, as we shall see, the participation of intelligent creatures in the eternal law) presupposes "God's vision of himself as imitable in a certain way in creation." For if moral law were solely contingent upon "God's arbitrary choice, it could be known only by revelation."[232]

However, in the very article in which Aquinas is arguing that "law is a function of reason,"[233] he concedes that "reason gets its motive force from the will . . . For it is because a person wills an end that his reason effectively governs arrangements to bring it about."[234] Hence reason is only concerned to achieve the ends decreed by the will and is thereby relative to it.

Thomas wants to guard against any notion of divine caprice by appealing to reason as that which governs the arrangements to bring about the end willed. He goes on to say that "To have the quality of law in what is so commanded the will must be ruled by some reason, and the maxim, the prince's will has the force of law, has to be understood with that proviso, otherwise his will would make for lawlessness rather than law." And yet if reason only serves the ends of the will in lawmaking, is not law, an important sense, grounded in will?

How then can humankind know the moral law apart from revelation? Humans, being rational, participate in the rational eternal law which God has ordained. They can thereby perceive the divine purpose in their own being and in the rest of the natural order. Yet this will not provide

---

229 96, 5 ad 3.
230 93, 3.
231 *Ibid.*
232 *History of Medieval Philosophy*, 191.
233 90, 1 sed contra.
234 90, 1 ad 3.

access to the being of God, but only to the particular rational ordering ordained by divine fiat.

The eternal law, being the divine providence governing the acts and motions of all creatures, proceeds from the will of God. As such, we should expect that God himself is not subject to it. And that is exactly what we find. The will of God in the sense of "his own willing" is "his very essence" and as such is "not subject to his government or to the Eternal Law, but is the Eternal Law." But "the things God wills in creatures" are subject to the eternal law.[235]

O'Donovan declares:

> Nothing could be clearer than that *lex aeterna* presupposes the free and omnipotent decree of God in creation, and so the complete contingency of creation. It is not a law of God's own being, but a law by which he orders the created world to its given destiny.[236]

William P. Lee argues that Aquinas is not a voluntarist, since for the latter the divine ideas are unchangeable and "somehow prior to God's free choice."[237] That the divine ideas[238] are immutable in Thomist thought seems clear enough.[239] But they do not govern all aspects of God's willing. Lee observes that "For St. Thomas the divine ideas are identical with God's essence as understood to be imitable in many ways."[240] To be sure, 1a.15,1 ad 3 does assert that "God is the likeness of all things according to his essence; therefore an idea in God is nothing other than his essence." But in the foregoing response Thomas inserts a crucial qualifier:

> Although God knows Himself and all else by His own essence, yet his own essence is the operative principle of all things, *except of Himself*. It has therefore the nature

---

235 *Summa*, 93, 4.
236 *Ibid.*, 133.
237 William Patrick Lee, "The Natural Law and the Decalogue in St. Thomas Aquinas," PhD dissertation, Marquette University, 1980, 117.
238 Cf. Copleston, *Aquinas*, 98, 142f; Gilson, *The Christian Philosophy of St. Thomas Aquinas*, 125-26.
239 See, e.g., 1a.15, 2 sed contra; cf. Harry Wolfson, *Religious Philosophy*, (Cambridge, Mass: Belknapp Press, 1961), 57-64.
240 Ibid., 124; cf. *On the Power of God*, 111.16.

of an idea with respect to other things, *though not with respect to God Himself*.[241]

It would seem that for Aquinas, the divine ideas do not comprehend the divine essence as such, but created things. They only, so to speak, touch the "hem of his garment." In 1a.15, 2 he goes on to explain that God knows his essence in two ways: as it is in itself, and as it can be participated in by creatures "according to some kind of likeness"[242] This second way of knowing his essence insofar as it is imitable Aquinas calls a knowing of an idea. The divine ideas, then, regulate creatures and not God. *They describe finite participations in the divine essence.* They do not, however, perfectly exemplify the divine essence,[243] and hence do not exhaust it.[244]

Lee wants to demonstrate that God does not permit dispensations from the natural law.[245] St. Thomas shared that same concern, but was not altogether successful in pursuing it. For the "divine reason" is perfect and immutable.[246] Nevertheless only two articles later he reasons that since natural law proceeds from the will of God, God can change it.[247] Thus he finds himself in the ironic position of arguing for God's freedom to command an act contrary to the *lex naturae* in the very passage in which he is defending the unchanging nature of natural law: "adultery is intercourse with another's wife; who is allotted to him by the law emanating from God. Consequently intercourse with any woman, by the command of God, is neither adultery nor fornication."[248]

Elsewhere treating the same issue, Thomas countenances the question whether such a command is in accord with "right reason." He

---

241 *Basic Writings of Saint Thomas Aquinas*, vol. 1, tr., ed. Anton C. Pegis (New York: Random House, 1945) 1a.15, 1 ad 2 (emphasis mine), henceforth, Pegis trans.

242 Pegis trans.

243 1a.47, 1 ad 2.

244 "In knowing himself, not as he is in himself, but as he can be participated in by creatures, God knows ideas" (Gilson, *History of Christian Philosophy in the Middle Ages*, (London: Sheed and Ward, 1958), 374).

245 *Ibid.*, 19.

246 1a2ae.97, 1.

247 1a2ae.97, 3 ad 1; 4 ad 3.

248 1a2ae.94, 5 ad 2 (Pegis trans.); cf. *On the Power of God*, 1, 6.

responds that God's will determines the nature of right reason; if God commands fornication it cannot be against right reason.[249]

Hans Meyer notes that by basing law both intellect and will, Aquinas "built a bulwark against legal Positivism and legal voluntarism which denied a universally valid legal objective order in the world."[250] And yet Meyer is also troubled by Aquinas' notion of divinely-ordained exceptions to the natural law.

> He adopts the viewpoint that the killing of the innocent, adultery, and theft are indeed violations of the natural law, but he tries to explain the difficulties by referring to God as the supreme Lord and Lawgiver, who has peculiar relations to men and things . . . These distinctions and explanations contribute no more to the solution of the difficulty than the simple reference to God's absolute sovereignty, and this latter explanation is an unintentional admission of moral positivism.[251]

Natural law thus is binding on humankind, but not on their Maker. When Lee argues that the divine ideas govern the being of God, he overlooks the fact that the Thomist God transcends these finite participations. In his innermost being, his will is, in a certain sense, prior.

Lee points us to 1a.25, where Thomas discusses the distinction between God's *potentia absoluta* and *potentia ordinata*.[252] But it is precisely there that a full-blown voluntarism comes to the surface. For God's omnipotence means that he can do anything that does not involve a contradiction in terms.[253] Brian Davies concludes that such a view calls into question the possibility of extrapolating from the observable world to the character of God.

> An implication of this position [concerning God's omnipotence] . . . is that from God's world we can

---

249 2a2ae.154, 2 ad 2.

250 Meyer, *op. cit.*, 457.

251 *Ibid.*, 496-97.

252 Lee, 135ff.

253 1a.25; cf. *On the Power of God*, 1, 2 et 3; *Summa Contra Gentiles*, 11, 22; cf. Anthony Kenny, "The Definition of Omnipotence," in Thomas V. Morris, ed., *The Concept of God*, (Oxford: Oxford University Press, 1988), 20-21, 33.

deduce nothing about his character, not as we would normally deduce character anyway. Something quite different from what we find could, in fact, have been God's world.[254]

Nonetheless Aquinas, as we have seen,[255] thinks he can deduce perfection, goodness, infinity, omnipresence, immutability, and simplicity from the natural world. And W. J. Hankey concludes: "When the Five Ways are taken together, they can be immediately seen to produce a considerable knowledge of God."[256]

Lee argues that among the classes of things that imply a contradiction for Aquinas are those which would "contradict God's wisdom and goodness." He cites 1a.25, 3 ad 2, where St. Thomas reasons that God cannot sin, for to be able to sin is to be able to fail by falling short of full activity, which would be incompatible with omnipotence. Clearly he does not want to attribute voluntarism to God, but it is significant that he appeals to God's power rather than his goodness as the reason he could not sin.

Furthermore, Lee refers to 1a.25, 3 ad 3, where it is affirmed that "the carrying out of divine mercy is at the root of all God's works," and that bringing men to share in "infinite good" is the "crowning effect of God's power." But does this mean that God's mercy and goodness are directed towards the salvation of all humankind? Back in 1a.21 Aquinas indicates that God's mercy is shown in different ways: by granting a human existence, by bestowing a penalty of damnation on the reprobate which is nonetheless 'lighter than deserved,' or by sparing evildoers. In this way he is able to hold that God is good to everyone, although he does not "will every sort of good to each."[257] And if pressed as to why this is so, Thomas will say that "eventually, all goes back to the simple will of God."[258]

---

254 Brian Davies, *The Thought of Thomas Aquinas*, (Oxford: Clarendon Press, 1992), 124.
255 Cf. supra, 54-55.
256 *God in Himself. Aquinas' Doctrine of God as expounded in the Summa Theologiae*, 41.
257 1a.23, 3 ad 1.
258 1a.19, 5 ad 3.

It is striking too that at the very point Thomas is arguing for mercy and goodness being in some way at the foundation of all God's works, he avers that God's forgiving sins freely "declares his supreme power; he that is bound by the law of a superior is not free to forgive offenses against it."[259] It would appear that divine forgiveness finds its underpinning in God's freedom from Law. While the Law is grounded in the being of God as rational, it nonetheless represents an order determined by the will of God. Therefore, in Thomas' thinking, God is above that particular order.

True, God is a God who is goodness in his inmost nature and thus cannot act without regard to goodness. But his relation to law as his ordained order for humans, and his forgiving breaches of it, are matters of his will. It would appear that we see here a parallel to his discussion of double predestination: "He who grants by grace can give freely as he wills, be it more or less, without prejudice to justice."[260]

If forgiveness is a matter for his omnipotence, and grace a decision of his will, and the eternal destinies of equally undeserving humans can be variously determined according to his will, it would seem that his division of the thought of the will of God from the self-disclosure of God in Christ has proven to be determinative.

Why is the overarching concept of the will of God so prominent in Thomas' thought? He is anxious to demonstrate that employing Aristotelian categories does not perforce entail a necessitarian view of the divine being.[261] Aristotle's God, in fact, has no true "will;" only an attractive power.[262] But Aquinas asserted that "God does not act from necessity of nature, but . . . his will is the cause of all things, and there is no natural drive that necessitates and determines and makes his will produce them." Thus we cannot say that there is a necessary relation between the "present course of things" and the being of God. Nor does God's wisdom 'require' that things be as they are, for His wisdom and power are one.[263] Indeed, in terms of God's *potentia absoluta*, he can do

---

259 1a.25, 3 ad 3.
260 1a.23, 5 ad 3.
261 Gilson, *The Christian Philosophy of St. Thomas Aquinas*, 79, 83.
262 Hans Meyer, *The Philosophy of St. Thomas Aquinas*, 272-303.
263 1a.25, 5.

anything that is consonant with being. Whatever God chooses to do is *conveniens et iustum* if he decides to do it.[264]

Nevertheless, the Eternal Law is the ideal order of the universe by which God's wisdom governs the acts and movements of every single creature.[265] And yet even this ordering of creation known as the *lex aeterna* cannot be known as it is in itself by anyone but God himself and the blessed, who see him in his essence. At the same time, "every rational creature can know about it according to some dawning, greater or less, of its light." Indeed, everyone knows at least the "general principles of natural law."[266]

Now, the Eternal Law governs the motions and actions of everything.[267] From this, all true laws descend.[268] But human laws are often imperfect, and fail to reflect the divine *ratio* ordained for the world; hence we must stipulate that "all laws, in so far as they share in right reason . . . derive from the Eternal Law."[269]

As rational creatures, humans have a share in the *ratio aeterna* whereby they are inclined to their proper acts and end, and this participation of the eternal law in the intelligent creature is called the 'natural law'. Thus "by the light of natural reason" they can "discern what is good and what evil."[270]

We have observed that Thomas has already ruled out any noetic effects of original sin on humanity. Humanity *qua* humanity is rational and as such participates in the Eternal Law. And yet post-lapsarian humans now have the potential of lessening that sharing.[271] By habitually sinning, humans can render their participation imperfect and corrupt, so that "their natural instinct for virtue is spoilt by vice and their natural knowledge of what is right is darkened by the passions and habits of sin.[272] Nevertheless, no person is so dominated by sinning that "his

---

264 1a.25, 5 ad 2, cf. O'Donovan, 41.
265 1a2ae.93, 1 et ad 1; cf. O'Connor, *Aquinas and Natural Law*, 59.
266 1a2ae.93, 2.
267 1a2ae.93, 1.
268 1a2ae.93, 3 sed contra.
269 1a2ae.93, 3.
270 1a2ae. 91, 2.
271 1a2ae. 91, 6.
272 1a2ae.93, 6.

essential soundness is destroyed; the instinct remains for doing what is according to Eternal Law.[273]

By synderesis, which is the "law of our understanding," we know the first precepts of natural law.[274] They are indemonstrable,[275] for these basic principles are grasped intuitively apart from formal moral training by an innate capacity of the mind.[276] Moreover, these precepts are by definition the same for everyone and recognized by all as such. There may be differences, however, with respect to particular conclusions drawn from these common principles; differences which deepen as we descend into details.[277]

In defining the content of *lex naturae*, Aquinas begins with Aristotelian teleology: "every agent acts on account of an end, and to be an end carries the meaning of 'to be good' . . . And so this is the first command of law, 'that good is to be sought and done, evil to be avoided'; all other commands of natural law are based on this." Since good is the end all seek after, reason by nature discerns what is good by apprehending the objectives humanity naturally tends toward, while apprehending their contraries as evil and so to be avoided. In fine, a human by the light of reason can discern the fundamental tendencies of his nature and by reflecting on them can come to a knowledge of the natural law. And since this law is a participation in the eternal law, humankind can know the basic divinely-given principles for all conduct.

Now, we perceive three stages in the order of the commands of *lex naturae*. First, humans, along with all substances, have an appetite for self-preservation. Secondly, they share with animals the drive towards procreation. Finally, there is in humankind an "appetite for the good of his nature as rational," such as to "know truths about God and about living in society." Natural law enters all three levels, but especially this third one,[278] for a human's "proper form" is the rational soul. Indeed, humanity has a "natural tendency to act according to reason," which is to act virtuously.[279]

---

273 1a2ae.93, 6 ad 2.
274 1a2ae.94, 1 ad 2.
275 1a2ae.91, 3.
276   Cf. Eardley and Still, *Aquinas: A Guide for the Perplexed*, 79.
277 1a2ae.94, 4.
278 1a2ae. 94, 2.
279 1a2ae.94, 3.

Nonetheless, in order for a human's natural aptitude for virtue to be perfected, he must be educated. For some, especially among the young, "fatherly admonition" is sufficient, but others, who are "headlong in vice", can only be held back through fear and force, which are the concomitants of the discipline of "human law." Eventually, they may become habituated to the point that they may voluntarily do what formerly they did out of fear.[280]

All laws are just insofar as they accord with right reason, the first rule of which is natural law. Hence to the extent that a given human or "positive" law derives from natural law, it has the force of law.[281] Having begun with common and indemonstrable principles, human reason arrives at the more specific arrangements known as human law. For support, Thomas quotes Cicero's assertion that "justice took its start from nature."[282]

Now, commands may be derived from the *lex naturae* in two ways. The first is the way of deduction from premises, such as the prohibition against murder, which is inferred from the natural law principle "you must do harm to nobody." The second involves specific determinations of natural law, such as particular penalties to be exacted for its breach. Of course, only the first has the force of natural law; the second carries the weight of human law.[283]

But natural and human law are insufficient to direct humans to the eternal happiness which is their end. Since it is the role of law to direct persons to "actions matching what they are made for," and what they are made for is "out of proportion to their natural resources," there must be a God-given law which is above natural and human law.[284] Conformity to natural law by one's native abilities will only carry a person so far. Then grace is introduced to perfect nature, "through the divine grant of an additional law which heightens their sharing in the eternal law."[285] This "divine law" directs them to their end in a four-fold way, as exposited in his interpretation of Psalm 19:7:

---

280 1a2ae.95, 1.
281 1a2ae.95, 3.
282 *De inventione oratoria* 11, 53, cited in 1a2ae. 91, 3.
283 1a2ae.95, 3.
284 1a2ae. 91, 4.
285 1a2ae.91, 4 ad 1.

The law of the Lord is unspotted, i.e., allowing no foulness of sin; converting souls, because it directs not only exterior, but also interior, acts; the testimony of the Lord is faithful, because of the certainty of what is true and right; giving wisdom to little ones, by directing man to an end supernatural and divine.[286]

It must be said that St. Thomas here envisages quite a comprehensive role for law. God is the Supreme Lawgiver who creates humans in some sense to conform to Law. Indeed, everything he wills for a person is accomplished by divine law: it proscribes all sinning, promulgates the *finis* of his life, and then sets forth the actions he must undertake in order to attain that end. As Gilson puts it, "Divine law is addressed personally to each human being in order to make him subject to God, to attach him to God and to unite him finally to God by means of love."[287]

Of course, this also reminds us that law is not the *summum bonum* of life; it is only a transient (albeit indispensable) stage along the way, which looks to its replacement one day by a state of union and communion with God in the beatific vision. But it is conformity to law that conducts a person there. In that sense, law is not only the means but also the goal. In this connection Thomas adduces Paul's declaration that "The commandment has charity as its goal" (I Tim 1:5) as proof that "all law tends of its nature to establish harmonious relationships between man and man or between man and God."[288]

In Thomas' thought, law is not limited to the three uses Calvin later expounded---as a mirror,[289] a curb,[290] and as a teacher for those "in whose hearts the Spirit of God already lives and reigns."[291] These are all Christocentric: the first two are ways in which the law serves as a schoolmaster, leading us to Christ, while the third indicates its use for the one who is united to Christ. Aquinas' four-fold function of law, as we shall see, bears certain resemblances to these, but since the Christ his

---

286 1a2ae.91, 4 (Pegis trans.).
287 *The Christian Philosophy of St. Thomas Aquinas,* 333.
288 1a2ae.99, 1 ad 2.
289 *Op. cit.,* II.vii.7.
290 *Ibid.,* II.vii.8.
291 *Ibid.,* II.vii.12.

law points to is not the one who is the sole foundation of the gospel,[292] but one who begins a work which we must complete by our obedience, the similarities prove superficial. For Thomas, our conformity to law has a predominant place in the Christian life.

> The Gentiles obtained salvation more perfectly and more surely through the observances of the Law than they would have if they had confined themselves to the natural law alone . . . In the same way now laymen enter the clerical state and the non-religious the religious state even though they could obtain salvation without this.[293]

Certainly the focus is here directed not to a salvation completed once and for all in the vicarious obedience unto death of Christ (as in Calvin and Campbell), but toward a work which must be fulfilled in us by our decision and activity (although with the assistance of grace). This accords, as we shall see, with the medieval conception of justification as the process whereby the individual is "made just" in his own personal history.

Thus Thomas will tell us that "the fulfillment of the commandments of the law . . . has the character of justification, inasmuch as it is just that man should obey God."[294] He was rightly concerned that the mighty salvation of Christ be related to the empirical experience of humans. But the emphasis on *experentia* all too easily becomes a doctrine of conditional grace in which our acceptance before God is contingent upon our merit and worthiness. And this loss of the freedom of grace in its *unmeritedness* stems, we think, from the separation of the concept of the will of God from the self-revelation of God in and through his Son.

Nevertheless, law has the wide-ranging character we have just observed in Aquinas' thought. Divine Law works all this in its two-fold form, namely, as "Old Law" and "New Law." They are related to one another as imperfect and perfect within the same species. Hence both are ordained to the common good, but in different ways: the Old Law is concerned with "material and earthly benefit" while the other envisages "spiritual and heavenly good." Moreover, Law's purpose is to direct

---

292 See *Institutes* II.x.4.
293 1a2ae. 98, 5.
294 1a2ae.100, 2 ad 1.

human acts, which the Old Law accomplishes by restraining exterior acts, while the New Law restrains interior acts. Finally, it belongs to law "to lead men into keeping its commandments. This the Old Law did through fear of penalty, but the New Law through the love shed in our hearts by the grace of Christ."[295]

Thomas exposits the Old Law in terms of the metaphysic of final causality. He affirms that the Old Law was good, but imperfectly so, in that while it was "of some assistance in attaining the end," it was not sufficient of itself to realize it. For the end of divine law is to bring humans to enjoy eternal happiness, and Old Law contributes to that goal by removing obstacles such as "sins which are contrary to reason."

However the Old Law is unable make persons completely fit to share in that *felicitatis aeternae*. For this, the grace of the Holy Spirit is needed, by which love is shed in our hearts, thereby fulfilling the requirements of the law. This grace is conferred by Christ in the New Law.[296] But this is not to say that Christ fulfills the requirements *for us*. He only bestows a grace which will "help" us bear the "yoke of the law."[297] This synergistic emphasis sounds the predominant note throughout the Thomist corpus, and qualifies everything said about grace.[298]

Already we are given a tell-tale sign that for Aquinas reconciliation is not achieved for us and in us in the vicarious obedience of the Man Jesus, as Calvin and McLeod Campbell would emphasize. Rather, as we shall see, the work of Christ is by his obedience unto death to merit grace so as to set up a potential relation with us, a relation whose fulfillment awaits our meritorious obedience assisted by his grace.

All of this presupposes a conditional view of grace. Obedience to Old Law could not take persons all the way, but it was a necessary stage along the way.[299] What then was the purpose of the *lex vetus*? In his commentary on Galatians he finds a fourfold function: first, to "suppress wickedness"; second, to "disclose human weakness"; third, to "tame the concupiscence" that evil people might not degenerate even further; and

---

295 1a2ae.91, 5.
296 1a2ae.98, 1.
297 1a2ae.98, 1 ad 3.
298 Cf. T. F. Torrance, *Theology in Reconstruction*, (London: SCM Press, 1965), 174.
299 St. Thomas Aquinas, *Commentary on St. Paul's Epistle to the Galatians*, trans. F. R. Larcher, (Albany: Magi Books, 1966), 142.

fourth, to set forth a "figure of future grace serving as a "shadow of the good things to come" (Heb. 10:1).[300]

The second purpose illuminates his conception of the relation between grace and law, for law's work of exposing human imperfection points the way to grace. When a person saw his inability consistently to avoid sinning, he would "more ardently yearn for grace."[301] Indeed, the Old Law was given that he might "seek the grace of a mediator." We are reminded of the Federal theologians' stress on the importance of a "law work" preceding true conversion.[302] Already in the thirteenth century, their scholastic forebear reasoned that "before they should receive grace, they had to be convinced by the law."[303]

What is more, Aquinas went so far as to set forth three eras in salvation history: the law of nature, followed by the Old Law---embodying the natural law and its applications in written form,[304] and then by the "law of grace."[305] Later Calvinists would refer to a "covenant of works" manifest in nature and discerned by the light of reason, republished at Sinai, and then displaced (for the elect) by a "covenant of grace."[306]

And he emphasizes that this ordering was intended by God as his way of leading persons to grace. Thus God granted his help in stages, "men being led to the perfect by means of the less perfect."[307] For after the sin of the first human, the guiding light of natural law had not yet been darkened by habitual sin."[308] But gradually, by the proliferation of sin, *lex naturae* became obscured enough that humankind became proud of their knowledge and power, thinking these were sufficient for salvation.[309] "And therefore, in order that it might be brought home to him that he was proud in this sense, man was left to the guidance of his

---

300 *Ibid.*, 95-97.

301 *Ibid.*, 96.

302 Cf. Bell, *Calvin and Scottish Theology*, (Edinburgh: Handsel, 1985), 53, 59, 77-78, 95, 139, 158, 165, 187-88.

303 *Ibid.*, 97.

304 1a2ae.99, 4.

305 *Ibid.*, 96; 1a2ae.98, 6.

306 For an extensive discussion of the place of *foedera* in Calvinist theology, see David A. Weir, *The Origins of Federal Theology in Sixteenth-Century Reformation Thought*, (Oxford: Clarendon Press, 1990).

307 1a2ae. 98, 6.

308 1a2ae.98, 6 ad 1.

309 *Commentary on Galatians*, 96.

own reason without the support of the written law." By observing the moral deterioration of humankind he could learn the deficiencies of his reason,[310] and thus his need of a written law.[311]

If the first era showed persons their lack of knowledge, the second (Old Law) "was given which would cause a knowledge of sin" and of their inability to avoid sin consistently without help. But the written law itself became an occasion for sin because "concupiscence, not yet healed by grace, lusted after what was forbidden, with the result that sin became more grievous, being now a violation of a written law." But, reasons Aquinas, God permitted this so that persons having recognized their own imperfection, "might seek the grace of a mediator."[312]

To be fair to the Angelic Doctor, he did not intend to place law prior to grace as a condition of it. He takes pains to emphasize that God did not give the Law to the Jews because of the latter's worthiness. Indeed, Scripture indicates that they turned to idolatry even after receiving the Law. No, God bestowed the Law and "other special advantages" to fulfill his promise to their forebears that Christ would be born of them. Thus we must confess that it was *ex sola gratuita electione* that the fathers received the promise and the people descended from them received the Law."[313]

This is the closest Aquinas appears to come to the *sola gratia* of the Reformation. But upon closer inspection, he says no more than that the first grace is unmerited. But if this grace is to flourish and come to fruition, it must be supplemented and in that sense sustained by human effort. In the final analysis, his seeming monergism drifts into synergism.

Thus he tells us that persons did not have sufficient powers to fulfill the Old Law by themselves and seeing that, they would turn to the *auxiliam gratiae*.[314] Grace does not stand alone as the only means of salvation; it is rather an *auxiliam*. Indeed, God provided *simul cum lege*, another kind of *auxiliam*: faith in the Mediator.[315] Consequently grace and law go hand in hand, cooperating together for justification.[316]

---

310 1a2ae.98, 6.
311 1a2ae.98, 6 ad 1.
312 *Commentary on Galatians*, 97.
313 1a2ae.98, 4.
314 1a2ae.98, 3 ad 3.
315 1a2ae.98, 2 ad 4.
316 Cf. 1a2ae.100, 2 ad 1.

Again we see that the freeness of grace in all its *unmeritedness* is lost in Thomas' theology. But Thomas believes that God willed it thus. And this is due to his separation of the thought of the will God from the self-disclosure of God in Christ.

Now, "just as grace presupposes nature, so it is right that the divine law should presuppose natural law."[317] But this does not mean that the two are completely distinct from one another. In fact, the Old Law merely re-publishes the obligations of natural law and then sets forth additional precepts.[318] Again we see the Thomist addition of grace to nature, and thus an innate capacity in humanity to come a certain distance toward God apart from revelation. It is true that reason "may" be hindered in the noetic process by "habitual sin" so that universally accepted principles are not correctly applied, but this is a hypothetical rather than a necessary outcome.

In addition to these commonly recognized principles are those precepts which are "deduced as conclusions from natural law": here too, the minds of "many" were led astray. Thus divine law was promulgated in order to overcome these deficiencies. For the same reason, *lex divina* also sets forth those truths accessible to human reason such as God's oneness, and those which are not, such as God's threeness.[319]

Moral Law

St. Thomas subdivides precepts of Old Law into three classes: moral, ceremonial and judicial. Moral law comprises those precepts "arising [directly] from the dictates of natural law."[320] Their locus of concern is with those matters pertaining by their very nature to right conduct. Furthermore, human actions are judged according to their conformity to right reason, which is itself grounded in the "natural knowledge of first principles" in the case of speculative reason, and in "certain naturally known principles" in the case of "practical reason." In the first instance, judgments of reason require a minimum of reflection, while in the second, much consideration on the part of the wise is needed.[321]

The inclusion of moral precepts in Old Law is a consequence of

317 1a2ae.99, 2 ad 1.
318 1a2ae. 98, 5.
319 1a2ae.99, 2 ad 2.
320 1a2ae.99, 4; 100, 3; 100, 3 ad 1.
321 1a2ae.100, 1.

the rationale of divine law itself, for the latter is "principally designed to establish loving and harmonious relations between man and God." Since we only love that which is like us, and God is good, we must also be made good. Virtue accomplishes this, and thus Old Law contains precepts about acts of virtue. These are the moral precepts of the Law.[322]

Moreover, since the image of God in humankind consists in their reason and they are "joined to God" by that reason, the divine law promulgates commands which will dispose[323] human reason for communication with God. This is accomplished through virtuous acts: "Intellectual virtues rightly dispose the acts of reason in themselves and the moral virtues dispose them aright in regard to the inward passions and outward actions."[324]

Although all the *moralia praecepta* belong to the law of nature, they do so in different ways. Some, such as "Honor thy father and mother," "thou shalt not kill," and "thou shalt not steal," are immediately self-evident to natural reason. But for some, human reason requires divine instruction, such as "Thou shalt not make thyself a graven image" or "Thou shalt not take the name of the Lord thy God in vain."[325]

Ceremonial Law

In addition to those principles arising directly from the dictates of Natural Law are derivative precepts, such as those embodying "concrete applications of the principle of divine worship."[326] These "ceremonial precepts" specify how God is to be worshiped,[327] but they are shaped by a particular goal, that of orientating persons towards God by the exercise of certain external actions.[328] In Thomas' view, God does not simply lay hold of someone and transform him. There must be preparation; the matter of which persons are composed must be predisposed to receive this new form. Consequently the Old Law was promulgated in order to

---

322 la2ae.99, 2.

323 Cf. Alister E. McGrath, *Iustitia Dei*, vol. I, Cambridge, Cambridge University Press, 1986, pp. 78ff.

324 la2ae.100, 2. For discussion of the intellectual virtues and moral virtues see la2ae.57-58.

325 la2ae.100, 1.

326 la2ae.99, 4.

327 la2ae.99, 3 ad 2.

328 la2ae.99, 3.

convict them of their sinful state,[329] and to prefigure not only the truth to be manifested in the heavenly country, but also Christ, the way leading to it."[330]

Yet it was not enough for one to know that there is a heavenly country and that Christ is the way to it and that his sinfulness keeps him from Christ. He must also be readied for Christ. Thus when humans in obedience to the law withdrew from idolatry to worship the one true God, they were thereby through the law "predisposed" for Christ.[331] Quite evidently, Thomas does not believe that the ceremonial law contained Christ. It was in that sense detached from him. Only the sacrifice of the New Law, the Eucharist, contains Christ.[332] Law prepares the way for grace.

Calvin would also speak of a dual role for ceremonial law, of disclosing human sin[333] and foreshadowing Christ.[334] However, the reformer went on to "utterly reject that Scholastic dogma...which notes such a great difference between the sacraments of the old and new law, as if the former only foreshadowed God's grace, but the latter give it as a present reality."[335] No, said Calvin, the fathers were sustained by the same spiritual food as we. They too fed on Christ. In partaking of the ceremonial rites of the Law of Moses,[336] the Jews received "Christ with his spiritual riches."[337]

But for Aquinas, the sacraments of the Old Law did not contain Christ; they merely prefigured him. Among these sacraments' or sacrifices was the sin offering. As the name indicates, it was offered because of the need for forgiveness of sin. When presented properly through the ministry of priests, it was a satisfaction for sin; God granted remission of sins. But does this mean that humankind has no part to play in salvation? Not at all! In fact, the peace offering affords a true picture: When it was offered to God it was divided into three parts: one was burnt in honor of God, one was allotted to the priests, and one went to the offerers. Now this, says Thomas, signifies that "the salvation of

---

329 1a2ae.98, 1 ad 1.
330 1a2ae.101, 2.
331 98, 2.
332 1a2ae.101, 4 ad 1.
333 *Institutes*, II.vii.17; IV.xiv.21.
334 *Ibid.*, II.vii.16; IV.xiv.20-26.
335 *Ibid.*, IV.xiv.23.
336 *Ibid*, IV.xiv.20.
337 *Ibid.*, IV.14.23.

humankind comes from God, under the direction of his ministers, and with the cooperation of those who are saved.[338]

Nevertheless, since the ceremonial laws did not contain Christ, they could not have had the power (*virtus*) which would flow from the incarnate and crucified Christ. Therefore they were unable to cleanse from sin. This *virtus* or *gratia* flows only from Christ. We must immediately add that the minds of the faithful found it possible to be united by faith to Christ. But this is a *iustificatio ex fide*. Indeed, the sacrifices themselves did not take away sin, but when offered properly they "were a kind of profession of faith which cleanses from sin."[339]

Aquinas even renders the Hebrew *wekipper* of Leviticus 4 and 5, usually construed as "to make atonement," in such a way as to find a reference to certain virtues in the priest rather than in the sacrifice: "The Law itself implies this in saying that in offering victims for sin 'the priest shall pray for him and it shall be forgiven him', as if the sin was forgiven not in virtue of the sacrifices, but through the faith and devotion of those who offered them."[340] He wants to emphasize that the law itself did not work justification, but only through its connection with Christ. But the way he connects the two is by the bridge of our faith and devotion. Even the grace by which we are saved is not seen as God's gift of himself in Christ, but as separate from Christ, "flowing" from him into those who by faith and devotion merit it.

Consequently the ceremonies of the Old Law served as the means by which persons professed their faith. Abraham was required to declare his faith by circumcision. But now that the mystery of Christ has been consummated, a new sign is required, namely, baptism.[341]

Judicial Law

The third and final subdivision of Old Law consists of judicial precepts, which as concrete applications of the dictates of natural law[342] regulate relations between humans.[343] They were instituted in order to

---

338 la2ae.102, 3 ad 8.
339 la2ae.103, 2.
340 *Ibid.*
341 la2ae.103, 3 ad 4.
342 la2ae.99, 4.
343 la2ae.104, 1.

govern the state of the people according to justice and equity.[344] That a state ought to be regulated by law can be seen not only from the principles of natural law, but from what a nation is by definition. Here Thomas cites Augustine: "a nation is a body of persons joined together in acceptance of a law and for the good of all."[345]

However, since the Law was a pedagogue leading persons to Christ, judicial precepts lost their binding force with Christ's advent, of course, justice is always to be observed, and thus a ruler may order their observance in any age so long as such laws are not alleged to be grounded in Old Law.[346] But since such precepts exist as concrete determinations of the natural law principle of justice, their precise form may vary in accordance with the type of government.[347]

Grace: New Law

We have already had occasion to observe that for St. Thomas, the final cause of humankind is to see God in His essence, an experience bestowed only on the good.[348] In order therefore to make persons good, God has instituted law in its various forms.

Delineating three periods in the history of salvation, he says that humankind was created under natural law, but took pride in their natural reason, thinking it could suffice for salvation. Consequently they were left to such knowledge alone that they might learn the deficiencies of it, especially as they found themselves sinking into idolatry. Then they were ready for the Old Law as a remedy for their ignorance. But this written law was not the complete answer either, for it exposed humanity's inability to put it into practice. Then came the New Law to complete the process.

Consequently, the three different eras of law actually served as stages, each serving as an *auxilium* in order that persons might be led from the less perfect to the perfect. The Old Law, then, was an intermediary stage between *lex naturae* and *lex gratiae*.[349] Indeed, the process may be likened to the gradual production of corn from a shoot: first we have the

344 la2ae.104, 2.
345 *De Civitate Dei* 11, 21, cited *in loc.*, la2ae.105, 2.
346 la2ae.104, 3.
347 la2ae.104, 3 ad 1 et 2.
348 Cf. *supra*, p. 27.
349 la2ae. 98, 6.

shoot, in the law of nature, then the ear, in the Law of Moses, and finally the full fruit, in the Gospel.[350]

Certainly we are here given a powerful exposition of the conviction that law precedes and prepares the way for grace. But we are bound to wonder whether this does not in the final analysis make grace conditional upon the fulfillment of the requirements of law. Aquinas clearly thinks that one must first be brought under the conviction of the law before he sees his need for grace. And he sees Old and New Law as stages along the way, each heightening one's sharing in the eternal law in order that a person might be directed to his supernatural end.[351] Aquinas is so concerned that humankind experience a justification that really makes just, that he directs our attention to human acts and human nature in the process of appropriating and actualizing this justification. But in this way our gaze is directed not so much to the saving humanity of Christ as to our actions and merits. Thus *gratia* loses its New Testament character as standing *sola* and instead becomes a part of a synergistic process depending on us as well as God.

If the Old Law, through its demands and threats, shows us our need of grace[352] the New Law is the very law of grace.[353] Through faith in Christ, the grace of the Holy Spirit is given, grace which constitutes the whole power of the New Law. At the same time, this is not to say that grace is the only note in the *lex nova*, for the latter also contains elements which "dispose" us for grace, and some which inform us how to use it.[354] Thus we may say that with regard to our intellect, we are disposed by faith, as the channel through which grace flows.[355] Indeed, faith constitutes a necessary condition for grace. Thus it is said that persons are accepted by God "because of" their faith.[356]

With respect to our affections, the New Law teaches us that contempt for the world is necessary in order that one might be fit to receive this grace. Finally, as regards our exercising grace, the scriptures of the New Law prescribe the virtuous actions by which this occurs.[357]

350 Ia2ae.107, 3.
351 Ia2ae.91, 4 ad 1.
352 Ia2ae.91, 5; 98, 1; 106, 3.
353 Ia2ae.106, 3.
354 Ia2ae.106, 1.
355 Ia2ae.106, 1 ad 1.
356 Ia2ae.107, 1 ad 3.
357 Ia2ae.106, 1 ad 1.

What does grace achieve? It justifies us,[358] and it helps us act as we ought.[359] Nevertheless, the grace of the New Covenant does not overpower us and confirm us in good. Only in the state of glory shall we be permanently established in good. It simply provides sufficient assistance so that we can avoid sin. Hence Thomas warns us that if someone sins after receiving grace, it is his own fault and he deserves a heavier punishment.[360]

Now, we must emphasize that grace comes through the incarnate Son of God alone: "grace first filled his humanity and thence was brought to us."[361] But grace did not reside in his humanity by nature. Grace is proper to God alone. Grace is a causal energy which achieves that which God intends, a thing almost substantival which can be said to "flow" from God to the humanity of Christ. For in Christ, his humanity served as the "instrument" of his divinity.[362] By the Spirit of God resting upon him, "habitual grace" was bestowed upon his humanity[363] in such an abundance that it could overflow to others.[364] But Christ is not only a passive human. "He gives the gifts as God and receives them as man."[365] Thus we can say that Christ's actions caused grace in us by meriting it as human and by some kind of efficient causation as God.[366]

Thomas' depiction of Jesus' natures as active causality on the one hand and instrumental causality on the other enables him to distinguish between his divine and human natures and to make sense of the God-humanward movement in reconciliation. But in consequence the human-Godward dimension is denigrated. If his humanity was only instrumental, we cannot speak of God as human responding to the action of God as God reaching down to humankind. And although his conception of the immutability of God rules out any divine suffering *a priori*, this division of the two natures only serves to strengthen the impression that this God does not come to share our plight; he rather joins himself to a human soul which experiences it.

358 1a2ae.106, 2.
359 1a2ae.106, 1 ad 2.
360 1a2ae.106, 2 ad 2.
361 1a2ae. 108,1.
362 3a.7, 2 ad 3.
363 3a.7, 1 sed contra.
364 3a.7, 1 et 9.
365 3a.7, 5 ad 1.
366 3a. 8, 1 ad 1.

This would seem to create problems for the orthodox conviction that God became human, but Thomas ingeniously argues that when we speak of the incarnation, we are predicating humanness of God in virtue of the union, which is a relation. And when predicates signify relationships, they can be newly attributed to a subject "without its being intrinsically changed." For example, a person can be made to stand on the right hand side without actually changing himself, simply by someone moving to his left. In that case an effect is caused by a change in something else. Now, he reasons, we are predicating just such a relation when we attribute "to be a man" to God. "Accordingly, without any change in God being implied, we newly predicate of him that he is a man by reason of the change occurring in the human nature which is assumed to the divine person.[367] Therefore we can and must affirm that "Christ, in his divinity, is incorporeal and not subject to suffering.[368]

Of course, this is Thomas' way of laying stress on the role of the humanity of the Savior in our redemption. It was through the passion of this Man that grace could flow from God to us. And this presents the question as to the precise nature of grace. What is this *gratia* which can be said to "flow", which is not inherent in Christ but received from God and passed on to those who are being saved? Is not this separation of grace from Christ a natural outcome of dividing the will of God from the revelation of God in Christ, such that God's will to bestow grace is not grounded in the nature of God disclosed in his Son?

In Question 110, article one of the *Prima Secundae*, it is asked, "does grace set up something (*aliquid*) in the soul?" The objection argues on the contrary that grace sets up (*pono*) nothing in the one who is said to have grace; it merely signifies divine acceptance. Furthermore, as the soul operates on the body, so God operates on the soul, without an intermediary, so grace "does not set up any created reality in the soul." Thirdly, when God forgives sins he does not set up anything in the soul; "grace" only points us to a reality in God, in his not imputing sin.

The ensuing discussion is most revealing. Thomas suggests that in common parlance, grace might be taken in one of three senses. First, we might use it to signify the love of someone, as in the case of a soldier who is said to have the king's grace and favor. Here clearly grace is

367 3a.16, 6 ad 2.
368 3a.16, 8 ad 2.

located in the king: he regards the soldier "favorably." Second, it is used to refer to a gift given freely, as one might say "I confer on you this grace." Finally, it is used to signify gratitude on the part of the one who receives a gift, as when we say grace for benefits.

Now surely, reasons Thomas, both of these latter two usages involve grace setting up something in the recipient of grace. Even in the first case there must be "something in him pleasing to the other," caused by grace.[369] So it is with God's bestowal of grace upon humans, except that the results are far greater, for "when a man is said to have God's grace, something supernatural is referred to, issuing in man from God."[370]

In response to the assertion that God operates on the soul without an intermediary, as the soul operates on the body, this analogy of similar relations is affirmed, but it is urged that the dissimilarity lies in the kind of operation or causation involved, for the soul serves as the formal cause of the body while God acts as the efficient cause of the soul. Consequently when God operates on the soul, he does so as an efficient cause, producing an effect--grace--which as an intermediary determines the form (i.e., the soul) of the human. At the same time, grace is not interposed between form and matter, for it informs the subject, not by its substance, but by the form which it causes.[371]

For article two, he considers whether grace is a "quality of the soul." He has already determined that for someone to have grace is to have an effect of God's will in him.[372] But this effect can be considered from the standpoint of God's efficient causation, and hence as a "movement of the soul" to know, will or do something. Or it can be seen from the perspective of God's formal causation, as a "habitual gift infused by God into the soul." As such, human souls receive a "supernatural form" which becomes an "originating principle of actions" so that by it God moves them "towards obtaining an eternal, supernatural good." In this sense, grace may be said to be a kind of quality.[373]

Therefore grace in humans cannot be seen as a substance, but an accident. Only in God is it to be found substantially.[374] Yet when persons

369 Ia2ae.110, 1 ad 1.
370 Ia2ae.110, 1.
371 Ia2ae.110, 1 ad 2.
372 Ia2ae.110, 1 et 2.
373 Ia2ae.110, 2 et ad 1.
374 Ia2ae.110, 2 ad 2.

begin to be in the mode of this accident, when they are "established in a new being, out of nothing, that is, not by their merits," we can say that grace is there "created." This enables Thomas to say that a person can cease to be in the mode of the accident we call grace without grace ceasing to be, because an accident does not possess the kind of independent being which can come to be or pass away.[375]

Although we may speak of grace as a quality or accidental form of the soul, it is never possessed independently of God. This is already indicated by its existence substantially in God alone, but Aquinas goes on to explain that grace exists in an accidental mode only in the soul which "participates in the divine goodness."[376] But this does not simply occur by divine fiat or action independent of humankind. First, there are the "acquired virtues", which, as the name indicates, are obtained by human action. These are "dispositions by which man is fittingly disposed with reference to the nature by which he is a man.

But in order that grace may perfect nature, humans are granted "infused virtues", which predispose them "in a higher way, and in view of a higher end", viz., participation in the divine nature. To put it another way, "just as the acquired virtues perfect a man so that he may walk in a way which befits the natural light of reason, so the infused virtues perfect a man so that he may walk in a way which befits the light of grace."[377] These infused virtues, he elsewhere tells us, include the theological triad of faith, hope and charity,[378] and other "corresponding" virtues as well.[379]

The Division of Grace

In customary medieval fashion, Aquinas defines grace more precisely by proposing certain distinctions. First, he divides it into *gratia gratum faciens* and *gratia gratis data*, sanctifying grace and freely bestowed grace. The first would of course literally be rendered "grace which makes pleasing." But we will follow the conventional translation.[380]

---

375 la2ae.110, 2 ad 3.
376 la2ae.110, 2 ad 2.
377 la2ae.110, 3.
378 la2ae.62, 2.
379 la2ae.63, 3.
380 Cf. Cornelius Ernest, trans. and ed. of vol. 30 (la2ae.106-114), p.125; Alister Mc-Grath, *Iustitia Dei*, Cambridge, Cambridge University Press, 1986, vol. 1, pp. 103ff.

Now, "sanctifying grace" is that "by which man himself is united to God."[381] The first objection argues that we cannot speak of a grace which makes one pleasing, since his being pleasing to God is a condition rather than a consequence of grace. Thomas replies that grace makes a person pleasing not by an efficient but a formal cause. In other words, the objector is interpreting him as holding that a person is made pleasing to God by that which he is given (i.e., grace) in itself. But as Thomas already said,[382] God works as the efficient cause, while sanctifying grace serves as the formal cause, disposing the form of the soul, such that "by it a man is justified and made worthy to be called pleasing to God."[383]

Secondly, grace may be considered as operating or as co-operating grace. Behind this argument lies a certain notion of divine causality, one which is carefully expounded back in Question 105, Articles Four and Five of the *Prima Pars*. For Thomas, the first principle of action is the end which moves the agent; the second is the agent; the third is the form of that which the agent applies to action. Thus a craftsman is moved to a certain action by a particular end: In order to make a bed (end) he (the agent) applies the axe (the form) to action. Now, this is how God works in every worker. Every agent works for the sake of some good, real or apparent, and every good is so only insofar as it participates in a likeness to the Supreme Good, which is God. Therefore God, as the end of every action, is the universal cause. All things were created for a *telos* which serves as the purpose of their operations.

But God is not only the end. He also moves in all things so that they have their proper operations. Thus He gives created agents their forms or principles of action and preserves their forms and powers. God as the Creator possesses the power of the First cause, and bestows active power on his created effects. Therefore we may say that humans are moved voluntarily, that is, by an interior principle, but this interior principle or power of willing is caused by an exterior principle. So in every human action we see two agents, God and a human. But God serves as the primary and humankind as the secondary agent.

As he begins his discussion of operating and co-operating grace, Aquinas enlists the support of Augustine, who explains that "By his

---

381 la2ae.111, 1.
382 la2ae.110, 1.
383 la2ae.111, 1 ad 1.

cooperation God perfects in us what he initiates by his operation; since by his operation he initiates our willing who, by his cooperation with us who will, perfects us."[384] Again we find this foundational conception of grace as that which functions, on the one hand as *causa* and on the other as *effectus*. For grace, whether considered as the divine help whereby "God moves us to will and do good" or as "the habitual gift implanted in us by God", can be taken in two ways: either as operating or as cooperating grace. As a cause achieving a certain effect, grace stands alone. In this act of operating grace, God is the sole mover: our mind is moved but does not initiate any movement. But in that effect in which both God and our mind move, the operation, Aquinas maintains, must be "attributed not only to God but also to the soul," and here we refer to cooperating grace.[385]

Now then, if grace is understood as God's "gratuitous motion" whereby he moves us to perform a "meritorious good", we must speak first of an "interior act of the will" in which the will is moved. *Gratia operans* is logically prior, for the initiative is God's. God moves a human mind which formerly willed evil to will good, and this movement is called operating grace. But then there is an external act, commanded by the will. Yet even in this act God helps us, both by strengthening our will within so that it might secure its end, and by supplying the means of acting outwardly. Thus we call grace "cooperating" with respect to this act.

At the same time, if grace is taken as habitual gift, once again there is a double effect: "the first is being, the second is activity." Concludes Thomas: "Thus if grace is understood as the gratuitous motion of God by which he moves us to perform a meritorious good, grace is satisfactorily divided into operative and cooperative grace."[386]

This argument is of fundamental importance for Thomas, because it enables him to find a role for both God and humankind in salvation. He hopes thereby to be true to *sola gratia* and yet preserve a place for human free will and action. Thus he offers his well-known declaration that:

> God does not justify us without us, since while we
> are being justified, we consent to God's justice by a

384 *De Gratia et Libero Arbitrio*, cited *in loc.*
385 la2ae.111, 2.
386 la2ae.111, 2.

movement of free choice. But that movement is not the cause but the effect of grace. Thus the whole operation belongs to grace.[387]

It should be noted that this formulation, while speaking of a grace which causes all our actions, nonetheless leaves room for our free choice. Hence our justification is not already complete before our decision. It is only a potential reality dependent upon our actions which are made possible by grace. And the loss of the sense of *unmeritedness* in the freeness of grace is due to Thomas' lodging of the gift of grace in the will of God[388] without reference to God's self-disclosure in Christ.

After distinguishing between prevenient and subsequent grace in a way which underscores the fact that God's grace both precedes a person to heal him and then follows him to make him strong,[389] he proceeds to discuss *gratia gratis data*, freely bestowed grace. This grace is granted that one might cooperate with another to lead him to God. Of course, only God can move someone internally (through sanctifying grace), and so humans are left with the role of teaching or persuading externally. To this end, one must possess a deep knowledge of things divine, be able to authenticate what he says, and be able to express it adequately. Therefore the Spirit bestows various graces, including faith, utterance of wisdom, utterance of knowledge, healing, working of miracles, prophecy and the discernment of spirits.[390]

Since freely bestowed grace is ordained to the common good of the entire church, while sanctifying grace is ordained only the good of an individual human being, can we not say that it is of more value than sanctifying grace? No, replies Aquinas, because we must evaluate virtues on the basis of the excellence of their ends, and sanctifying grace orders a person to union with the last end which is God, while freely bestowed grace only orders one to "preparatory stages" on the way to that objective. Surely the end is greater than the means, and so we must say that that grace which causes union with God is greater than the grace which causes certain dispositions for this.[391]

387 la2ae.111, 2 ad 2.
388 la2ae.110, 1 et 2.
389 la2ae.111, 3.
390 la2ae.111, 4.
391 la2ae.111, 5 et 5 ad 2.

A central point emerging from our investigation here is the conception of grace as a kind of causal energy. It is not so much embedded in the personality of God as his self-giving as it is that which produces a certain effect. And yet grace itself is an effect, caused by God. Question 112 asks "Whether God alone is the cause of grace." Grace must be caused by either a created or divine nature. But since grace exceeds the capacity of created nature, it must be caused by divine nature. Indeed, this must be so since "it is nothing other than a certain participation in the divine nature."[392]

Participation

But what is the nature of this *participatio*? Is this a relational term, connoting some kind of personal sharing in the life of God? Despite the mystical ring of the term, we are meant to take it in a much different sense. For at the heart of Thomist metaphysics lies the conviction that God is the *causa efficientis* of all things. Aquinas' Second Way of proving God's existence reasons from finite effects to their first efficient cause.[393] Now, the universe of created things is ordered in a chain of causes because it is hierarchized in a scale of being from those things which are almost totally matter and as such mostly potential, to those which are almost pure form and thus largely actual. Change is the movement from potency to act, and those beings which are the most actual are also the most perfect, having realized the most potentiality, while the converse is true for those having achieved the least actuality. Now God, as the efficient cause of all things, must therefore be the most perfect.[394]

This conception of God as containing all perfections is grounded in Thomas' Fourth Way of demonstrating the existence of God. There he begins with an observation of the degrees of being or perfection found in created things and he argues in a manner reminiscent of Plato[395] that we can only compare things by a standard of comparison. And this standard, itself containing all perfections in the highest degree must be the cause of them in creatures, since "when many things possess some property in

392 la2ae.112, 1.
393 la.2, 3.
394 la.4, 1.
395 *The Christian Philosophy of St. Thomas Aquinas*, p.74; Copleston, *Aquinas*, p. 121.

common, the one most fully possessing it causes it in others." Therefore the perfections found in second things, whether being or goodness or some other, must be caused by this First Being, which we call God.[396]

Thus we may say that created things receive their act of existing from God. Their essence is other than their existence, for the latter is derivative. But God's essence is his very existence. The very condition of his existence is that no addition can be made to it, for he possesses no unactualized potentialities. There can be no perfection lacking in pure existence; on the contrary, God embraces to the most excellent degree the perfections found in all classes.

Now, that which is perfect and actual is by definition good; in fine, it attracts as a final cause.[397] Since only God possesses every kind of perfection by nature, he alone is by nature good.[398] On the other hand "the goodness of a created thing is not its nature but something additional: either its existence, or some added perfection, or some relatedness to a goal."[399] They are only "good by divine goodness," for God is the "pattern, source and goal of all goodness."[400]

This brings us directly to Thomas' conception of participation, for only God is his very existence (*ipsum esse per se subsistens*), while others share (*participio*) in existence. They are caused by one First Being, who possesses being most perfectly. Thus they only participate in being, which is by nature God's alone.[401] That is to say, they possess to a finite degree those perfections which are found to an unlimited degree in God.[402] Participation is therefore not a category of personal relations, as when one might say that he participates in a friendship with another. It is rather a logical and causal category denoting the (limited) extent to which one thing partakes of another.

But since the creature participates in that which God possesses essentially, there is a basis, as we saw earlier for analogical predication. We might summarize it this way. Whatever perfection a thing participates

---

396 Ia.2, 3.
397 Ia.5, 1 et 4.
398 Ia.6, 3.
399 Ia.6 ad 3.
400 Ia.6, 4.
401 Ia.44, 1.
402 Cf. Charles A. Hart, *Thomist Metaphysics. An Inquiry into the Act of Existing*, Englewood Cliffs, Prentice Hall, 1959, p. 89.

in, it receives via efficient causality from that which possesses it essentially.[403] But since every agent makes its like (*omne agens agat sibi simile*),[404] we must predicate goodness of created things, not by extrinsic denomination, but by intrinsic denomination. Their goodness, although derived, is nonetheless theirs inherently.[405] Although in the instance of goodness both Creator and creature possess the same perfection, they do so to (qualitatively) different degrees. This is the basis for analogy. And since creation and God are united by a logical relation of ontological participation, in which effects participate in their cause, our predications concerning them are governed by an analogy of intrinsic attribution.[406]

What then does Thomas have in mind when he describes grace as "a certain participation in the divine nature?" He means that to have grace is to have a certain effect, namely, to approximate to a certain degree the likeness of God. As a formal cause, grace disposes the form of the soul, justifying a person and thereby making him pleasing to God.[407]

By creation we already participate in the being of God. But grace brings about a heightened participation. Grace does not destroy nature, it perfects it. That is why we are told that "the goodness of a created thing is not its nature but something additional (*superadditum*): either its existence, or some added perfection, or some relatedness to a goal." Participation means that God infuses in the form of a created, analogical likeness, an accidental quality upon the soul.

Now God, as "an agent of infinite power," could simply cause this participation directly, without any chain of intervening causes. He could, that is, in terms of his own capability. But within the order of things he has established,[408] he cannot. The trouble with such a division is that it means that what God is toward us in his earthly activity bears no necessary resemblance with what he is in himself, in his own being.

And it is precisely this division between the will of God (as demonstrated in his actions) and the nature of God, which, we argue, leads to restrictions and qualifications on the extent and nature of God's

---

403 la.3, 4.
404 la.6, 1; cf. 4, 3.
405 la.6, 4.
406 Mondin, *op. cit.*, pp. 63-66.
407 la2ae.111, 2 ad 1.
408 This is, of course, another instance of the distinction between the *potentia absoluta* and the *potentia ordinata* of God.

grace. Only when our knowledge of God is controlled by the self-disclosure of God in Christ is grace seen in all its unrestrictedness and unmeritedness.

For Aquinas, matter must be properly disposed if it is to receive a form.[409] Therefore, the indispensable condition for divine infusion of grace into the soul, is that the soul be disposed for it.[410]

Behind this notion of disposition lies the view that a person, in order to attain an end, must arrange his acts by method. Indeed, his very soul is composed of parts, viz., mind, will and passions, all of which must be disposed or positively oriented in view of his end. As a hylomorphic entity, his "matter" must be given the "disposition" to a given "form." His matter or its constituent parts---mind, will and passions---must be organized in order to receive the form which is grace.

Now, for a thing to require a disposition, it must be related to that form to which it is disposed "as potentiality is to act." To be more precise, it must be "capable of determination in several ways and to various things."[411] Which form will in fact perfect it is determined by the disposition.[412]

Among things needing to be disposed are powers which may be variously directed to act. And of these powers, our attention is directed to the will.[413] Because of the universality of reason and the free indeterminacy of the will (it may be ordered to vice or virtue in any number of ways), it must be disposed or prepared in order to receive a given form so that it may act in a given direction.[414] Thomas suggests the analogy of an arrow, which must take the right course if it is to strike the target. In the same way, the will must be inclined rightly for happiness (which is attained through choosing the good).[415] A disposition, therefore, serves as an intermediary between the power, say, of will and its action.

However, when the end in view is that of humankind's eternal happiness, such a *telos* "exceeds the proportion of human nature."[416] If

409 1a2ae.4, 4; 112, 2 ad 3.
410 1a2ae.112, 2 ad 3.
411 1a2ae.49, 4.
412 1a2ae.49, 4 ad 1.
413 1a2ae.50, 5.
414 1a2ae.49, 4, 5.
415 1a2ae.4, 4 ad 1.
416 1a2ae.51, 4.

we are to attain it, grace must perfect nature. Grace exists as a form in the subject who receives it. But there must be a disposition to this form. The proximate disposition to supernatural grace is a person s act of free will in accepting this grace. Yet this act itself is prompted and caused by a divine motion.[417]

Thomas is not anticipating Calvin's conviction that "God, whenever he wills to make way for his providence, bends and turns men's wills even in external things; nor are they so free to choose that God's will does not rule over their freedom."[418] Calvin would not speak, as Aquinas does, about a *liberum arbitrium*,[419] but rather a *libertate abdicatum voluntatem*.[420] It is true that Thomas says that a person's *libero arbitrio* "can only be turned to God when God turns it to himself."[421] But he is able to separate a human's free activity from God's action. Thus he can say that "man does not necessarily receive grace from God, however much he prepares himself."[422] And preparation as "arising from free choice" in contradistinction to preparation "considered as from God the mover" is not proportionate to the gift of grace.[423]

For Aquinas, the *imago dei* signifies a person's freedom to "judge what he shall do" and his "power to act or not act."[424] A human *per se* is the "master of his actions through his reason and will."[425] True, God as the first Mover moves the will to the universal good. Without such a motion, one could not will anything. "But man by his reason determines himself to will this thing or that thing, which is either a true good or an apparent good. However, sometimes God particularly moves some to will a determinate good; in this case He moves them by grace..."[426] But

---

417 la2ae.109, 6.
418 Calvin, *op. cit.*, II.iv.7.
419 la2ae.109, 6 ad 1.
420 *Ibid.*, II.iii.5, Ioannis Calvinus, *Institutio Christiane Religionis*, ed. A. Tholuck, London, D. Nutt, 1846; cf. John H. Leith, "The Doctrine of the Will in the *Institutes of the Christian Religion*," Reformatio Perennis, ed. Brian Gerrish, Pittsburgh, Pickwick Press, 1981, pp. 52-53.
421 la2ae.109, 6 ad 1.
422 la2ae.112, 3 sed contra.
423 la2ae.112, 3.
424 Prologue to la2ae, *Treatise on Happiness.* la2ae, 1-21, trans. by John A. Oesterle, Notre Dame, University of Notre Dame Press, 1983.
425 la2ae.1, 1, cf. 1, 2; 21, 2 (Oesterle trans.).
426 la2ae.9, 6 ad 3, (Oesterle trans).

this does not mean that God overrules human freedom; only that God, as the external mover, is the originating principle of a person's willing anything at all.[427]

Indeed, when God moves the will, he "so moves it that He does not determine it to one thing necessarily, but leaves its movement contingent and not necessarily, except in regard to what is moved naturally."[428] The reason for this lies in the nature of things, for God moves things in a manner consistent with their own principles. Divine providence does not destroy nature, but works in a manner appropriate to it. For the will to be moved with necessity would not be proper to its nature, for it is "an active principle which is not determined to one thing, but is related indifferently to many."[429] The will can tend to anything the reason apprehends as good, and since all things contain some good, it can tend to any of them.[430] For Thomas, "ought" implies "can." Acts are blameworthy or praiseworthy when the agent committing them possesses the power to choose.[431]

However, as we have observed, in order that a person might move toward a good, he must be disposed to that end. Philosophically, it is the ordering of his matter to receive a given form. Theologically, this *dispositio* is in fact *preparatio*. One's preparation for grace is constituted by his act of free will in accepting it. That such a *preparatio* is necessary is indicated in Amos 4.12, "Prepare to meet your God, O Israel," and I Samuel 7.3, "Prepare your hearts unto the Lord."[432]

Such preparation on the part of humans is not possible without the assistance of grace. Indeed, the fundamental principles of final causality indicate this, for God, as the Primary Mover or final cause, turns his effects toward himself as their end. But this does not exclude human action, for "man is turned to the ultimate end by the motion of the primary mover, but to the proximate end by the motion of a subordinate mover." By the divine motion, all things are turned to God in so far as they are set in a natural tendency to the good. But God turns "just men to himself as to a special end." Even this does not exclude human action, since

---

427 1a2ae.109, 2 et ad 1.
428 1a2ae.10, 4, Oesterle trans.
429 *Ibid.*
430 1a2ae.13, 6.
431 1a2ae.21, 2; 83, 1.
432 1a2ae.112, 2 sed contra.

even while God is moving a person within, the latter is also preparing himself.[433] This preparation is a kind of turning to God, which one may do "by his free decision." And yet "the free decision can only be turned to God when God turns it to himself."[434] God's grace liberates him that he may have the freedom to choose at all. Thus, should he decide for God, he owes it to the divine assistance.[435] It is in this connection that Thomas is willing to affirm the scholastic axiom, *Facienti quod in se est, Deus non denegat gratiam* (God does not refuse grace to him who does what he can).[436] For such he is able to do "in so far *as* he is moved by God."[437]

Walter Farrell explains this dual action of God and humankind:

> In the supernatural order we prepare ourselves for grace by our own actions proceeding from our own free will, under our control. They are ours. But we are only seeing half the truth if we do not see that these actions are also God's, that behind our causality is the causality of the first cause, necessary for every instant of our causality.[438]

How this relates to the *facere quod* in Thomas' thought is further explained in this manner:

> Each can prepare himself for sanctifying grace, can increase that grace in his soul. To each God gives grace in proportion to the preparation made by the help of that divine movement. It is strictly true that to a man doing his best, doing what is in him [i.e., *facere quod in se est* in Ia2ae.109, 6 ad 2], God does not deny grace; the very

---

433 Ia2ae.109, 6.

434 Ia2ae.109, 6 ad 1.

435 Ia2ae.109, 2 et ad 1.

436 Cf. Heiko Oberman, "Facientibus Quod in Se Est, Deus Non Denegat Gratiam. Robert Holcott, O.P. and the beginnings of Luther's Theology," *Harvard Theological Review*, vol. lv, 1962, pp. 317-42; Alister E. McGrath, *Iustitia Dei: A history of the Christian doctrine of Justification*, vol. II, Cambridge, Cambridge University Press, 1986, pp. 129f.

437 Ia2ae.109, 6 ad 2.

438 Walter Farrell, *A Companion to the Summa*, vol. II, New York, Sheed and Ward, 1939, pp. 426-27.

doing of his best is already an evidence of the rain of grace falling on the soil of his soul.[439]

This is typically Thomist in its positing a cooperation between divine and human activity, while insisting that even that human activity is enabled by grace. The intent is surely to expound *sola gratia* over against the notion that humans can by proper preparation merit the 'first grace'---a position formerly held by the Angelic Doctor himself in his early commentary on the *Sentences* of Peter Lombard.[440]

But the assumption is that grace is a kind of causal energy working within a human, gradually transforming him as he, through grace, exercises his free will[441] and so merits an increase of grace. In this way, grace is seen to depend in some sense on human accomplishment. Even more seriously, grace is thereby detached from Christ. Only when the will of God is seen in the light of the self-disclosure of God in and through Christ is grace seen in its character as standing *sola*, because the exegesis of *sola gratia* is *solus Christus*.

But because grace is detached from Christ, its continued presence in the life of the *viator* is not assured. Thomas believes that sin takes away grace and disorders human nature so that one's will is no longer automatically subject to God. But God can work a twofold restoration of humankind; first, by bestowing grace as a habitual gift and second, by drawing a person's will to himself, so that rectitude may be restored to his nature.[442] Does this relegate human beings to a passive role in salvation? Far from it. A person for his part is called to undertake by an *actum liberum arbitrii* to try to rise up again from sin. "When a man tries to rise from sin by a free decision moved by God, he receives the light of justifying grace.[443]

Divine grace, while indispensable and powerful, is not the only thing needful. Human decision and effort are also required. For "the withdrawal of grace has its primary cause in us, but the bestowal of

---

439 *Ibid.* p. 428.
440 In his *Commentary on the Sentences* of Peter Lombard, he argued that a person can prepare himself for the reception of the 'first grace' of justification (*Scripta super libros Sententiarum*, II. dist. xxviii.1, 4, cited in McGrath, *op. cit.*, p. 81).
441 la2ae.109, 6 ad 1.
442 la2ae.109, 7.
443 la2ae.109, 7 ad 1.

grace has its primary cause in God."[444] If we receive grace, our decision is only the proximate cause while God is the ultimate cause. Even so, our deciding against grace can frustrate it. And our sinning can drive it away altogether. The ineluctable conclusion here is that Aquinas, while wanting to affirm *sola gratia* in human salvation, nevertheless wants to preserve a large province for a person's freely choosing whether or not to avail himself of divine assistance and then to act accordingly.

Justification

Alister McGrath[445] has shown that within the early Dominican school, the application of Aristotelian physics to the transition from nature to grace led to a quadripartite *processus iustificationis*, with a twofold motion of free will. Although Albert the Great had already related the Aristotelian maxim *omne quod movetur ab alio movetur* to an analysis of the inner psychological structure of the motion of justification in defining justification as a motion from sin to grace,[446] the explicit correlation between Aristotle's theory of generation and the *motus* of justification is especially found in Thomas Aquinas.

As one surveys the exposition of the doctrine in Question 113 of the *Prima Secundae*, he is immediately struck by the paucity of references to Christ. There is, in fact, but one--and it says no more than that for justification, an unrighteous person "should believe that God is he who justifies men through the mystery of Christ."[447] Thomas grounds his doctrine of *iustificatio* elsewhere, in a semantic analysis of contemporary usage, and in Aristotelian physics.

M. D. Chenu argues that "the Incarnation is.. .a contingent event, and it enters.. .only as an absolutely gratuitous work of God's absolutely free will." Indeed, the tract of grace makes no mention of the Mediator because "grace, as such, has its own nature, its own structure, its own laws, beyond the temporal conditions of its realization; in due course, filial adoption in Christ will follow."[448] Certainly Thomas agrees. But

---

444 la2ae.112, 3 ad 2.
445 Iustitia Dei, vol. 1 pp. 43ff.
446 *In IV Sententiarum*, dist. xviiA a.15, cited in *ibid.*, p.44.
447 la2ae.13, 4 ad 3.
448 *Toward Understanding St. Thomas*, trans. Albert M. Landry and Dominic Hughes, Chicago, Henry Regnery, 1964, pp. 314-15.

we wonder whether allowing grace that kind of independence from Christ has not in fact, profoundly altered its character.

At any rate, Thomas opens Article One with the observation that "justification implies a movement towards justice, just as heating implies a movement towards heat." Aristotle's analysis of motion is as applicable to the *motus* of physical objects as it is to spiritual processes. And what is the intrinsic meaning of *iustitia*? "Rightness of order," or rightness in a person's relations with others. It can also mean, as Aristotle says, rectitude in a person's interior dispositions, in which his lower powers are subject to his higher power, namely, reason. Such can come about either through "simple generation", as when Adam received *originalis iustitia*, or through a *motus* "from contrary to contrary, in which a person moves from the state of injustice to the state of justice." This, maintains Aquinas, is the New Testament understanding of the justification of the unrighteous.[449]

Since every movement takes its name from its *terminus*, justification may be said to consist in the remission of sin. But this is not to say that *iustificatio* is simply a forensic declaration. Rather, it is a process which consists in *remissio peccatorum*.[450]

Moreover the indispensable condition of forgiveness is the infusion of grace. This is not so that God can love us, for his nature as *purus actus* means that his love endures eternally without change. And yet we may fail to receive it because of our sins. Here Aquinas offers a characteristic analysis of the life of the *viator*: "as to the effect which [God's love] impresses on us, it is sometimes interrupted, namely, when we sometimes fall away from it and sometimes regain it." The sporadic nature of the would-be Christian's life, not (we might say) unlike a flickering light suffering from a loose connection (with grace), will be more fully explored in Thomas' doctrine of Penance. But since the effect of divine causality, the grace by which a person "becomes worthy of eternal life" is taken away by mortal sin, it must somehow be restored. This God accomplished by an *infusio gratiae*. Of course, the presence of divine grace within the soul means that God's love, in which reconciliation and peace consist, is being received again. And

449 1a2ae.113, 1.
450 *Ibid.*

when God is reconciled to us, sin is said to be remitted to us. Therefore, *remissio peccatorum* requires the infusion of grace.[451]

But the *processus iustificationis* entails more than divine action. Human acts are also necessary. If we take it as axiomatic that "God moves all things according to the mode proper to each," we must affirm that God moves humans according to the conditions of their nature, that is, in a manner consistent with human free will.

And so we must speak, not only of a "motion from God towards justice", but also of a motion of free will on the part of the human person. Indeed, God so infuses justifying grace that at the same time "he also moves the free choice to accept this gift of grace."[452] We recall our discussion of the *liberum arbitrium*, in which it became evident that for Aquinas, God moves the free will contingently, with an indeterminate movement, so that a person could turn away from the gift of grace. But in so far as he freely moves to accept it, his *motus* must be attributed to the First Mover.

That this is Thomas' meaning here is supported by the response to the first objection, wherein he considers cases in which individuals are incapable of exercising free will, e.g., infants or the insane. God simply moves them towards justice by impressing the form of grace upon their souls (albeit via a "sacramental act"). That is to say, he chooses for them. And if someone loses his power of free choice through sickness or unconsciousness, he will not receive justifying grace by any sacrament "unless he had earlier had the intention of receiving the sacrament; and this cannot happen without the exercise of free choice."[453]

The third objection had maintained that grace could be infused "from the start" without a *motu liberii arbitrii*. In reply Thomas says that "There is a certain transformation of the soul when justifying grace is infused into it; and so an appropriate movement of the human soul is required, such that the soul moves in the mode proper to it."[454] A condition must be fulfilled if the soul is to receive the form which is grace: it must move in the appropriate mode, which is free will.

Next Aquinas considers the question whether a *motus fide* is required for justification. For this is the way in which a person, in a moment of

---

451 la2ae.113, 2.
452 la2ae.113, 2.
453 la2ae.113, 3 ad 1.
454 la2ae.113, 3 ad 3.

free choice, turns to God. Believing is an act of the will[455] assenting voluntarily[456] to a proposition.[457] One must believe the "primary points or articles of faith" explicitly, and implicitly be prepared to believe whatever is contained in the Scriptures,[458] such as the mystery of Christ,[459] or the Trinity[460] because it is revealed by God.[461] But this is not to say that the beginning of faith is from ourselves. The *causa fidei* is "God moving man inwardly by grace."[462] For a human to assent to such teachings proposed to him, he must be raised above his nature.[463] This does not pre-empt human decision: "To believe does indeed depend on the will of the believer: but man's will needs to be prepared with grace."[464] Indeed, a person, though unable to acquire or deserve grace of his own free will, can nevertheless "stop himself from receiving it...to obstruct or not to obstruct the entrance of divine grace lies in the power of man s own free will..."[465]

If it be urged that one is justified, not only by faith, but by fear, charity, humility or mercy as well, Thomas replies that underlying all these virtues is one movement of free will towards God, a movement initiated by the turning of faith.[466] "For one and the same act of free choice can engage different virtues.[467]

But a *motus fidei* toward God must be accompanied by a movement of free choice away from sin, since justification is a movement from the state of sin to the state of justice. There is then a twofold movement of *liberum arbitrium*, "one in which one reaches out for God's justice by desire, and one in which sin is renounced."[468] The latter necessarily

---

455 2a2ae.2, 1 ad 3.
456 2a2ae.1, 4.
457 2a2ae.1, 2.
458 2a2ae. 2, 5.
459 2a2ae. 2, 7.
460 2a2ae. 2, 8.
461 2a2ae . 1, 1.
462 2a2ae.6, 1, trans. Fathers of the English Dominican Province [henceforth D.F.], London, Burns Oates and Washbourne, 1916.
463 *Ibid.*
464 2a2ae.6, 1 ad 1, D.F.
465 *Summa Contra Gentiles*, III, 160.
466 la2ae.113, 4.
467 la2ae.113, 4 ad 1.
468 la2ae.113, 5.

entails renouncing every sin we can remember as well as those we are unable to recall, "for a man in this state is so disposed that he would be contrite even about those sins which he does not remember if he could recall them."[469]

The fourth and final requirement for *iustificatio* is the forgiveness of sins, for this is the *finis* of the process.[470] But in order to reach the end-term, "many other things are required"--viz., the infusion of grace, a movement of the will towards God by faith and a movement of the will away from sin.[471] Thomas defends this on the basis of the Aristotelian theory of motion:

> Now in any movement in which something is moved by something else, three elements are required: firstly, the motion given by the mover; secondly, the movement of that which is to be moved; and thirdly, the completion of the movement, that is, the arrival at the end. As regards the divine motion, then, we have the infusion of grace; as regards the free choice set in movement, however, we have two movements, in the sense of a departure from the initial term and of an approach to the end term; the completion of the movement, or its arrival at its term, is implied in the forgiveness of sin, for in this justification is completed.[472]

This is not to say that justification takes place in successive stages over time; it is instantaneous with the infusion of grace, "for it is through this that free choice is moved and sin forgiven."[473] Even human consent, which constitutes the movement of free choice, takes place in a moment. There may be a time of deliberation prior to this, but "this is not of the substance of justification but a way to it."[474] The order of the elements of the *processus iustificationis* then is not temporal but natural. By nature, cause is prior to effect. Thus, in the *motus qui est de statu peccati in statum iustitiae*, the motion of the mover must come first, followed

469 1a2ae.113, 5 ad 3.
470 1a2ae.113, 6 sed contra.
471 1a2ae.113, 6 et ad 1.
472 1a2ae.113, 6.
473 1a2ae.113, 7
474 1a2ae.113, 7 ad 1.

by the disposition of the matter or the motion of that which is to be moved, followed by the end-term of the movement.[475] We may place the movement of the free will towards God prior to the movement against sin, since, as Aristotle says, "in movements of the mind the movement to the principle of understanding or to the end of action comes first absolutely.[476]

In expounding his doctrine of justification, Thomas is caught in a dilemma. On the one hand he wants to affirm that "the whole operation [of our justification] belongs to grace,[477] that justification is the effect of "operative grace,"[478] and that any preparations required of us are performed by God himself.[479] Yet on the other hand he maintains that humans, far from being passive, actively do their part---preparing themselves,[480] trying to rise up from sin,[481] exercising free will to accept God's grace,[482] and believing all the primary articles of faith. Indeed, the "precepts of the Law, which man is bound to fulfill, contain certain acts of virtue (e.g., faith) which are means of obtaining salvation.[483]

How can all be attributed to God and yet humans be held responsible to do so much? Part of the answer lies in the Thomist view of human nature: *naturaliter anima est gratiae capax*. If the soul is naturally capable of receiving grace, then grace and nature work hand in hand to achieve the justification of the unrighteous. Secondly, when our attention is averted from the self-revelation of God in Christ, the notion of grace in its *unmeritedness* is lost. Looking away from Christ as the sole source of justification and toward human actions and powers, albeit supplemented and empowered by God, we are left with a conditional conception of grace.

---

475 la2ae.113, 8.
476 *Physics* II, 9.200a10, cited *in loc*.
477 la2ae.111, 2 ad 2.
478 Prologue to la2ae.113.
479 la2ae.112, 2 et ad 3; 113, 7.
480 la2ae.112, 2.
481 la2ae.109, 7 ad 1.
482 la2ae.113, 2 et 3.
483 2a2ae.2, 5 D.F.

Merit

If justification is an effect of operative grace, "merit" is an effect of cooperative grace.[484] Although grace, considered as operative or cooperative, remains the "same grace,"[485] it may be distinguished by its different effects. In the former, the primary accent falls on the initiative and activity of God as the mover, while the human mind is moved. Even there, a place is reserved for the *liberum arbitrium*, since a person must consent to the divine *motus*, but the emphasis is on the divine movement.

Yet the connection between justification and merit is closer than a common origin in grace. For if justification is the process of moving from the state of injustice to justice, merit becomes possible upon its completion.[486] Prior to that, when one is in a state of sin, sin itself is an impediment to his meriting grace. Hence the "first grace"--justification--cannot be merited by fallen humans.[487] However, it has been merited by Christ for us.[488]

Within the state of justice, a person may be "repaid" "in return for work." Such a reward is itself an "act of justice." We must admit that such a work on the part of a human is not intrinsically deserving of divine reward, because "there is the greatest inequality between God and man; they are infinitely far from each other and man's whole good is from God." Nonetheless, God can and does ordain that "by his work and action man is to obtain from God as a sort of reward that for which God has allotted him a power of action."[489] God is not bound in advance by any given order, since all order proceeds from his will. But given the presupposition of a divine ordination, God will act in a way consistent with it--infallibly, but not coercively. And God has ordained reward for merit.[490]

Because no relation of equivalence is possible between God and humankind, we may speak only of justice in a restricted, proportional sense. That is to say, in the relationship between God and a human,

---

484 Prologue to la2ae.113 and prologue to la2ae.114.
485 la2ae.111, 2 ad 4.
486 la2ae.114, 1.
487 la2ae.114, 5.
488 la2ae.114, 6.
489 la2ae.114, 1.
490 la2ae.114, 1 et ad 3; cf. la2ae.112, 3; cf. John Farthing, *Thomas Aquinas and Gabriel Biel*, pp. 160-62.

"each works in his own mode." But God ordains the "mode and measure of human capacity" and so human merit presupposes the divine ordering such that "by his work and action" a person is to obtain from God as a kind of reward that for which God has allotted him a power of action."[491] A person must move himself into action by free choice, or else his "act of justice" will not be meritorious. Moreover, he must do what he can.[492]

To say that God allots a person a "power of action" is not to posit a capability independent of grace by which eternal life could be merited. Fallen humans must first receive forgiveness of sins and be reconciled to God, and this happens by grace. Only in the state of grace can a person merit eternal life.[493] Hence it is not as if a person can by sheer effort earn his way into the grace of God. "For man's whole power to do good he has from God... and so man can only merit something from God by his gift."[494]

And yet there seems to be a fundamental ambivalence in Thomas' notion of merit through co-operative grace. One's meritorious work, he tells us, can be viewed in two ways: either as it proceeds from free will or as it proceeds from the grace of the Holy Spirit. In terms of the first, "if a man does what he can,"[495] God will in turn reward him according to the greatness of his power. But from the vantage point of the second "now the value of the merit is assessed by the power of the Holy Spirit moving us to eternal life." And the value of the work depends on the "worth of grace, by which man, having become a sharer in the divine nature, is adopted as a son of God, someone to whom the inheritance is owed by the very right of adoption.[496]

How are we to reconcile the two? Does eternal life hang on how well a person utilizes the grace he is given, or is it grounded in the gracious activity of God? To affirm both is to qualify the second by the first.

Thomas tries to avoid contradiction by saying that the mercy of God is the "primary cause" of our reaching eternal life, while our merit is a "secondary cause."[497] But is it meaningful to say that God's mercy is

---

491 1a2ae.114, 1.
492 1a2ae.114, 1 et ad 1; 114, 3.
493 1a2ae.114, 2.
494 1a2ae.114, 2 ad 3.
495 1a2ae.114, 3 D.F.
496 *Ibid.*
497 1a2ae.114, 3 ad 2.

the primary cause--viz., that our reaching everlasting bliss is ultimately attributable to the *miseratio dei*, while also affirming that, down the causal chain, our merit--depending by definition partly and therefore necessarily on our best efforts, initiated by our free will, is a secondary cause?

> Although by his death Christ sufficiently merited salvation for the whole human race, each of us must there seek his own cure. Christ's death is like the universal cause of deliverance...Nevertheless, even a universal cause must be applied to be effective."[498]

No doubt Aquinas is quite concerned to attribute all to grace, but at the end of the day he expounds the Gospel of grace in the language of merit. And the latter, it would seem, has the last word.

So persons by their freely-chosen movements and actions in accord with the divine ordination and enabled by grace, merit eternal life. But not all human works are worthy of reward. Only those springing from virtues as their operative principles are such. And since the end of meritable human working is eternal life, which consists in the enjoyment of God, our attention is directed to that virtue serving as the principle of motion towards the good which is God, namely, charity. The motion or act toward God which is "proper to charity" in turn directs the other virtues to the same end. "And so the merit of eternal life belongs primarily to charity."[499] Even the virtue of faith is not meritorious unless it works through charity.[500]

But what is a person to do who turns away from justice and falls into sin? He cannot merit restoration for himself, since sin interrupts the motion of divine grace which would have conferred merit on his works.[501] Indeed, even the eternal life he previously merited can no longer be in prospect so long as he remains in his fallen state, because "by a subsequent sin an impediment is put in the way of the preceding merit, such that it does not obtain its proper effect."[502]

---

498 *Summa Contra Gentiles* IV.55.
499 1a2ae.114, 5.
500 1a2ae.114, 5 ad 3.
501 1a2ae .114, 7.
502 1a2ae.114, 7 ad 3.

Consequently, one cannot merit, in this life, perseverance. Perseverance on the way to glory is only the gift of God[503] which we are enjoined to ask God for.[504] However, perseverance in glory, when our free will is at last "brought down on the side of good" by the final consummation, *does* fall under merit. In this life we can never be sure of our eternal salvation, but should beseech God for the grace of perseverance, that we might at last be found having attained it.[505]

Grace and Christ

We have seen that eternal life depends on our meriting it through the enabling of grace. Moreover, grace comes to us via Christ, who sufficiently merited salvation for all humankind. Now we must investigate more closely the relation between grace and Christ. Thomas affirms that Christ is true God and true man. He bestows grace as God and receives it as man.[506] What does it mean to say that he "receives" grace? We are given a three-fold answer. First, in the union of his (human) soul with God, he was thereby as a man drawn close to the "cause" acting on him--viz., grace. Second, this grace, in the form of a habit, enabled him to know and love God intimately. Third, "he must have had grace to such an extent that it would overflow to others."[507] But he dispenses grace through his humanity, which serves as the "instrument of the divinity."[508]

What are we to say to this? One can appreciate that his concern here is to underscore grace's origin in God, and the initiative of God in our salvation. But does not conceiving of the humanity as the instrument or organ of the divinity not detract from the full humanity of the Savior, and thus relegate it to a lesser role? Oliver Quick thinks that Thomas' doctrine of the incarnation leaves us with a divine Christ

---

503 1a2ae.114, 9.
504 1a2ae.114, 9 ad 1.
505 1a2ae.114, 9 et ad 1.
506 3a.7, 5 ad 2.
507 3a.7, 1.
508 3a.7, 1 ad 3.

whose "humanity is but a mask."[509] In so saying, Quick is not charging Thomas with docetism; he recognizes the constant emphasis on the reality of Christ's suffering manhood. But at the same time he finds in the theology of Aquinas, and in medieval thought generally, the sense in which so far as the incarnation is concerned, Jesus Christ "remains God."[510]

That Aquinas should find difficulty in formulating his conception of the incarnation was already anticipated in his doctrine of God. As we saw earlier, God, being pure act, is immutable. Therefore the incarnation cannot introduce any change in the divine being. For an eternal being, temporal sequence has no meaning; it only has significance for time-bound creatures such as us. Thus there can be no mutual relations between God and humans. In Thomas' words, "Being related to God is a reality in creatures, but being related to creatures is not a reality in God." The only change possible is in the creature. Thus a pillar can change from being on my left to being on my right simply by my motion rather than by any change in the pillar.[511] Thomas recalls that discussion later in his interpretation of the hypostatic union:

> Now, as was said above [1a.13, 7], every relation which we consider between God and the creature is really in the creature, by whose change the relation is brought into being; whereas it is not really in God, but only in our thinking, since it does not arise from any change in God. And hence we must say that the union of which we are speaking is not really in God, except in our way of thinking; but in the human nature, which is a creature, it is really.[512]

---

509 Oliver Chase Quick, *The Doctrines of the Creed. Their Basis in Scripture and their Meaning To-day*, (London: Nisbet and Co., 1938), 125-6; cp. Rik Van Nieuwenhove, "Bearing the Marks of Christ's Passion: Aquinas' Soteriology, in Rik Van Nieuwenhove and Jospeh Wawrykow, eds., *The Theology of Thomas Aquinas*, (Notre Dame: University of Notre Dame Press), 2005, 293-294; cf. Jean-Pierre Torrell, O.P., *Aquinas' Summa: Background, Structure, and Reception*, trans. Benedict M. Guevin, O.S.B. (Washington: Catholic University of America Press, 2005), 55-56.
510 *Ibid.*, 127.
511 1a.13, 7.
512 3a.2, 7.

Certainly Thomas adheres to the full deity and humanity within the person of the Savior. But he seems to have difficulty in formulating a doctrine of the *assumptio carnis* which testifies to a God who lives, acts, and experiences, not only as God, but as man. Instead, we are presented with a Christ who from his conception was almost omniscient.[513] And His humanity, though passible, "could have prevented these passions from coming upon it, and especially by the divine power; yet of his own will He subjected himself to these corporeal and animal passions."[514] Consequently the manhood of Christ becomes but the "instrument" of the divinity--a living instrument, to be sure, which acts as well as receives action.[515] The analogy cited is of the body of a man, or his members. Presumably we are to think of the soul which, though inseparably united to the body as the latter's form, directs the action of its limbs.[516] The humanity therefore, is said to be "so acted upon [by the Godhead] as to act." Indeed,

> [T]he human nature in Christ is assumed with the result that instrumentally He performs the things which are the proper operation of God alone: to wash away sins, for example, to enlighten minds by grace, to lead into the perfection of eternal life.[517]

That is to say, Christ as God gives grace "authoritatively", while as man he bestows it "instrumentally."[518] It must be said that for all Thomas' support of *enhypostasia*[519] and even his declaration that "Christ had the most perfect obedience to God,"[520] the accent falls on the passive obedience of Christ as man.

---

513 3a.7, sed contra; 7, 7 ad 3, 4; 10, 2; 11, 1; 15, 3 D. F.; cp. 9, 4; and 13, 1: Jesus "could know all things, but not in every way", i.e., he could know all actual existents, but not all possibles as God alone knows them, and thus could neither be said to have faith (3a.7, 4 D. F.).

514 3a.15, 4 ad 1 D. F.

515 3a.7, 1 ad 1 D. F. For a similar criticism, see Otto Weber, *Foundations of Dogmatics*, vol. 1, trans. Darrell L. Guder, (Grand Rapids: Eerdmans, 1981), 121-124.

516 Cf. 3a.8, 2; *Summa Contra Gentiles*, IV.41.

517 *Summa Contra Gentiles*, IV.41.

518 3a.8, 1 ad 1 D. F.

519 3a.2, 6 ad 2 et 4; 3a.16, 12; 17, 1.

520 3a.7, 3 ad 3 D. F.

Now Christ, as he has said, received habitual grace. He also received "sanctifying grace" so as to perform meritorious acts, and "gratuitous grace" for the working of miracles. His power for effecting all these acts he received from the divine motion. But unlike other saints, who are moved by God as "separated instruments", he was moved as a "united instrument" in virtue of the hypostatic union.[521]

How did Christ receive grace? From his proximity to the "cause of grace," because "the nearer a recipient is to the inflowing cause, the more it receives. And hence the soul of Christ, which is more closely united to God than all other rational creatures, received the greatest outpouring of His grace." But we must immediately go on to say that Christ is the conduit of grace, receiving it in such a way that it is "poured out" from his soul to others.[522]

A quasi-material conception of grace seems very much in evidence here, since it is something distinguishable from God which can be poured out from God to Christ and then to humans. What is more, it can be dispensed in varying quantities.[523]

As a priest, Christ is a "mediator between God and the people" inasmuch as he "bestows divine things on the people," "offers up the people's prayers to God," "makes satisfaction to God for their sins," and we can even say that "He reconciled the human race to God."[524] He is a lawgiver, priest and king.[525] He was both priest and victim, having offered himself for us.[526]

By the "virtue" of his priestly work, grace is given us, a grace by which our hearts are turned to the Lord that we might receive remission of sins. This, as we have seen, transpires in the *processus iustificationis*. But in all this saving activity, the divinity of Christ, while remaining, recedes from center stage. Thomas is unambiguous at this point: "Although Christ was a priest, not as God, but as man, yet one and the same was both priest and God."[527] As man, and not as God, he exercises his mediatorial office. Augustine's testimony is called upon: "Not

---

521 3a.7, 7 ad 1 D. F.
522 3a.7, 9 D. F.
523 3a.7, 10; 7, 12.
524 3a.22, 1 D. F.
525 3a.22, 1 ad 3.
526 3a.22, 2.
527 3a.22, 3 D. F.

because He is the Word, is Christ Mediator, since He Who is supremely mortal and supremely happy is far from us unhappy mortals; but He is Mediator, as man."[528]

Of course, Aquinas already has this notion in his Aristotelian doctrine of the impassibility of God. As pure act, God does not change. He is incapable of suffering or of any feelings as we experience them. Therefore Christ cannot undertake the bearing of the cross as God, but only as man. And as man, he offers "satisfaction and prayers to God for men" and communicates to fellow humans "both precepts and gifts."[529] No wonder Quick concludes his summary of Thomist Christology thusly: "While in the medieval doctrine of the incarnation Jesus Christ remains God, in the medieval doctrine of the atonement he remains man."[530]

When Christ's redemption is linked to a process awaiting our acting for completion, when it is seen as a potential reality requiring our act of free will to obtain the grace of the passion of Christ;[531] indeed, when the "sacrifice which is offered every day in the Church is not distinct from that which Christ Himself offered" but is commemorated on behalf of those unbelievers who are unwilling to be "participators in His Sacrifice," or those "who, after taking part in this sacrifice, fall away from it by whatsoever kind of sin," the consequence is that salvation is not complete in Christ, as it is in Calvin's theology. Furthermore, the Priesthood of Christ does not, for Thomas, exclude others from exercising a priesthood "in His stead." This is because Christ unites men to God "perfectively" in that it is by his death that the human race is reconciled to God. "However, nothing hinders certain others from being called mediators in some respect, between God and man, forasmuch as they co-operate in uniting men to God . . . ."[532] Such are "priests of the New Law."[533]

---

528 *De Civitate Dei*, ix.15, cited in 3a.26, 2 sed contra D. F.
529 3a.26, 2 D. F.
530 Oliver C. Quick, *The Doctrines of the Creed. Their Basis in Scripture and Their Meaning To-day*, (London: Nisbet and Co., 1938), 127, but cp. 3a.45, 5; 47, 3 ad 2.
531 3a.8, 3 et ad 2 D. F.
532 3a.26, 1 D. F.
533 3a.26, 1 ad 1 D. F.

The Passion of Christ

Now Christ, as we have said, was given grace that it might flow from him to others. And since he was in the "state of grace," his suffering "merited" eternal salvation for "all who are his members," viz., potentially, everyone.[534] Absolutely speaking, it was not "necessary" that Christ should suffer, for there was no compulsion either internal or external to that end.[535] Indeed, "God could have freed men otherwise than by Christ's passion, for 'nothing is impossible with God.'"[536] He could simply have remitted sins by fiat, without satisfaction and yet not in so doing violate justice. After all, "God has no one above him, for He is himself the supreme and common good."[537]

We must conclude that the sole reason Christ had to suffer to free humankind is that God foreknew and willed it in advance.[538] Again we witness a reduced kind of voluntarism in Aquinas' suggestion that when it comes to the dispensation of grace, God can give it in whatever manner he wills.

Now, Christ actually merited eternal salvation for us from the moment of conception.[539] This he accomplished in virtue of a two-fold movement. At the first instant of the creation of Christ's soul [i.e., his human nature], Christ was "sanctified by grace" by reason of his (simultaneous) *motus* of free will towards God. Since that movement was undertaken in a state of grace, it was meritorious.[540] Does his meriting salvation at his conception rule out his meriting it by his passion? Not at all.

> Nothing prevents the same thing belonging to someone from several causes. And thus it is that Christ was able by subsequent actions and sufferings to merit the glory of immortality, which He also merited in the first instant of His conception: not, indeed, so that it became thereby more due to him than before, but so that it was due to Him from more causes than before.[541]

534 3a.48, 2.
535 3a.46, 1.
536 3a.46, 2.
537 3a.46, 2 ad 3.
538 3a.46, 2.
539 3a.48, 1 ad 2.
540 3a.34, 3.
541 3a.34, 3 ad 3 D. F.

And yet we are not to conclude that the sufferings of the Savior were superfluous. For there were particular "obstacles" which kept us from enjoying the *effectum* of his previously acquired merits. Thus in order to remove these impediments Christ had to suffer.[542] Now among these *impedimenta* are the guilt of original sin and our own personal sins.[543] By his passion Christ merited for us both the grace of justification and the glory of beatitude.[544] But there is only one way in which we may take our share in the *passio Christi*, and that is the way of "faith, love, and the sacraments of the faith."[545] Since only the just have a place in the heavenly kingdom, we must be made just. Thus we may say that our salvation is perfected in our loving God. And our "obedience, humility, constancy, justice" (as well as other virtues) are necessary for our salvation.[546]

Consequently there is a twofold movement of merit going on. On the one hand Christ merits justification and eternal life for us. Yet, as Marie-Dominique Chenu reminds us, the basic Thomist principle of grace perfecting nature applies to our salvation:

> Once again, in this delicate question of human agency, we observe that for St. Thomas the sign of the gospel's influence in history is the subtle harmony of grace and nature. Better, it is the perfecting of nature in and through grace. *Gratia non tollit naturam sed perficit* (Grace does not destroy nature, but completes it)...The gospel absolutes lose nothing in being expressed in the available reality of human cooperation and freedom.[547]

Christ's meriting justification and eternal life for us is not sufficient for our salvation. Having received that "first grace" (justification), we must do our part by grace in order to merit eternal life. Hence "By the performance of good works, the patriarchs merited entry into the

542 3a.48, 1 ad 2.
543 3a.49, 5.
544 3a.46, 3.
545 3a.49, 5.
546 3a.46, 3.
547 Marie-Dominique Chenu, *Aquinas and His Role in Theology*, trans. Paul Philibert (Collegeville, Minnesota: The Liturgical Press), 2002, 116-117.

heavenly kingdom through faith in Christ's passion . . ."[548] But prior to that (in nature though not in time) Christ's passion removed the obstacle of guilt by meriting the grace of justification.

Thomas does employ imagery other than merit in his exposition of the passion: satisfaction (by "suffering in a loving and obedient spirit [Christ] offered more to God than was demanded in recompense for all the sins of mankind");[549] sacrifice ("he delivered himself up for us");[550] redemption ("his passion was as it were the price of punishment by which we are freed" from slavery to sin and consequent punishment);[551] and causation (his divine power caused salvation as an efficient cause working instrumentally by his humanity)."[552]

His discussion of the suffering of Christ is thus rich in biblical metaphor. Yet it would seem that the two concepts most determinative for his soteriology are those of causation and merit. Causation fits most naturally into his Aristotelian metaphysics and seems to provide a consistent thread throughout his theology, from creation as effects caused by an uncaused First Cause to the Law in its various forms as an unfolding of the principle of final causality, to salvation as the effect of an efficient cause. And merit, as the "effect" of cooperative grace dovetails neatly as well.

The Sacraments

Predominant in the Thomist doctrine of the work of Christ are the two notions of potentiality and actuality. As we saw earlier, all things are comprised of form (actuality) and matter (potentiality). In this way, Aristotle sought an answer to the problem of change, for a thing contains within itself principles which determine it to be the particular thing that it is, as well as principles which govern what it may become. Now Christ, by his passion, has become the Head of all humankind, which with him comprise his "mystical body." But obviously, protests the objector, not all are united to Christ in present experience. How then can they without exception be said to be part of his body and he their head? Well, says

---

548 3a.49, 5 ad 1.
549 3a.48, 2.
550 3a.48, 3.
551 3a.48, 4.
552 3a.48, 6.

Thomas, "We must consider the members of the mystical body not only as they are in act, but as they are in potentiality."[553]

And wherein does this potentiality consist? "First and principally, in the power (*virtus*) of Christ, which is sufficient for the salvation of the whole human race; secondly, in free will."[554] Of course that "power" for salvation resides principally in the passion of Christ.[555] For "Christ's flesh, wherein He endured the passion, is the instrument of the Godhead, so that His sufferings and actions co-operate with Divine power for expelling sin."[556] Therefore Aquinas maintains that Christ's passion establishes a potential relation between Christ and the human race which awaits actualization by the response of an individual's free will. By his passion Christ established the cause of our deliverance. But it is a cause which "must be applied specially to each one that he may receive the effect" of this cause.[557]

The grace Christ died to secure is compared to a medicine by which potentially all sickness might be cured. But each patient must take the prescription; "it needs to be applied to each individual for the cleansing of personal sins."[558] And this, declares Thomas, "is done by baptism and penance and the other sacraments, which derive their power from Christ's passion."[559]

Thus great emphasis is placed upon the efforts of the individual in his salvation. "Every single one," we are admonished, "must seek the remedies of his own salvation."[560] And it is not simply a matter of fleeing to Christ. One must seek him where he is to be found, namely, in the sacraments. And even there one must not come as he is. A sinner with an "ill-disposed will" is thereby unable to "co-operate with God," and so cannot be justified in baptism.[561] If however, his "will is set on renouncing sin,"[562] he has in this respect prepared himself. This the minister must

---

553 3a.8, 3 D. F.
554 3a.8, 3 ad 1 D. F.
555 3a.62, 5 D. F.
556 3a.49, 1 D. F.
557 *Summa Contra Gentiles*, IV.55.
558 3a.49, 1 ad 3 D. F.
559 3a.49, 1 ad 4 D. F.
560 *Summa Contra Gentiles*, IV.55.
561 3a.68, 4 sed contra D. F.
562 3a.68, 4 ad 1 D. F.

discern by looking for a "sign" of his "interior conversion," even as a doctor will only administer medicine to a sick man who manifests some "sign of life."[563]

What is more, other dispositions for the efficacious reception of the effects of the passion applied in the sacraments are necessary as well, viz., faith and charity.[564] For "it is by charity that we procure pardon of our sins, according to Luke 7:47, 'Many sins are forgiven her because she hath loved much.'"[565] But the benefits of Christ's passion are received through faith, though not lifeless faith, which can exist even with sin, but faith living through charity.[566]

Here we have Thomas' notion of "formed faith." By "form" he does not have in mind his hylomorphism, but his doctrine of final causality, according to which voluntary actions are shaped or determined by their end or form. "Each thing works through its own form. Now faith works through charity. Therefore the love of charity is the form of faith."[567] Now the form or end of faith is the "Divine Good," the "proper object of charity." When that act of faith is "perfected" or completed by charity, it is said to be "formed" faith.[568] If one has faith without charity, it is lifeless, unformed faith.[569] Nevertheless living and lifeless faith exist as "perfect and imperfect within the same species," the former being completed by charity, the latter not.[570]

Now faith comes from God "moving man inwardly by grace,"[571] in that God "prepares" him with grace, but it also "depends" on the "will of the believer."[572] Lifeless faith is from God since God has granted the one having it to believe. But its lifelessness is not a positive distortion, only a "privation" of the form of charity. Hence there is nothing wrong with it in itself; it is only incomplete, unperfected. God has granted such a one to believe, yet he has not also given the gift of charity. At the same

---

563 3a.68, 4 ad 2 D. F.
564 3a.49, 3 ad 1; 49, 5.
565 3a.49, 1 D. F.
566 3a.49, 1 ad 5.
567 2a2ae.4, 3 sed contra.
568 2a2ae.4, 3 D. F.
569 2a2ae.4, 4 ad 4.
570 2a2ae.4, 5 ad 3 D. F.
571 2a2ae.6, 1 D. F.
572 2a2ae.6, 1 ad 3 D. F.

time, this privation may be attributed to the presence of sin, with which charity cannot coexist.[573]

And what is faith's object? The coming and passion of Christ. The sacraments function as "signs in protestation of the faith whereby man is justified."[574] Now, a sacrament is a "sign of a holy thing so far as it makes men holy."[575] As such it signifies three aspects of our sanctification; viz., its cause, which is Christ's passion; its form, which is grace and the virtues; and its final end, which is eternal life.[576] Sacraments are necessary for salvation, because human nature ascends to "spiritual" and "intelligible" realities by means of "corporeal" and "sensible" things.[577] While it is true that Christ's passion is the sufficient cause of salvation, God has ordained that humans should receive this effect through the sacraments.[578]

Although Bernard argued that grace was not intrinsic in the sacraments; God only wills to cause grace when they are employed, Thomas firmly rejected such a view. That would make of them "mere signs," but in fact "the Sacraments of the New Law not only signify, but also cause grace."[579] Indeed, grace is their "principle effect."[580] And that grace itself is a "participated likeness of the Divine Nature," caused by God via the instrumentality of the sacraments.[581] Thus it exists both as cause (in God) and effect (in humans).[582] From sacramental grace flow not only virtues and gifts, by which the soul's powers are perfected in relation to their actions, but also "a certain Divine assistance in obtaining the end of the Sacrament" which is, as the objector observes, the "perfecting of the soul."[583] Negatively, sacramental grace is ordained to remove "defects" remaining as the result of past sin.[584]

---

573 2a2ae.6, 2 ad 3 D. F.
574 3a.61, 3 sed contra; 61, 3 ad 2; 61, 4; 62, 5 ad 6 D. F.
575 3a.60, 1 sed contra D. F.
576 3a.60, 3 sed contra D. F.
577 3a.61, 1 D. F.
578 3a.61, 1 ad 2 et 3 D. F.
579 3a. 62, 1 D. F.
580 3a. 62, prologue D. F.
581 3a .62, 1 D. F.
582 3a. 62, 1 ad 1 D. F.
583 3a.62, 2 D. F.
584 3a.62, 5 D. F.

The "other effect of the sacrament," says Thomas, is "character," which is a "kind of sealing" by which "God imprints his character upon us."[585] It distinguishes the recipient from others not so marked.[586] But it is also a certain spiritual "power" ordained to assist in divine worship, that the recipient may receive "Divine gifts" or give them to others. Indeed, it "disposes" the soul towards such worship.[587] Now this power is only instrumental in virtue of the power in the sacraments.[588]

This sacramental character is also the character of Christ, the eternal likeness of God.[589] By this, the recipients are made to be like Christ.[590] Therefore we can say that the faithful are likened to Christ by sharing in the spiritual power of the sacrament. And this likeness, as for any sanctification wrought by the priesthood of Christ, is enduring and therefore indelible.[591] For this reason even former apostates are not rebaptized.[592]

On the other hand, the primary effect of the sacrament, grace, subsists as a form in the soul, and as such depends on the "condition of the subject." And the soul this side of heaven is "changeable in respect of free will," so grace is similarly changeable.[593] When grace is taken away by sin, only character remains. Do all the sacraments confer character? No, for character, embodying a spiritual power ordained to assist a person to further sacramental acts or benefits, is implanted only by the sacraments of Order, Baptism, and Confirmation.[594] Of the seven sacraments Thomas enumerates (Baptism, Extreme Unction, Eucharist, Order, Penance, Matrimony and Confirmation)[595] we will particularly investigate Baptism, Eucharist and Penance, for in those three is gathered up his conception of the relation between grace and law.

---

585 3a.63, 1 sed contra D. F.
586 3a.63, 2 sed contra.
587 3a.63, 4 ad 1.
588 3a.63, 2.
589 3a.63, 3 sed contra.
590 3a.63, 3 ad 2.
591 3a.63, 5.
592 3a.63, 5 ad 2.
593 3a.63, 5 ad 1 D. F.
594 3a.63, 6.
595 3a.65, 1.

Baptism

In the sacrament of Baptism, we are told, there are three matters to be considered, viz., the "sacrament only" (sacramentum tantum); "reality and sacrament" (*res et sacramentum*); and "reality only" (*res tantum*). The first, sacrament only, is the "outward and visible sign" of "inward effect." As such it is not just the water, but the application of it to the person---the "washing." The reality and sacrament is the "baptismal character," for it is something real attested to by the external washing, and yet it is also a sacramental sign of the real something--- inward justification. Thus, of course, the reality itself of the sacrament of Baptism is justification. As we saw earlier with reference to all the sacraments, character, being indelible, remains, while justification "can be lost." What does it mean to say that a person is justified in baptism? He is regenerated, ushered into a "life of righteousness." This spiritual life is entered by faith and so we can consider Baptism as a "sort of protestation of faith."[596]

But, of course, Baptism, while possessing the power of conferring grace, derives its efficacy from beyond itself. We noted earlier that by all the sacraments the effects of the passion of Christ are applied instrumentally. Yet this sacrament was instituted by Christ at his Baptism. At that moment, it received the "power of producing its effect." The connection with the death of Christ inheres in Baptism's effect of making a person "conformable to Christ's Passion and Resurrection, in so far as he dies to sin and begins to live anew unto righteousness." Moreover it proclaims to him his "obligation" of so "conforming himself."[597] But Baptism's power to cleanse from sin comes from the power of Christ's blood.[598]

Baptism effects what it signifies. It is a "spiritual regeneration, inasmuch as a man dies to the old life and begins to lead the new life." Therefore a number of arguments may be marshaled against rebaptism: (1) One can only be begotten once (whether physically or, in this case, spiritually); (2) Christ, into whose death we are baptized, died once; (3) Baptism imprints an indelible character which does not require

---

596 3a.66, 1 et ad 1 D. F.
597 3a.66, 2 et ad 1 D. F.
598 3a.66, 3 ad 3 D. F.

renewing; and (4) Baptism is chiefly a remedy against original sin. Once the latter is removed it cannot recur.[599]

This line of reasoning would seem to argue for an unshakable, enduring new life for the one baptized, but no, Aquinas in typical fashion says that while the virtue of the *passio Christi* and hence of Baptism cannot be canceled by subsequent sins, they can block (*impedio*) its effect. Such sins must be blotted out in Penance.[600]

This suggests that, for all its connection with the regenerating effect of the unrepeatable death of Christ, Baptism is nevertheless attached by some very weak links, viz., human actions. Our sins, while not actually severing the connection, can certainly render it useless. What is more, Baptism is not simply about the saving passion of Christ. It is also about certain "conditions" which must be "fulfilled" in order for the sacrament to produce its "effect."[601] It requires, for example, one's faith. Before Christ's coming, persons were "incorporated into Christ by faith." In the same way, since his advent, persons are still incorporated into Christ by faith. Previously this faith was "manifested" by the "sign" of circumcision; now it is attested to by Baptism.[602] Indeed, faith is "something without which grace, which is the ultimate effect of the sacrament, cannot be had."[603] Of course for Aquinas, faith and sin are antithetical: for one to be present is for the other to be absent.[604] Therefore we are really bound to Christ's passion by our faith and separated from it by our sin. Baptism only bestows potential power, or grace, which we must make use of in order to actualize it in ourselves.

Thus, Thomas says that receiving the sacrament is not the pivotal issue in relation to a person's incorporation into Christ; rather, the "desire" on the part of those who "have the use of free will" is the *sine qua non*. If one should want to be baptized but die before having the chance, he could still obtain salvation "on account of his desire for Baptism, which desire is the outcome of faith that worketh by charity

---

599 3a.66, 9 D. F.
600 3a.66, 9 ad 1.
601 3a.68, 8.
602 3a.68, 1 ad 1 D. F.
603 3a.68, 8 D. F.
604 3a.68, 4 ad 3.

. . . ." For God's power is not "tied" to the sacraments; he is free to dispense grace when and where he wills.[605]

Furthermore the indispensability of human actions is underscored by Thomas' treatment of the question, "Whether sinners should be baptized." He quotes St. Augustine,[606] "He Who created thee without thee, will not justify thee without thee." And a sinner's will is "ill-disposed" so that he does not "co-operate with God." Hence Baptism cannot be employed as a means of justification for such a one.[607] Christ, the "Physician of souls," prepares a person's will so that it wills good and hates evil.[608] But this disposing, as noted earlier, does not exclude but requires free consent.

On the other hand, the grace-dimension to Baptism is seen in Thomas' conviction that no "works of satisfaction" are to be required of those right after Baptism, because "Christ's death satisfied sufficiently for sins;" to enjoin any such deeds would be to "dishonour" the Passion and imply its insufficiency.[609]

But Christ's full satisfaction for sin does not obviate the need for a baptismal candidate to confess his sins to God and sorrow over them beforehand, since, as Augustine declared, "he cannot begin the new life except he repent of his former life."[610] Indeed, he who can exercise free will must also "in order to die to the old life," "will to repent of his former life,"[611] and "intend to lead a new life."[612] The objection argues that the one baptized is a "patient" in the sacrament and therefore is passive, which would preclude requiring intentions and resolutions of him. But Thomas responds: "When a man is justified by Baptism, his passiveness is not violent but voluntary: wherefore it is necessary for him to intend to receive that which is given him."[613]

---

605 3a.68, 2.
606 *Sermon* 169, cited *in loc.*
607 3a.68, 4 sed contra D. F.
608 3a.68, 4 ad 2.
609 3a.68, 5 D. F.
610 *Sermon* 351, cited *in loc.* at 3a.68, 6.
611 Augustine, *op. cit.*
612 3a.68, 7 D. F.
613 3a.68, 7 ad 1 D. F.

What are the effects of Baptism? Since therein one dies to sin and begins to live a new life of grace, every sin is taken away at Baptism.[614] And Christ's passion is a sufficient satisfaction for all sins, so all debt of punishment is taken away as well.[615] Furthermore, the "grace of the Holy Spirit" and the virtues, which flow from Christ the Head to all His members, are received in Baptism.[616]

Also, the baptized are "born again unto the spiritual life" by their incorporation in Christ as his members, which happens in Baptism. And they are "enlightened by Christ as to the knowledge of the truth" and made "fruitful in good works" by the infusion of grace.[617] To be enlightened as to the knowledge of the truth is to be "prepared" in one's heart to receive the "doctrines of the truth."[618] The final effect of Baptism is to open the gates of the heavenly kingdom.[619]

In Thomas' exposition of Baptism, as elsewhere, we find a fundamental ambivalence about grace and law. On the one hand we find all the above gracious effects in the recipient of the sacrament. It can even be said that "Baptism has an equal effect in all."[620] And yet the measure of grace received is relative to the disposition of the one baptized.[621] While children, being equally disposed due to their Baptism in the faith of the Church, actually receive an equal effect, adults, approaching Baptism "in their own faith," are not equally disposed, "for some approach thereto with greater, some with less, devotion." And consequently, "some receive a greater, some a smaller share of the grace of newness."[622]

To be sure, this is not due to a lesser measure of grace being bestowed on certain ones. Grace flows equally from the passion through the sacrament to all. But prior conditions and subsequent actions make all the difference. Receiving grace, we are told, is like sitting near a fire: "some receive a greater, some receive a smaller share of the grace

---

614 3a.69, 1 D. F.
615 3a.69, 2 D. F.
616 3a.69, 4.
617 3a.69, 5 D. F.
618 3a.69, 5 ad 2 D. F.
619 3a.69, 7 D. F.
620 3a.69, 8 sed contra D. F.
621 3a.69, 8 D. F.
622 *Ibid.*

of newness; just as from the same fire, he receives more heat who approaches nearest to it, although the fire, as far as it is concerned, sends forth its heat equally to all."[623] But even should they receive equal grace, they must still utilize it as best they can, for the one who "applies himself more to advance therein" will progress more, while one who is negligent thereby "baffles grace."[624]

Finally, the effect of grace may be hindered (*impedio*) by "insincerity." If a person is to be justified in Baptism, God will not compel him: "his will must needs embrace both Baptism and the baptismal effect." Should his will be in contradiction to either, he is said to be "insincere."[625] He is not made sincere in this sacrament; he must come in sincerity in order to be justified.[626] But as soon as he becomes sincere, the obstacle to grace's effect is removed. And this obstacle is removed by Penance.[627]

Eucharist

Before examining that particular sacrament, however, we turn our attention to the sacrament of the Eucharist. Like the other sacraments, it is "ordained for helping man in the spiritual life." The assistance it offers in common with baptism may be compared to the help required by the body, for it needs generation in order that life may begin and food that it may be sustained. The former is supplied by baptism, the latter by the Eucharist.[628] The "spiritual food" of the Eucharist imparts a perfection to the recipient.[629] However the great difference between the two is seen in the fact that while Baptism contains its "sacred thing", viz., "sanctifying power" only in relation to its application to the individual, the Eucharist contains its "sacred thing", "Christ's own body" absolutely, as soon as it is consecrated. For in the Eucharist, that which is both "reality and sacrament" (*res et sacramentum*) is "in the matter itself," bread and wine, while that which is reality only (*res tantum*), namely, grace, is in the recipient; whereas in Baptism both are in the recipient.[630]

---

623 *Ibid.*
624 3a.69, 8 ad 2 D. F.
625 3a.69, 9 D. F.
626 3a.69, 9 ad 2.
627 3a.69, 10 D. F.
628 3a.73, 1 D. F.
629 3a.73, 1 ad 1 D. F.
630 3a.73, 1 ad 3 D. F.

Like Baptism, the Eucharist is necessary for salvation, and also in common between the two is the sufficiency of having the desire of receiving it "if there be no occasion for the actual reception of the sacrament."[631]

As we have noted, Aquinas maintains that the Eucharist contains the very body and blood of Christ. This presence is neither detectible by sense nor by understanding; but by faith alone, which rests upon divine authority, viz., "This is My body."[632] In defending this position, it is urged that in this way the "sacrifice of the New Law" fulfills the "sacrifices of the Old Law." The former contained Christ crucified figuratively, while the latter contains him "in very truth."[633]

Now, Christ's body does not come to be present in the sacrament by "local motion," for then it would have to leave heaven and traverse the places in between, and moreover, it would not be able to terminate its movement locally in different places at the same time. Therefore we must conclude that Christ's body begins to be anew in the sacrament by a change of the "substance" of the bread.[634] Such a conversion is "not like natural changes, but is entirely supernatural, and effected by God's power alone." In fact, it transcends "nature's laws" by the action of God, who is "infinite act." Natural agents can only act by a change of form, but God converts the very being, so that "the whole substance of one thing" is "changed into the whole substance of another." Thus it can be called *transubstantio*.[635]

Although the substance is changed, our sense perception informs us that the accidents remain. And this is beneficial, since our receiving the Lord's body and blood "invisibly" by faith is meritorious.[636] It may even contradict the natural order, in which substance is logically prior to accidents. But God's power, the universal First Cause, can ordain that the accidents remain while the original substance is taken away.[637]

Over what period of time is this change brought about? Since it is effected by an Infinite Power, it is instantaneous.[638] When the minister

631 3a.73, 3 D. F.
632 3a.75, 1 sed contra D. F.
633 3a.75, 1.
634 3a.75, 2 D. F.
635 3a.75, 4 D. F.
636 3a.75, 5 D. F.
637 3a.75, 5 ad 1; 77, 1 et ad 1 D. F.
638 3a.75, 3 D. F.

utters the words of Christ, "This is my body," and "This is the chalice of my blood," which together comprise the "form" of the sacrament, the matter (bread and wine) is thereby consecrated. And this consecration "consists in the miraculous change of substance, which can only be done by God."[639] In the words of the form of the sacrament resides a "created power" which causes transubstantiation, but this cause is instrumental, deriving its power[640] from Christ[641] whose power is infinite.[642]

The "power" of the passion works in this sacrament toward a threefold end: (1) to secure our "eternal heritage;" (2) "for justifying by grace, which is by faith;" and (3) "for removing sins which are the impediments to both of these things."[643] Yet as (2) indicates, faith is required. Like Baptism, the Eucharist is a sacrament of faith, "because by faith alone do we hold the presence of Christ's blood in this sacrament. Moreover Christ's passion justifies us by faith.[644]

What are the effects of this sacrament? Since it contains Christ, who, with his passion, is the cause of grace, it must bestow grace.[645] Thus, so long as a person comes with "his own desire," he will "procure" grace by which he is "enabled to lead the spiritual life." But he already received grace at his baptism, and so by the sacrament of the Eucharist "grace is increased" and the "spiritual life is perfected."[646] This sacrament also confers the "virtue of charity."[647]

Another effect is the "attaining of eternal life," the approach to which Christ opened to us by his passion.[648] Yet we must add that while Christ's passion is the "sufficient cause" of attaining eternal life, it does not infallibly secure it for us. It "bestows on us the power of coming into glory." But we must first suffer with him in order afterwards to be glorified with him.[649] And this effect will not come to those who receive the sacrament "unworthily," who fail to "keep innocence."[650]

639 3a.78, 1 D. F.
640 3a.78, 5.
641 3a.78, 4.
642 3a.78, 5.
643 3a.78, 3 D. F.
644 3a.78, 3 ad 6 D. F.
645 3a.79, 1.
646 3a.79, 1 ad 1 D. F.
647 3a.79, 1 ad 2 D. F.
648 3a.79, 2 D. F.
649 3a.79, 2 ad 1 D. F.
650 3a.79, 2 ad 2 D. F.

One receives the Eucharist unworthily by taking it while in "mortal sin." Although the sacrament derives from the passion the power of forgiving all sins, mortal sin constitutes an obstacle (*impedimentum*) to receiving the sacrament's *effectum*. Such a person "cannot be united with Christ, which is the effect of this sacrament, as long as he retains an attachment towards mortal sin." Nor can he receive forgiveness for that sin.[651]

However, if one in mortal sin desires to receive the effect of the sacrament (and thus, presumably, also desires to forsake his sin), he will do so. Also, if he comes with a mortal sin without knowing it and for which he has no "attachment," he can be forgiven. Or if he (presumably in Penance) was not "sufficiently contrite at first," he may still approach the Eucharist "devoutly and reverently," and by this "he obtains the grace of charity, which will perfect his contrition and bring forgiveness of sin."[652]

"Venial" sins, on the other hand, are forgiven by this sacrament because they are those which only "lessen the fervour of charity," while this sacrament not only bestows, but also kindles charity, and "by this means venial sins are forgiven."[653] But venial sins still being committed do partly hinder the effect of the sacrament since they "distract the mind" and hinder the fervour of charity.[654]

Does the Eucharist remit all punishment due to sin? It cannot, because it was not instituted for "satisfaction" but for spiritual nourishment. It is from the fervour of charity, as we have observed, that humans obtain forgiveness. And even while charity is bestowed in the sacrament, it is incumbent upon the recipient to exercise it fully.[655] It is by the charity he offers, along with the grace he receives that remission of punishment is obtained. Indeed, Thomas goes so far as to say that the amount of such remission is "according to the measure of his devotion and fervour." The "affection of the offerer is weighed" in determining how far the "satisfactory power" contained in the sacrament shall go in remitting punishment due to sin.[656] If only part of his punishment is taken away,

651 3a.79, 3 D. F.
652 3a.79, 3 D. F.
653 3a.79, 4 D. F.
654 3a.79, 8 D. F.
655 3a.79, 5; cf. 79, 6 ad 2 D. F.
656 3a.79, 5 D. F.

"it is due to a defect not on the part of Christ's power, but on the part of man's devotion."[657] In fact, even the reception of forgiveness of sins and the attaining of glory, twin effects of the Eucharist, are only for those who are "united with Christ's passion through faith and charity" and then only in relation to the "measure of their devotion."[658]

Another effect of the sacrament is preservation from future sins. This is accomplished in two ways: (1) by uniting a person with Christ through grace, it strengthens his spiritual life; (2) since by Christ's passion "the devils are conquered," it wards off "all assaults of demons."[659] Nevertheless, cautions Thomas,

> The effect of this sacrament is received according to man's condition: such is the case with every active cause in that its effect is received in matter according to the condition of the matter. But such is the condition of man on earth that his free will can be bent to good or evil. Hence, although this sacrament of itself has the power of preserving from sin, yet it does not take away from man the possibility of sinning.[660]

In Thomas' theology, a great emphasis is placed upon the condition, the attitudes, the feelings of the individual. While he does not doubt Christ's power to save, he clearly thinks that the condition of the would-be recipient of this power can make all the difference. There may be a tremendous reservoir of grace available in the Eucharist, but one who sins mortally cannot receive it. In fact, "if anyone, while in mortal sin, receives this sacrament, he purchases damnation, by sinning mortally."[661] The reason is that the recipient is by his reception testifying that he is united with Christ and his members, and this union only takes place by living (i.e., formed) faith, which a mortal sin cannot have. Such "lying to the sacrament" profanes it and thereby constitutes a mortal sin.[662]

While it is true that Eucharistic grace is a "medicine," "every medicine does not suit every stage of sickness." Baptism and Penance

657 3a.79, 5 ad 3 D. F.
658 3a.79, 7 ad 2 D. F.
659 3a.79, 6 D. F.
660 3a.79, 6 ad 1 D. F.
661 3a.80, 4 sed contra.
662 3a.80, 4 D. F.

take away the "fever of sin," but this medicine is administered to strengthen, and thus "ought not to be given except to them who are quit of sin."[663] Ignorance is no excuse either. Violations based on lack of knowledge of the law still incur the above penalty. When one fails to examine his conscience, he commits sin in receiving Christ's body.[664]

At the same time Thomas' pastoral concern emerges in his discussion of the one who sorrows over his sin, but is not "sufficiently contrite." He would not be wrong to partake, because "a man cannot know for certain whether he is truly contrite." It is enough that he find in himself the "marks of contrition," such as grieving over past sins and intending to avoid them thenceforth.[665] Furthermore, the priest ought not to withhold Holy Communion from any but notorious sinners, so long as the recipients have been baptized.[666] And he should give the sacrament to those who are feeble-minded so long as they can "conceive some devotion towards this sacrament."[667]

Christ even gave his body and blood to Judas; it was Judas who "separated himself" from Christ, and not Christ who "excluded him." "Therefore," says Thomas, "Christ for his part drinks the wine even with Judas in the Kingdom of God, but Judas himself repudiated this banquet."[668] Nevertheless, the priest must warn all openly in public, not to approach the Lord's table until they have repented of their sins.[669]

Now, the priest performs this sacrament "as in the person of Christ," receiving the power of consecrating it on Christ's behalf at his ordination.[670] He stands as the "appointed intermediary between God and the people; hence as it belongs to him to offer the people's gifts to God, so it belongs to him to deliver consecrated gifts to the people."[671] When he celebrates the sacrament, Christ himself is sacrificed.[672] But a devout layman is not united to Christ by such sacramental power, and hence must not seek to accomplish the Eucharist.[673]

---

663 3a.80, 4 ad 2 D. F.
664 3a.80, 4 ad 5.
665 3a.80, 4 ad 5 D. F.
666 3a.80, 6 D. F.
667 3a.80, 8 D. F.
668 3a.81, 2 ad 1 D. F.
669 3a.80, 6.
670 3a.82, 1 D. F.
671 3a.82, 3 D. F.
672 3a.83, 1.
673 3a.82, 1 ad 2 D. F.

Penance

Penance, like Baptism, is a sacrament whereby we may be cleansed from sin.[674] But in all other sacraments save Matrimony, human acts are not the "essential matter" of the sacrament, but dispositions to it. Here in Penance, the human act "stands in the place of the matter." Thomas again appeals to a medical analogy, comparing the first kind of sacraments to "medicines applied externally," while Penance is more like a cure which requires certain acts on the part of the person such as exercises.[675] What is more, Baptism is ordained to cleanse from original sin, but Penance is for taking away mortal sin.[676]

If the actions taken by the penitent are the "matter" of the sacrament, its "form" is supplied by the priest who, on the authority of Christ, says "I absolve thee."[677] This does not supplant the prerogative of God, who alone absolves from sin. In pronouncing the words of absolution, the priest thereby works as an instrument of divine power, having been entrusted with the power of the keys.[678] However, in common with all the sacraments of the New Law, Penance has of itself a certain effect via the power of Christ's passion. But that effect may be impeded (*impedio*) on the part of the recipient.[679]

Is this sacrament necessary for salvation? In an "absolute" sense it is not, for what is necessary is that one be born again in Christ, and this happens by Baptism. But given the supposition that mortal sin has been committed subsequently, Penance is essential for salvation. The only way such sin can be taken away is through this sacrament, wherein the power of Christ's passion works through the priest's absolution and the penitent's action in co-operating with grace for the elimination of his sin. However we must again distinguish between the absolute and ordained powers of God, for he can, as he did when Christ forgave the adulterous woman of John 7, by the "excellence" of his power, grant forgiveness without Penance.[680]

---

674 3a.84, 1 sed contra, D. F.
675 3a.84, 1 ad 1; cf. 84, 5.
676 3a.84, 2 ad 3.
677 3a.84, 3 sed contra; 84, 3.
678 3a.84, 3 ad 3 D. F.
679 3a.84, 3 ad 5 D. F.
680 3a.84, 5 ad 3 D. F.

For Thomas, justification is not by definition a process producing an enduring state of affairs. Although it is rooted in the passion of Christ, the power of which causes a sure effect, its *terminus* is located in humans, whose actions determine whether the divine *motus* reaches that *terminus*. And even should it, it is quite possible for a given *viator* to exist in a state of justice only occasionally, for each time he sins mortally, he must seek justification all over again---through Penance.[681]

Penance serves, as Jerome[682] says, as a "second plank after shipwreck."[683] The first help for those are shipwrecked is the plank of baptism, which removes all sin. But if that plank no longer avails because their integrity is destroyed by sin, they must strive to regain it by seizing the second plank, viz., Penance.[684] One's obligation to do penance is not discharged fully by the sacrament. It is true that "exterior penance" whereby one shows outward "signs of sorrow," confesses his sins to the priest and "makes satisfaction" for his sins, need not be prolonged until the end of life, but "only for a definite period according to the measure of sin." But "interior penance," in which one grieves over sins committed, ought to be lifelong. Indeed, if he ever stopped being displeased over sinning, "by this very fact he would incur a new sin and he would lose the fruit of pardon."[685] In this sense Thomas exhorts the individual to "persevere in penance lest he again fall into sin."[686]

Another example of Thomas' pastoral intent may be seen in his teaching that penance can be repeated many times, because of the "infinity of divine mercy which is beyond all number and magnitude of sins."[687] And even should a person sin after penance "by act or intention: it does not call into question the sincerity or validity of his former penance."[688]

In order adequately to do one's part in this sacrament, he must deplore his past sins and while doing so, not repeat them either by act

---

681 Cf. 3a.84, 5 ad 2.
682 *Letters*, 130, cited *in loc.*
683 3a.84, 6 sed contra D. F.
684 3a.84, 6.
685 3a.84, 8 D. F.
686 3a.84, 8 ad 1 D. F.
687 3a.84, 10.
688 3a.84, 10 ad 4.

or intention.[689] This deploring, this sorrow, is both a "passion of the sensitive appetite," and an act of the will,[690] which involves choice. Now Aristotle defines "virtue" as "the habit of choosing according to right reason."[691] Therefore penance must be an act of virtue.[692] Yet penance as an act also springs from charity, for it is grounded in a love for the good and grief for what is contrary to it.[693] For the matter of that, penance involves all the theological virtues, including faith "in Christ's passion, whereby we are cleansed from our sins," hope "for pardon," charity, in that one hates vice, as well as the moral virtues.[694]

In Article 5 of Question 85 it is asked "whether Penance originates from fear?" The objector reasons that Penance springs from love, since it comes from displeasure at sin, which belongs to charity. Thomas replies that sin rather begins to displease a person out of fear of punishment before it displeases him because of its being an offense against God.[695]

But another objection is raised, namely, that "men are induced to do Penance, through the expectation of the heavenly kingdom, according to Matthew 3:2 and 4:13, "Do Penance, for the kingdom of heaven is at hand." To this Thomas replies "By the approach of the kingdom of God is understood not only the advent of a king who rewards, but also of one who punishes."[696]

It would seem that no more striking or telling contrast with Calvin could be found. For in Book III, Chapter 3 of his *Institutio*, he would offer an extensive critique of the medieval sacrament of Penance. And he expressly says concerning the Matthaean text, "For while Christ the Lord and John preach in this manner: 'Repent, for the kingdom of heaven is at hand,' do they not derive the reason for repenting from grace itself and the promise of salvation?"[697]

Nevertheless, for Thomas, repentance is the way to forgiveness. And this forgiveness, contained in Penance, is powerful enough to take

---

689 3a.84, 10 ad 4.
690 3a.84, 10 ad 3.
691 *Ethics* ii.6, cited *in loc.*
692 3a.85, 1.
693 3a.85, 1 ad 1.
694 3a.85, 3 ad 4 D. F.
695 3a.85, 1 ad 1.
696 3a.85, 1 ad 2.
697 *Institutes*, III.iii.2.

away all sins. In this life there is no sin so great it cannot be repented of. True, this requires a movement of free will, but the will of the wayfarer is "flexible about good and evil." Yet the power of grace is able to move the heart of any sinner to repent. To say that any sin is beyond pardoning would be to derogate the mercy of God and the power of Christ's passion.[698]

Now Penance, as we have said, is the process whereby one who sins after baptism is justified. And both God and humans have indispensable parts to play, for sins are "remedied by an act of man co-operating with God for his justification."[699] Of course, Penance as a habit is "infused immediately without our co-operating as principal agents," and even this divine *motus* does not take place "without our cooperation preparing us through certain acts," such as faith, servile fear, hope, charity and filial fear.[700]

We earlier saw that in the *processus iustificationis* a motion of the free will towards God and away from sin is required. Now we learn that this is because "it cannot happen that God pardons an offense without change in the offending person's will." And mortal sin arises when a person's will turns away from God and towards a mortal good. "Hence, for pardon of this offence against God, it is required that man's will be so changed that it be turned to God and renounce having turned away, together with the purpose of amendment." And that is the nature of Penance. Without it, it is "impossible" for God to forgive sin.[701] Impossible, that is, on the supposition of the *potentia ordinata*.

Can one sin be pardoned without others being pardoned? Not at all, since sin is "taken away by grace." And every mortal sin is opposed to grace and excludes it. Besides, true Penance, motivated by a love for God above all things, is displeased with all sin.[702] Yet even when all sin is taken away, all its remnants are not necessarily removed. Sometimes God first takes away guilt by "operating grace and afterwards by co-operating grace, removes the remnants of sin by degrees."[703]

---

698 3a.86, 1.
699 3a.85, 2 ad 2 D. F.
700 3a.85, 5 D. F.
701 3a.86, 2 D. F.
702 3a.86, 3.
703 3a.86, 5 ad 1.

For Aquinas, release from sin does not entail release from punishment. After David repented he was forgiven and yet there remained a "debt of punishment."[704] Every mortal sin is a turning away from the "immortal good," God, and thereby incurs a "debt of eternal punishment." God's justice must still be satisfied. The disorder of sin upsets the "balance of justice," which can only be tilted back by punishment. Since venial sins do not involve turning away from God, they only earn a finite punishment. And when mortal sin is forgiven by grace, the soul is turned back to God so that the debt of eternal punishment is removed, although "the debt of some finite punishment may remain."[705]

This may seem to qualify the sufficiency of the *passio Christi*, but in fact it is "sufficient of itself to remove all debt of punishment." Nonetheless, a person receives release from the debt of punishment "according to the way a man shares in the power of Christ's passion."[706] For remission of punishment belongs to co-operative grace, which means that both God's grace and human free will are involved.[707] Therefore "one benefits by the power of Christ's passion according to the measure of personal acts which are the matter of Penance." Only after one has fulfilled all the penitential acts is the extra debt of punishment remitted.[708]

Now venial sin separates one from God incompletely, in contrast with mortal sin, which effects an absolute separation. But forgiveness comes for both kinds of sin "by reason of repentance, since in repentance the will is turned to embrace God, and sin "cannot be pardoned as long as the will clings to sin."[709]

But because the separation is absolute in the case of mortal sin, a greater repentance is called for, viz., his detesting "actually" every mortal sin he has committed. He must try to remember each one of these sins. Yet he need not worry about the sins he fails to remember after a scrupulous self-examination. Such is not necessary for venial sins. But he should always see to it that his affections tend towards God and the things of God, so that were he to commit any sin which would hinder

---

704 3a.86, 4 sed contra.
705 3a.86, 4.
706 3a.86, 5 ad 3.
707 3a.86, 5 ad 2.
708 3a.86, 5 ad 3.
709 3a.87, 1.

that tendency it would grieve him.[710] Also, "striking one's breast" and reciting the Lord's Prayer "cause the remission of sins." Such actions are evidence of the infusion of grace and a detesting of sin which together work in Penance.[711]

If a person commits a sin again after Penance, the old sin itself does not return, but the debt of punishment is greater the second time, on account of the second sin's being aggravated in view of his earlier sin.[712] Moreover, if he demonstrates ungratefulness to God after receiving forgiveness by committing more mortal sins or by "doing something against the form received," e.g., by failing to forgive his brother, he incurs a debt of punishment for sins previously pardoned.[713]

In addition to forgiveness of sin, the recovery of all virtues is an effect of Penance. This is because remission of sin requires the infusion of grace, from which all the virtues flow.[714] Yet the penitent always "rises again to less virtue," since grace is infused relative to the strength of the free will which constitutes the disposition to it: "In Penance, according to the degree of intensity or remissness in the movement of free will, the penitent receives greater or lesser grace." Again Thomas brings in the notion of an *impedio* on the part of the recipient to account for the variability in the face of the power of Penance to "bring all defects back to perfection."[715]

Nevertheless, and seemingly inconsistently, Thomas says that the "predestined," regardless of how often they fall, will rise again to more abiding grace because they will be more "careful and humble" and therefore "more steadfastly . . . abide in grace."[716]

If through sin one loses his place among the children of God, he can recover it through Penance. He cannot be restored to his former innocence but he gains "something greater."[717] But should he fail to do

710 3a.87, 2 D. F.
711 3a.87, 3.
712 3a.88, 1 D. F.
713 3a.88, 2 D. F.
714 3a.89, 1 D. F.
715 3a.89, 2 ad 2 D. F. This variability of the intensity of free will reinforces the impression that justification, while the effect of operative grace, also entails a flexible free will and hence requires human co-operation which the person may or may not render.
716 3a.89, 2 ad 1 D. F.
717 3a.89, 3 D. F.

Penance for sin, even deeds done in charity will no longer merit eternal life, since the effect of those works is "hindered" by mortal sin.[718] Such meritorious works previously deadened can be revived by Penance, which removes the impediment.[719] At the same time, subsequent Penance cannot vivify "dead works," i.e., those not done in charity.[720]

Aquinas assigns to the sacrament of Penance the traditional three-fold partition, viz., contrition, confession and satisfaction. Considered as parts, they constitute the material cause," for human acts are the matter of this sacrament. As a whole, they are a "kind of formal cause."[721]

In Penance, the "scales are righted" according to both the will of the sinner and the judgment of God, because the goal is reconciliation of friendship. Thus the requirements of the penitent are, first, the "intention of making amends," or contrition; second, submission to the judgment of the priest standing in the place of God, or confession; and third, recompense according to the judgment of the priest, or satisfaction.[722]

Contrition is itself a sort of "inner repentance, including the "resolve to confess and make satisfaction."[723] Satisfaction includes both an inner willingness to atone and its external accomplishment.[724] Confession, of course, is "in word."[725] And these three parts answer to sin in all its forms, viz., thoughts, words and deeds; or a combination thereof.[726]

Thomas does not fully develop these three parts, since he left his *Summa* unfinished at this point. But he does indicate that satisfaction includes making "some kind of compensation" for one's offence.[727] Indeed, when justice is to be sought between unequal parties "he that falls short must do whatever he can,"[728] including "weeping and tears." Such work will be rewarded by the "full remission of sin both as to guilt and as to punishment."[729]

718 3a.89, 4 D. F.
719 3a.89, 5 D. F.
720 3a.89, 6 D. F.
721 3a.90, 1 D. F.
722 3a.90, 2 D. F.
723 3a.90, 2 ad 1 D. F.
724 3a.90, 2 ad 2 D. F.
725 3a.90, 2 ad 4.
726 3a.90, 3 ad 1 D. F.
727 3a.85, 3.
728 3a.85, 3 ad 2 D. F.
729 3a.84, 9 ad 1 D. F.

Conclusion

The freshness of Thomas' approach, the profundity of his insights into classic Christian beliefs, and above all, the consummate skill with which the Angelic Doctor fuses together nature and grace into an all-embracing world view covering nearly every intellectual and theological question of his day constitute a masterly work in whose shallows most of us, this writer included, are condemned to paddle. One gains an increasingly vivid sense of his own limited grasp of the sweep of the history of theology and of the depth of the questions raised in the scholastic dialogue with that history as he peruses the work of this intellectual giant.

And yet, for all that profundity, certain nagging problems would appear to remain. Thomas' reasoning backward, *via analogiae*, from effect to cause, leads him to an abstract, impersonal God.[730] He then argues downward, from the First Cause, to construct a chain of cause and effect between Creator and creature in a way which does not seem to do justice to the relation of persons which God has graciously established in the life, death and resurrection of his only Son. And the mechanical, abstract categories under which God and humankind are subsumed would seem to hinder a warm, personal relationship between God the Father and his children. For that to take place, a mutual relation of knowing is necessary, but such knowing is ruled out by the discontinuity between God as he is in himself according to his *potentia absoluta*, and as he is in his actions in the world on the basis of his *potentia ordinata*.

His doctrine of God as the Pure Act of Being, who could save without the Cross, who in an exercise of "soteriological voluntarism" can predestine some for everlasting joy and reprobate others with equanimity does not seem to take fully into account the God revealed as the eternal Father of our Lord Jesus Christ.

What is more, the fundamental ambivalence in notion that God has willed a system of merit through co-operative grace appears to call into question the graciousness of grace. Eternal life in some sense hangs on how well a person utilizes the grace he is given, rather than being grounded in the gracious activity of God. While it would be too much to argue that grace is actually a "thing" for Aquinas, it certainly can in his

---

730 Cf. T. F. Torrance, "Scientific Hermeneutics According to St. Thomas Aquinas," *Journal of Theological Studies*, New Series, vol. xiii, pt. 2, October, 1962, 289.

thought be detached from Christ, and even considered as an accidental characteristic of a human habit, it remains something other than God himself. No doubt he is quite concerned to attribute all to grace, but at the end of the day St. Thomas expounds the Gospel of grace in the language of merit, and the latter, it would appear, has the last word.

In all of this we have detected in discussions of grace, law, and predestination, an emphasis on the will without reference to God's nature as revealed in Christ. In this way, despite Thomas' intellectualism,[731] the will of God seems to assume an undue primacy at times. Father D'Arcy thinks that Thomas' God enjoys the complete freedom of self-determination:

> God is not determined by anything outside himself, and we must not think even of his own nature as lying heavily upon his acts. That nature is wholly active and is taken up into his will. Hence he is independent of all else save himself; he has full charge over his nature, and he does what he does solely because he wills it.[732]

D'Arcy may be overstating his case, in light of Thomas' constant insistence on the goodness of God being at the root of all his actions. And yet sometimes we wonder whether Goodness becomes simply defined as whatever God does, in a circular fashion, and Will becomes in some sense the primary determinant. All definitions are finally in some sense circular, but we think that the doctrines of the Christian faith are located in a circle not "vicious" when interpreted in the light of the self-disclosure of God in Christ. We have seen in the theology of Aquinas that when the thought of the will of God is detached from the revelation of God in and through Christ, the consequence is that the freeness of grace in its *unrestrictedness* as well as in its *unmeritedness* can be lost.

We will attempt to show that John Calvin, and more successfully, John McLeod Campbell, sought to interpret the will and nature of God in the light of his self-disclosure in Christ. In this way we see the nature of grace as nothing other than the self-giving of God in redemptive activity for a sinful human race. If God is gracious in his inmost character, then all of his willing is informed by that grace, and he takes the plight of

---

731 Cf. Blanchette, *The Perfection of the Universe According to Aquinas*, 268-305.
732 M. C. D'Arcy, *Saint Thomas Aquinas*, 130-131.

all people upon himself in his inhomination. Moreover our response is therefore not to actualize a "potential" salvation, but to embrace in faith a reality *extra nos*, already there for us in Christ, to devote a lifetime to gratitude and glorifying God.

CHAPTER 2

THE DIVIDED GOD OF CALVIN

Introduction

By considering Calvin after the Angelic Doctor, we are not intimating that the former consciously undertook a comprehensive assessment of St. Thomas. In fact, he rarely mentions him by name. In Calvin's day Peter Lombard, the Master of Sentences, still reigned supreme.[733] Nevertheless, it will be shown that Calvin's theology constitutes an evangelical critique of many of the doctrines taught by (among others) St. Thomas, especially as they relate to Grace and Law.

If we bear in mind that Calvin presented his first edition of the *Institutio* a mere nineteen years after Luther posted his Ninety-Five Theses on the door of the Schlosskirche in Wittenberg, we will not permit his thoroughgoing doctrine of the Double Decree (which was already found in milder terms in Augustine, Aquinas and Luther)[734] to detract from his central insights regarding the grace and knowledge of God, and the sacraments as powerful witnesses to the evangelical content of the Gospel. In fact, it will be shown that Calvin's twofold predestination is motivated by a desire to defend the freeness of grace, for it is his concern that divine election not be predicated upon foreknowledge of merit--even in the form of a decision to accept grace.[735]

However, in the process, he divides the thought of the will of God from the self-revelation of God in Christ. His doctrine of election, so far as it concerns those predestined to glory, *is* anchored in God as disclosed

---

733 Copleston, *Aquinas*, 9; Armand Aime LaValee, "Calvin's Criticism of Scholastic Theology" (Ph.D. dissertation, Harvard University, 1967), 23.

734 See J. B. Mozley, *A Treatise on the Augustinian Doctrine of Predestination*, Second Edition, (New York: E. P. Dutton, 1878). Mozley can find no substantial difference between Aquinas and Calvin regarding their doctrines of predestination (267, 393ff). But, as we shall seek to show, this overlooks the clear note of *sola gratia* which pervades Calvin's discussion, in contrast to the mixture of grace and merit which characterizes Thomas' treatment.

735 John Calvin, *Concerning the Eternal Predestination of God*, trans., ed. J. K. S. Reid, (Cambridge: James Clarke, 1961), 149.

probation is grounded elsewhere, in an abstract God
...er grace when and where he wills.

...should make this move is somewhat surprising in light of
h...   ..r programmatic statements that the whole of our knowledge
of Go...   ...st be derived from and bounded by his self-revelation in and
through Jesus Christ. Moreover, he is sure that the disclosure of the
Father by the Son gives us a true apprehension of God's inner nature
as loving, gracious, and fatherly. He even goes so far as to propound a
doctrine of universal atonement.

For the Genevan reformer, we are only permitted to hold a
Christological doctrine of grace. Thus, God's grace is not something
which is dispensed in different manners, sometimes
unconditionally, while at others, contingently, awaiting meritorious use
of the "first grace." Rather, grace is constituted by God's self-giving[736]
in the humanity of his Son and as such can never be distinguished or
divided from Jesus Christ.

Moreover, knowledge of God is not the product of abstractive
extrapolation from effects to the First Cause, even if supplemented
by Scripture. The noetic effects of original sin and the lowly estate of
humankind rule out any movement of knowing anchored on the human
side, apart from a bare *sensus divinitatis*, an awareness always distorted
and turned into idolatry apart from a saving union with Christ.

Calvin's strong emphasis on the pervasive sinfulness of human
nature likewise shapes his doctrine of human will. Although under
no external compulsion, postlapsarian persons are not free to choose
from a range of choices, but are drawn to evil. As such they are in no
position to originate motions toward God, even with the "assistance" of
"cooperating grace." Therefore Calvin has no use for the formula, *deus
non denegat gratiam facere quod in se est*. Any good in us contributory
to our responding to the divine initiative is itself the sole consequence
of grace.

A proper understanding of Calvin's doctrine of grace must bear in
mind that law and Gospel are not contraries. The law is and always has
been grounded in the grace of God, for God gives what he demands.
Therefore, there is but one covenant, a covenant of grace, administered

---

736 Cf. John H. Leith, "The Doctrine of the Will in the *Institutes of the Christian Religion*," *Reformatio Perennis*, ed. Brian Gerrish, (Pittsburgh: Pickwick Press, 1981), 57.

in two dispensations, the Old and New Testaments. It is evident that the Genevan reformer would look askance at later Federal attempts to posit a Covenant of Works, predicated on obedience to law as a condition of grace, prior to the Covenant of grace, governed by *sola gratia*.

Calvin's insistence on grace as God's self-giving in Christ also gives his soteriological doctrine a richer content. While he employs sacrificial and legal metaphors, he continually places them in the context of the saving humanity of Christ. The latter provides his true theme, for in Christ God becomes human, bone of our bone, flesh of our flesh that he might take what is ours upon himself, and impart what is his to us. It seems evident that for Calvin, God's work in Christ embraces the entire human race. Yet only certain ones are chosen by God to be awakened by the Spirit to the faith that knows what God has accomplished for them.

There is a tension between these two doctrines--universal atonement and selective election--indeed, arguably an unbearable one. Calvin propounded them not as inescapable correlates of the logic of his system, for they were not, in fact, compatible with it,[737] but rather as the teaching of Scripture and as a defense of the unconditional freeness of grace.

Calvin's mistake, it seems to us, lies in detaching the thought of the will of God from the revelation of God in and through Christ. As a consequence, the freeness of grace in that it is *unrestricted* is missing in Calvinian[738] thought. However, since he does anchor his understanding of the will of God *toward the elect* in the self-disclosure of God through His Word, the freeness of grace in all its *unmeritedness* is preserved.

Although John Calvin bristles at the accusation of voluntarism, we will show that vestiges of such a doctrine remain in such a way as to create a troublesome cleavage in his conception of God. For all his decided accentuation on the nature of God as a Father who loves his offspring unconditionally, he defends the widespread want of knowledge of, or trust in God with the declaration that God decides whether to disclose himself as Father or as Judge. In this way he treads precipitously near the

---

737 Cf. Anthony Hoekema, "The Covenant of Grace in Calvin's Teaching," *Calvin Theological Journal*, vol. 2, 1967, 134-35; Charles Partee, "Calvin's Central Dogma Again," *Sixteenth Century Journal*, vol. xviii, no. 2, 1987, 182.

738 I use the term 'Calvinian' to designate features of Calvin's thought, in distinction to 'Calvinist,' which I use in reference to certain self-designated followers of Calvin who, in their espousal of a limited atonement, it will be argued, departed from Calvin's teaching.

notion that God is not fatherly in his innermost life, but only determines (arbitrarily?) to be fatherly toward a given person.

Before creation God determines to reprobate certain sinners while being gracious towards other, equally undeserving sinners. In the arena of election, it would seem, God's will reigns supreme. Yet Calvin is sure that God is justice in his innermost life and never does anything without reference to his own nature as just. Thus we must charge him, as well as Thomas, not with a thoroughgoing voluntarism, but with a kind of 'soteriological voluntarism.'

In the early nineteenth century, McLeod Campbell would insist on a more consistently Christological understanding of the will of God *vis a vis* the human race. Jesus Christ came solely to do the will of God, and as the consubstantial Son of the Father, discloses the heart and mind of the Father in all his works and ways. Consequently, the freedom of the grace of God in all its *unrestrictedness* as well as its *unmeritedness* is upheld.

The Nature of God

Calvin is sure that God possesses "infinite goodness."[739] He is not arbitrary in his commands to his creatures. He asks nothing of them which is not consistent with his inner being as infinitely good. More than a First Cause, he is a Father.[740] He is eternally "Father"[741] because of his "reciprocal relationship to the Son."[742] When he created the human race, he was their common Father,[743] but that relationship was lost in the Fall.

739 "John Calvin to the Reader," *Calvin: Institutes of the Christian Religion*, two vols, ed. John T. McNeill, trans Ford Lewis Battles, (Philadelphia: Westminster Press, 1960), 3, 4.

740 Charles Partee in his "Predestination in Aquinas and Calvin," suggests that "Thomas' view of providence and predestination is an exposition of the rational understanding of God's causality and Calvin's is an exposition of man's experience of God's care" (*Reformed Review*, vol. 39, 1978, 17). This would seem on the whole a fair assessment, although the latter's doctrine of reprobation seems grounded partly on another kind of experience, that of the rejection of the Gospel on the part of some, as well as on deductions from the divine omnipotence with its attendant notions of causality.

741 *Ibid.*, 5; cf. T. F. Torrance, *Calvin's Doctrine of Man*, (London: Lutterworth Press, 1949), 23-25, 147-48.

742 *Institutes*, II.xiv.7. Future references to this work will eliminate the title, *Institutes*, and simply indicate book, chapter and section. Thus, this entry would be: II.xiv.7.

743 II.xiv.5.

Therefore, the Son who was "begotten of the Father before all ages took human nature in a hypostatic union," becoming our brother[744] that he might make us once again sons of God. Even the patriarchs of old were sons of God, calling on him as their Father. But it was not until the only Son of God came into the world that "the heavenly fatherhood became more clearly known."[745]

God is infinitely wise.[746] Indeed, all "goodness, virtue, righteousness, and wisdom" originate in God.[747] These attributes are seen in God's providential governance of the universe. There his "fatherly goodness and his beneficently inclined will are repeatedly extolled." Of course, there also is displayed his "severity" toward those who commit evil or who obstinately resist him despite his forbearance.[748] Lists of divine characteristics crop up frequently in the *Institutio*, and their contents will vary, naturally depending on the biblical text cited or the context of the discussion. But Calvin is quite clear that God is both mercy and justice in his innermost being. Ford Lewis Battles notes that for Calvin, "the Fatherhood of God…has a universal reference in the creation itself."[749] Calvin even avers that "His nature is to show Himself gracious and gentle to all His creatures."[750] The "fatherly care" manifested in his providence[751] is grounded in his nature as the only true father.[752] He is the "fountain of all goodness, and of all happiness."[753]

In fact, Calvin's chief charge against medieval theology is that it holds a defective doctrine of God. God is not an idle bystander,

---

744 Sermon IV, *Sermons on Isaiah's Prophecy of the Death and Passion of Christ*, trans., ed. T. H. L. Parker, (London: James Clarke, 1956), 98, (*Calvini Opera*, vol. xxv, 636ff, *Corpus Reformatorum*).

745 II.xiv.5.

746 "Subject Matter of the Present Work" (from the French edition of 1560), 6.

747 "Prefatory Address to King Francis I of France," 13.

748 I.x.i.

749 Ford Lewis Battles, *Interpreting John Calvin*, ed. Robert Benedetto (Grand Rapids: Baker, 1996), 126.

750 Sermon 3, "Blessed is the Man Whom God Corrects," *Sermons From Job*, trans. Leroy Nixon, (Grand Rapids: Baker, 1952), 39, Sermon 21 in *Calvini Opera, Corpus Reformatorum*, vol. 33, 258-270.

751 Sermon 6, "If God Were Our Adversary," *Sermons from Job*, 79, Sermon 55 CO, 68-92.

752 Sermon 1 on II Timothy, *John Calvin's Sermons on Timothy and Titus*, trans. L.T., (1579 Facsimile edition), (Edinburgh: Banner of Truth, 1983), 665.

753 *Ibid.*, 670.

watching human struggles and intentions and efforts.[754] He is an active, purposeful, powerfully involved God. Here, of course, is the doctrine of the almighty will of God. But this will is not divided from his grace toward the elect. He graciously intervenes, bringing them solely in his mercy to salvation. Similarly in Calvin's doctrine of repentance, he vigorously maintains that forgiveness and grace must precede and then accomplish our renewal, not only because sinners could never hope to repent in any other way, but also because God is forgiveness and grace *in se*.[755] For the witness of the Psalmist is true, "There is propitiation with thee . . . that thou mayest be feared." Our willing obedience to God's law is anchored in our trust that "God is propitious."[756]

Calvin's complaint against the "Papists" was that they espoused a doctrine of conditional grace, "mingling their own merits, satisfactions, and worthy preparation--as they term it--with the grace of God," and therefore remained in doubt respecting their reconciliation with God. But when the psalmist confesses that "with thee there is forgiveness," he "declares that God's mercy cannot be separated or torn from himself." He found assurance, not in his works, but in *who God* is: 'As soon as I think upon thee,' he says in amount, 'thy clemency also presents itself to my mind, so that I have no doubt that thou wilt be merciful to me, it being impossible for thee to divest thyself of thy own nature: the very fact that thou art God is to me a sure guarantee that thou wilt be merciful."[757]

Of course, Calvin's opponents argued that he was actually positing the divine will as *prior* to his mercy such that God could create the vast bulk of the human race for the sole purpose of perdition. "But," they protested, "to create men for perdition is not an act of love, but of hatred. Therefore God did not create anyone to perdition."[758]

754 Cf. William J. Bouwsma, *John Calvin: A Sixteenth Century Portrait*, (New York: Oxford University Press, 1988), 168.

755 Cf. Albert-Marie Schmidt, *John Calvin and the Calvinistic Tradition*, trans. Ronald Wallace, (London: Longmans, 1960), 87-88.

756 III.iii.2; cf. Ronald S. Wallace, *Calvin's Doctrine of the Christian Life*, (Edinburgh and London: Oliver and Boyd, 1959), 96-97.

757 Commentary on Ps. 130:4, *Commentary on the Book of Psalms*, vol. IV, trans. James Anderson, (Edinburgh: Calvin Translation Society; Grand Rapids: Baker n. d., reprinted 1989).

758 "The Secret Providence of God," *Calvin's Calvinism*, trans. Henry Cole, (London: Sovereign Grace Union, 1927), 264.

Calvin bristles at such a "calumny." In the "original creation" of the human race, "the love of God shines in all its brightness."[759] And even since the Fall, "proofs of the love of God towards the whole human race exist innumerable."[760]

In a sermon on Deuteronomy he goes to great length to persuade his congregation that God is loving and merciful in his heart of hearts:

> Now when Moses saith, 'The Lord thy God is merciful, and therefore he will not forsake thee nor cast thee off,' he bringeth the people back to the nature of God . . . . God's nature is loving and gentle, and . . . he is ready to forgive the faults of such as acknowledge them . . . . But whatsoever be said to us concerning his goodness: yet can we not trust in him as we ought to do. There is not anything harder to us than to assure ourselves of the goodness and fatherly love of our God. It is a great thing that when God shall have avowed a hundred thousand times, that he loveth us and will be favorable to us: yet we continue still in a wavering, and stand disputing upon the matter, and feed our own distrustfulness, as though we would need disable the record that God giveth us of his goodness.
>
> Now then, it is not more than needeth, when Moses telleth us that God of his own nature is pitiful. It is a property that is evermore attributed unto him, and that not only in this text, but also in other places . . . the Scripture is full of the same doctrine. And why? Because that else it were not possible to assure men, forasmuch as they be so given to unbelief, as they still martyr themselves, and are always in perplexity and unquietness, [telling themselves] that God will never be at one with them . . . . Not without cause therefore doth Moses say here that God is merciful, to the end that the people might

---

759 *Ibid.*, 270.

760 *Ibid.*, 268. In the light of this and other passages, it is surprising that Ralph Roger Sundquist, Jr. should conclude that "Calvin did not argue that God loves everyone," but that God is loving toward certain ones: "The Third Use of the Law in the Thought of John Calvin: An Interpretation and Evaluation" (Ph.D. dissertation, Columbia University, 1970), 87f.

conceive God's nature and take hold of it . . . . So then
let us hearken to the texts of Holy Scripture, where God
telleth us that he is slow to wrath, patient, and ready to
forgive the faults that are committed against him.[761]

Clearly the Genevan theologian holds that God is loving and merciful in
his inmost being.[762] But he charges his opponents with failing to realize
that God ever remains free to bestow his love as he chooses. When he
adopted the family of Abraham as his own, he clearly testified that "He
did not embrace the whole of mankind with an equal love."[763] Here we
recall the teaching of Aquinas that while God loves all people, he does
not love them all in the same manner.

For John Calvin, the love which God bestows upon the elect is given
"freely." When he rejected Esau and chose Jacob, "He gave a manifest
and signal proof of His free love, of that love with which He loves none
others than those whom He will."[764] His 'calumniator' accuses him of
propounding a "pure and mere will" in God, but Calvin rejoins that God
never does anything that is not "wise, holy and just," although the cause
may lie hidden from mortals.[765]

Explaining how a loving God might not choose everyone, he begins
by affirming the love of God which moved him to send Jesus Christ:
"That is the only wellspring." Indeed, when John writes that "God so
loved the world that he spared not his only son," the word "world" is
not to be restricted to a few, but refers to all in general. Why? "For
Jesus Christ offereth himself generally to all men without exception to
be their redeemer." This love embraces the entire world.

761 Sermon 26, given on June 3, 1555, *Sermons on Deuteronomy* (facsimile of 1583
edition), trans. Arthur Golding, (Edinburgh: Banner of Truth, 1987), 156-57.
762 Yet R. N. Carew Hunt alleges that the "root of Calvin's error is that he predicates
only a single attribute of God. God is indeed Majesty and Power . . . . But so equally is
He Justice, Mercy and Truth, and we may not isolate these attributes, each of which is
transcended in the divine simplicity", *Calvin*, (London: Centenary Press, 1933), 123.
Surely the above citations prove the inaccuracy of the charge, although there is some
truth to the implication that at times Calvin speaks of the will or power of God without reference to his love. Calvin is unequivocal in his affirmations concerning love as
God's essential nature.
763 *Ibid.*
764 *Ibid.*
765 *Ibid.*, 266; cf. J. K. S. Reid's Introduction to Calvin's *Concerning the Eternal
Predestination of God*, 15.

But we must speak of "three degrees of the love" shown to us in Christ. First, because Christ died for the world, we affirm a universal love.

> The first is in respect of the redemption that was purchased in the person of him that gave himself for us, and became accursed to reconcile us to God his father. That is the first degree of love, which extendeth to all men, inasmuch as Jesus Christ reacheth out his arms to call and allure all men both great and small, and to win them to him.

But the second degree of love is limited to those who hear the Gospel. Calvin is here trying to account for the fact that the news of what God has done in Christ has not been proclaimed in every place and time.[766] Yet the Bible knows no such distinction, between a universal love in the atonement and a "special love," for auditors of the Evangel. Rather, Christ commanded a world-wide proclamation, thereby implying that God's love is not content with anything less.

Nevertheless, Calvin continues, there is also a "third love that God showeth unto us," whereby he not only causes the Gospel to be preached unto us but also "maketh us to feel the power thereof so as we know him to be our father and saviour, not doubting but that our sins are forgiven us for our Lord Jesus Christ's sake." This highest form of love is manifested in God's gift of the Spirit, by whom we come to the faith which apprehends God's fatherliness.[767]

Calvin is careful to state that he is not really describing three different loves, as though God has "divers affections," for all these loves are single in God. Yet, we may wonder whether such an exegesis takes with full seriousness the import of John 3:16. To divide the love of God for the world from its explicit objective, viz., that whoever believes might have eternal life, is to miss John's logic. The reformer's concern, however, is to maintain the unconditional freeness of grace.[768] Why has God chosen us rather than someone else?

> Let us not make long circuits to find some reason in ourselves: but let us hold us contented with the free love

---

766 Cf. *Concerning the Eternal Predestination of God*, 149.

767 *Ibid.*, Sermon 28, preached on June 5, 1555, 167.

768 Cf. Emmanuel Stickelberger, *John Calvin*, trans. David Georg Gelzer, (Cambridge: James Clarke, 1977), 31-33.

of God, for he is not bound to any man. He might destroy all mankind by justice: but yet for all that he had pity on us. And whereas he pitieth not all alike, but letteth whom he list alone: therein he intendeth to give the greater show of his goodness . . . .[769]

Calvin never tires of arguing that if God's love is predicated on "some reason in ourselves," it becomes contingent and the burden of our salvation is in this way shifted from God to humankind.[770] But in ourselves there is nothing but "wretchedness and misery . . . there is neither life nor strength, nor else whatsoever." Therefore, if someone should ask why God has enlightened us while leaving others in their blindness, "we cannot say, that we are better than they, and therefore God preferred us before them . . . neither are we worthier than they . . . . Who can brag, that he hath brought any thing of his own, that he may say, that God should be moved to love him more than other?"[771]

Consequently Calvin rejects a universal reference for God's desire that "all men be saved" (I Tim. 2:3-5). In a sermon he told his auditors that "all" does not mean "all people", but "all sorts" of people. Again we recall Thomas suggesting a similar approach.

The reformer from Geneva then takes to task those who misuse this passage "to make the election of our God, a thing of naught, and utterly take it away." They say that God's will is, in fact, indifferent, so that "it standeth in the choice of men to save themselves, and that God letteth us alone, and waiteth to see whether we will come to him or not, and so receiveth them that come unto him." But in so doing they "destroy the ground of our salvation," which is God's grace, and they fail to take into account that all people are "so contrary and such enemies to God that we cannot but resist him." Thus, our only hope is that God draw us by his Holy Spirit to partake of that salvation.[772]

This brings us to a consideration of Calvin's understanding of the nature of God as will. Given that God is loving and gracious in himself, how is it that he has determined to express his nature in one way to some

---

769 *Ibid.*, 166.
770 Cf. Sermon 1, *John Calvin's Sermons on the Epistles to Timothy and Titus*, 8.
771 *Ibid.*, Sermon 8, 88-89.
772 *Ibid.*, Sermon 13, 148.

and in another to others? The Fall itself was in some sense decreed by God. He chose to give humans a "mediocre and even transitory will," which was capable of being swayed to one side or the other. He did this knowing that they would sin, "that from man's Fall he might gather occasion for his own glory."[773]

Did Calvin favor a supralapsarian understanding of the decrees of God? Several passages substantiate it. For example, he reasons that "surely the fall of Adam is not presupposed as preceding God's decree in time; but it is what God determined before all ages . . . when he willed to heal the misery of mankind." At the same time, the favored few were elected in Christ "before time began."[774]

Yet God continues to watch over all of Creation by his providence,[775] which embraces not only his sustaining the motion of the universe, but also the action by which "he sustains, nourishes, and cares for, everything he has made, even to the least sparrow." However, within this providence there is a "special care" toward the elect, "by which alone his fatherly favor is known."[776]

Divine providence is not equivalent to blind fate or chance. "All events are governed by God's secret plan." And this notion of a secret plan, while giving due weight to the unsearchableness of God's essence, also provides Calvin the opportunity to posit another, hidden will for the world other than that disclosed in Christ.

He argues that although each individual nature has its own properties, "it does not exercise its own power except in so far as it is directed by God's ever-present hand." So it emerges that these are only "instruments", given a carefully measured effectiveness and bent and turned to particular actions as God wills. This is true not only for the regular rhythms of nature but also for miraculous events such as the sun standing still for Joshua. But there is no discontinuity, no interruption here. God is always governing the course of the rising and setting of the sun. Each day "is governed by a new, a special, providence of God."[777]For

---

773 I.xv.8.

774 II.xii.5.

775 Cf. Timothy George, *The Theology of the Reformers*, (Nashville: Broadman, 1988), 204-213.

776 I.xvi.1; cf. Richard Muller, *Christ and the Decree: Christology and Predestination in Reformed Theology from Calvin to Perkins*, (Grand Rapids: Baker, 1988), 22-27.

777 I.xvi.3.

Calvin, the omnipotence of God requires that he not remain "empty, idle, and almost unconscious," as the events of the world march by unaffected, but rather that he be "watchful, effective, active . . . engaged in ceaseless activity."[778] And this activity is guided purposefully and specifically by God's providence such that "nothing takes place without his deliberation," and his knowing and willing decree.

The world does not continue to operate by some divinely established "universal law of nature," but by God's intimate, purposeful involvement in all that happens. Thus, experience teaches us that some mothers' breasts are full of milk while others are not, because God wanted it that way. Pastorally, the doctrine of providence means that God is powerful enough to do good for those who are obedient to him, and to grant total safety and protection for his own.[779]

The implications of this for human actions is now apparent. More than "bare foreknowledge", providence is "lodged in the act." That is to say, Calvin rejects the suggestion that God decrees that which he already foresees will take place by human free will.[780] Aquinas would side with the reformer on this score, but not on the next, for Calvin goes on to decry the notion that God governs by a "general motion" the actions of the universe and its constituent parts, that he gives individual creatures their efficacies and the freedom to carry out their own choices. Such persons, says Calvin, "teach that nothing hinders all creatures from being contingently moved, or man from turning himself thither by the free choice of his will." To qualify this by adding that in the case of particular human acts, God does intervene and specifically direct, fails to undo the damage. God's will is all-embracing such that "nothing takes place by chance."

What is Calvin's concern here? The will of God is qualified by human will. Things belonging to God are "apportioned" between God and humanity. Thus human acts are "governed by God's might, but not by his determination." This would rob him of "the chief thing: that he directs everything by his incomprehensible wisdom and directs it to his own end."[781]

---

778 I.xv.3; cf. Bouwsma, *op. cit.*, 171-73.
779 I.xvi.3.
780 Cf. Wilhelm Niesel, *The Theology of Calvin*, trans. Harold Knight, (London: Lutterworth Press, 1956), 175-79.
781 I.xvi.4.

In seeming anticipation of McLeod Campbell's later charge, Calvin vigorously rejects any parallel between his doctrine of providence and the "Stoics' dogma of fate." For the Stoics find necessity in an impersonal nature, bound up in its own perpetual chain of causation, while Calvin believes in a personal God, mighty in power and perfect in wisdom, who actively and wisely decrees the future course of all motions, and then accomplishes it.[782] P. H. Reardon has shown that Calvin, in his doctrine of providence, is seeking to steer a course between the *necessitas* of the Stoics and the *fortuna* of the Epicureans, such that God is active in nature and history while remaining distinct from them both.[783]

At the same time, this providential will of God is not accessible to us. We do not ground our confidence in the rightness of God's actions upon our ability to see why he does things. Indeed, "the order, reason, end, and necessity of those things which happen for the most part lie hidden in God's purposes, and are not apprehended by human opinion."[50]

Here we find one of many references to Calvin's doctrine of the "secret will" of God. It serves as a cautionary word, which would dissuade us from presuming to search out the essence of God's majesty. Yet it also becomes a defense against the charge that the doctrine of reprobation does not square with God's self-disclosure in Jesus Christ. And we may wonder whether it is satisfactory to posit some other will, some other attitude in God than that found in his only Son.

Nevertheless, Calvin's God is not capricious. By his providence God reveals "his concern for the whole human race, but especially his vigilance in ruling the church." All that he does is thus motivated by his "fatherly favor and beneficence or severity of judgment."

God never acts out of bare volition, without reference to his nature. While the causes of certain events may remain hidden, "God always has the best reason for his plan." We must reverently confess that all events are determined by a will that is "truly just." Even when terrible storms arise, we know that "God out of the pure light of his justice and wisdom

---

782 Cf. John Verhy, "Calvin's 'Treatise Against the Libertines," *Calvin Theological Journal*, vol. 15, no. 2, November, 1980, 198.

783 "Calvin on Providence: The Development of an Insight," *Scottish Journal of Theology*, vol. 28, 1975, 517-534. For insights on Calving s early, although guarded, sympathy towards stoicism, cf. Quirinius Breen, *John Calvin: A Study in French Humanism*, (Grand Rapids: Eerdmans, 1931), 69-77.

tempers and directs these very movements in the best-conceived order to a right end."[784]

Therefore Calvin takes issue with the scholastic voluntarists who posited a purely arbitrary, absolute power in God. Although the divine will we delineate, he says, is indeed the "sole rule of righteousness," it is not to be equated with

> that absolute will of which the Sophists babble, by an impious and profane distinction separating his justice from his power--but providence, that determinative principle of all things, from which flows nothing but right, although the reasons have been hidden from us.[785]

The voluntarists or nominalists sought to provide for a uniformity of nature on the one hand, and the consistency of divine activity in relation to the human race on the other, by differentiating between two powers in God, the *potentia absoluta* and the *potentia ordinata*. By the former they meant the pure, absolute power of God as he is in himself. In himself, God can do anything, for that is what it is to be God. But God does not act in a haphazard, chaotic manner in the universe. The second power is that by which God deigns to act in relation to the events of nature and of humans. Absolutely, God could do anything, but in view of his ordination, there are only certain things which he can do.

Albrecht Ritschl and others attributed Calvin's doctrine of the double decree to the nominalist dialectic of the two powers.[786] Richard Muller, however, writes of Calvin's "sharp declamation against the distinction between *potentia absoluta* and *potentia ordinata*."[787] He is not the first to have contended that Calvin always saw the power of God as directed by his justice. Emile Doumergue adduced the following passage:

---

784 I.xvii.1; cf. Herman Bavinck, "Calvin and Common Grace," *Calvin and the Reformation*, ed. William Park Armstrong, (New York: Fleming Revell, 1909), 114.

785 I.xvii.2.

786 "Geschichtliche Studien zur christlichen Lehre von Gott," *Jahrbuscher fur deutche Theologie*, vol. 13, Gotha, 1868, 107; cf. Williston Walker, *John Calvin, the Organizer of Reformed Protestantism*, London, 1906; R. Seeberg, *Die Theologie des Joh. duns Scotus*, Leipzig, 1900, 163ff. These references are cited in Francois Wendel, *Calvin. The Origins and Development of His Thought*, trans. Philip Mairet, (London and Glasgow: Fontana, 1965), 127f.

787 Richard A. Muller, *The Unaccomodated Calvin*, (Oxford: Oxford University Press, 2000), 47.

> We do not approve of the dream of the Papist theologians touching the absolute power of God; for their ramblings about it are profane . . . . Nor do we imagine a God without any law, seeing that he is law to himself.[788]

Calvin considers an assertion by Augustine that God could if he willed immediately impart to mortal man angelic purity. Augustine hastens to add that God never would act contrary to his declared will in the Scriptures.[789] This would seem to agree with the later medieval dialectic of the two powers. To this remark Calvin says, "I do not deny this, but yet add that it is ill-advised to pit God's might against his truth." This looks like a clear refutation of voluntarism, but in fact he is only speaking in terms of the ordained power of God, cautioning us against pitting God's might against his *revealed* truth. Thus the quotation continues: "Therefore, if someone says that what the Scriptures declare will not be, cannot be, such a statement is not to be scoffed at."[790]

Furthermore, there are many other passages where Calvin seems to adopt a voluntarist line of thinking. For example he asserts that

> the will of God is so much the supreme and sovereign rule of justice that whatever he wills must be held to be just in so far as he wills it. So that when one asks, Why did God do this? we must reply, Because he willed it. If one goes further and says, Why did he will this?, that is asking for something greater and higher than the will of God, which there cannot be.[791]

In the same manner Calvin comments upon Exodus that God "is free from laws, because He is a law unto Himself, and to all."[792] It seems clear that he regards God's will as the sole explanation for everything he does. But does this mean that God could be unjust? One may suspect as much on the basis of passages such as the abovementioned one.

---

788 III.23.2, cited in Wendel, *op. cit.*, 127. Doumergue's discussion is found in his work, *Jean Calvin--Les hommes et les choses de son temps*, vol. iv, 119.
789 *On Man's Perfection in Righteousness*, iii.8, cited *in loc.*
790 II.vii.5.
791 III.23.2.
792 Commentary on Exodus 3:22, *Commentaries on the Last Four Books of Moses*, vol. I, trans. Charles William Bingham, (Grand Rapids: Eerdmans, 1950).

Indeed, the justice God decrees for the human race does not apply to God himself. The Genevan reformer told his congregation that

> God is not like creatures who ought to be obedient to the common rule in such manner that they may be brought to account and measured by the Law which He has given us; to us, I say, He has squared out his Law to be our measure, and not to be subject to it himself. [793]

But in order to understand this point in the broader context of Calvin's doctrine of God, we need to recall his constant conviction that God does nothing in disregard of his justice. His argument against the nominalist theologians was that the god of the *potentia absoluta* was a "hateful fiction." "We fancy no lawless god who is a law unto himself . . . the will of God is not only free from all fault but is the highest rule of perfection and even the law of all laws."[794]

That is to say, all justice is grounded in God, who is himself the "highest rule of perfection." When Calvin warns his listeners that God has given "Law to be our measure, and not to be subject to it himself," he does not mean that God disregards justice, but that it is not our place to measure him by his justice. We will not always know why God does things as he does, but we must content ourselves with confessing that he always acts justly. Thus in his lecture on Genesis 18:25, "Shall not the Judge of all the earth do right?" we are told that Abraham

> reasons from the nature of God, that it is impossible for Him to do anything unjust . . . . it was impossible for God, who is the Judge of the world, and by nature loves equity, yea, whose will is the law of justice and rectitude, should in the least degree swerve from righteousness.[795]

Of course, the charge of espousing an unjust, tyrannical god was leveled against Calvin by his detractors, who rejected his doctrine of the Double Decree. In response Calvin penned the lines cited above, to the

793 Sermon 5, *Sermons From Job*, (Sermon 50 in *Calvini Opera, Corpus Reformatorum* vol. 33, 617-630); cf. Sermon 18, 268, CO vol. 35, 168-179.
794 III.xxiii.3.
795 Commentary on Genesis 18:25, *Commentaries on the First Book of Moses called Genesis*, vol. 1, trans. John King, (Grand Rapids: Baker, 1989); cf. Sermon 18, *Sermons from Job*, 267ff.

effect that God is not the god of the *potentia absoluta*, a lawless god, for his will is the "highest rule of perfection and even the law of all laws." When God predestines some to eternal death, he does so with perfect justice, since they are sinners and deserve nothing else.[796]

David Steinmetz argues that Calvin attacks the medieval distinction between the two powers "as a speculative doctrine which separates the omnipotence of God from his justice and which transforms the compassionate Father of the biblical narratives into an arbitrary tyrant."[797] He acknowledges that Calvin shares with thinkers such as Duns Scotus and William of Ockham the concern to preserve the transcendent freedom of God and the radical contingency of the world, but in a careful analysis of several passages in the Calvinian corpus, he demonstrates that Calvin consistently rejects a division between the power of God and the justice of God.

Where Steinmetz is less successful, it would seem, is in establishing that Calvin's rejection of the twofold dialectic was further motivated by a concern to safeguard the compassionate fatherhood of God. In the passages adduced, we find nothing concerning the love or compassion of God. For example, in the *Commentary on Genesis*, Sarah's laughter at the promise of a child in her old age betrays a failure to recognize the "greatness of [God's] power." But the 'Papists' are equally wrong in considering the power of God apart from the 'lamp' of his Word.[798] The love of God is unmentioned.

Similarly, in his *Commentary on Jeremiah*, Calvin finds the prophet disconcerted by the prosperity of the wicked. Yet in his pleading with God, he does not "set up the judgments of men against the absolute power of God, as the sophists under the Papacy do, who ascribe such absolute power to God as perverts all judgment and all order." Again, Calvin makes no effort to defend the *compassion* of God, only his *justice*. In fact, in this very passage, he twice explicitly rejects any attempt to

---

796 III.xxiii.3; cf. Alister McGrath, *A Life of John Calvin*, (Oxford: Basil Blackwell, 1990), 167-69.
797 D. C. Steinmetz, "Calvin and the Absolute Power of God," *Journal of Medieval and Renaissance Studies*, vol. 18, no. 1, Spring 1988, p. 65.
798 John Calvin, Commentary on Genesis 18:13, *Commentaries on the First Book of Moses called Genesis*, vol. 1, (Grand Rapids: Baker, 1984), cited in Steinmetz, *op. cit.*, 73-74.

construe the love of God (toward the wicked) from the governance of God.[799]

The problem for Calvin, it would seem, is not a separation between justice and power, but between justice and love.[800] Has he taken with full seriousness his own conviction that God is a loving Father in his inmost nature? We earlier saw how Calvin tried to differentiate between "degrees" of love, so that God could in some sense be said to love the world, and yet in another, indeed all-important sense, he loves only the elect. In expounding Deuteronomy 4:37, he tells us, "God of his own free mercy chose them, not for that they were better than other nations . . . or for that there was more nobleness, worthiness or virtue in them: but for that it pleased him to love their fathers . . . it pleased him of his own good will."[801]

For Calvin the very Gospel is at stake. If God's election were universal, then the only explanation for the lack of universal response would be that all did not possess sufficient virtue. But once election is conditioned upon merit, the graciousness of grace is lost and the center of gravity in the divine-human relationship shifts from God to humankind.[802] So he attempts to hold onto the freeness of grace and

---

799 Commentary on Jeremiah 12:1, *Commentaries on the Book of Jeremiah and Lamentations*, vol. II, trans. John Owen, (Grand Rapids: Baker, 1984), cited in Steinmetz, *op. cit.*, 74-75.

800 Allen Verhy reminds us that Calvin strenuously resists any separation between God's power and goodness. He adduces the latter's "Treatise Against the Libertines," chapter XIV as support. But what does this mean for God's relations with the human race? Says Calvin in that very chapter, God "causes [his creatures] to serve His goodness, righteousness, and judgment according to His present will to help His servants, to punish the wicked, and to test His faithful." This accords with his assertions in the *Institutes*, that God can administer his goodness as he sees fit, helping his servants (the elect) while punishing the wicked (the reprobate). It still fails to answer why God withholds his redeeming love from a select portion of the human family. Cf. John Calvin, *Treatises Against the Anabaptists and Against the Libertines*, trans., ed. by Benjamin Wirt Farley, (Grand Rapids: Baker, 1982), 242-248, Farley's comments on pp. 178-79, and Allen Verhy, "Calvin's 'Treatise Against the Libertines,'" *Calvin Theological Journal*, vol. 15, no. 2, November, 1980, 198-99; cf. Anna Case-Winters, *God's Power*, (Louisville: Westminster/John Knox, 1990), 59-61.

801 Sermon 28, *Sermons on Deuteronomy*, 165.

802 Cf. Calvin's commentary on Romans 3:19, wherein he decries the "schoolmen['s] . . . well-worn cliché that works are meritorious not by any intrinsic worthiness, but by the covenant of God. They are mistaken, since they do not see that our works are

the inherent love of God by attributing the empirical disparity among humans to the sovereignty of God.[803] "What was the cause that [God] chose [Israel's] forefathers? Even his own love . . . that is to say, because he marked them of his own free mercy to select them from amongst the rest of the world.[804]

But we must ask Calvin whether it is meaningful to say that a God who is loving in his inmost life can exercise a selectivity toward a world of sinners, none of whom deserve grace more or less than the others. Is that loving, or is that not a capricious exercise of the will? If indeed God's inner reality is pure, compassionate love, does this compromise his freedom? Not if we say that his freedom is his love and his love is his freedom.[805] Calvin comes close to this when he says in a sermon that God

> does not wish to keep the good which He has in Himself as it were locked up and hidden; but he wishes that it may be poured out upon us, and that we may be partakers of it . . . . So is He also in everything and through everything: it is that He takes pleasure in stretching out His benefits to give us such enjoyment of them, that He joins Himself to us, and us to Him.[806]

But alas! Such freely chosen love is only for the benefit of the elect. God does not will to be gracious toward the rest. Calvin's further positing of a God unbounded by his own love constitutes an abstraction untrue to God's self-revelation in Christ.[807]

---

always corrupted by vices which deprive them of any merit" (*The Epistles of Paul the Apostle to the Romans and to the Thessalonians*, trans. Ross Mackenzie, eds. David W. Torrance and Thomas F. Torrance, (Grand Rapids: Eerdmans, 1973).

803 So also John H. Leith, *John Calvin's Doctrine of the Christian Life*, (Louisville: Westminster/John Knox, 1989), 122.

804 Sermon 28, *Sermons on Deuteronomy*, 165; cf. Ronald S. Wallace, *Calvin, Geneva and the Reformation*, (Grand Rapids: Baker, 1988), 79.

805 Cf. Colin Gunton, *Becoming and Being. The Doctrine of God in Charles Hartshorne and Karl Barth*, (Oxford: Oxford University Press, 1978, reprinted 1980), 187-207.

806 Sermon 10, "Man Profitable to God?," *Sermons from Job*, 143; Sermon 83 in CO, vol. 34, 267-79.

807 Niesel, *The Theology of Calvin*, 165-69. Paul Helm says that if Calvin is to be called a voluntarist, then so also should Augustine and Aquinas (a conclusion he re-

In any ease, Calvin is convinced that God accomplishes all things by his will, and that nothing happens without his decree. And "nothing is more profitable than the knowledge of this doctrine" of providence.[808] For the Lord watches over his own with such care that they are prevented from stumbling over stones. Therefore we can take refuge in him, knowing he will take care of us even more faithfully than a mother will her young.[809] Our proper response to divine providence as creatures is humbly to submit ourselves in "fear and reverence."[810]

He explains the way in which God's ordination does not do violence to individual responsibility and action by distinguishing between two levels of causation. Ultimately, God is the "principle cause" of things, and yet there are also "secondary causes."[811] Thus he sends Satan to put lies into the mouths of Ahab's prophets and he even permits individuals "to attempt what their lust and madness has prompted."[812]

With this in view, we are not surprised that Calvin has no use for the distinction between doing and permitting. In all human actions God's will is sovereign. He turns the efforts of people so that they carry out his decrees. Indeed, "it would be ridiculous for the Judge only to permit what he wills to be done, and not also to decree it and to command its execution by his ministers." This explains the crucifixion: the Jews wanted Christ killed, the Romans were compliant, but Scripture declares that God decreed it.[813] Many other biblical examples could be adduced.[814] Summing up, Calvin says

> since God's will is said to be the cause of all things, I
> have made his providence the determinative principle for
> all human plans and works, not only in order to display
> its force in the elect, who are ruled by the Holy Spirit,
> but also to compel the reprobate to obedience.[815]

sists). Of course, we are attempting to demonstrate that, in an important but qualified sense, both Calvin and Aquinas espouse a kind of voluntarism which divides God's will from his love. Cf. Helm, *Calvin at the Centre* (Oxford and New York, Oxford University Press, 2010), 171-181.
808 I.xvii.3.
809 I.xvii.6.
810 I.xvii.2.
811 I.xvii.6; cf. "The Secret Providence of God," *Calvin's Calvinism*, 230-255.
812 I.xvii.7.
813 Calvin refers to Acts 4:28.
814 I.xviii.1.
815 I.xviii.2.

Much has been made of the fact that Calvin expounds the doctrine of election, not in connection with providence in Book I, but in Book III, where it is considered as a part of the redemptive work of the Holy Spirit.[816] The argument is that predestination is now grounded in Christ rather than in some abstract will of God. This is in a sense true, so far as the elect are concerned. But reprobation is still grounded elsewhere, in the "secret will" of God. And Calvin tells us that "election precedes this grace of God,"[817] suggesting that even in the case of the elect, God's will is primary, and Christ only comes in to execute the decrees. Moreover, strong, all-encompassing declarations such as the quote in the preceding paragraph are unambiguous in their conviction that divine providence determines everything, including election and reprobation.[818]

Is God then in possession of two contrary wills, since "by his secret plan he decrees what he has openly forbidden by his law"? Calvin will have none of it. God's will is single and simple, although because of our finite mental capacity we cannot grasp how something can happen which he both wills and does not will. The same event is looked at from different aspects, that of God's intention and of human intention. He willed that his Son be delivered up with a view to our redemption, but he did not will that Judas betray Jesus for his own evil purposes.[819]

However, because divine election is bestowed gratuitously upon undeserving sinners, we need to consider in some depth exactly why, in Calvin's thought, humankind is unable to construct a bridge back to God. His understanding of the nature of fallen mortals stands in sharp contrast to that of Aquinas, and helps explain why his emphasis on *sola gratia* becomes so uncompromising.

---

816 Cf. e.g., J. T. McNeill's comments in his edition of the *Institutes*, 197 n.1; James B. Torrance, "Strengths and Weaknesses of Westminster Theology," *The Westminster Confession in the Church Today*, ed. Alisdair I. C. Heron, (Edinburgh: St. Andrews, 1982), 46; John H. Leith, *Calvin's Doctrine of the Christian Life*, 125-26.

817 III.xii.1., cf. Sermon on Ephesians 1:4-6, *Sermons on The Epistle to the Ephesians*, (Edinburgh: Banner of Truth, 1975), 46, "God has accepted them of his own pure goodness and grace because he had elected them already."

818 Cf. Charles Partee, "Calvin and Determinism," *Christian Scholars Review*, vol. 5, no. 2, 1975, 124-26.

819 I.xviii.3, 4.

The Knowledge of God

Calvin inaugurates the body of his *Institutes* with a discussion of the *duplex cognitio*. We cannot know God without knowing ourselves, and yet it is equally true that we cannot know ourselves without knowing God. Our very existence is nothing but a "subsistence" in God.

Edward Dowey finds in this *duplex cognitio Domini* an indication that Calvin conceived of "two kinds of revelation: the revelation of God as Creator, and as Redeemer."[820] In Dowey's mind, Calvin teaches that even fallen humans can, through "empirical observation and ratiocination" in reflection upon the "objective revelation in creation,"[821] deduce "a number of attributes of God." He cites the *Commentary on Romans*, where Calvin says that Paul "plainly testifies that God introduces the knowledge of himself into the minds of all, *that is, he so points to himself through his works* that they must necessarily see what of their own accord they do not seek, that there is some God . . . . It is not possible to conceive of God without holding his eternity, power, wisdom, goodness, truth, righteousness and mercy."[822]

Dowey continues the quotation, including the part which he seems to have overlooked in his conclusions: "Therefore, whoever has received the knowledge of God ought to praise him for his eternity, wisdom, goodness and righteousness. *Since men have not recognized these attributes in God, but have dreamed of him as an empty phantom, they are deservedly said to have piously robbed God of his glory* [emphasis mine]." The Latin itself reads *ergo qui conceptam Dei notitiam habet*,[823] which suggests a focus on the activity of the human subject in forming a concept of God, rather than passively "receiving the knowledge of God," as Dowey's translation interprets it.[824] In fact, the whole thrust

---

820 Edward Dowey, *The Knowledge of God in Calvin's Theology*, (New York: Columbia University Press, 1959), 41; cf. William F. Keesecker, "The Law in John Calvin's Ethics," *Calvin and Christian Ethics*, (Grand Rapids: Calvin Studies Society, 1987), 20.

821 *Ibid.*, 75. So also, Alister McGrath, in *A Life of John Calvin*, (Oxford: Basil Blackwell, 1990), 152-54.

822 *Ibid.*, 80-81, italics his.

823 Ioannis Calvini, *In Novum Testamentum Commentarii*, vol. v, ed. A. Tholuck, *in loc.*

824 Indeed, R. Mackenzie renders it, "Those, therefore, who have formed a conception of God ought to give Him the praise due to His eternity, [etc]," Commentary on Romans 1:21, *The Epistles of Paul the Apostle to the Romans and Thessalonians*, ed.

of Calvin's argument seems to be predicated, not on *fallen humanity's knowledge of God*, but rather on *fallen humanity's culpable ignorance of God*.[825]

Dowey argues that "a number of attributes of God are known to men," while Calvin says the opposite: "Since men have not recognized these attributes in God, but have dreamed of him as an empty phantom, they are deservedly said to have impiously robbed God of his glory." Commenting on the preceding verse, Calvin declares that the fault lies not in the revelation of God, which is sufficiently clear. Rather, it is

> inadequate on account of our blindness. But we are not so blind that we can plead ignorance without being convicted of perversity. We form a conception of divinity, and then we conclude that we are under the necessity of worshipping such a Being, whatever His character may be. Our judgment, however, fails here before it discovers the nature or character of God.[826]

Calvin's doctrine of the knowledge of God through creation is steeped in the recognition of the pervasive fact of sin. The "miserable ruin" of our postlapsarian state compels us to look upward,[827] but it also dooms any attempt to obtain positive knowledge of God from the human side.[828]

To be sure, the very order of nature points us to a certain knowledge of God,[829] but such knowledge is ruled out, as John T. McNeill observes,[830] by Calvin's crucial qualifying phrase, *si integer stetisset Adam*, "if Adam had remained upright." Indeed, "in this ruin of mankind no one now experiences God either as Father or as Author of salvation, or favorable

---

David W. Torrance and Thomas F. Torrance, (Grand Rapids: Eerdmans, 1973).

825 Cf. Ronald S. Wallace's discussion of the *perversitas* of the human mind as a "barrier to any true knowledge of God outside of Christ", *Calvin's Doctrine of Word and Sacrament*, (Grand Rapids: Eerdmans, 1957), 69-70.

826 Commentary on Romans 1:20, Mackenzie translation.

827 I.i.1.

828 Cf. Brian Gerrish, *The Old Protestantism and the New*, (Chicago: University of Chicago Press, 1982), 58-59; Bouwsma, *John Calvin: A Sixteenth Century Portrait*, 103.

829 *Ibid.*

830 *Ibid., in loc.* (40).

in any way, until Christ the Mediator comes forward to reconcile him to us."[831]

There is not the slightest doubt in Calvin's mind that God reveals himself in the wonderful theater of creation. The light of God shines daily, but humankind shuts its eyes to it. "It is therefore in vain that so many burning lamps shine for us in the workmanship of the universe to show forth the glory of its author." God's nature is manifested there, but "we have not the eyes to see this unless they be illumined by the inner revelation of God through faith."[832]

The failure is not to be attributed the revelation of God, for it continues.[833] Nor does it lie in our nature as originally created, for as such we could comprehend something of who God is in the world around us and in our own hearts. Our ignorance is blameworthy. Our failure to receive and accept God's self-manifestation is culpable. "The fault of the dullness is within us." Paul goes to great length to demonstrate that what is known of God is plainly revealed in the universe, not in order to postulate a sort of natural theology, but to prove the entire race "inexcusable."[834] Human nature being what it now is, all knowledge of God is anchored on the divine side. "No drop will be found either of wisdom and light, or of righteousness or power of rectitude, or of genuine truth, which does not flow from him, and of which he is not the cause."[835] As T. H. L. Parker puts it, "the problem of the knowledge of God is the problem of revelation."[836] Only God can reveal God, and for that disclosure we must wait.

This brings us to a crucial point. For the Calvinian human, the problem is not whether or not God is gracious or merciful or kind or fatherly. It is rather *whether he is one of those given to know it.* All people are sustained by God's "fatherly care", but some never see it.[837]

Therefore, so oft as we will have God to receive us, and
we will also come boldly to him, we must have this word

---

831 *Ibid.*
832 I.vi.14.
833 Cf. Benjamin B. Warfield, "Calvin's Doctrine of the Knowledge of God," *Calvin and the Reformation*, ed. William Park Armstrong, 145ff.
834 I.vi.14-15.
835 *Ibid.*
836 T. H. L. Parker, *The Doctrine of the Knowledge of God. A Study in the Theology of John Calvin*, (Edinburgh: Oliver and Boyd, 1952), 10.
837 I.vi.15.

Father before our eyes, which cannot be, unless we have Jesus Christ for our Mediator . . . we cannot conceive that God is our Father, unless our Lord Jesus Christ present himself and show himself to be the only Son, and we are ingrafted into his body by faith.[838]

Indeed, "unless God confronts us in Christ we cannot know that we are saved." Christ does not create a new attitude in God, he discloses it. God is already watching over us in fatherly care, governing and nourishing us. But "apart from Christ the saving knowledge of God does not stand." Here a paradox in Calvin occurs. Although God is fatherly, and has acted for the salvation of the world, Christ is set before the elect only as an object of faith.[839]

The problem for those ignorant of Christ is not that God is devoid of mercy in his heart, nor is it that he is not truly fatherly within his own being. It is rather that they have not been permitted to know the heart of God. Before the coming of Christ it was not possible for humans "truly to taste God's mercy and thus be persuaded that he was their Father . . . . Accordingly, because they did not hold Christ as their Head, they possessed only a fleeting knowledge of God" and even that knowledge degenerated into superstition and ignorance.[840]

In his discussion of the sacraments, Calvin responded to those who argued that the reception of the sacraments by the wicked proved that grace is not offered in those sacraments. One might have expected him to respond that God never offers grace to the wicked, that he is not gracious toward them anyway, and that what he has done in Christ was not for the reprobate. But this is precisely the line which he does not follow. The grace of God toward all is independent of their recognition of it, just as an official document will have the authentic seal attesting the will of the prince which is toward all. Yet some will scorn it as not applying to them, while others will accept it. So it is that

the Lord offers us mercy and the pledge of his grace both in his Sacred Word and in his sacraments. But it is understood only by those who take Word and sacraments

---

838 Sermon 1 on II Timothy, Sermons on Timothy and Titus, 669; cf. Institutes, I.i.1.
839 II.vi.4.
840 Ibid.

with sure faith, just as Christ is offered and held forth by the Father to all unto salvation, yet not all acknowledge and receive him.[841]

Again we have the paradox that the grace of God in Christ is there for the wicked, and yet they never receive it. Why? Because "faith is the proper and entire work of the Holy Spirit, illumined by whom we recognize God and the treasures of his kindness, and without whose light our mind is so blinded that it can sense nothing of spiritual things."[842] The Spirit has not enlightened them to come to know the Father and his grace through the Son.

Moreover, even through Christ we are not given to know all there is of God. "His essence is incomprehensible . . . his divineness far escapes all human perception."[843] When Moses describes Jehovah as merciful and gracious, patient and compassionate, forgiving the iniquities of thousands and visiting the iniquity of the fathers upon future generations, God is "shown to us not as he is in himself, but as he is toward us."[844]

Is this the crack through which his notions of a God who is restrictive in his grace may slip? Is there another, darker side to God than that which we see in Christ? Such an inference is not logically necessary. It may be no more than a devout and humble recognition of the majesty of God which far exceeds any mortal's poor ability to apprehend. If it is not logically necessary, however, it remains logically possible. And the crucial question we must put to Calvin is whether there is not a terrible

---

841 IV.xiv.7.
842 IV.xiv.8. Calvin is making precisely this point in his treatise, "The clear explanation of sound doctrine concerning the true partaking of the flesh and blood of Christ in the Holy Supper, to dissipate the mists of Tileman Heshusius," *Calvin: Theological Treatises*, ed., trans. J. K. S. Reid, (Philadelphia: Westminster Press, 1954), 257-324. Calvin asks "how the wicked can eat the flesh of Christ which was not crucified for them?" (285). Bell, in his *Calvin and Scottish Theology. The Doctrine of Assurance*, (Edinburgh: Handsel Press, 1985), 16-17, rightly reminds us that Calvin affirms a genuine offer of Christ in the Sacrament to the wicked but contends that they, lacking faith, do not partake of him (283). Therefore he cannot have denied that Christ died even for those who reject him. Rather, Calvin poses a "rhetorical" question which represents a view which he rejects (17). We will take up the question of the extent of the atonement later.
843 I.v.1.
844 I.x.2.

difference between saying on the one hand, that God's disclosure in Christ does not *exhaust* the essence of God, while on the other, saying that such a disclosure is, in fact, *contradicted* by other aspects of his essence.

Calvin would bristle at such a suggestion. He saw no contradiction in the being of God. All such apparent antinomies are no more than apparent. If our minds were great enough we would see that God is consistent.

In our opinion Calvin is right in that general assertion but wrong in its application. Christ not only discloses a God who is love in his innermost being. He reveals a God, who will go to any length to suffer for the fallen race of humankind, and moreover, who desires that all should come to him on the basis of his actions. This would be McLeod Campbell's point, although he despaired of finding much positive in the writings of Calvin.

Calvin's impatience with "idle speculation" is well known. We must not "dream up" for ourselves some god which suits us, but instead fix our minds on "the one and only true God."[845] The God we meet in the face of Christ[846] is a merciful Father known for his loving-kindness and trustworthy guidance and protection. He is also "a righteous judge, armed with severity to punish wickedness", but the pious mind is "not so terrified by the awareness of his judgment as to wish to withdraw . . . because it loves and reveres God as Father" and worships and adores him as Lord."[847] This piety, we must add, is not human in origin. It arises from the knowledge of God's benefits, of his fatherly care, an apprehension mediated only through Christ."[848]

What knowledge of God is then left to fallen humankind apart from his self-disclosure in Christ? Nothing more than a *sensus divinitatis*, a bare awareness that there is a God who made them. Yet a signal illustration of the fallenness of our race is provided by the fact that this sense of divinity is amply attested in idolatry.[849] The world of unbelievers tries with all its might to rid itself of all knowledge of God and to corrupt what

---

845 I.ii.2; cf. I.v.9.
846 I.i.1.
847 I.ii.2.
848 I.i.1.
849 I.iii.1.

knowledge remains.[850] Indeed, "all degenerate from the true knowledge of him." Rather than rest content with God's disclosure in their hearts, they foolishly proceed to invent a god of their own imagining.[851] "As soon as we conceive any whit of the divine majesty: by and by we be gadding after idols, and turn away from the living God."[852]

Fallen humanity's mind is like a labyrinth. Once a person tries to find the way to a true conception of God by his own mental power he immediately finds himself lost in a maze, for which he does not possess the map. The better part of wisdom would be for him to confess, "The longer I consider this, the more obscure it seems to me."[853]

We have seen that the Genevan reformer does not deny the objective reality of natural *revelation*. The glory of God continues to shine forth in the whole of creation and in the crown of his creation, humankind. What Calvin does reject, and emphatically so, is the possibility for fallen humanity to engage in natural *theology*. As Wilhelm Niesel helpfully puts it:

> The self-disclosure of God in the worlds of nature and history is objectively real, but the knowledge which we may acquire from his works and deeds is subjective and unreal. It would only be fully real for us if Adam had not fallen but had 'remained in his primal perfection' [I.ii.1].[854]

---

850 I.iii.3.

851 I.iv.1.

852 Sermon 17, *Sermons on Deuteronomy*, 101; cf. I.xi.8.

853 I.v.12; cf. I.xiii.21. It is interesting that Gerald J. Postema should adduce I.v.6 as proof that "Calvin's view of God's revelation in nature, if not identical, is at least rather close to that of Aquinas." There, Postema finds "an abbreviated argument from causation to a First Cause." Calvin does say that "he from who all things draw their origin must be eternal and have beginning from himself. If this is an argument from causation, it begins by assuming what he intends to prove! His reasoning is rather that, "there is one God who so governs all natures that he would have us look unto him, direct our faith to him, and worship and call upon him." But sections 11 and 12 soon follow, indicating the failure of humanity, in the darkness of its mind, to know and worship God. Cf. "Calvin's Alleged Rejection of Natural Theology," *Scottish Journal of Theology*, vol. 24, no. 4, 1971, 424-434. Cf. T. F. Torrance's incisive contrast between the epistemologies of Thomas and Calvin in his book, *The Hermeneutics of John Calvin*, (Edinburgh: Scottish Academic Press, 1988), 86-87.

854 *The Theology of Calvin*, 43-44.

The point of this thorough rejection of natural theology is that only God can reveal God. This is a fundamental principle for Calvin. "It remains for God himself to give witness of himself from heaven."[855] "God himself is the sole and proper witness of himself."[856] The human mind is too puny to attempt any searching out of the divine essence. We must remain content to conceive God to be as he reveals himself to be in his Word without inquiring about him elsewhere.[857]

This God accomplishes through the Scripture, which "clearly shows us the true God." But even here, the knowledge of God through his Word cannot be independently extracted by human minds apart from a divine operation. Only those whom it pleased God to gather unto himself and instruct, that is to say, only the elect, are given to know God through the Scripture.[858] And Scripture serves not as a supplementary, second step in the knowledge of God after nature, but as a first step.

> Now, in order that true religion may shine upon us, we ought to hold that it must take its beginning from heavenly doctrine and that no one can get even the slightest taste of right and sound doctrine unless he be a pupil of Scripture.[859]

Of course, in the light of his Word, we may go back to nature and apprehend the true and vivid description of God contained therein.[860] But this must ever remain a subsequent step, undertaken with the illumination of the Scripture, rather than a first step, positing certain prior notions of God which are then permitted to control our interpretation of biblical revelation or even of God's self-disclosure in Christ.

Moreover, the biblical message will not be received without the inner testimony of the Spirit. God's self-revelation is mediated by the written word and Spirit joined together by a "mutual bond." The Spirit confirms the Word, illuminating the truth so that we may contemplate God's face imaged in the same Word. Proclaiming the law apart from Christ and His grace leaves the human heart untouched, and becomes

855 I.v.13.
856 I.xi.1.
857 I.xiii.21.
858 I.vi.1; cf. I.vii.5.
859 I.vi.2.
860 I.vi.3.

nothing more than sounds in the ear. "But if through the Spirit it is really branded upon hearts, if it shows forth Christ, it is the word of life "converting souls . . . giving wisdom to little ones."[861]

Yet for the Word to be operative in human hearts, converting souls to God, not only the Spirit's branding it upon the heart is needed. The Scripture must also "show forth Christ." St. Paul contended in II Corinthians against those who commended the law "apart from Christ." Only when the Word is seen as a witness to Christ, pointing persons to that saving work whereby God engraves his law upon the heart, can Christ's grace be received.[862]

Strongly emphasizing that God is known solely through Christ, Calvin marshals Cyprian's declaration that "one must listen to Christ alone, for Scripture says, 'Hear him'; and that we need not be concerned about what others before us either said or did, but only about what Christ, who is the first of all, commanded."[863]

As we have seen, this is acutely true for fallen humans, but even in its pristine condition humankind would have required epistemological mediation because of the majesty of God.[864] Our faith is directed through Christ to the Father. But we never reach the point where Christ is left behind or extraneous in our knowing God the Father. Jesus Christ bids us trust in himself, because even faith in God "will gradually disappear unless he who retains it in perfect firmness intercedes as mediator. Otherwise God's majesty is too lofty to be attained by mortal men . . . ."

A major theme in Calvin's writings concerns the divine accommodation. Because of his majesty and our lowliness, only through God's condescension may we come to know him. Thus Irenaeus explains that an infinite Father becomes finite in the Son in order to make himself known to finite minds.[865] Therefore, declares Calvin "God is comprehended *in Christ alone.*

---

861 I.ix.3.

862 *Ibid.* In this light, it is puzzling that Hugh Y. Reyburn should allege that Scripture for Calvin "ceased to be a means of grace bringing the heart and conscience into connexion with the Divine Author. It became a dead law-book whose pages had to be consulted for precedents and instructions", *John Calvin: His Life. Letters and Work,* (London: Hodder and Stoughton, 1914), 353.

863 Prefatory Address to King Francis I of France, 22, citing Cyprian, Letters lxiii.14, cited *in loc.*

864 II.xii.1; cf. Parker, *The Doctrine of the Knowledge of God,* 11.

865 Irenaeus, *Adversus haereses* IV.iv.2, cited by McNeill, *Institutes,* II.vi.4, n. 14.

John's saying has always been true: 'He that does not have the Son does not have the Father.'"[866]

In this connection Calvin expounds the prophetic office of Christ. Although J. F. Jansen[867] has shown that in the Reformer's exposition of the *triplex munus*, the prophetic is de-emphasized, it nonetheless plays an important role in establishing a Christological understanding of doctrine. For Christ "was anointed by the Spirit to be herald and witness of the Father's grace." It is this teaching office which he carries on the "continuing preaching of the gospel."

Embodied in this role is the *revelation of all that God would have us know concerning himself*. In fact, "in him are hid all the treasures of wisdom and understanding." Does this mean that in Christ God has disclosed, not everything we need to know, perhaps, but certainly the crucial facts of the Gospel? No, far more than that, it means, "That is, outside Christ there is nothing worth knowing, and all who by faith perceive what he is like have grasped the whole immensity of heavenly benefits."[868]

All those who fail to be content with the "perfect doctrine" which he has brought and therefore "patch it with something extraneous to it, detract from Christ's authority." God's self-disclosure in his Son is so comprehensive, so fulsome, that we only denigrate it by adding doctrines from other sources. Calvin concludes: "And the prophetic dignity in Christ leads us to know that in the sum of doctrine as he has given it to us all parts of perfect wisdom are contained."[869]

Of course, Calvin's insistence on a Christ as the locus of God's self-revelation is grounded in his conviction that the Son is consubstantial with the Father. John depicts Christ as the Word who was there in

---

866 I John 2:23, cited in II.vi.4 (italics mine).

867 J. F. Jansen, *Calvin's Doctrine of the Work of Christ*, (London: James Clarke, 1956), 20-38.

868 II.xv.2.

869 II.xv.2, contra James Mackinnon, who asserts that "absolute predestination in virtue of God's sovereign will occupies the central place in [Calvin's] thought, whereas the 'gracious God,' whom Luther had long sought and at last found in 'the Gospel of Jesus Christ,' stands at the centre of his", *Calvin and the Reformation*, (New York: Russell and Russell, 1962), 216; cf. Basil Hall, "Calvin Against the Calvinists," *John Calvin*, ed. G. E. Duffield, (Berkshire: Sutton Courtenay, 1966), 24-25, correcting his own previous assertions contained in *John Calvin: Humanist and Theologian*, (London: Routledge and Kegan Paul, 1956), 20-21.

the beginning of God the Father. The Word and the Father shared in common the work of creation for no other reason than that the two abide everlastingly together, and indeed, the Word "is God himself." Therefore "this substantial Word is properly placed at the highest level, as the wellspring of all oracles." All of God's revelations are made through him.

Indeed, although Christ was not yet manifested, even the Old Testament prophets "spoke by the Spirit of Christ just as much as the apostles did."[870] When God revealed himself by an angel to Abraham and other patriarchs, that angel was none other than

> God's Word, who already at that time, as a sort of a foretaste, began to fulfill the office of Mediator. Even though he was not yet clothed in flesh, he came down, so to speak, as an intermediary, in order to approach believers more intimately.[871]

Creation and Fall

But the human dilemma is more than ignorance. It is culpable ignorance. Postlapsarian humans do not know God because of the darkened minds that are in them. They were not created so. When God created the human race, he made them in his own likeness.

If we are to comprehend what that means, we begin not in Thomist fashion, with some prior, abstract definition of humanness. Indeed, in keeping with his Christological epistemology, he tells us that the image of God "can be nowhere better recognized than from the restoration of his corrupted nature." Since the goal of regeneration is "that Christ should reform us to God's image," we must look to the kind of persons humans become when renewed through Christ.

Whereas for Paul renewal in Christ's image comprises knowledge, righteousness and holiness, we may infer that "to begin with, God's image was visible in the light of the mind, in the uprightness of the heart, and in the soundness of all the parts." Correspondingly, Christ comes as the Second Adam to restore us to our "true and complete integrity."[872]

---

870 I.xiii.7.
871 I.xiii.10; cf. I.xiv.5.
872 I.xv.4. For an illuminating, detailed study of Calvin's doctrine of the *imago dei*, cf. T. F. Torrance, *Calvin's Doctrine of Man* 61-82.

Although in Calvin's thought the *imago dei* found its primary locus in the mind and heart, there were traces of God's glory in every part, even the body. The likeness extended to the "whole excellence" by which his nature surpassed that of all other living creatures. But Calvin's central definition of the *imago dei* runs thusly:

> he had full possession of right understanding . . . his affections kept within the bounds of reason, all his senses tempered in right order, and he truly referred his excellence to exceptional gifts bestowed upon him by his Maker.[873]

This highly rational definition of the image of God helps us understand the epistemic effects of the Fall. If by nature humans were governed by reason and their reason submissive to their Maker, we would expect that a fallen nature would entail fallen reason disobedient to that Maker. God's image was not completely obliterated, "yet it was so corrupted that whatever remains is a frightful deformity."[874]

The results of the Fall may be further explained as the corruption of the "natural gifts," so that "soundness of mind and uprightness of heart" were withdrawn, and the loss of the supernatural gifts," such as the "light of faith" and righteousness. Therefore all qualities proper to a citizen of the Kingdom of God have been extinguished, including "faith, love of God, charity toward neighbor, zeal for holiness and for righteousness."

For Calvin "total depravity" does not mean that nothing positive remains in humanity, but that every aspect of humanity's being is corrupted to a significant degree.[875] So fallen humans are not totally irrational--" something of understanding and judgment remains as a residue along with the will" --yet the mind is "weak and plunged into deep darkness," and the will is depraved.

Calvin's gloomy conclusion is that human nature is so fallen as to require total renewal of mind and will.[876] The entire race of Adam's

---

873 I.xv.3.

874 I.xv.4.

875 Cf. Torrance, *Calvin's Doctrine of Man*, 88-97; Ronald S. Wallace, *Calvin, Geneva and the Reformation*, 224-25.

876 Cf. Francois Wendel, *Calvin: The Origins and Development of His Thought*, 185-196; cf. Wilhelm Niesel, *The Theology of Calvin*, 80-91.

children bears depraved natures. Their souls are "utterly devoid of all good."[877] The will is in such bondage to sin that it cannot undertake any movement toward good without conversion, which is accomplished solely by divine grace.[878] Only through Christ could we be restored to the original integrity of God's image.[879] In the garden Adam was tested to see whether he would remain willingly under the divine command. He should have been contented with his humble place, but instead he rose up in pride, disobedience, and contempt for the truth. At the root of all other sins was his unfaithfulness, his unwillingness to live in dependence upon the Word of God.[880]

What is more, by his rebellion Adam consigned his entire race to ruin. His guilt spread to all his offspring. This inherited corruption, or original sin, refers to the "depravation of a nature previously good and pure." It communicates, not by imitation, but by propagation. However Calvin is careful to emphasize that original sin is not spread by the physical act of procreation, but by divine ordinance.

> For the contagion does not take its origin from the substance of the flesh or soul, but because it had been so ordained by God that the first man should at one and the same time have and lose, both for himself and for his descendants, the gifts that God had bestowed upon him.[881]

Fallen humankind has ever since been infected by a fundamental perversity, giving rise to all kinds of evil works. Calvin is willing to accept the scholastic definition of original sin as "concupiscence", provided it be acknowledged that it affects the whole person, "from the understanding to the will, from the soul even to the flesh." For Ephesians 2:3 declares that we are by nature "children of wrath." And yet he carefully qualifies what is meant by that verse. God is "hostile toward the corruption of his work rather than toward the work itself."[882] This is a negative way of saying that God still loved us, even though we

---

877 II.iii.2.
878 II.iii.5, 6.
879 I.xv.4.
880 II.i.4.
881 II.i.7.
882 II.ii.11.

were terribly fallen. The Genevan reformer assured his congregation that "the enmity which God bears us, is not in respect of our nature, but in respect of our corruption, for, since God created us, it is certain that he cannot hate us."[883]

Nevertheless, original sin affects our entire nature, including our wills. We can no longer exercise freely our wills in order to choose right conduct. For medieval theologians to speak of a mere "wounding" of human reason was to fail to come to terms with the effects of the Fall.

Thomas Aquinas, says Calvin, attributes freedom to the will, so that free will becomes a "power of selection." It is derived from a "mingling of understanding and appetite", while inclining more to appetite.[884] Moreover, three kinds of freedom are differentiated by the scholastics: "first from necessity, second from sin, and the third from misery." If the first were lost, humankind would no longer be human, so it is retained, while the latter two have been robbed by sin.

Calvin will accept this so long as necessity is not confused with "compulsion."[885] Because the will is depraved, it is drawn to evil of necessity. That is its natural, automatic inclination. "Necessity," therefore describes human beings under the conditions of original sin. As such, humans willingly choose to sin--they are not under external compulsion. Yet they necessarily choose it by virtue of their fallen nature.[886] Of course, such a severe qualification of Thomas' position here actually turns it on its head, so that free will is no longer truly free to choose the good.[887]

What kind of ability have we to do good works? The distinction employed by the schoolmen (including St. Thomas) between "operating" grace, which initially ensures that we will to do good and "cooperating", which follows good will as an assistance, carries an unfortunate implication: "that man by his very own nature somehow seeks after the good--though ineffectively." Thus the notion emerges that "we co-operate with the assisting grace of God, because it is our right either to render it ineffectual by spurning the first grace, or to confirm it by following it."[888]

---

883 Sermon on Ephesians 1:4-7, *op. cit.*, 50.
884 See *Summa*, Ia.83, 3.
885 II.ii.6.
886 II.iii.5.
887 Cf. Torrance, *Calvin's Doctrine of Man*, 90-91.
888 II.ii.6.

If there were freedom of the will, the reason could deliberate between alternate possibilities. This, of course, is Thomas' view.[889] But Calvin will only concede that humans have a natural desire for good understood as that which they perceive to be for their own well-being.

> But man does not choose by reason and pursue with zeal what is truly good for himself . . . nor does he use his reason in deliberation or bend his mind to it. Rather, like an animal he follows the inclination of his nature, without reason, without deliberation.[890]

What is the point of this sustained attack upon reason and free will? "To sum up, much as man desires to follow what is good, still he does not follow it. There is no man to whom eternal blessedness is not pleasing, yet no man aspires to it except by the impulsion of the Holy Spirit."[891] That is to say, grace is at stake. If humankind by its own decision and efforts (albeit with the assistance of grace) can raise itself to an acceptable level of goodness, then grace becomes conditional. In fact, they cannot, and the situation would be hopeless were it not for the operation of the Holy Spirit.

Our entire being is enslaved by the power of sin, and this includes especially the will, which is the "chief seat" of sin. Therefore, no positive movement of the will can precede the grace of the Spirit.[892] "Away then with all that 'preparation' which many babble about."[893]

It becomes evident that Calvin takes a dim view of the suggestion that humans might make *any* contribution to their salvation. That this is so can be seen first in his conviction that the entire human nature is enslaved to sin, and secondly, in his emphasis on all-encompassing nature of the Gospel of grace, which will brook no rivals.

> Because of the bondage of sin by which the will is held bound, it cannot move toward good, much less apply itself thereto; for a movement of this sort is the beginning

---

889 *Summa*, la.83, 3.
890 II.ii.26.
891 II.ii.26.
892 Cf. T. H. L. Parker, *The Oracles of God. An Introduction to the Preaching of John Calvin*, (London: Lutterworth, 1947), 83-84.
893 II.ii.27.

of conversion to God, which in Scripture is ascribed entirely to God's grace.[894]

Indeed, the operation of grace itself bears eloquent testimony to the depths of our "destitution." The divine work of conversion begins in the human will, "bending, forming, and directing" so that we desire righteousness, and then completes it by "confirming us to perseverance." Such a spiritual renovation is not a matter of strengthening an inclination already present, but of a thoroughgoing transformation. Therefore, concludes the Genevan Reformer, "let us not divide between him and us what he claims for himself alone." *Sola gratia* rules out any human contribution, however slight or hesitant, to the salvific process. "Everything good in the will is the work of grace alone."[895]

Yet Calvin is not finished criticizing the view held, among others, by Thomas. The distinction between the "first grace," wrought by the power of the Lord alone, and the "second grace", which, as "co-operating grace" strengthens the will's "own part in the action," flies in the face of the true nature of grace. For grace means that God first extinguishes our will and then substitutes a good one from himself.[896] And even the cause of election lies not in humans, but in God only, in his election before creation.

When those who by nature are inclined to evil begin to will what is good, they do so "out of mere grace." For it is God who takes out the stony heart, replacing it with a heart of flesh. This work of conversion accomplishes nothing less than the creation of a new spirit, a new heart. And this is from God alone.[897]

It will be seen that this concern for *sola gratia* shapes Calvin's doctrine of election as well.[898] For God does not move the will such that

---

894 II.iii.5.

895 II.iii.6.

896 II.iii.7.

897 II.iii.8.

898 Cf. Parker, *The Oracles of God*, 84-85; John H. Leith, *John Calvin's Doctrine of the Christian Life*, (Louisville: Westminster/John Knox Press, 1989), 122. Cf. Georgia Harkness, who thinks predestination is merely the inexorable conclusion of his doctrine of divine omnipotence, *John Calvin: The Man and His Ethics*, (New York: Abingdon, 1958), 72-78, and Leroy Nixon, who considers predestination a "corollary of the doctrines of the absolute sovereignty of God and the total inability of man", *John Calvin--Expository Preacher*, (Grand Rapids: Eerdmans, 1950), 86.

we then have the option whether to accept it or not. He gives us more than an ability to do good works. God gives "a new Spirit to the elect" so that they will actually walk rightly. He does not "indiscriminately deem everyone worthy of this grace" as that late medieval saying claimed: "grace is denied to no one who does what is in him." In the *Summa*, Thomas had accepted the notion, with the stipulation that "Man can do nothing unless moved by God . . . . Hence when a man is said to do what is in him to do [*facere quod in se est*], this is said to be in his power according as he is moved by God."[899] In other words, having received the first grace, *gratia operans*, he then is bestowed *gratia cooperans*, with which he may or may not choose to cooperate and so "do what is in him." Thus, as we have seen, despite St. Thomas' firm emphasis on God's grace as prevenient and even making possible any human response or merit, grace becomes contingent upon human sincerity, good works, and piety.

This key idea, which appears frequently in scholastic writings in the form, *deus non denegat gratiam facere quod in se est*[900] is explicitly rejected by Calvin. While it is true that God's lovingkindness is not denied to those who seek it, the only ones who do seek it are the "elect, that, regenerated through the Spirit of God . . . are moved and governed by his leading.[901]

Perseverance, therefore, is not granted according to human merit, not even when it is conceived as a receptivity to the first grace. This embodies two errors: first, that our proper use of the first grace is "rewarded by subsequent gifts" and second, that additional (i.e. cooperating) grace comes not independent of our activity, but "is only a coworker with us."

Calvin is willing to say that we receive different graces. He prefers, however, to speak of new gifts of grace, since grace is one and the same while having different manifestations at various times along our spiritual pilgrimage. But they never come as rewards for past usage, nor could a human be in a position to determine whether God's grace would be effective in his life. God's grace is always and ever must remain "free grace." Calvin is uncompromising: "if they mean that man has

---

899 *Summa*, la2ae.109, 6 ad 2.
900 Cf. Heiko Oberman, *The Harvest of Medieval Theology. Gabriel Biel and Late Medieval Nominalism*, third edition, (Durham: Labyrinth Press, 1983), 129-153.
901 II.iii.10; cf. Sermon on Ephesians 3:13-16, *op. cit.*, 278; Sermon 5 on II Timothy in *op. cit.*, 745.

in himself the power to work in partnership with God's grace, they are most wretchedly deluding themselves."[902]

Grace in the Old Testament

Charles Partee rightly avers that "The central theological point of [Chapters VI through XI of Book III of the *Institutes*] is that God's grace is the result of God's love and is extended to humanity before instruction in behavior is given. Even more important is Calvin's focus on Jesus Christ as the promise of the law and the fulfillment of the Gospel."[903] In fact, as Christopher Elwood says, for Calvin, "redemption in Christ is the heart of all of Scripture."[904] In the 1536 edition of the *Institutes* he began with Law, and then turned to Grace.[905] But by his final, definitive 1559 edition, he reorganized its architectonics within a Trinitarian scheme, considering our knowledge of God the Creator first, and then our knowledge of God the Redeemer. And he subsumes his investigation of Law under the latter.[906] Now he is teaching that grace precedes law, in both Testaments of the Scriptures.

McNeill aptly comments that the insertion of Chapter VI in Book II, "Fallen Man Ought to Seek Redemption in Christ," along with sections 1 and 2 of Chapter VII (entitled "The Mediator helps only fallen man" and "The law contains a promise"), thereby enables Calvin to introduce soteriology, "not by law, but by this radical *in Christo* passage, which brings the law within the context of the promise of the gospel."[907]

Calvin opens Chapter VI by stating that because of the Fall, the original excellence of the divine image would only serve for our

---

902 II.iii.ii.

903 Charles Partee, *The Theology of John Calvin* (Louisville and London: Westminster John Knox Press, 2008), 137.

904 Christopher Elwood, *Calvin for Armchair Theologians* (Louisville: Westminster John Knox Press, 2002), 71.

905 In his 1536 edition, Chapter I is entitled, "The Law: Containing an Explanation of the Decalogue," while Chapter II is "Faith: Containing an Explanation of the Creed (Called Apostolic)." See *Institutes of the Christian Religion*, Basel, 1536, trans. Ford Lewis Battles, (Grand Rapids: Eerdmans, 1975).

906 James B. Torrance, "The Unconditional Freeness of Grace," *Theological Renewal*, no. 9, June/July 1978, 12.

907 *Institutes*, vol. 1, 340 n. 1.

greater condemnation were it not for the fact that the Creator came as the Redeemer "in the person of his only-begotten Son." The entire knowledge of God the Creator which we ought to have had but lost in the Fall "would be useless unless faith also followed, setting forth for us God our Father in Christ."

Again we note that God is known as a Father *in Christ*, and not elsewhere. Although God displays his "fatherly favor" in various ways, because of our dullness "we cannot by contemplating the universe infer that he is our Father." The Genevan Reformer clearly intends to establish a familial intention in Creation. God made us to be his sons and daughters. His fatherliness is objective and universal and prior to our knowing it, but due to the Fall, we no longer apprehend God as such. Now it is only in his Son that we are given to know it.

Consequently, "if we desire to return to God our Author and Maker, from whom we have been estranged, in order that he may again begin to be our Father," we must embrace the preaching of the cross. As Christ declares in John 17:3, eternal life means knowing the Father "to be the one true God" and Jesus Christ, whom he has sent. Only those who are "engrafted into the body of the only begotten Son" may become children of God.[908]

This radically Christological prolegomena for discussing the Law dramatically highlights the fact that for Calvin the Law should never be discussed starkly alone, in abstraction from Christ and His Gospel.[909] It never was an alternate means of salvation or merely a negative preparation for the Good News to follow:

> Apart from the Mediator, God never showed favor toward
> the ancient people, nor ever gave hope of grace to them.
> I pass over the sacrifices of the law, which plainly and
> openly taught believers to seek salvation nowhere else
> than in the atonement that Christ alone carries out. I am

---

908 II.vi.1.
909 Thus it is surprising that Ronald S. Wallace, in his careful exposition of *Calvin's Doctrine of the Christian Life*, which notes that the sanctification of the church is "in Christ" (3-47) and that the Christian life is nothing but a "dying and rising with Christ," overlooks the crucial Christological focus of Calvin's doctrine of law (112-122) for the Christian life.

only saying that the blessed and happy state of the church always had its foundation in the person of Christ.[910]

Even in Old Testament times Law was never a way to obtain grace. Rather, it was grounded in grace, the grace of Christ. And the grace Christ provides through his atonement is provided in his person at the same time. Here as elsewhere Calvin refuses to separate the work from the person of Christ.

Thus he explains in the prior paragraph that "life was in Christ from the beginning, and all the world fell away from it." Therefore "it is necessary to return to that source. So also, Christ, inasmuch as he is the propitiator, declares himself to be 'life.'" In fact Calvin would appear to be tiptoeing on the edge of universalism. For Christ, by virtue of who he is and what has done *is* that life from which all the world had fallen away. It would seem that all the world is restored in the[911] person of Christ. But Calvin hastens to add that only by faith are persons engrafted into Christ. We find already the tension between salvation being complete in Christ and faith-union with Christ being required in order to enjoy those benefits.[912]

In any case, the thrust of Calvin's argument here is that "under the law Christ was always set before the holy fathers as the end to which they should direct their faith."[913] The Old Testament prophecies were intended by God to direct the eyes of the Jews to Christ "in order to seek deliverance." Into his "freely given covenant" God had "adopted his elect," pledging to deliver them through Christ.

Consequently, Christ serves as the proper object of faith. While it is true that "faith rests in God, it will gradually disappear unless he who retains it in perfect firmness intercedes as Mediator. Otherwise, God's majesty is too lofty to be attained by mortal men, who are like grubs crawling upon the earth."

---

910 II.vi.2.

911 II.vi.1.

912 Cf. Wilhelm Niesel, *Reformed Symbolics*, (Edinburgh: Oliver and Boyd, 1962), 181ff.

913 II.vi.2; cf. I. John Hesselink, "Christ, the Law and the Christian: An Unexplored Aspect of the Third Use of the Law in Calvin's Theology," *Reformatio Perennis*, ed. Brian A. Gerrish, (Pittsburgh: Pickwick Press, 1981), 11-26.

What is of particular interest here is that God's majesty's not set over against his disclosure in Christ as polar opposites, as though we never know God in his majesty, but only as he stoops to us in Christ. There is a truth in that, as already noted, but God's mercy and fatherliness are part of his majesty, and not separate, chosen but non-essential, ways of dealing with humankind. That this must be Calvin's meaning is seen in the fact that he continues the above quote by saying

> For this reason [i.e., since our knowledge of God's majesty must originate in the Mediator] I subscribe to the common saying that God is the object of faith, yet it requires qualification. For Christ is not without reason called "the image of the invisible God." This title warns us that, unless God confronts us in Christ, we cannot come to know that we are saved.[914]

And what is the content of this knowledge we are given in Christ? "Let the first step toward godliness be to recognize that God is our Father to watch over us, govern and nourish us. Hence what we have recently said becomes clear, that apart from Christ the saving knowledge of God does not stand." That is why the Father comes to disclose himself to us in the Son. Indeed, "God is comprehended in Christ alone."[915]

The dilemma in Calvin's thought is that God has not given himself to be known by all people in Christ. God is by nature merciful and Fatherly, but only some are elected to learn this and taste of it. Those who claimed to worship the "Supreme Majesty, the Maker of heaven and earth" suffered this deprivation. "Because they had no Mediator, it was not possible for them truly to taste God's mercy, and thus be persuaded that he was their Father."[916] In this way, Calvin has detached the thought of the will of God from the self-revelation of God in Christ.

Yet Christ is the focal point of the Law, as the divinely appointed Mediator of the knowledge and redemption of God. But what, exactly, is

---

914 II.vi.4.

915 *Ibid.*

916 II.vi.4. That last quote would doubtless be seized upon by those arguing for a limited atonement in Calvin's thought. Is not Calvin telling us that some "had no Mediator"? But Calvin's argument concerns not the extent of the atonement, but the extent of its disclosure. Christ has not mediated knowledge of his saving person and work to all people. We will take up the issue of the scope of the atonement later.

the Law? In present context, Calvin tells us that he means to comprehend under the rubric not only the Ten Commandments, but also the "form of religion handed down by God through Moses."[917]

If we are to understand what the law is, we should "look to the Lawgiver, by whose character the nature of the law also is to be appraised."[918] The law is grounded in who God is, in his very nature. Indeed, the entire purpose of the law may be described as forming human life "to the archetype of divine purity. For God has so depicted his character in the law that if any man carries out in deeds whatever is enjoined there, he will express the image of God, as it were, in his own life." To that end we are called to embody his holiness in all our actions. And holiness is perfected in a twofold way: "First, indeed, our soul should be entirely filled with the love of God. From this will flow directly the love of neighbor."[919] Surely Calvin is here saying that the believer is called to live out the innermost character of God, *which is love*. Everything in the way of duty and right living flows from that.

Since Law is rooted in the character of God, we should expect to find that it is grounded in the grace of God. And that is exactly what we find. Calvin finds it significant the Law was given four hundred years after the "freely given covenant" was made with Abraham and the other patriarchs. It served not as an abrogation of the grace there promised, but as a renewal of the promise.

To be sure, the cultus of the law was never intended to be the thing itself, as if by sacrifices the people could reconcile themselves to God." The law rather served as so many shadows and figures referring to the Christ who was coming.[920] Therefore for Calvin grace clearly precedes and undergirds law. Law is grounded in the nature of God and his freely given covenant, a covenant which finds its fulfillment and its efficacy in Christ.

Thus the proleptic nature of law is emphasized. All the sacrifices were for naught apart from the One True Sacrifice, by which all evil deeds were atoned. The ceremonies were "worthless and empty until the time of Christ." Even its moral imperatives would only constitute an

---

917 II.vii.1.
918 II.viii.6.
919 II.viii.51.
920 II.vii.1.

"intolerable yoke and burden" and God's demands would be useless to know were it not that Christ was coming to succor his people.

In this way Calvin powerfully expounds his conviction that even under the law, all was of grace, from first to last. What does he do with the New Testament teaching that the law was also promulgated to convince people of their sin? Yes, concedes the Reformer, but this was in order to prepare them to seek Christ. What was at stake here was the refutation of meriting righteousness by the works of the law. "Consequently, to refute their error [Paul] was sometimes compelled to take the bare law in a narrow sense, even though it was otherwise graced with the covenant of free adoption."[921]

Calvin affirms a condemning function in the law. The law sets forth a standard such that perfect compliance would constitute righteousness before the Great Assize. When Moses published the law, he indicated that obeying it would merit life, eternal life. But all of us fail to observe the law, and are thereby "excluded from the promises of life." Therefore by instruction in the moral law our shortcomings are exposed, that "our guilt may arouse us to seek pardon."[922]

But the law has more than a negative function. Although we can never fulfill the conditions, God in his "free goodness" and apart from our works, receives us, and we in faith embrace that same goodness promised in the Gospel. Then the Lord freely supplies what is lacking in our imperfect obedience, treating us as if the conditions of the law had been fulfilled by us. This of course refers to the work of Christ, and Calvin promises to take it up later under the consideration of justification by faith.[923]

Full observance of the law is impossible, even for the saints. "There will be no one hereafter who will reach the goal of true perfection without sloughing off the weight of the body." Every person on earth remains unrighteous in the eyes of God. Even for the Christian, the "flesh lusts against the Spirit." Because of the weakness of our nature, we can never in this life reach perfection.[924]

Calvin proceeds to expound his familiar three uses of the law. First, it condemns humans for their unrighteousness, serving as a mirror of

---

921 II.vii.2.
922 II.vii.3.
923 II.vii.4; cf. III.xi.1-7.
924 II.vii.3.

our weakness. It shows us our infirmity that we might flee to grace. It also exposes the guilt of the reprobate, while leaving them in despair.[925]

Secondly, the law restrains evil persons from giving full rein to their depraved natures. In this function, the law employs the threat of punishment. Of course this only curbs outward wickedness, while being wholly ineffective in eliminating inner lusts and rebellion. Positively, it keeps some of the unregenerate from plunging wholly into "forgetfulness and contempt of God" until the day when they are awakened by the Spirit.[926]

However, the third is the principle use of the law, by which it admonishes believers in the way of upright living. For those in whose hearts the Spirit lives and reigns, the law serves to teach concerning the Lord's will and ways. By frequent meditation upon the law, the believer will be "aroused to obedience . . . strengthened in it, and be drawn back from the slippery path of transgression."[927]

It becomes evident that Calvin has no use for antinomians, who would "rashly cast out the whole of Moses, and bid farewell to the two Tables of the law." Throughout our lives we must continually meditate upon the law of the Lord, and endeavor to follow its pattern of righteousness.[928]

However, ceremonial laws, with their ritual cleansings and sacrifices, have been done away by the coming of Christ. Being "shadows", whose "substance" is Christ, they are outmoded. The promise of atonement for sins contained in the ancient sacrifices was "grounded in the grace of Christ, in whom one finds perfect and everlasting stability."

By his death Christ has accomplished redemption for the sins which could only be confessed in the ceremonial law. Therefore, concludes Calvin, the Jews under the ceremonial law "also were partakers in the same grace with us. For they attained that in Christ, not in the ceremonies . . . ." For Calvin, grace is not an independent something, standing apart from Christ, which is conferred upon the fulfillment of certain conditions. Grace is Christ himself. It was in Christ that Old

---

925 II.vii.7-9; cf. Wendel, *Calvin*, 198ff.
926 II.vii.10.
927 II.vii.12; cf. Sermon 20, "The Lord Answers Job," *Sermons from Job*, 290ff, CO vol. 35, 351-362.
928 II.vii.13.

Testament believers would find their sins atoned for, and in him they found grace.[929]

In Old Testament days, God "willed through expiations and sacrifices to attest that he was Father, and to set apart for himself a chosen people." That is to say, God wanted them to know through the provisions of ceremonial law that in his fatherliness he would provide a way for them to return to his heart and once again live as his sons and daughters. And so the grace anticipated by the ancient people and witnessed to by the prophets finally came in Christ.[930]

The word "gospel" in its widest connotation "includes those testimonies of his mercy and fatherly favor which God gave to the patriarchs of old. In a higher sense, however, the word refers, I say, to the proclamation of the grace manifested in Christ." In Christ the promises made to the patriarchs and the Jews have been fulfilled, for "the truth of his promises would be realized in the person of the Son." And "in the person" means nothing other than in the being, in the very humanity of Jesus, since "he has in his flesh accomplished the whole of our salvation."[931]

By now it will be evident that law and gospel are not contraries, nor is the Old Testament dispensation one of "works" while the New is of grace.[932] This is Calvin's continual theme, but lest there be any confusion, he takes pains to stress the point. "We refute those who always erroneously compare the law with the gospel by contrasting the merit of works with the free imputation of righteousness.

If by that comparison, one is only underscoring the graciousness of grace and the universal failure to completely observe the law, Calvin has no quarrel. "But the gospel did not so supplant the entire law so as to bring forward a different way of salvation. Rather, it confirmed and satisfied whatever the law had promised, and gave substance to the shadows."[933]

---

929 II.viii.17.
930 II.ix.1.
931 III.ix.2.
932 Cf. Andrew J. Bandstra, "Law and Gospel in Calvin and in Paul," *Exploring the Heritage of John Calvin*, ed. David E. Holwerda, (Grand Rapids: Baker, 1976), 22-23.
933 II.ix.4; cf. Sermon 3 on I Timothy, *Sermons on the Epistles to Timothy and Titus*, 29: "The Gospel is but a simple expounding of that which Moses preached before."

This would seem to present a fundamentally different view of grace and law than that propounded later by the Federal theologians. Calvin would appear resolutely opposed to the idea of a "covenant of works" promulgated in Eden, and republished at Sinai.[934] While he acknowledges, as we have seen, that by keeping the law in its entirety, one could receive eternal life, *he never views law as an alternate means of salvation.* Grace has always been the ground of God's dealings with the human race. Nor does he ever see the law as propounding conditions to grace. Grace precedes, undergirds and gives substance to law. In fact, the main distinction between law and gospel lies in the fullness of revelation: "where the whole law is concerned, the gospel differs from it only in clarity of manifestation."[935]

Moreover, Calvin only conceives of *one* covenant in two dispensations. All those adopted by God into his people since Creation were "covenanted to him by the same law and by the bond of the same doctrine as obtains among us . . . . God's people have never had any other rule of reverence and piety."[936] Indeed, "The covenant made with all the patriarchs is so much like ours in substance and reality that the two are actually one and the same. Yet they differ in the mode of dispensation.

To prove his point, the Reformer continues by showing how at every point the grace of God preceded and gave the very substance to the covenant the Lord made with the Israelites. First, the oracles, the law and the prophets all testified to the fact that they were "adopted into the hope of immortality." It was God's gracious action which took them into his family and gave them a sure hope of eternal life. Second, "the covenant by which they were bound to the Lord was supported, not by their own merits, but solely by the mercy of the God who called them." Third, "they had and knew Christ as Mediator, through whom they were joined to God and were to share in his promises." Clearly Calvin is here propounding the Gospel of *sola gratia* wholeheartedly: "all those blessings which the Lord has ever given or promised to his people arose

---

934 So also David Weir, *The Origins of the Federal Theology in Sixteenth-Century Reformation Thought*, 2-10.
935 Cf. M. Charles Bell, *Calvin and Scottish Theology. The Doctrine of Assurance*, 30-31; Wendel, 2P. cit., 208- 214.
936 II.x.1.

solely out of his goodness and kindness.[937] But *sola gratia* is always grounded in *solus Christus*:

> The Old Testament was established upon the free mercy of God, and was confirmed by Christ's intercession. For the Gospel preaching, too, declares nothing else than that sinners are justified apart from their own merit by God's fatherly kindness; and the whole of it is summed up in Christ. Who, then, dares to separate the Jews from Christ, since with them, we hear, was made the covenant of the gospel, the sole foundation of which is Christ? Who dares to estrange from the gift of free salvation those to whom we hear the doctrine of the righteousness of faith was imparted?[938]

The Mediation of Christ

And so the people of God under both dispensations looked in faith to one and the same Mediator, Jesus Christ. But why should this Mediator be both God and Man? There was no "absolute necessity." "Rather," he tells us, "it has stemmed from a heavenly decree, on which men's salvation depended."[939]

It may be thought that Calvin is thus grounding his doctrine of election upon some metaphysical speculation about an abstract God who issues decrees. And he does speak about an eternal decree before creation.[940] But, as Niesel shows, "it is just Calvin's doctrine of election which proves that he is not primarily a speculative thinker."[941] The Genevan reformer frequently warns us against a speculative contemplation of God and his eternal counsels. Investigating God's eternal plan engulfs one in a "deadly abyss."[942]

Christopher Elwood notes that "[i]n some interpretations of Calvin, predestination is understood as the defining theme of his theology." He

---

937 II.x.2.

938 II.x.4.

939 I.xii.1; cf. *Sermons on the Saving Work of Christ* trans. Leroy Nixon, (Hertfordshire: Evangelical Press, 1980), "The nativity of Jesus Christ," 49; "Fourth Sermon on the Ascension of our Lord Jesus Christ," 237.

940 III.xxi.5.

941 Niesel, *The Theology of Calvin*, 160.

942 III.xxiv.4; cf. numerous citations in John H. Leith, *Calvin's Doctrine of the Christian Life*, 132-133 and Niesel, *op. cit.*, 160-61.

points out that in fact, the doctrine is not located at the beginning of his *Institutio*, but "toward the end of the book dealing with 'The Way in Which We Receive the Grace of Christ.'"[943]

We are not permitted to examine predestination abstractly, in relation to God apart from his Son. Since Christ is the

> eternal wisdom of the Father, his unchangeable truth, his
> firm counsel, we ought not to be afraid of what he tells us
> in his Word varying in the slightest from that will of the
> Father which we seek. Rather, he faithfully reveals to us
> that will as it was from the beginning and ever shall be.[944]

Calvin tells us clearly that he intends to interpret the will of God in light of Christ, the "eternal wisdom of the Father," his "firm counsel." If we seek to know the will of God "as it was from the beginning," we must look to what Christ tells in his Word. Christ, indeed, is the "mirror by which the will of God is presented to us," and the one in whom we are elected.[945] Because Calvin grounds the will of God in the self-disclosure of God in and through his Son, so far as the election to eternal life is concerned, the freeness of grace in all its unmeritedness is, as we shall see, upheld. However, it will also become apparent that when he turns to the doctrine of reprobation, he departs from his own stated parameters, anchoring the will of God for the damned elsewhere than in his Son.

But so far as the elect are concerned, the way our merciful Father has decreed is best for us. God was too lofty for any human to serve as

---

943 Christopher Elwood, *Calvin for Armchair Theologians* (Louisville: Westminster John Knox Press, 2002), 98.

944 I.xxiv.5.

945 John Calvin, *Instruction in Faith (1537)*, trans. Paul T. Fuhrman, (London: Lutterworth, 1949), 37; III.xxiv.5. J. K. S. Reid's valuable study of "The Office of Christ in Election" seems to have overlooked this crucial role of Christ as *disclosing* the election of the Father, indeed, disclosing the will as grounded in the heart of the Father as love (II.vi.4). Reid complains that "despite all that is said concerning the place of Christian election, the *Leitmotiv* of Calvin's presentation of the doctrine is that Predestination belongs to God . . . a God into whose counsels Christ has not been admitted, and the inmost recesses of whose wisdom Christ has not illuminated". *Scottish Journal of Theology*, vol. 1, no. 1, 12. Rather, it would seem that the problem for Calvin is that Christ *is* admitted into the counsels of God, but for the elect only. In other words, the will of God is grounded in his self-disclosure in Christ only so far as the elect are concerned.

intermediary, and no member of Adam's race could bear the sight of God.

> The situation would surely have been hopeless had the very majesty of God not descended to us, since it was not in our power to ascend to him. Hence, it was necessary for the Son of God to become for us "Immanuel, that is, God with us" and in such a way that his divinity and our human nature might by mutual connection grow together. Otherwise the nearness would not have been near enough . . . so great was the disagreement between our uncleanness and God's perfect purity![946]

When Calvin takes us to the heart of God's saving work in Christ, it is not the language of external relations that he employs, but the language of being--of God's divinity and our human nature by mutual connection growing together. This is ontological language with a vengeance! To be sure, the vocabulary of the courtroom, of the marketplace and the altar each have their important place in Calvin's thought for illuminating aspects of the deeds of God in his Son. But when he is sketching the inner reality, he directs our attention to the mystery of the hypostatic union, wherein our flesh was in some wonderful way healed and united to the very nature of God himself.[947]

Where then is grace in all of this? It is everywhere, for it is not an "it," but a person. For Calvin, grace is nothing other than the action of God on our behalf. Soteriology finds its ground in the God who descends, the God who becomes--so that he might be the God who dwells with us. Indeed, should anyone be troubled regarding what path he must take to the Mediator, the path has already been taken to *him*, because "he is

---

946 II.xii.1.

947 The Calvinian corpus is filled with similar references. To sample a few: "He willed that assuming our nature He might have true brotherhood with us" (Sermon 1, *Sermons on the Saving Work of Christ*, 14; CO vol. 47, 465-484); "Christ justifies us, not only in that He is God, but also in that He is man; for He acquired for us righteousness in His flesh," Commentary on Isaiah 53:11, trans. T. H. L. Parker, Sermons on Isaiah's Prophecy of the Death and Passion of Christ, (London: James Clarke, 1956), 119; "We do not have to look far for our righteousness, since we find it in the person of our Lord Jesus Christ, in that He has put on our nature and made Himself our brother," Sermon VI, on Isaiah 53:11, Ibid., 125, CR 661ff.

near us, indeed touches us, since he is our flesh."[948] Grace, therefore, is God's self-giving.

To put it another way, grace is the God-man himself, for in that union rests our salvation. The Mediator's task was nothing less than "to restore us to God's grace", and by this Calvin does not mean infusing us with a supernatural habit, as Aquinas teaches, but rather retrieving us and bringing us near himself where grace is. And the nearness achieved is again described in terms of the *assumptio carnis*:

> Who could have done this had not the self-same Son of God become the Son of Man) and had not so taken what was ours as to impart what was his to us, and to make what was his by nature ours by grace? Therefore, relying on this pledge, we trust that we are sons of God, for God's natural Son fashioned for himself a body from our body, flesh from our flesh, bones from our bones, that he might be one with us. Ungrudgingly he took our nature upon himself to impart to us what was his, and to become both Son of God and Son of man in common with us.[949]

Calvin here affirms the ancient Athanasian doctrine of the 'great exchange,' that God takes our humanity that we might, by grace, share in his divinity.[950] Sharing in his nature means sharing in his sonship. Christ becomes a Son of Man that we might become Sons of God. Here again the Fatherhood of God is close at hand, and his familial intentions in creation, which we noted earlier, are realized in the new creation accomplished when the Creator becomes the Redeemer and so gives us to share in a "holy brotherhood."[951] That accomplished, Christ can declare that he is ascending to "my Father and your Father, to my God and your God" (John 20:17).[952]

At this point we might think that the atonement was accomplished by the incarnation alone, since Calvin has already told us that our

---

948 II.xii.1.
949 II.xii.2.
950 *The Orations of Athanasius Against the Arians*, 1.39, London, Griffith, Farran, Okeden and Welsh, n. d.
951 Cf. Wallace, *Calvin, Geneva and the Reformation*, 242-46.
952 II.xii.2.

uncleanness was dealt with in the hypostatic union by bringing it into contact with God's purity. Although we are not to think of an instantaneous action (his nature and ours were "by mutual connection to grow together"), neither has anything been said regarding outward actions of the God-man.

But for Calvin, the person and the work of Christ are inseparable. The faith which knows him, receives him "as he is offered by the Father: namely, clothed with his gospel."[953] Who he is, is expressed in what he does, and what he does is part of who he is. And more than the assumption of our humanity was required in order to fulfill the office of Mediator.

And so Calvin comes to the "second requirement of our reconciliation with God," namely, the obedience of Christ taking the place of our disobedience. So it had to be "that man, who by his disobedience had become lost, should by way of remedy counter it with obedience, satisfy God's judgment, and pay the penalties for sin." Christ comes as the second Adam, presenting "our flesh" to satisfy God's judgment.

Calvin's continual insistence that it was precisely "our flesh" which God assumed, that he took "Adam's place." that he took "our nature", that the gulf between our "uncleanness" and "God's perfect purity" was overcome *in the hypostatic union* strongly suggests that the humanity which our Lord took upon himself was fallen humanity, humanity dominated by original sin.

He even declares that Christ was "suffering in his soul the terrible torments of a condemned and forsaken man,"[954] that Christ prayed "not to be spared death, but he prays not to be swallowed up by it as a sinner because he there bore our nature."[955]

To pursue this would be beyond the scope of this book,[956] but elsewhere he appears to reject the notion decisively: "We make Christ

---

953 III.ii.6.

954 II.xvi.10.

955 II.xvi.11; cf. II.xvi.12.

956 See further Paul van Buren's *Christ in our Place. The Substitutionary Character of Calvin's Doctrine of Reconciliation*, (Edinburgh: Oliver and Boyd, 1957), and Harry Johnson's, *The Humanity of the Savior*, (London: Epworth, 1962). David Dorries' "Nineteenth Century British Christological Controversy Centring Upon Edward Irving's Doctrine of Christ's Human Nature", (Ph.D. thesis, Aberdeen University, 1987), 155ff contains a valuable survey of the views on the nature Christ assumed, of divines from the days of the early church through the Reformation and then that propounded by Edward Irving.

free of all stain . . . because he was sanctified by the Spirit that the generation might be pure and undefiled as would have been true before Adam's fall . . . no infection came to Christ . . . . No wonder, then, that Christ, through whom integrity was to be restored, was exempted from the common corruption!"[957]

Nonetheless, it was in our flesh that Christ offered the one true sacrifice, "that he might wipe out our guilt by his act of expiation and appease the Father's righteous wrath." Calvin is at home with penal-substitutionary terminology. To atone for our sin, Christ presented "our flesh as the price of satisfaction to God's righteous judgment, and, in the same flesh," went so far as "to pay the penalty that we had deserved.[958]

Of course, the connection here emphasized is between the sacrificial system in the Old Testament and the Perfect Sacrifice of Christ Himself, who alone could atone for sin. The shedding of blood itself is a "sign of expiation." But in this case, says Calvin, the Priest becomes the victim. This interpretation radically qualifies the penal-substitutionary language here utilized. It is not as if God could only be gracious if a penalty were exacted, so he punishes the Son to that end. Penal language is couched in the passive tense, and it is God himself who receives it, by becoming the victim. In fact, argues Calvin, Christ's priestly self-offering served as a "mirror" of "the goodness of God," and "his boundless love."[959]

In this light we must interpret the discussion of Christ's priestly office. For he begins by saying that "God's righteous curse bars our access to him, and God in his capacity as judge is angry toward us. Hence an expiation must intervene in order that Christ may obtain God's favor for us and appease his wrath."[960] We are not to think of the love and the justice of God as antinomies, so that the cross becomes some kind of "battle of the attributes."

Nor are we to picture an angry, legally-minded God the Father and a loving, gracious Son changing his mind. "An expiation must intervene" because God's boundless love would have it no other way. Calvin's high Christology will not permit a dualism of Father and Son. At the same time God's justice is also real. His eyes are too pure to look upon evil.

---

957 II.xiii.4.
958 II.xii.3.
959 II.xii.4.
960 II.xvi.6.

Sin is contrary to his very being as holy and righteous. Therefore we cannot come into his presence. Our relationship as children to the Father has been utterly broken. So God comes forward in "fatherly mercy" and dons our human flesh that he might offer himself as the sacrifice.

By that sacrifice, Christ "sanctifies us and obtains for us that grace from which the uncleanness of our transgressions and vices debars us." This does not mean that grace is separated from Christ and that he must go through a struggle in order to reach it. Grace is Christ, for it is God's self-giving. Grace is not removed from Christ but from *us* and by his assumption of our flesh and self-offering on our behalf he is able to release his grace into our life, which is to say that he is able to shower the blessings of his presence upon us.

Calvin quotes Augustine as saying that Christ, our "Head," is "the very foundation of grace." Everyone who becomes a Christian owes that transformation to the "same grace whereby that Man from his beginning became the Christ."[961] That is to say, God, who *is grace*, by his grace unites himself to humanity in the incarnation that he may work graciously to join human beings as members of his Body.

In this context we can talk about a kind of "merit" in Christ. For God, as the "First Cause", ordained in his grace and mercy that Christ should be our Mediator. By God's grace, Christ's saving work constituted his merit which intervened on our behalf.[962] In this sense we may say that "by his obedience . . . Christ truly acquired and merited grace for us with his Father." And Christ "deserved" the salvation he acquired by his making satisfaction for our sins, suffering for the unrighteous.[963]

But we are not permitted to take this guarded use of the term "merit" as connoting any kind of conditionality in divine grace. For Christ is none other than *Deus in carne*, and as such is giving gifts as God and receiving them as man. Even here, therefore, the controlling conviction is that grace is the self-giving of God. Thus Calvin explicated the Christmas message "The Saviour is born to us," as meaning, "He gives Himself to us."[964] In the coming of his only Son, God "shed his grace",

---

961 II.xvii.1, citing Augustine, *On the Predestination of the Saints* xv.30, 31, cited *in loc.*

962 II.xvii.1.

963 II.xviii.3.

964 Sermon on Luke 2:9-14, Appendix 1, *The Oracles of God. An Introduction to the Preaching of John Calvin*, by T. H. L. Parker, (London: Lutterworth Press, 1947), 151

for in that mighty event he deigned to "give himself to us."[965] When God graciously bound himself to Israel and Israel to himself on Mount Horeb, he did it out of his own "infinite goodness." But he showed himself more fully to be our gracious father and Savior in the incarnation, for "God hath given us his own heart in the person of the Lord Jesus Christ."[966]

In fact, it was this guiding conviction that grace is God's redemptive action on behalf of a sinful race in the humanity of Christ that shaped his critique of medieval theology. In that Man, the "whole fullness of grace is presented to us."[967] In giving us Christ, God gives us grace, and he never gives it apart from himself. Therefore the whole system of preparations and merit and a person "doing what is in him" as a way of cooperating with grace so as to earn more grace is overturned. In "our Lord Jesus Christ our salvation is already perfect." When through faith we are united to him we possess him, and in possessing him we lack nothing. "We must not imagine as the Papists do, that Jesus hath but opened us the gate of salvation, and that it in our power to enter it if we list: and that he hath begone, and it is in us to make an end."[968] For God in giving himself, has given us all things.

This means that not only are our sins expiated, but our very being is sanctified in the God-man. He "sanctifies us", we are "consecrated through him", indeed *in him*. In our flesh Christ comes to sanctify himself. He comes as "comrade and partner in the same nature with us", and "of his boundless grace joins himself to base and ignoble men."[969]

But this sanctification effected in his priestly intercession is not past tense only. Calvin takes great pains to stress the *on-going priesthood of Christ*.[970]

By his incarnation in our humanity Christ is able
to receive us as his companions in this great office.

(CR vol. 46), 285-298.
965 Sermon 1, *Sermons on Deuteronomy*, 4.
966 Sermon 30, *Sermons on Deuteronomy*, 179-180; cf. Sermon 46.
967 Sermon on Ephesians 2:1-5, *Sermons on The Epistle to the Ephesians*, 128.
968 Sermon 16 on Titus, *John Calvin's Sermons on Timothy and Titus*, 1230.
969 II.xiii.1-4.
970 Cf. the profound treatment of this theme in James B. Torrance, "The Priesthood of Christ," *Essays in Christology*, ed. T. H. L. Parker (Lutterworth, 1956), 155-73 and his essay on "The Vicarious Humanity of Christ," in *The Incarnation*, ed. T. F. Torrance (Handsel, 1981), 127-147.

> For we who are defiled in ourselves, yet are priests in
> him, offer ourselves and our all to God, and freely enter
> the heavenly sanctuary that the sacrifices of prayers
> and praise that we bring may be acceptable and sweet-
> smelling before God.[971]

This means that the Christian life is not simply a matter of looking
backward to Golgotha and Easter. It is one of daily drawing strength
from the living Christ, and sharing in his Priesthood in our life before
God and our life before the world.

All of this flows from Calvin's belief that the Person of Christ cannot
be separated from the Work of Christ. Christ accomplishes reconciliation
in his own being, and even in his fulfilling of the law in his death, he
is there as God, taking the consequences upon himself. But Calvin
does not "jump" from the cradle to the Cross, from the incarnation to
the atonement. Between those points lay a long struggle which Christ
undertook in our flesh on our behalf.

Thus, the general answer to the question concerning how Christ has
conquered the sin and separation and acquired righteousness for us, is
that "he has achieved this for us by the whole course of his obedience."[972]
The "active obedience" of the God-man in our place was lifelong, so
that he daily substituted his righteousness, for our unrighteousness, his
obedience for our disobedience, his faithfulness for our unfaithfulness,
his fellowship with the Father for our alienation from him. Even his
baptism was part of this vicarious obedience. "In short," declares Calvin,
"from the time when he took on the form of a servant, he began to pay
the price of liberation in order to redeem us.

Standing in our humanity proved to be a struggle for Christ, since
it entailed taking upon himself our weaknesses. He had to "wrestle
with terrible fear", and to "cast off all concern for himself" even to the
point of "disregarding his own feelings." These are powerful words,
and indicate that Calvin wanted to take the humanity of Christ with full
seriousness.

We must nonetheless recognize that in a "peculiar and proper"
fashion the Scriptures attribute our salvation to Christ's death, since it

971 II.xvi.6.
972 II.xvi.5.

was necessary to take away our sins. "Yet the remainder of the obedience that he manifested in his life is not excluded" from his saving work. Indeed, the death itself gained its efficacy from "his willing obedience." Were it not voluntary, his sacrifice could not have accomplished righteousness for us.[973]

This emphasis on the voluntary aspect of the Son's obedience is an important one, for it is controlled by the ontological oneness of Father and Son. McLeod Campbell would later carry this point further and insist that we see no other mind in God than in the mind of the Son manifested throughout his life and on the cross, and that oneness of mind requires that we believe in an all-embracing love of God which could not bear to live without any of his creatures. That is to say, the will of God must be grounded in the self-disclosure of God.

Calvin also employs the imagery of the courtroom. All humankind stands guilty and condemned before the divine judgment seat. But Christ interposes himself, taking our penalty upon himself. A way had to be chosen by which our condemnation could be transferred to himself. Thus, as he stood before Pilate's judgment seat as a criminal, "we know by these proofs that he took the role of a guilty man and evildoer." Yet he was carrying the sin of another rather than his own. And by this "substitution," our acquittal was won, for "the guilt that held us liable for punishment has been transferred to the head of the Son of God."[974]

Yet even here we are not to think of Father and Son as, so to speak, in opposition to one another. On the Cross, "The Father" was the one who "destroyed the force of sin when the curse of sin was transferred to Christ's flesh." Or, from the Son's perspective, we may say that "we must not understand that he fell under a curse that overwhelmed him; rather--in taking the curse upon himself--he crushed, broke, and scattered its whole force."[975] Calvin is even clearer when he says that when Christ uttered the anguishing cry of dereliction, "we do not suggest that God was ever inimical or angry toward him. How could he be angry toward his beloved Son, 'in whom his heart reposed?'"[976] Indeed, observes Calvin, anticipating McLeod Campbell, "he did not cease to call him his God, by whom he cried out that he had been forsaken."[977]

---

973 *Ibid.*
974 *Ibid.*
975 II.xvi.6.
976 II.xvi.11.
977 II.xvi.12; cf. McLeod Campbell, *The Nature of the Atonement*, 275-281.

Calvin's ringing conclusion to his discussion of salvation is found in Book II, chapter xv, section 19: "We see that our whole salvation and all its parts are comprehended in Christ." Therefore, he argues, we ought not seek it anywhere else. If we seek salvation, it will be found in him. If we seek spiritual gifts, they are in his anointing by the Spirit. Similarly, he locates strength in Christ's dominion, purity in his conception, gentleness in his birth, redemption in his passion, acquittal in his condemnation, remission of the curse in his cross, and so on. "In short," urges the Reformer, "let us drink our fill from this fountain, and from no other." For sorry is the story of those who strayed from the true path by "turning some part of their thinking in another direction."[978]

A Universal Atonement

Corresponding to Calvin's insistence on the love and mercy and fatherhood of God in his inner life is his conviction that God's work in Christ embraces the entire human race. Universalist passages abound in the Calvinian corpus. Many of them refer expressly to God's intentions in our creation. All humans, he declares, "are born and live to the end that they may know God."[979] Our greatest joy lies in the knowledge of God, and "lest anyone, then, be excluded from access to happiness," God planted in human minds the "seed of religion" and daily reveals himself in the great theater of the universe.[980] And again, "there is one God who so governs all natures that he would have us look unto him, direct our faith to him, worship and call upon him."[981]

And the Fall was no insurmountable obstacle to the divine intention. The Cross itself bears eloquent testimony to the prior love of God, since the giving of his Son could only constitute a pledge of his love to us if his "free favor" had preceded it.[982] This is not to soft-peddle God's just wrath and hatred of sin. A righteous God cannot love the wickedness imbedded in all of us. We all "have in ourselves something deserving of God's hatred." All humankind stands before God guilty and deserving of damnation.

---

978 II.xvii.19.
979 I.iii.3.
980 I.v.1.
981 I.v.6.
982 II.xvi.2.

But Calvin waxes eloquent in his exposition of the eternal love of God which would not be defeated by the creature's sin:

> But because the Lord wills not to lose what is his in us, out of his own kindness he still finds something to love. However much we may be sinners by cur own fault, we nevertheless remain his creatures. However much we have brought death upon ourselves, yet he has created us unto life. Thus he is moved by pure and freely given love of us to receive us into grace.[983]

Therefore God takes away all the "cause for enmity" and by the death of his Son wipes away all the sin and reconciles us completely to himself.

In this manner the Reformer makes crystal clear his conviction that God's love is not conditional. He loved us before creation itself, and his love is unchangeable. Therefore, the purpose of the Son's reconciling work was not so that God could love us. Rather, "he has loved us before the world was created, that we also might be his sons along with his only-begotten Son--before we became anything at all."[984]

Although Calvin presses into service a wide range of images to express something of the depth and breadth of what God has accomplished in his Son, including metaphors from the marketplace, the law court, and the Temple, he continually draws us back to the saving humanity of Jesus Christ. Our joy is grounded in the fact that

> [A]lthough He was eternal God, He clothed Himself with our flesh and cur nature, in order to be our brother. And He has even taken the curse our sins upon Him and has carried the burden which would have crushed us all, in order that we may no more be found guilty before God and that our sins may no more be accounted or remembered. He has also clothed us with His righteousness.[985]

This was wrought for "us all," and not merely in a forensic fashion, in which case the number and even the names of the guilty parties whose

983 II.xvi.3.
984 II.xvi.4. Calvin is quoting Augustine, *John's Gospel* cx.6, cited in McNeill, *op. cit.*, 507.
985 Sermon on Luke 2:9-14, Appendix I, *The Oracles of God*, 150.

plight Christ assumes as their substitute might well be a matter of arbitrary determination. There is a crucial judicial dimension, to be sure, but it is never to be thought of in abstraction from the saving humanity of Jesus. In becoming our brother, Christ unites himself with the world of sinners in a fraternity of flesh, in a brotherly knot, and heals our sinful humanity in his person and in all that he does in his obedience unto death, even death on a Cross.

If this is so, faith does not create a new reality, but apprehends a reality already existing independent of its knowledge. And this is what Calvin tells us. For the joy which the Gospel brings to us "has its foundation in our Lord Jesus Christ. Whoever does not know the office of Jesus Christ, can never trust in God."[986] And this joy was not for a few, but for "all people." It is true, admits the reformer, "that all have not rejoiced. But from God's side the joy has been offered to them. So unbelievers must be made inexcusable, seeing they are deprived by their own malice of the grace of God offered them."[987]

If Calvin, as has been alleged[988] taught a limited atonement, his argument for the culpability of the lost would not be predicated on their "unbelief" in one who was not their savior, nor would he charge them with "depriving themselves of the grace God offers." Among those espousing a particular redemption in Calvin, P. Helm may be taken as representative in his reasoning: "If Christ is the author of election and the elect are a definite number, how can it be that Christ would die for some whom he had not elected?"[989] There is certainly an inconsistency in holding these two convictions, one which Beza and other Calvinists sought to eliminate in favor of a relentlessly logical system derived from the assumption that God is absolute will in his inmost being.

---

986 *Ibid.* 150-151.

987 *Ibid.*, 149-150.

988 E.g. by R. B. Kuiper, *For Whom Did Christ Die?*, (Grand Rapids: Eerdmans, 1959), 66, 91; Richard A. Muller, *Christ and the Decree. Christology and Predestination in Reformed Theology from Calvin to Perkins*, (Grand Rapids: Baker, 1988), 33f; Paul Helm, *Calvin and the Calvinists*, (Edinburgh: Banner of Truth, 1982), 16ff.

989 *Op. cit.*, 20. In a similar vein Timothy Paul Jensen argues that "Calvin's logic is on the side of particular atonement . . . . If he believed Christ intended to save all people by his death, he also necessarily believed that Christ failed in that intention, but he never remotely suggests that Christ failed in any of his acts or intentions". "Calvin and Turretin: A Comparison of Their Soteriologies," (Ph.D. dissertation, University of Virginia, 1988), 146-47.

But the question before us is not whether the two concepts are incompatible, but whether John Calvin taught them. And the answer it would seem, must be in the affirmative. Jesus is the "Redeemer of the world,"[990] who stood before Pilate "in the person of all cursed ones and of all transgressors," and as such "bears the burdens of all those who had offended God mortally."[991] Commenting on Isaiah 53:12, "He bore the sin of many," Calvin says, "I approve of the ordinary reading, that he alone bore the punishment of man, because on him was laid the guilt of the whole world. It is evident from other passages . . . that 'many' sometimes denotes 'all.'"[992]

Preaching on the same text, Calvin reiterates that Christ bore the sins of all and proceeds to remind us that "our Lord Jesus was offered to all the world. For it is not speaking of three or four when it says: 'God so loved the world, that he spared not his only Son.'" True, he admits, it is only those who believe who receive eternal life. But that is the point: "Our Lord Jesus suffered for all and there is neither great nor small who is not inexcusable to-day, for we can obtain salvation in Him. Unbelievers who turn away from Him and who deprive themselves of Him by their malice are today doubly culpable."[993]

So the reformer urges his hearers to "pray generally for all men," especially for "wretched unbelievers" and the "ignorant." For what else could we do watching "souls in peril, which are so precious to God, as he has shown in that he has ransomed them with the blood of his own Son? If we see then a poor soul going thus to perdition . . . should we not desire God to apply the remedy?"[994] If it be argued that we are only told that these souls are "going" toward perdition, and therefore, having been ransomed, will surely be called and saved before actually arriving, Calvin will tell us that in fact some "poor souls whom our Lord Jesus Christ has bought so dearly that he did not spare himself to save them, perish and are given into Satan's possession. Yet we remain quite indifferent."[995]

---

990 Sermon 7, *Sermons on the Saving Work of Christ*, 126, CO vol. 46, 887-901.
991 Sermon 5, *op. cit.*, 95, CO vol. 46, 859-873.
992 John Calvin, *Commentary on the Book of the Prophet Isaiah*, vol. 3, trans. William Pringle, (Grand Rapids: Baker, 1989).
993 Sermon VII, *Sermons on Isaiah's Prophecy*, 141, CO xxxv, 675.
994 Sermon on Ephesians 6:18-19, *Sermons on Ephesians*, 684-85; cf. Sermon on Ephesians 5:11-14, 521.
995 Sermon on Ephesians 5:11-14, *Sermons on Ephesians*, 525.

We must bear in mind that for Calvin, while God has accomplished the whole of our salvation in the person of his Son independent of our recognition of it, we only share in that salvation by faith. And faith, as we have observed, is knowledge of that objective reality. So the Genevan reformer declares:

> It was not enough that our Lord Jesus should have fulfilled in his person everything necessary for our salvation, but that we must grasp it by faith. This is the knowledge that is needed. For how many unbelievers do we see perishing, for whom the death and passion of our Lord Jesus Christ serves only for more severe condemnation, because they trample underfoot His sacred blood and reject His grace offered to them . . . we on our side can receive no profit by Him save by the knowledge of Him.[996]

Many other passages could be adduced which make the case for universal atonement, in this writer's mind, incontrovertible.[997] When Calvin exegetes II Peter 3:9, which states that God is not willing that any should perish, he does not restrict the word "any" to the elect, for "This is His wondrous love towards the human race, that He desires all men to be saved." Then he countenances the natural question as to why so many do in fact perish:

> My reply is that no mention is made here of the secret decree of God by which the wicked are doomed to their

---

996 Sermon on Isaiah 53:11, *Sermons on Isaiah's Prophecy of the Death and Passion of Christ*, 126.

997 Cf. Sermons 13 and 15, *John Calvin's Sermons on Timothy and Titus*, 159, 177; Sermon 17, *Sermons on the Saving Work of Christ*, 263; Sermon on Ephesians 2:16-19, *Sermons on The Epistle to the Ephesians*, 202; and the passages cited in M. Charles Bell, *Calvin and Scottish Theology*, 13-18 and in R. T. Kendall, *Calvin and English Calvinism to 1649*, (Oxford: Oxford University Press, 1981), 13-21. Richard Muller, *op. cit.* ventures the strange distinction between "sins" and "sinners," suggesting that Calvin holds to "the complete expiation or satisfaction for sin," while restricting the benefits of such a satisfaction to certain sinners, viz., the elect (p. 34). But Calvin refuses to separate the benefits of Christ from Christ, and speaks, as we have seen, of "souls going to perdition" whom God has "ransomed with the blood of his Son". True it is that he proceeds to speak of a restrictive election and a limited awakening, but that must never distract us from his emphatic stress on the fact that Christ died for the whole world.

own ruin, but only of His loving-kindness as it is made known in the Gospel. There God stretches out His hand to all alike, but He only grasps those (in such a way as to lead to Himself) whom He has chosen before the foundation of the world.[998]

Selective Election

That Calvin did not hold that all are elect in Christ is well known. While God is love in his inmost being, and therefore loves the "whole human race", he "did not embrace the whole of mankind with an equal love."[999] For reasons mysterious to mortal minds[1000], God has by his secret election deigned to grant his grace to a few. The rest are justly reprobated on the basis of their sinfulness. And these are not merely left to their own devices. They are actively, willingly hardened by God. "The nature of this activity is by no means explained if we take refuge in foreknowledge or permission."

This is wholly consistent with the position earlier expounded, according to which divine providence entails the notion that God actively decrees every motion in the universe. But it is not consistent with the will of God as revealed in Jesus Christ, not even according to Calvin's account of it.

He has forbidden us to examine predestination abstractly, in relation to God apart from his Son. Since Christ is the "eternal wisdom of the Father, his unchangeable truth, his firm counsel" what "he tells us in his Word" will not be found varying in the slightest from that will of the Father which we seek. Rather, he faithfully reveals to us that will as it was from the beginning and ever shall be."[1001]

But now we find that Calvin grounds the will of God in the self-disclosure of God in and through his Son, *only so far as the elect are concerned*. But when he turns to the doctrine of reprobation, he departs

---

998 Commentary on II Peter 3:9, *The Epistle of Paul The Apostle to the Hebrews and the First and Second Epistles of St Peter* trans. William B. Johnston, (Grand Rapids: Eerdmans, 1963).

999 "The Secret Providence of God," *Calvin's Calvinism*, 268.

1000 However, we must go on to confess that "God doth nothing without the highest of reasons" (*Ibid.*, 247).

1001 I.xxiv.5; cf. T. H. L. Parker, *John Calvin*, (Hertfordshire: Lion Publishing, 1982), 48.

from his own stated parameters, anchoring the will of God for the damned elsewhere than in his Son.

In fact, Calvin asserts that "Satan intervenes to stir up the reprobate whenever the Lord by his providence destines them to one end or another." Of course, in that same action there is a wide disparity between what God does and what Satan and evil people seek to do. But "God makes these evil instruments, which he holds under his hand and can turn wherever he pleases, to serve his justice."[1002] Their nature is already depraved, but God hardens it further.

Hardening takes place in two ways: (1) removing the light of the Spirit; and (2) arousing their evil wills and strengthening their evil endeavors. By the first is meant that God takes away their spiritual sight, and their ability to obey. By the second is meant that God renders their hearts "obstinate" in evil.[1003] So for Calvin, reprobation is not only the passive activity of abandoning a person to his own sinful inclinations, but the active movement of confirming him in them.

But it must be stressed that this obstinacy is not merely externally caused. "The cause of their obstinacy was their own perverse will. If they find the source of evil within themselves, why do they strain after external causes so as not to seem the authors of their own destruction?"[1004] In other words, the fact that God has confirmed them in their hardness does not remove blame from them since their hardness is nonetheless also self-chosen.[1005] Striking it is, that Calvin employs personal and familial categories to describe God's calling of the elect, but turns to mechanistic and impersonal and legal concepts to account for reprobation.

Yet Calvin frequently uses other language to describe those who are not saved. While from the divine side, their condemnation was decreed before time, from the human side it is due to their fault. We have already seen how this thought is developed in the discussion of providence and secondary causation. Although God wills the damnation

---

1002 II.iv.5.

1003 II.iv.3.

1004 II.v.11.

1005 John Murray observes that the symmetry between election and reprobation breaks down in the case of their respective grounds, since election is grounded in the goodness of God while reprobation is based on human guilt. *Calvin on Scripture and Divine Sovereignty*, (Grand Rapids: Baker, 1978), 60-64; cf. Calvin's *Commentary on Romans 9, op. cit.*

of certain unregenerate, they willingly resist him and thus can only blame themselves. But Calvin also speaks at times as if Christ truly is their Savior, but they have rejected him. Thus Calvin says that "the moment we turn away even slightly from [Christ], our salvation, which rests firmly in him, gradually vanishes away. As a result, all those who do not repose in him voluntarily deprive themselves of all grace."[1006]

Of course, Calvin also says that God decreed their rejection before time, and that they reject him because God never deigned to give them his Spirit, by whom alone sinners are awakened to faith. It almost seems as if for Calvin God's universal love is somehow frustrated by his will.

> God is not bound by any law that should compel Him to show mercy unto all men indiscriminately and alike; but . . . He is the Lord of His own will, to impart pardon to whom He will and to pass by others as He will.[1007]

Calvin faces the tension between universal atonement and selective awakening in Book III, Chapter 1:

> As long as Christ remains outside of us, and we are separated from him, all that he has suffered and done for the salvation of the human race remains useless and of no value for us.[1008]

It would seem to this writer that he has here taken an unequivocal stand. What Christ did was not for the elect only, but for the "human race." Yet it does us no good so long as Christ remains outside of us. All that Christ has done in our flesh for us is of no value until Christ dwells within us. This in mind, Calvin expounds the doctrine of union with Christ, setting forth how we are united to him as members to the Head. For some reason not all embrace this "communion with Christ which is offered through the gospel." That is to say, the Gospel of reconciliation is held out to *all*, because Christ died for all. And yet all do not accept it, for it is only by the Spirit that "we come to enjoy Christ and all his benefits."[1009] As Dennis Tamburello summarizes Calvin's teaching on

---

1006 II.xvi.1.
1007 "The Secret Providence of God," *Calvin's Calvinism*, 282.
1008 III.i.1.
1009 *Ibid.*

this point: "The Holy Spirit brings the elect, through the hearing of the Gospel, to faith; in so doing, the Spirit engrafts them into Christ."[1010]

It is the office of the Spirit to attest to the reality of Christ's cleansing and sacrificial work in the heart of the individual. And Christ, by the Holy Spirit "effectually unites us to himself."[1011] The Holy Spirit is he who works faith in us. Faith is not a human work, for it is "a supernatural gift that those who would otherwise remain in unbelief receive Christ by faith."[1012] As Paul Helm explains it, for Calvin, it is "[n]ot that faith is a ground or basis of justification; it is merely its instrument."[1013] And faith looks to Christ.

Because Christ alone knows the Father, "Paul declares that he considers nothing worth knowing save Christ." We come to know God through the God-man, and nowhere else.[1014] Looking elsewhere will only result in wandering through endless labyrinths. But "faith rests on knowledge . . . knowledge not only of God but of the divine will." And what is the content of this knowledge mediated by Christ? That "God is our merciful Father . . . and that Christ has been given to us as righteousness, sanctification and life."[1015] Clearly, faith is knowledge, and knowledge of the nature of God, and what it knows about God is that he *is* a merciful Father *in se*.

Since "faith consists in the knowledge of God and Christ,"[1016] we see the dilemma posted by Calvin's soteriology. Faith does not create a new reality in God; it knows an already existing reality, namely, the Fatherly heart of God, and the finished work of Christ. And this work was done for the entire human race, but only some are permitted to know it.

Sometimes Calvin seems to imply a division between God as he is in himself and as he is toward us:

1010 Dennis E. Tamburello, *Union with Christ: John Calvin and the Mysticism of St. Bernard* (Louisville: Westminster John Knox Press, 1994), 86.

1011 *Ibid.*
1012 III.i.4.
1013 Paul Helm, *Calvin: A Guide for the Perplexed* (London and New York: T & T Clark, 2008), 73.

1014 III.ii.1.
1015 III.ii.2.
1016 III.ii.3.

In understanding faith it is not merely a question of knowing that God exists, but also--and this especially--of knowing what is his will toward us. For it is not so much our concern to know who he is in himself, as what he wills to be toward us.[1017]

It seems that Calvin here means to remind us that we cannot plumb the depths of God. His essence will always far transcend us. Therefore it is not for us to claim in our faith to know all that there is of God, but only how he has chosen to act toward us. But this leaves open the question whether there might be a contradiction between the divine love we see manifested toward ourselves and perhaps a quite different attitude towards others. Calvin seems to believe not that God contradicts himself, but that at one time he manifests one attribute--e.g., love (toward certain ones) while at others he manifests another--e.g., justice. Thus, he says that "the solid pledge of [God's] love is Christ, without whom the signs of hatred and wrath are everywhere evident."[1018] If we demur, he replies that it is not our business to question God. He is right, but has he been true to his conviction that "God is comprehended in Christ alone"?[1019]

For Calvin, "only those predestined to salvation receive the light of faith." Moreover, since true faith is knowledge, it is "a sure persuasion,"[1020] "a firm and certain knowledge of God's benevolence toward us."[1021] Since Christ died for the world, the faith which the Spirit awakens need not continually be subjected to wavering and uncertainty. Yet this does not preclude times of doubt and struggle.[1022]

1017 III.ii.6.

1018 III.ii.7.

1019 II.vi.4.

1020 III.ii.12.

1021 III.ii.7.

1022 III.ii.15. Helm contends that Calvin's definition of faith as "a firm and sure knowledge of the divine favour toward us, founded upon the truth of a free promise in Christ, and revealed to our minds and sealed on our hearts, by the Holy Spirit" (III. ii.7, *Institutes of the Christian Religion*, trans. Henry Beveridge (Edinburgh, 1845, reprinted London, James Clarke & Co, 1949) is "not a definition in the sense of a set of necessary and sufficient conditions for the presence of faith to any degree. It is the definition of an ideal, of what faith is supposed to be like, of what its best is." He goes on to argue that for Calvin, there are "degrees of faith," and even "weak faith" (See *Calvin: A Guide for the Perplexed*, 81-82). It appears that Helm is anxious to qualify

Carl Trueman contends that "Calvin and the earlier reformers, in their reaction against the medieval church's virtual denial of any assurance, tended to emphasize this point somewhat in their rhetoric of faith."[1023] Yet, Calvin's emphatic insistence on assurance as the very essence of faith was far more than rhetorical. It was grounded in his conviction that Christ died for the world and that therefore the believer had a warrant to be sure of his salvation by looking to Christ.[1024]

At the same time, faith can find repose not only in the work of Christ, but also in its ultimate grounding in the very nature of God:

> He alone is truly a believer who, convinced by a firm conviction that God is a kindly and well-disposed Father toward him, promises himself all things on the basis of his generosity; who, relying upon the promises of divine benevolence toward him, lays hold on an undoubted expectation of salvation.[1025]

Although faith does not "comprehend" in the same way the mind does through sense perception, and it has to go beyond and above the

---

Calvin's strong statement regarding the certitude of faith because of his contention that for Calvin, Christ only died for the elect (*Calvin and the Calvinists*, 30). If Calvin taught a limited atonement, one could not look to Christ and there find assurance of salvation, because that would beg the question whether Christ in fact died *for that individual.* Thus, Calvinists like Helm, make much room for weak faith and the like and encourage one to look, not solely at Christ, but at empirical evidence "of our own spiritual and moral renovation" for signs of election (*Calvin and the Calvinists*, 26-28). Yet this would not yield certainty. So why would Calvin, if he thought of faith as a "firm and sure knowledge" also speak of weak faith? Perhaps he is speaking of our emotional struggles as we sometimes do not *feel* that we are in union with Christ. As a description of psychological states, faith can vary. But we are not saved by psychology, by the feeling of trusting. Calvin insists that we are saved by Christ *alone*, and in believing we are looking *away* from our deeds, our actions, and our feelings, and to the Christ who died for all, and the sure promises of God's Word concerning what Christ has done for us.

1023 Carl R. Trueman, "Historically---Calvin and Reformed Orthodoxy," *The Calvin Handbook*, ed. Herman J. Selderhuis, trans. Henry J. Baron, *et. al.* (Grand Rapids and Cambridge: William B. Eerdmans, 2009), 474.

1024 It is astonishing that in the course of a 395-page book, *The Quest for Full Assurance: The Legacy of Calvin and His Successors* (Edinburgh and Carlisle, Pennsylvania: Banner of Truth, 1999), Joel R. Beeke does not discuss the pastoral difficulties for assurance presented by the Calvinist doctrine of limited atonement.

1025 III.ii.16.

human mind in order to attain what it knows, it does, nevertheless, include a certain persuasion. "For the knowledge of faith consists in assurance rather than in comprehension."[1026]

Such a faith is not preoccupied with inner changes, or even "evidences" of election. Aquinas, in his treatment of the question, "Whether a Man Can Know that He Has Grace"[1027], argues precisely the opposite. But Calvin declares, "Hence we may judge how dangerous is the Scholastic dogma that we can discern the grace of God toward us only by moral conjecture, according as every man regards himself as not unworthy of it."[1028] By such a method, we could never be sure as to how the Lord feels toward us.

But that would be to turn grace on its head and the Gospel into works. For our righteousness is grounded solely in God's mercy, and participated in through union with Christ. This, faith apprehends.[1029] Faith is not grounded *intra nos*, but *extra nos*, such that we are bid to look away from ourselves to Christ, in whom all parts of our salvation are comprehended. This looking, however, must never turn upon itself such that the looking--i.e., the believing--becomes itself the ground for assurance. There were those in Calvin's day who taught this. "If, they say, you contemplate Christ, there is sure salvation: if you turn back to yourself, there is sure damnation."

No, says Calvin, Christ is not standing afar off, being somehow spiritually appropriated by earnest endeavors at believing on him. For a real change has taken place in the believer through Christ's engrafting him into his body. In this way we are made "participants not only in all his benefits, but also in himself." For Christ and his benefits cannot be separated for his Person and Work, Being and Act are one. And when by the Spirit Christ awakens faith within us, he also unites us with himself and gives us to participate, not in some distinct, isolated, or separate benefits or merits or grace, but in *himself, who is grace*. And this "fellowship by which he has bound himself to us" deepens day by day, so that "he grows more and more into one body with us until he becomes completely one with us."[1030]

1026 III.ii.14.
1027 *Summa*, la2ae.112, 5.
1028 III.ii.38.
1029 III.xv.1.
1030 III.ii.24.

Evangelical and Legal Repentance

Although Calvin has already expounded the doctrine of union with Christ by faith, the discussion would be incomplete without an "explanation of the effects we feel." What is the relation between the faith that embraces Christ and the godly life we are called to live? The cruciality of the topic can be seen in the fact that "the sum of the Gospel is held to consist in repentance and forgiveness of sins." But what is their relation?

Calvin's short answer is that "both repentance and forgiveness of sins--that is, newness of life and free reconciliation--are conferred on us by Christ, and both are attained through faith." This Christological perspective will control all that is said subsequently on the subject. Repentance and forgiveness are not human attainments, merited even partially by our works. They are gifts of Christ, conferred by him alone, and even their appropriation has no merit, but is by faith alone.

In a direct refutation of the doctrine held by Aquinas, Calvin countenances the argument that repentance must precede grace: "Christ, they say, and John in their preaching first urge the people to repentance, then add that the Kingdom of Heaven has come near."[1031] To which the Genevan reformer observes that mere order of syllables is no indication of logical thrust.

> For while Christ the Lord and John preach in this manner: "Repent, for the Kingdom of Heaven is at hand", do they not derive the reason for repenting from grace itself and the promise of salvation?" Accordingly, therefore, their words mean the same thing as if they said, "Since the Kingdom of Heaven has come near, repent."[1032]

These are momentous words. They constitute Calvin's "evangelical critique" of medieval theology. The "reason for repenting" is *not* so that grace may come, but because grace is here. Grace is not somehow achieved by human acts, for it is *logically and ontologically prior to repentance*. The only possibility of human repentance is constituted by grace. Because the Kingdom had arrived in the person of Christ, who *is grace*, he could summon people to repentance.

1031 III.iii.1; cf. *Summa*, 3a.85.
1032 III.iii.2.

Indeed, Calvin makes an even more startling statement: "a man cannot apply himself seriously to repentance without knowing himself to belong to God." Medieval preaching assumed that it was the individual's responsibility to cooperate with grace in order to *become* one of God's own, but Calvin says that they begin by knowing they already are. Since faith is knowledge, and is given in union with Christ, Calvin is saying that according to the Gospel, only the person who in faith knows himself to belong to God through the reconciliation accomplished in Christ can begin to repent. Therefore, rather than preceding salvation as a means to obtain it, repentance flows from it![1033] Calvin does not deny that empirically some may be smitten in conscience prior to coming to know or even taste grace. Christ uses all kinds of ways to draw us to himself. But even then, whether we know it or not, grace precedes true repentance, and indeed, even leads to repentance.

But Calvin traces it one important step further. Not only is grace prior to law, grace is anchored in the very being of God. Thus he quotes Psalm 130:4, "There is propitiation with thee . . . that thou mayest be feared." No one will ever reverence God or seriously apply himself to obedience unless he first trusts that God is "propitious" to him.[1034] The Christian life is not lived independently of God, striving as best one might. It is carried out with faith in the forgiveness, the propitiousness, indeed, the "fatherly favor" there already in the heart of God. And his nature is more than an inspiration. It is the ground of the entire Christian life, for God is gracious.

In light of the foregoing, Calvin's critique of the sacrament of penance proceeds along predictable lines. The "Scholastic Sophists," he observes, divide repentance into contrition, confession and satisfaction. A careful scrutiny of their doctrine is necessary, since they "torment themselves greatly with a gross error, that repentance is the 'second plank after shipwreck.'"[1035]

Calvin cautions his readers that this is no debate "over the shadow of an ass" since they claim that this three-fold penance comprises things necessary for forgiveness of sins. And so the Reformer's complaint is

---

1033 Cf. David C. Steinmetz, "The Theology of John Calvin," in *The Cambridge Companion to Reformation Theology*, ed. David Bagchi and David C. Steinmetz (Cambridge: Cambridge University Press, 2004), 124-125.
1034 III.iii.2.
1035 III.iv.1.

that free grace has thereby become conditional. And when conditions are placed upon the reception of forgiveness, "the conscience can have no rest at all, no peace with God, no assurance or security; but it continually trembles, wavers, tosses, is tormented and vexed, shakes, hates, and flees the sight of God."[1036] The acuteness of the problem lies in the fact that, for all these conditions intended to spell out clearly the way to grace, the individual is still left unsure as to whether he has adequately fulfilled these conditions.[1037]

To this position Calvin offers an evangelical critique. The Gospel is founded not upon human actions, but divine. Refreshment, rest, freedom, forgiveness, are all to be sought in God's mercy alone. Repentance for sins there must be, but such is never the cause of forgiveness. Indeed, "We have taught that the sinner does not dwell upon his own compunction or tears, but fixes both eyes upon the Lord's mercy alone."[1038] Therefore contrition is not a condition of forgiveness.

As for the second of the constituent parts of the medieval sacrament of penance, Calvin finds confession to priests nowhere enjoined in Scripture. Besides, "All priestly offices have been transferred to Christ and are fulfilled and completed in him."[1039] The sole priesthood of Christ is his response, because Christ as the One True Priest has offered himself as the victim, thereby taking all of our sins and guilt upon himself. Forgiveness of sins is found *in him*.

If we have sins, advises the Reformer, let us take them to the one who "forgives, forgets and wipes out, sins, let us confess our sins to him in order to obtain pardon. He is the physician: therefore let us lay bare our wounds to him." Therefore, a human priest is superfluous. We can take refuge in the Lord's goodness and mercy and lovingkindness.[1040]

As for the third part of penance, satisfaction, Rome taught that God relieves only the guilt of sins, but not the punishment. This latter must be redeemed by satisfaction. Pardon thus is contingent upon merit, upon human actions. To this Calvin replies that the free remission of sins is everywhere taught in Holy Writ. And the "cause and foundation of forgiveness are to be sought in [God's] goodness alone."[1041]

1036 III.iv.2.
1037 *Ibid.*
1038 III.iv.3.
1039 III.iv.4.
1040 III.iv.9.
1041 III.iv.24.

And God's goodness manifested itself in Christ, in whose name forgiveness is preached. Thus when Acts 10:43 says that forgiveness of sins is "by the name of Christ," declares Calvin:

> [I]t means that we bring nothing, we claim nothing of our own, but rely solely upon the commendation of Christ, as Paul declares, "God was in Christ reconciling the world to himself, not counting their trespasses against men on his account." And he immediately adds the how and the why: "For our sake he made him to be sin who was without sin.[1042]

Therefore, says Calvin, the Roman doctrine of penance deprives Christ of the honor due him. For those who (like Thomas) argue that in the initial forgiveness of sins, bestowed through baptism, "only the grace of God operates, but if we have fallen afterward, our works co-operate in obtaining the second pardon," are depriving the biblical testimony concerning Christ's offering a full satisfaction of its force. For there is a wide difference between saying that Christ has expiated our sins in himself and saying that we must expiate them by our works.[1043]

But for Calvin, the cross of Christ brooks no rival. When John announces that "If anyone has sinned, we have an advocate with the Father, Jesus Christ," and "he is the propitiation for our sins (I John 2:1-2)," and "I am writing to you, little children, because your sins are forgiven in his name (I John 2:12),"

> Surely he is addressing believers for whom, while he sets forth Christ as the propitiation of sins, he shows that there is no other satisfaction whereby offended God can be propitiated or appeased. He does not say: "God was once for all reconciled to you through Christ; now seek for yourself another means." But he makes him a perpetual advocate in order that by his intercession he may always restore us to the Father's favor; an everlasting propitiation by which sins may be expiated . . . he alone is the Lamb of God, he also is the sole offering for sins, the sole expiation, the sole satisfaction.[1044]

1042 III.iv.25.
1043 III.iv.27.
1044 III.iv.26.

Before concluding his debate with Rome concerning penance, he countenances one final objection, namely, that many scriptural testimonies suggest that God does indeed, having forgiven sin, proceed to inflict penalties. In a revealing passage, Calvin reasons that there are "two kinds of divine judgment," corresponding to two different groups of people. Toward God's enemies, he inflicts the "judgment of vengeance," while toward believers, he applies the "judgment of chastisement." By the first, God weighs the crimes and applies the penalties to them. But by the latter, he undertakes "correction and admonition."[1045]

And then Calvin tells us that "the one act is the act of a judge, the other, of a father."[1046] While intended to explain the different ways in which God deals with sins, one might wonder whether such a distinction is, at the end of the day, all that helpful. For it implies that God has two faces, indeed, almost two separate and contrary roles. Calvin even says that in the case of the chastisement of the saints, "there God takes upon himself the person of Father . . . " almost as if Fatherhood were a mask to be donned or set aside when it suits the divine will.[1047]

Yet Calvin attributes the distinction between the two roles to human perception:

> For he who, struck by the hand of God, thinks God a punishing Judge, cannot conceive of him as other than wrathful and hostile, cannot but detest the very scourge of God as curse and damnation. In short, he who feels that God still intends to punish him can never be persuaded that he is loved by God. But he who in the end profits by God's scourges is the man who considers God angry at his vices, but merciful and kindly toward himself.[1048]

For Calvin, God's love and mercy reside in His nature, but only the believer can see it. And this disparity is of course elsewhere attributed

---

1045 III.iv.31.

1046 *Ibid.*

1047 III.iv.33.

1048 Cf. III.xi.1, wherein Calvin avers that through union with Christ we "have in heaven instead of a Judge a gracious Father . . . ." In Sermon 25 on Deuteronomy, he warns his congregation that if they continue in their sins, and show themselves to be "unamendable", God will "lay away the person of a Father, and show himself to be a judge" and consume them by his fire. *Sermons on Deuteronomy*, 151.

to the will of God. So again we must ask Calvin whether this confidence in the will of God as somehow deeper than and separate from his love is warranted in light of the incarnation and all that he has said regarding Christ as the sole possibility of knowing God. Furthermore, is it helpful to see God as playing different roles, so that at times he is a Father while at others he is not?

Is there not a way to interpret the persistent stubbornness of the sinner in light of the fatherliness of God, such that God the Father weeps over the willful estrangement of his children? For Calvin, this could only be done at the expense of the sovereignty of God on the one hand and the freeness of grace on the other. The latter, Calvin believes, is manifested in the fact that if God is pictured as no more than hurting over his children's rejection, then it implies either an incapacity in God to effect his will, or a capacity in humans to choose whether or not to place themselves into grace. But perhaps Calvin has not taken seriously enough his own insistence that the only God we know is the God who has disclosed himself in Christ. Christ, it may be argued, embodied the divine love for everyone, and not a select few.

Nevertheless, Calvin's pastoral concern to help the Christian to see that God has born the guilt and the penalty of all his wrongdoing is evident on every page. And his further intent to assure the believer that he could look into the heart of God and see love and mercy there for him was also a tremendous contribution. He was right, it seems, to appeal to the person and work of Christ in his critique of penance. One only wishes he had carried it even further.

Justification by Faith

For Calvin, all that God has given to us of himself is enclosed in Christ. And by participating in a faith union with Christ, "we principally receive a double grace," justification and sanctification.[1049] Calvin tells us that he elected to discuss sanctification prior to justification in order to make clear that free grace did not preclude but rather led to holiness of life. Now he turns his attention to "the main hinge on which religion turns," which is justification by faith. From the vantage point of what God has done for us in Christ, all Christian piety is to be understood.[1050]

1049 Cf. Paul Van Buren, *Christ in Our Place. The Substitutionary Character of Calvin's Doctrine of Reconciliation*, 118-124.
1050 III.xi.1.

It will be recalled that for Thomas, justification embraces the movement from injustice to justice in the life of the individual. Thereby our attention is directed to the empirical changes which must transpire in the human person in order for this to happen. In this way, for all the wonders of God's grace, certain requirements and conditions emerge as necessary in order that his grace be actualized.

But Calvin turned resolutely away from medievalism on this score.

> Justified by faith is he who, excluded from the righteousness of works, grasps the righteousness of Christ through faith and clothed in it, appears in God's sight not as a sinner but as a righteous man. Therefore, we explain justification simply as the acceptance with which God receives us into his favor as righteous men. And we say it consists in the remission of sins and the imputation of Christ's righteousness.[1051]

This must be interpreted with constant reference to the saving humanity of Christ. When he assumed our flesh he stood in our place and offered up a life of faithfulness and obedience acceptable to the Father, culminating in his Cross.[1052] He is our righteousness by virtue of his obedience in our humanity. Consequently, "we must seek all the parts of our salvation in Jesus Christ, for we shall not find one drop of it anywhere else."[1053]

And now, Christ is "grasped and possessed by us in faith," and in that faith union what we are in him becomes ours in experience.[1054] Calvin's doctrine of justification is not a "legal fiction" as McLeod Campbell would later charge. Rather, it is God's acceptance of us for what we are in Jesus Christ. By his life of obedience in our flesh he sanctified himself. As such he is our sanctification. Yet his obedience

---

1051 III.xi.2.

1052 Cf. T. F. Torrance, "Justification: Its Radical Nature and Place in Reformed Doctrine and Life," *Theology in Reconstruction*, 155-156.

1053 Sermon 16 on Titus, *John Calvin's Sermons on Timothy and Titus*, 1224.

1054 Charles Partee thinks that "union with Christ" could be considered Calvin's "central dogma," in the sense that it serves as a "viewing point . . . present in Calvin's thinking about every other doctrine" (*The Sixteenth Century Journal*, vol. xviii, no. 2, 191-199). This is a helpful suggestion, since for Calvin even our knowing of God is never permitted outside of our *insitio in Christum*. However, it is lost sight of in his doctrine of reprobation.

was also our justification. Calvin quotes Romans 5:19, "We are made righteous by Christ's obedience," interpreting it as saying that "we are reckoned righteous before God in Christ and apart from ourselves. Christ's righteousness is therefore imputed to us, not as a way of obscuring our true condition, but as a way of underscoring who we are in Christ, because he has taken our place in his Person, and of drawing our attention to what we will be like, for he is our future.

Calvin explains that when God justifies us by Christ's intercession, "he absolves us not by the confirmation of our own innocence, but by the imputation of righteousness, so that we who are not righteous in ourselves may be reckoned as such in Christ."[1055] For justification has nothing to do with our performing "works of the law." It is rather "the mere benefit of Christ . . . received by faith."

In his dispute with Andreas Osiander, Calvin found occasion to clarify the nature of this union of the believer with Christ. While Osiander alleged that our unity with Christ is constituted by an intermingling of Christ's essence with ours, Calvin argues that we are "united with Christ by the secret power of his Spirit."[1056] In this way, the union is a relational one, upheld by the Spirit.

Osiander further said, according to Calvin, that "we are substantially righteous in God by the infusion both of his essence and of his quality." To this the Reformer responded that we become like Christ, not by a transfusion of essence, but by the power of the Spirit in such a way that our righteousness is always "in his person", viz., in Christ. And we are "justified by the grace of the Mediator alone," and not by any essential righteousness of our own.

Calvin also charges Osiander with confusing justification with sanctification, for by the former Christ's righteousness is imputed to us, while by the latter we are remade in the image of God by the Spirit. But both of these are to be found in Christ.[1057]

> [A]s Christ cannot be torn into pieces, so these two
> which we perceive in him together and conjointly are
> inseparable --namely, righteousness and sanctification.
> Whomever, therefore, God receives into grace, on them

1055 III.xi.3.
1056 III.xi.5.
1057 Cf. III.xvi.1.

he at the same time bestows the spirit of adoption, by
whose power he remakes them to his own image.[1058]

Therefore justification is not by essential righteousness, but by faith. Yet
faith itself does not confer justification, for human faith will always be
weak and imperfect. "God alone justifies." Faith is more like a vessel:
we come "empty and with the mouth of our soul open to seek Christ's
grace . . . ."[1059]

The heart of Osiander's error is his grounding our redemption in
the deity of Christ rather than in his humanity. In so doing he would
"lead us away from the priesthood of Christ." For Christ, declares
Calvin, reconciled us to the Father "in his flesh" and in that way gave
us righteousness. His divinity was also crucial, however, that he might
serve as Mediator between God and humankind, and as the only source
of righteousness. For Christ gives righteousness as God and receives it
as man.[1060]

When we are joined to Christ as members to their Head, then, what
is his becomes ours. In that "mystical union" we are given to share
in Christ's gifts. Our righteousness is therefore not merely a matter
of imputation while we contemplate him outside ourselves from afar.
Rather, we are engrafted into his body and so made one with him. But
that union is such that we never live out of our powers, even acquired
ones. Our life is in Christ, in fellowship with him.

Alister McGrath shows that justification in Calvin's theology is
grounded in the union of the believer with Christ:

> Through faith, the believer is united with Jesus Christ
> in a spiritual union, in such a way that we are not only
> partakers of all his benefits, but also of himself (III.ii.24).
> All that Christ is becomes ours through faith. Through
> participating in him, we share in his benefits.[1061]

Yet the requisite faith is not a work performed in order to merit grace:
"By faith we come empty to him to make room for his grace in order

---

1058 III.xvi.6.
1059 III.xvi.7.
1060 III.xi.8.
1061 McGrath, *A Life of John Calvin*, 166.

that he alone may fill us." For grace is not an accidental quality of the human soul, but is none other than Christ himself. When he fills us, we receive all that there is of grace.[1062]

And the actual process of becoming righteous continues throughout life. At times the progress is slow, and our faith will totter if it pays attention to our performance.[1063] But faith knows that Christ is our future because he is our history.[1064]

The Double Decree

Not until Book III, Chapter 21, does Calvin broach his explication of "Eternal Election, By Which God Has Predestined Some to Salvation, Others to Destruction." Locating it as a subdivision of his discussion of salvation underscores his pastoral and evangelical concern to defend the doctrine of *sola gratia*.[1065] He is not concerned to address reprobates, but believers, and to assure them that their salvation is anchored securely in the unconditionally free grace of God. To that end, of course, he finds it necessary to refute detractors, who would ground election in foreknowledge of merit.

It is of more than passing interest that Calvin inaugurates his discussion of election by appealing to experience:[1066] "In actual fact, the covenant of life is not preached equally among all men, and among those to whom it is preached, it does not gain the same acceptance."[1067] Calvin, it seems, was confronted with a dilemma. God so loved the entire world that he gave his only Son that all aspects of our salvation

---

1062 III.xi.10.
1063 III.xi.11.
1064 Cf. Francois Wendel, *Calvin. The Origins and Developments of His Thought*, 255-262.
1065 Cf. T. F. Torrance, Introduction, John Calvin, *Tracts and Treatises on the Reformation of the Church*, vol. I, trans. Henry Beveridge, (Grand Rapids: Eerdmans, 1958), vi.
1066 Cf. III.xxii.7. Wendel thinks that Calvin developed his doctrine of reprobation from the experience of the rejection of the preaching of the word by so many (*op. cit.*, 266-67). Against him, Harro Hopfl thinks that Calvin simply interpreted Scripture as faithfully as he knew how. *The Christian Polity of John Calvin*, (Cambridge, Cambridge University Press, 1985), 228-32. Certainly Calvin *did think* his doctrine was scriptural. But he also seems to take his empirical observation as in some sense a starting point: "If all men in general bowed the knee before Christ, election would be general; now in the fewness of believers a manifest diversity appears" (II.xxii.7).
1067 III.xxi.1; cf. III.xxii.1.

might be accomplished in him. The atonement is universal in scope. Yet empirical observation proves that all have not accepted this gospel.[1068] If we attribute the diversity to human freedom, then we underestimate the depravity of human nature on the one hand and the graciousness of grace on the other. For if human aspirations and inclinations and decisions are permitted to forge the final link between God and humankind, then grace becomes little more than assistance and individuals are at the end of the day left to their own resources.

Calvin already had at his disposal a ready answer in his doctrine of providence. Although discussed half a volume earlier, its influence is never far away.[1069] For God actively governs and decrees all motions in the entire universe. Therefore his will alone is the explanation for the disparity. And so Calvin says,

> In this diversity the wonderful depth of God's judgment is made known. For there is no doubt that this variety also serves the decision of God's eternal election. If it is plain that it comes to pass by God's bidding that salvation is freely offered to some while others are barred from access to it, at once great and difficult questions spring up, explicable only when reverent minds regard as settled what they may suitably hold concerning election and predestination.[304]

This is not a doctrine Calvin arrives at lightly or casually. Despite the caricatures, he is never the cold logician or the legally-trained jurist whose stern objective it is to exact the full penalties of the law upon sinners.[1070] He acknowledges that the issue is "baffling" to many.

His prime concern is for believers, that they not fall into the trap of works-righteousness. Indeed,

> [W]e shall never be clearly persuaded ... that our salvation flows from the wellspring of God's free mercy until we come to know eternal election, which illumines God's grace by this contrast: that he does not indiscriminately

---

1068 Cf. Charles Partee, "Calvin and Experience," *Scottish Journal of Theology*, vol. 26, no. 2, (1973), 180-181.
1069 Cf. Richard Muller, *Christ and the Decree*, 22-23.
1070 III.xxi.1.

adopt all into the hope of salvation but gives to some what he denies to others.[1071]

Indeed, God "utterly disregarded works" in his election. He was not concerned with any prior actions or attitudes or intentions we might hope to contribute. Not a smidgeon of our salvation is due to us. It comes "solely from God's mere generosity."[1072] Calvin is clearly the pastor here, reassuring his flock that their redemption is sure, directing them away from their own efforts to the grace of God in Christ.[1073] He is also the evangelist, urging sinners to embrace the gospel of free grace and come to God through the Lord Jesus Christ.

Before carrying the discussion further, Calvin issues a familiar *caveat*. There is no place here for human curiosity, for inquiring minds to wander dangerously and proudly, seeking in vain to scale the heights and sound the depths of "the sacred precincts of divine wisdom." God has revealed in his Word as much as he would have us know, and we must be content with that. Calvin, of course, was convinced of the scriptural basis for his doctrine of predestination.[1074]

Now, predestination is not grounded in foreknowledge. It is not as if God, seeing what individuals will do, merely ratifies their decision. By such reckoning, God "adopts as sons those whom he foreknows will not be unworthy of his grace; he appoints to the damnation of death those whose dispositions he discerns will be inclined to evil intention and ungodliness." But Calvin denies this completely. God is always free to grant or withhold grace as he chooses.[1075]

Even the "subtlety of Thomas"[1076] that while foreknowledge of merits does not cause predestination, God nonetheless predestines persons to glory because of merits which he has decreed to bestow upon them in grace such that they will merit glory, is to be rejected. The grammar of merit is inappropriate here. "The Lord wills that in election we contemplate nothing but his mere goodness."

1071 *Ibid.*
1072 *Ibid.*
1073 So also T. H. L. Parker, *The Oracles of God,* 82-85; John H. Leith, *John Calvin's Doctrine of the Christian Life,* 122.
1074 III.xxi.2-xxii.7; cf. Hopfl, *The Christian Polity of John Calvin,* 227-239.
1075 III.xxii.1.
1076 III.xxii.9; cf. *Summa,* 1a.23, 5.

Calvin does teach a kind of foreknowledge, however. When he uses the word, he explains, "we mean that all things always were, and perpetually remain, under his eyes, so that to his knowledge there is nothing future or past, but all things are present." And predestination is nothing other than

> God's eternal decree, by which he compacted with himself what he willed to become of each man. For all are not created in equal condition; rather, eternal life is foreordained for some, eternal damnation for others. Therefore, as any man has been created to one or other of these ends, we speak of him as predestined to life or death.[1077]

The problem which emerges for Calvin, it would seem, is that there is nothing here about the love of God. His will is spoken of in abstraction from the rest of his nature, as if it were, so to speak, located in an inner layer, while the outer layer of goodness, justice, love and grace is only addressed according to the divine decision. Thus with respect to one individual God may choose to act in a loving way, and with respect to another, in a just way. In this way Calvin can protect his understanding of the freeness of grace, but at the expense of taking with full seriousness the boundless love of God, his familial purposes in creation, and the universality of his work in Christ. Calvin has here departed from his own insight that the will of God be must comprehended in the light of the self-disclosure of God in Christ. And as a result, *the freedom of grace in its unrestrictedness* is lost.

This disparity in the way God's will interacts with different aspects of his nature is seen throughout Calvin's treatment of the doctrine. The Israelites were chosen "solely by God's freely given love," as were the patriarchs. Love here is the same as grace, for it is freely given, unmerited, and bestowed upon the unworthy. At the same time God chose not to elect others who were equally unworthy.[1078]

Voluntaristic leanings are evident in the entire notion that in God's election, his will is the sole cause. He even makes explicit reference to such a notion. In the election of Israel

---

1077 III.xxi.5; cf. *Concerning the Eternal Predestination of God*, trans. J. K. S. Reid, (London: James Clarke, 1961), 121.
1078 III.xxi.5.

God has already shown that in his mere generosity he has not been bound by any laws but is free, so that equal apportionment of grace is not to be required of him. The very inequality of his grace proves that it is free.[1079]

But this is true not only of nations, but of individuals as well. By his "secret plan," God freely decides whom he will elect and whom he will reject. And this election embraces perseverance as a necessary corollary. Those whom God foreordains to salvation are "engrafted to their Head", Christ, and as such are "never cut off from salvation." Their election is therefore "effectual." This does not mean that Christ did not atone for the sins of the world after all. Salvation is complete in Christ. But the reprobate are never engrafted into Christ, which is to say, they are denied the working of the Spirit whereby the individual is united to Christ through faith.[1080]

In tandem with his doctrine of universal atonement was his conviction that all are summoned to come to Christ. For later Calvinists to teach that all ought to be commanded to come to a Christ who did not die for them is puzzling at best and pastorally cruel at worst. At least Calvin did hold that on the basis of Christ's saving work, all are invited to come.[1081]

Yet Calvin's position was not without its problems, as others were wont to point out: "Some object that God would be contrary to himself if he should universally invite all men to him but admit only a few as elect." In reply the Genevan Reformer takes refuge in a sort of voluntarism:

For he who threatens that while it will rain upon one city there will be drought in another, and who elsewhere announces a famine of teaching, does not bind himself by a set law to call all men equally. And he who, forbidding Paul to speak the word in Asia, and turning him aside from Bithynia, draws him into Macedonia thus shows that he has the right to distribute this treasure to whom he pleases.[1082]

1079 III.xxi.6; cf. *On the Eternal Predestination of God*, 115-120.
1080 III.xxi.7.
1081 III.xxii.10; cf. Sermon 13, *Sermons on Deuteronomy*, 77.
1082 III.xx.ii.10.

What is more, God does not give the rest the eyes and ears necessary to receive the word. Therefore they are blind because the Lord wanted them to be blind. They are obstinate because he ordained it so. We are "warned" to "seek no cause outside his will."[1083] If the sheer will of God is insufficient to silence detractors, Augustine will be summoned to the witness stand: "You wish to argue with me? Marvel with me, and exclaim, 'O depth!' Let both of us agree in fear, lest we perish in error."[1084]

Calvin is right in reminding us not to presume to pass judgment upon the Majesty of God. His judgments are inscrutable, his ways past finding out. But if such an interpretation of the divine majesty flies in the face of God's self-disclosure in Christ, ought we not take a second look at the doctrine?

It will already be seen that Calvin sees the divine will as equally active in reprobation. It is not an incidental accompaniment to the central doctrine, which is election. Both decrees are mandated with equal ultimacy by God.[1085]

> Election itself could not stand except as set over against
> by reprobation . . . . Therefore those whom God passes
> over, he condemns: and this he does for no other reason
> than that he wills to exclude them from the inheritance
> which he predestines for his own children.[1086]

When Calvin is charged with making God look more like a capricious tyrant than a law-abiding judge, he replies that God retains the right to do what he likes. It would seem as if Calvin is conceding the criticism. For he says that investigating the causes of God's will is "very wicked." After all,

> His will is, and rightly ought to be, the cause of all things
> that are. For if it has any cause, something must precede
> it, to which it is, as it were, bound; this is unlawful to
> imagine. For God's will is so much the highest rule of

1083 III.xx.ii.11.
1084 III.xxii.10, quoting Augustine's *Sermons* xxvi.12, 13, cited by McNeill, *in loc.*
1085 *Concerning the Eternal Predestination of God*, 68; cf. Heinrich Quistorp, *Calvin's Doctrine of Last Things*, trans. Harold Knight, (Richmond: John Knox Press, 1955), 145-46.
1086 III.xxiii.1.

righteousness that whatever he wills, by the very fact that he wills it, must be considered righteous.[1087]

This could be interpreted as thoroughgoing voluntarism. God can do whatever he likes. He is bound by no rules. Everything he wills, simply by virtue of the fact that he wills it, is right. So if he has willed a double decree, its apparent injustice is irrelevant. But Calvin goes on to attack the notion of the *potentia absoluta*:

> And we do not advocate the fiction of "absolute might"; [*absoluta potentia*] because this is Profane, it ought rightly to be hateful to us. We fancy no lawless god who is a law unto himself . . . but the will of God is not only free of all fault but is the highest rule of perfection and even the law of all laws.[1088]

In saying that God is not a law unto himself but the law of all laws, he seems to be arguing that there is a continuity between the laws he has ordained for the world and the law by which he himself abides. Both stem from the same source, and God's law, rather than operating on some other self-defined perfection, abides by the same perfection which is embodied in his law. In fine, there is no dualism of ordained and absolute powers, there is only one realm, in which God wills and acts in harmony with his being. Yet this still does not explain what appears to be injustice in the twin decrees. Calvin says concerning Jacob and Esau, "In them all things are equal, yet God's judgment of each is different. For he receives one and rejects the other."[1089]

Nevertheless Calvin wants to say that God's treatment of the reprobate is not above justice. Reasoning that since the reprobate are "vitiated by sin" and therefore by "condition of nature subject to the judgment of death," God's rejection of them is in accordance with "the fairest reckoning of justice."[1090]

Calvin can argue each side of the decree with compelling logic. The elect are predestined to glory because God in free mercy wills it so. The

---

1087 III.xxiii.2.
1088 *Ibid.*
1089 III.xxii.5; cf. Benjamin Charles Milner, Jr., *Calvin's Doctrine of the Church*, (Leiden: Brill), 1970, 12-16.
1090 III.xxiii.3.

reprobate are foreordained to wrath because God wills that they receive what their natures deserve.[1091] Calvin occupies less certain ground when he attempts to make both statements, for he has difficulty in finding consistency in such a God. Moreover he is unable to tell us why God's nature as boundless love and mercy and grace has no effect on his reprobation of the wicked before the foundation of the world.

So anxious is Calvin to subject all to the will of God, that he even avers a thoroughgoing supralapsarianism: "in this miserable condition wherein men are now bound, all of Adam's children have fallen by God's will."[1092] If it is argued that Scripture nowhere says that God decreed the Fall, and that Adam had free choice to shape his own destiny, Calvin responds "where will that omnipotence of God be whereby he regulates all things according to his secret plan, which depends solely upon itself?"[1093] Clearly, there is an unbroken line in Calvin's thought from providence to predestination.

Indeed, the only reason Adam's fall "irremediably involved so many peoples, together with their infant offspring, in eternal death" was that "it so pleased God." Calvin admits that "the decree is dreadful," but he is undaunted. When God decreed the Fall, he did not merely permit it to happen: "what he has willed will of necessity come to pass."[1094]

It may seem that such a doctrine would be unpreachable, but Calvin frames it in such a way as to be less devastating. Following Augustine,[1095] he tells us not to address the people in this way: "If you do not believe, the reason is that you have already been divinely destined for destruction." This could drive them to despair or even outright evil. But since we are not privy to the divine ordination concerning individuals, we should always preach a universal invitation.[1096]

Indeed, in a sermon on Deuteronomy Calvin even went so far as to say that each of his listeners ought to apply God's promises of mercy to themselves in particular: "It is to thee that he speaketh when he saith,

---

1091 Cf. e.g., III.xxiii.8.
1092 III.xxiii.4.
1093 III.xxiii.7.
1094 *Ibid.*
1095 *On the Gift of Perseverance* xiv.37; xv.38; xvi.40, referred to in III.xxiii.14, cited by McNeill *in. loc.*
1096 III.xxiii.14.

Come unto me all ye that are weary and overladen and I will refresh you. *Thou art of that number.*"[1097]

Conclusion

In reading Calvin, one is continually impressed by the pastoral concern underlying his entire theology. Impatient with abstract speculation, uninterested in philosophical systems, he wants to preach and teach the Gospel in terms of *sola gratia*. God has already given himself to the world in the person of his Son, accomplishing a costly atonement in his life, death and resurrection. All that remains is for hearers of this Good News to "come to our Lord Jesus Christ." He alone is the Savior.

Furthermore, Christ is not only the exclusive way to God soteriologically, but epistemologically as well: "The sole means of retaining as well as restoring pure doctrine is to set Christ before our eyes, just as He is with all His blessings."[1098] In fact, "God is comprehended in Christ alone."[1099] Therefore, we must not contemplate the will of God in abstraction from Christ. Christ "faithfully reveals to us that will as it was from the beginning and ever shall be."[1100]

Following this theological program, Calvin anchors the concept of the will of God in the self-revelation of God in and through Christ so far as election is concerned. His wholehearted promulgation of unconditional election is nothing other than a defense of *sola gratia*. But for him, *sola gratia* ever remains the exegesis of *solus Christus*, for grace is not detachable from Christ, either as an infused habit, as in Aquinas, or as a "principle" of divine favor, as some Federal theologians would have it. Thus, by grounding the thought of the will of God in the self-disclosure of God in Christ, the freeness of grace in that it is *unmerited* is upheld.

It is true that his thoroughgoing defense of two-fold predestination is intended as a powerful emphasis on the undeserved, unconditional

---

1097 Sermon 26, *Sermons on Deuteronomy*, 157.

1098 Commentary on Colossians 1:12, *The Epistles of Paul the Apostle to the Galatians Ephesians, Philippians and Colossians*, trans. T. H. L. Parker, ed. David W. Torrance and Thomas F. Torrance, (Grand Rapids: Eerdmans, 1974).

1099 II.vi.4.

1100 I.xxiv.5; cf. T. H. L. Parker, *John Calvin*, (Hertfordshire: Lion Publishing, 1982), 48; T. F. Torrance, Introduction, *Tracts and Treatises on the Reformation of the Church*, v-xii.

grace of God which elects us, not in ourselves, but in Christ. He never tires of arguing that if it be conceded that all are elect in Christ, then the lack of faith on the part of some would be attributable to a defect in the grace of God, and the presence of faith in others must, at least partially, be attributed to human merit, whether conceived as better intentions or qualities or "use" of grace.

But where, theologically, does the Genevan reformer ground his concept of reprobation? He has forbidden us to examine predestination abstractly, in relation to God apart from his Son. And yet Calvin does just that! He supports his doctrine of the *decretum quidem horribile*, not on the basis of the Gospel, but of the absolute freedom of God, in a way that makes no reference to Jesus Christ at all. Instead he appeals to the naked will of God, who can do as he pleases.[1101]

It is true that Calvin carefully attempts to protect this doctrine from the charge of voluntarism, for God's might must not be seen as clashing against his justice. God cannot issue any decree without reference to his own being as just. But for all that, his refuge in the notion of a "secret will" of God, a will which bears no apparent relation to God's self-disclosure in his Son, and his frequent depiction of God as one who needs no reason other than that he wills a thing, would seem to substantiate our charge of "soteriological voluntarism."[1102]

Thus we see that when Calvin grounds his concept of the will of God in the self-disclosure of God the Father in his Son, the freeness of grace in all its *unmeritedness* is upheld, as is the case in his doctrine of election. Yet in his notion of reprobation, he departs from his own insights, basing his doctrine on an abstract will of God known apart from Christ. Consequently, the freeness of grace in all of its *unrestrictedness* is lost.

1101 Hence we cannot accept Alister McGrath's assertion that "Calvin's thought is thoroughly Christocentric" *(A Life of John Calvin*, 149).

1102 Gordon Spykman thinks that in Calvin's thought, God's sovereignty is "not one among several attributes of God: He *is* the sovereign, always in everywhere sovereign in creation, sovereign in our fall into sin, sovereign in the history of our redemption". "Sphere Sovereignty in Calvin and the Calvinist Tradition," *Exploring the Heritage of John Calvin*, ed. David E. Holwerda, (Grand Rapids: Baker, 1982), 188. Yet this overlooks Calvin's equal stress on God's fatherly nature disclosed in Christ, which significantly qualifies such a claim. God is not, as we have demonstrated, the absolute potentate of the voluntarists in Calvin's theology.

Moreover, we become unsure as to whether God-as-he-is-in-himself is truly merciful and fatherly and loving or not. We noted that Calvin speaks of God assuming the person of a father towards one human, while assuming the person of a judge to another. He tells us that while God is a father in himself, the reprobate are never given to know it. They only know him as a judge.

Are we to think of "layers" or "tiers" in the being of God such that God's innermost being is nothing other than Absolute Freedom, while the outer layer might comprise characteristics such as forgiveness, grace, and judgment? But once we say that God can choose whether to act in a loving or a judging manner, it is not clear that we can continue to maintain that God is truly loving in his heart at all. And so Calvin's Double Decree would seem to drive a wedge between God in himself and God as disclosed in his Word, in a way that calls into question the integrity of this revelation.

It now remains for us to demonstrate how McLeod Campbell's theology, by recalling Calvin to his premises concerning revelation, addresses caveats in both Aquinas and in the Genevan Reformer. For the Scottish preacher, all of our knowledge of God must be controlled by the disclosure of the Father in and through the Son. The consequences of this for Campbell's interpretation of the will of God as it relates to grace, law and the character of God will now be explored.

CHAPTER 3

THE CHRIST-CENTERED THEOLOGY
OF MCLEOD CAMPBELL

Introduction

We have explored some of the ways in which Aquinas and Calvin ground their doctrines of predestination in a will of God known outside of Christ. But the result has been a significant diminution of the freeness of grace. In the thought of Aquinas, God as the Uncaused Cause governs the motions of all creatures by his active will, predestinating some to eternal loss and others, equally undeserving, to eternal bliss. Thus the freedom of grace in its *unrestrictedness* is lost. Moreover a certain "soteriological voluntarism" has been detected therein.

Furthermore, while Thomas wants to attribute the whole of salvation to grace, he concedes enough to notions of cooperative grace and merit, to deprive grace of *unmeritedness* in the fullest sense of the term. Here, too, it would seem that the concept of the will of God has been separated from the self-revelation of God in Christ.

Calvin's critique of medieval theology is anchored in his insistence on the centrality of Christ as the only means of restoring and upholding true doctrine. God is not to be apprehended anywhere but in Christ. Thus he understands the will of God for the elect in the light of God's self-revelation, upholding the unconditional freeness of grace in all its *unmeritedness*.

But his argument shifts when he turns to the notion of reprobation. This is not a doctrine he learns from the self-revelation of God in Christ. It is rather based on an abstract will of a God who can do as he pleases. This kind of 'soteriological voluntarism' results from Calvin's dividing the thought of the will of God from the self-disclosure of God in Christ. In this way the freeness of grace in all its *unrestrictedness* is lost in Calvin's theology.

Having compared the two great systematic thinkers of the Christian Church, we are prepared to consider the contributions of this unusual nineteenth-century Scottish preacher, John McLeod Campbell. Although reared and schooled in a Calvinist church, he did not develop a fondness for Calvin's theology. He does not seem to differentiate between the teachings of the Reformer and those of his later proponents. For him, Calvin and Calvinism were of the same cloth, and neither were altogether true to the Scriptures. His theology was self-consciously shaped by the Bible in the light of his parish ministry.[1103]

And yet, for all that, Campbell's insights bear remarkable similarities to many of Calvin's. Although the former had no use for the *decretum quidem horribile*, he shared with the Genevan Reformer the great concern for the nature of God as gracious within his heart of hearts. Calvin had set out to confine all knowledge of God within Christological bounds, he at times departed from his own premises and lapsed into a kind of voluntarism abstracted from God's nature as love.

Campbell met such teachings in his day with a stout insistence on beginning and ending with the self-revelation of God in Christ.[1104] In this manner, he was really recalling Calvin to his own premises.

॰ Calvin taught that grace was not a state into or out of which one may fall, a gift separate from God with which one must cooperate in order for justification to result. Grace cannot be divided or distinguished from God because it is nothing more than God's self-condescension in Christ, his self-giving for sinful humankind. This represents a sharp contrast with St. Thomas, who undertook complicated investigations into how Christ merited grace for us and then mediates it to us through the sacraments. But the moment grace is detached from the being of God, it becomes subject to prior conditions. It was Campbell who exposed the ironic position of the Calvinists, who wanted no truck with Rome, and yet often adopted similar positions. They, like Aquinas, taught that there were certain things which the would-be Christian must do in order to actualize salvation. At times they spoke of faith as if it were a condition of justification.[1105]

Their doctrine of the double decree gave them no assurance, and so they proposed a system of evidences, which could be discerned through

---

1103 *Memorials of John McLeod Campbell, D. D.*, vol. I, ed. Donald Campbell, (London: Macmillan, 1873), 18-19.
1104 John McLeod Campbell, *Reminiscences and Reflections*, (London: Macmillan, 1873), 132-33.
1105 *Nature of the Atonement* [henceforth, *Nature*], (London: James Clarke, 1959), 98-100, 394; *Reminiscences and Reflections*, 129-34.

self-examination in light of God's law. Unfortunately such investigation only tended to fling the inquirer further into his despair, because no one finds perfect righteousness in his empirical performance.[1106] But Campbell insisted, along with Calvin, that assurance is of the essence of faith, for faith's focus is not upon oneself and one's attainments but upon the righteousness of God in Christ.[1107] Justification is being accepted for who we are in Christ.

Calvin taught a universal atonement, and in this Campbell is in full accord. The mind of the Father disclosed in the Son is one of pure love, and God so loved the world that he gave his only son so that whoever believes in him should not perish but have eternal life.[1108]

But Campbell saw clearly that even a universal atonement will not calm the conscience apart from a clear apprehension that God in Christ invites every sinner home to himself. And this invitation is anchored eternally in the very nature of God, for God is love, is grace, in his innermost being.[1109]

This is precisely where his interpretation of the will of God is so important to Campbell, because the Calvinists of his day did not deny the love of God.[1110] Some argued that love is not a "necessary" divine attribute, as justice is. It remains 'there' in the divine being, but God does not necessarily will to act in love. Therefore God may not will to express his love in the histories of some individuals.[1111]

But, contends Campbell, an act willed by God "simply because he wills it, ---can never, by any light in it, make the character of him whose act it is known to us." Thus presented, "the atonement *ceases to reveal* that *God is love*." To be elected by a mere act of will gives no indication as to who God "essentially is."[1112] In this way, Campbell's opponents had detached the thought of the will of God from the self-revelation of

1106 *Reminiscences and Reflections*, 147-151; cf. *Nature*, 223.
1107 *The Whole Proceedings Before the Presbytery of Dumbarton and the Synod of Glasgow and Ayr in the Case of the Rev. John McLeod Campbell, Minister of Row*, (Greenock: R. B. Lusk, 1831), 44-50.
1108 *Nature*, 59-64, 73.
1109 *Ibid.*, 76-103.
1110 *Ibid.*, 67-68.
1111 See Michael Jinkins' Ph.D. thesis, "Atonement and the Character of God: A Comparative Study in the Theology of the Atonement in Jonathan Edwards and John McLeod Campbell," University of Aberdeen, 1990, 172-188; 203-212; 311-319.
1112 *Nature*, 64-65.

_od in Christ. "It would be well that these deep reasoners had used the life of Christ more as their light."[1113]

For the Scottish preacher, "the Son alone could reveal the Father." Therefore Jesus continually reminded his disciples that "in that perfect obedience to the will of God which they saw in Him, they were contemplating the doing of the will of the Father by the Son."[1114]

Investigating Campbell's concept of the will of God in relation to his doctrine of revelation in Christ sheds light on the heart of his theology, because he is sure that Jesus Christ, in all his teaching and action, leads us straight as an arrow to the will of God, which always expresses the loving heart of God.[1115] In the Son's revealing the Father, "we have to do directly with the will of God; that is to say, His will as His mind and character, ---that in respect of which we say, God is love."[1116] For McLeod Campbell, there is no will in God that is not the will of the Father, who is love. As we shall see, the implications of this for our understanding of grace are profound, for by grounding his concept of the will of God in his self-revelation in and through the Son, the freeness of grace in all its *unmeritedness* as well as its *unrestrictedness* is upheld.

In his thought, the reciprocity and constitutive identity of the Father-Son relation are fundamental for our apprehension of God: "We see the Father when we see the Son, not merely because of an identity of will and character in the Father and Son, but because a father as such is known only in relation to a son."[1117] What do we see concerning the Father through the Son? We see that God *is love*. The incarnation discloses the "love of the Father of Spirits to men his offspring," and all interpretations of the atonement which fail to reckon with that love are to be rejected.[1118]

In fact, "the Scriptures represent the love of God as the cause and the atonement as the effect."[1119] The deep-seated conviction that love

---

1113 *Ibid.,* 64.

1114 *Ibid.,* 73.

1115 Cf. Jinkins, *Love is of the Essence: An Introduction to the Theology of John McLeod Campbell* (Edinburgh: St. Andrews Press, 1993), 8-10.

1116 *Ibid.,* xxxvi, xxxvii.

1117 *Ibid.,* lii.

1118 *Ibid.,* xxviii.

1119 *Ibid.,* 20.

is God's fundamental nature will determine the whole of McLeod Campbell's theology, although not in the manner of a relentless pursuit of a chain of logical deductions, but by "reverently learning" from the history of our redemption recorded in Holy Writ.[1120]

Our investigations into Campbell's understanding of grace will not be restricted to those texts in which the actual word appears, because the concept of grace is everywhere present. He affirms in common with high Calvinists the "sinner's dependence upon free grace for pardon,"[1121] but wishes to probe more deeply into the relation between incarnation and atonement, between the being of God and the actions of God for our salvation in order to expose what he believes to be the true nature of God as a Father who has opened the way to his very heart by his accomplishments in his Son.

In Christ, God has sent, not another, but himself for us and for our salvation. The powerful emphasis on Christ as "God in our nature"[1122] sounds throughout his Row Sermons, to the point where he will speak of the "blood of God shed for the remission of sins,"[1123] God's love is "self-sacrificing love."[1124] In the New Testament, the atonement is not depicted as the "sacrifice [of] one creature for another, for 'Christ is God,' and "*God* takes credit to *Himself* for the love that Christ manifests in dying for us."[1125]

When McLeod Campbell wrote to his daughter in 1871 that "I see the grace of God in the gift of eternal life,"[1126] he was not saying anything other than he had been saying all along as Pastor of Row parish, as the minister of Blackfriars Street Chapel, or as the writer of *Nature of the Atonement, Thoughts on Revelation,* or *Christ the Bread of Life.* The thread that runs so true through all of his teaching is that *grace is God's self-giving in and for humanity.* This can be seen in his exposition of I

1120 *Ibid.,* xxix.

1121 *Ibid.,* 12.

1122 Sermon VIII, *Inghin an Reachdaire,* no. 140, (London: F. Collins, J. Nisbet, and T. Flinn, n. d.), 21. See Peter Kenneth Stevenson, *God in our Nature. The Incarnational Theology of John McLeod Campbell,* (Eugene, Oregon: Wipf and Stock, 2006).

1123 Sermon III, *ibid.,* 7.

1124 *Nature,* 25.

1125 *Ibid.,* 26-27.

1126 *Memorials of John McLeod Campbell, D.D.,* ed. Donald Campbell, vol. II, (London: Macmillan, 1877), 320.

John 5:11, "And this is the record, that God hath given to us eternal life, and this life is in his Son." Eternal life is not a future happiness which an individual might possess only in hope in the present. "Eternal life . . . [is] that life which was with the Father before the world was, and which is manifested in the Son."[1127] Indeed, eternal life is the life that God lives, the blessedness, the happiness and holiness which are all one in him by virtue of the undivided simplicity that is in Him.

Therefore, explains McLeod Campbell to his parishioners, "when God declares that he has given us eternal life, I understand him as meaning nothing less than his giving us a participation in this very life which he had from all eternity."[1128] Indeed, the entire "history of the incarnation" was motivated by this single purpose. God's "high purpose" was not that we might receive safety, or be delivered from penalties, although these are accomplished in Christ. Rather, God came and took our flesh so that we might become "partakers of the divine nature," and in this way share in his holiness, his happiness, his love.[1129]

If grace is God's self-giving, then it cannot be something other than God, detachable from his being and therefore perhaps subject to conditions for its bestowal:

> When we hear of 'grace given to us,' we are apt to think of some endowment bestowed on ourselves, some *portion* of grace intrusted to us to profit withal, and so when we speak of the 'grace of baptism' as a thing which we may stain, the gift appears to be thought of as something which we may *possess*, instead of something which has been revealed in Christ, and which we can only *abide in* by abiding in Christ . . . .[1130]

1127 *Nature*, 14.

1128 Sermon I, *Sermons and Lectures*, vol. I, (Greenock: R. B. Lusk, 1832), 8-9; cf. Sermon III, *Inghin an Reachdaire*, 7.

1129 *Ibid.*, cf. Sermon XIII, *Sermons and Lectures*, vol. I, 303; Sermon XVI, *Sermons and Lectures*, vol. I, 352.

1130 *Bible Readings*, (Edinburgh: Edmonston and Douglas, 1864), 116. This book, although published anonymously, was bound together with *Fragments of Truth*, published by David Douglas (Edinburgh, 1898). The latter was, as the preface by Donald Campbell tells us, largely composed of expositions by John McLeod Campbell. Two were authored by A. J. Scott and one by Thomas Erskine of Linlathen. *Bible Readings* was, in this writer's opinion, also mostly written by McLeod Campbell, in light of the many phrases and thoughts characteristic of his writing, e.g., the "yearnings of a true

We can only abide in grace by abiding in Christ, God incarnate, because grace is God in his self-giving. Thus eternal life, seen as the "righteousness of the Son of God in humanity," is "itself the gift of God to us in Christ--to be ours as Christ is ours--to be partaken in as He is partaken in--to be our life as He is our life."[1131]

Grace, for Campbell, is love in action. Love is the nature of God, which pursues humankind even in the face of its determined enmity against Him. Supremely, the human race is given to see the very grace of God in the "blood of God shed for the remission of their sins."[1132] In the atoning life and death of Christ we find that God's love is not a love which can be contented to remain within itself.[1133]

Furthermore, love is not an occasional posturing of the divine will. This was Campbell's great criticism of Jonathan Edwards, that the latter made love a sporadic act of God's will rather than his innermost nature. For John McLeod Campbell, God *is* love. There is no more profound predication of the divine being than this. He embraces other characteristics as well, but they equally express this love of God. Therefore we must confess that "every attribute of God tells one tale-- and that is that God desires to bless him."[1134] For this one attribute, that God is love, is the "foundation of all."[1135] Beyond or beneath this we cannot go, for our doctrine of God must be controlled by the incarnation and cross: "on *this foundation all rests*, in Christ's having declared the Father's name; Christ having shewn us what the Father's love is, that he yearns over us with a love that was contented to die for us . . ."[1136]

father's heart" (2); the serpent in the Garden casting doubt on "God's fatherliness" (28); that in Christ which pleased the Father was "the spirit of perfect filial trust---the spirit which did not its own will but the will of Him who sent Him . . ." (58); "conscience is the ear of the Spirit" (76); the blood of Christ enables us to come to God, not by "changing God's heart toward us, but by so revealing it that we can venture back to Him; and more than that, by making for us--in our name, that confession which the righteous Father requires" (78). Stevenson, in his *God in our Nature*, (117-118), notes several references implying feminine authorship of Lesson VIII (43, 49, and 51-52), and suggests Miss Jane Gourlay, who recorded and edited *Fragments* as the writer. The other lessons bear strong evidence of being written by McLeod Campbell.
1131 *Nature*, 154.
1132 Sermon III, *Inghin an Reachdaire*, 7.
1133 Sermon XX, *Sermons and Lectures*, vol. II, 28.
1134 Sermon IX, *ibid.,* vol. I, 190.
1135 *Ibid.,* 191
1136 Sermon XIII, *Ibid.,* 307.

But love is nothing other than God himself in his self-giving. Therefore "Jesus Christ is the gift of the Father's love, because Jesus Christ is God, who is love." We cannot understand the incarnation or the sufferings of Christ, the just for the unjust apart from this. "There is no explanation but this, 'God is love.'"[1137]

Indeed, Campbell sees it as the most compelling evidence of our fallenness that people are naturally "unwilling to be taught" that God is love to them individually:

> The great thing which each man is unwilling to admit is God's love to *himself*--God's *free, unbought--unmerited love*--God's love to man, independent of what man is--a pure feeling coming out upon him, even when there is nothing in him that God can esteem.[1138]

We resist God's love more than anything else, because it constitutes an assault on our pride, and exposes our guilt. What is more, we do not want to know ourselves to be debtors "for a love which [we] have never yet acknowledged, never yet returned . . ."[1139]

But the practical consequences, Campbell realized, were very great. It meant that God's love is universal.

> If love be of God's character--if it be of God's substance--if God *is love*, then God loves every man. Yea the person who limits the love of God to some, has actually denied that there is love in God at all, for it would not be love, but mere partiality or caprice.[1140]

And as the young pastor in his kirk by the Gareloch looked out at his congregation, filled with desperate hearts, who could not venture to say whether Christ loved them or not, whether Christ died for them or not, whether there was forgiveness in the heart of God for them, he knew that it led to a spiritual despair, and worse, to all kinds of wicked living.[1141]

1137 Sermon IX, *Ibid.*, 188.

1138 Sermon XVI, *Ibid.*, 382-3.

1139 *Ibid.*

1140 *Ibid.*, 386.

1141 John McLeod Campbell, *The Everlasting Gospel. Notes of a Sermon by the Rev. J. M. Campbell, Minister of Row*, Dumbartonshire, pamphlet published by R. B. Lusk: Greenock, 1830, 30-31.

But if God is love, then he is loving in all his works and ways, and the Cross becomes the signal disclosure of his heart as loving towards every individual without exception.[1142]

So McLeod Campbell told his Row parishioners that in all his preaching, "my great object [has] been to direct your hearts into the love of God."[1143] In expounding the inner nature of God as unconditionally loving, he sought to persuade them that each of them had a warrant for coming to God the Father, for trusting in him wholeheartedly. But their trust was not directed to a naked majesty, awesome in power and inscrutable in his innermost attitude toward puny humanity. "What then is trusting in God? Is it merely trembling because he is stronger than I? Is this trusting God? Surely not. To trust in God is to *repose* on the bosom of infinite and eternal love."[1144]

In words now seen to be prophetic, Campbell told his parish in Row that the implications for theological understanding which arise from the simple conviction that God in his nature is love are far-reaching indeed: "There is no one part of God's acting, from the beginning to the end, that any man can have a right apprehension of who does not know that God is love."[1145]

By now it will be evident that the theology of John McLeod Campbell was not the result of academic speculation. He was throughout his adult life a pastor, and his fresh contributions to the doctrines of the Trinity and the atonement stemmed from his reflections on the spiritual life of his congregation in the light of Scripture.[1146] As he went about his

---

1142 *Nature*, 63ff.

1143 Sermon IX, *Sermons and Lectures*, vol. I, 187.

1144 *Ibid.*, 189.

1145 *Ibid.*, 189-90.

1146 This raises the question of influences upon McLeod Campbell, a topic considered at some length by George M. Tuttle in his book, *John McLeod Campbell on Christian Atonement: So Rich a Soil* (65-75). Tuttle thinks that Campbell and Thomas Erskine manifest a number of similar views on the atonement. And even a casual examination of the latter's book, *The Brazen Serpent* (originally published in 1831; our edition was published by David Douglas in Edinburgh in 1879) confirms this. Erskine speaks of Christ as one who comes "from the bosom of the Father's love" (35) to redeem sinners by "bearing the condemnation, and thus manifesting, through sorrow and death, the character of God, and the character of mans rebellion" (37-38). Moreover, the oneness of the flesh unites all men with the head [Christ] . . . . Just as the continuous texture of the vine unites the branches with the root" (61). Yet the extent of Erskine's influence on Campbell's early formulation of his views remains unclear, since Campbell wrote in 1826 to his father about having read Erskine's *Remarks on the Internal Evidences for the Truth of Revealed Religion* (1820). He mentions that Erskine phrased his ideas in "language which you remember was mine" (*Memorials of John McLeod Campbell, D.D.*, vol., 27, cited in Tuttle, 67). Certainly they must have influenced one another as their close friendship developed (see Tuttle, 66), but which way that influence went on a given subject is difficult to determine. Cf. Robert Mackintosh, *Historic Theories of the Atonement* (London: Hodder and Stoughton, 1920), 240; Robert S. Franks, *The Work of Christ*, (London: Thomas Nelson, 1962), 655; Eugene Bewkes, *The Legacy of a Christian Mind*, (Philadelphia: Judson Press, 1937), 7; Nicholas R. Needham, *Thomas Erskine of Linlathen. His Life and Theology 1788-1837*, (Edinburgh: Rutherford House, 1990), 468-73. Tuttle also shows, in the case of Frederick Dennison Maurice, that the dependence is likely to have been that of Maurice upon Campbell (69-70). Friedrich Schleiermacher is not likely to have been a great influence, since Campbell did not read German and the former's important work on the atonement was translated after Campbell's *Nature of the Atonement* (71). Campbell acknowledges Martin Luther as one to whom he turned for help, especially his volume, *A Commentary on St. Paul's Epistle to the Galatians*. Tuttle finds numerous phrases in Campbell's Row preaching which are reminiscent of Lutheran theology, such as references to God's 'strange work' and the notion that God's forgiveness must be seen as 'for me.' Yet Campbell, while not finding a "clear intellectual apprehension of the nature and essence of the atonement" in Luther (*Nature of the Atonement*, 32), appreciated many of the latter's insights (*ibid.*, 47). As Tuttle says, "Luther's emphasis on the love of God, and his understanding of the believers appropriation of Christ, entirely suited Campbell . . . . The next steps were his own" (73). Another possible influence, not mentioned in Tuttle, is that of Edward Irving. Certainly they possessed some common views. If a sermon Irving published in 1828 be taken as representative, "The Doctrine of the Incarnation Opened: Sermon 1, *The Collected Writings of Edward Irving*, ed. G. Carlyle, vol. v, (London: Alexander Strahan, 1865), we note that he strongly emphasizes the manifestation" of the eternal nature of God in the flesh: the incarnation is the "mystery of God manifest in the flesh (59);" "Christ manifested the name of the Father by setting forth every word as proceeding from the Father's will, and every act as the demonstration of His power and testifying of Him always, and always doing His will (70);" "The manifesting the name of God, therefore, I consider to be the manifesting the essence, or power, or nature of God, which Christ had done by every action of his life (70)." There is a pronounced similarity here to the thought of Campbell, as we shall see. But can we take it that Irving influenced Campbell on this score? The two first met in June, 1828, and despite Mrs. Oliphant's mistaken report of Campbell's recollection, *The Life of Edward Irving*, vol. II, (London: Hurst and Blacket, 1862), 24-25, Campbell shared with his new friend his insights regarding assurance of salvation as grounded in a universal atonement. Irving said, "I believe you are right, and that you were sent to show me this." "From that time," recalls Campbell, "he preached the Atonement as for all". *Memorials of John McLeod Campbell, D. D.*, vol. I, 53-54; cf. vol. II, 79. What of Irving's stress on Christ as the consubstantial Son of God disclosing the will which

pastoral visitation, he had discovered an absence of joy and assurance among his people. That God had sent Christ as his provision for sinners, that the righteousness of Christ was imputed to those who believed, they had no doubt. *"All their doubts were as to themselves."*[1147]

They had been taught the tenets of Federal Calvinism, as embodied particularly in the Westminster Confession of Faith (1647). In order to appreciate the pastoral and theological issues raised by the Confession, it might be useful to trace some of the antecedents of the so-called Federal Theology.

Federal Theology

For Calvin, there was only one eternal covenant of grace promised in the Old Testament and fulfilled in the New, in Christ. The two Testaments therefore describe, not separate and distinct covenants, but one covenant in two modes of dispensation. Indeed,

> . . . all men adopted by God into the company of his people since the beginning of the world were covenanted to him by the same law and by the bond of the same doctrine as obtains among us.[1148]

---

was grounded in the nature of God the Father? In 1831, Campbell recalled two "circumstances" which influenced his theological development as he began his ministry at Row in 1825: his confining his pulpit preparations to the study of the Bible without commentaries, and his ministerial visits. By late 1826, he was urging his people to rest "assured of [God's] love in Christ to them as individuals," and by late 1827, he taught a universal atonement, which consequently meant that they could rest "on the character of God as revealed in Christ," that manifested character being "forgiving love". "Extract of a Letter from the Revd. John McLeod Campbell, Minister of Row," prefixed to the book, *Notes of Sermons by the Rev. J. Mc. L. Campbell, Minister of Row, Dumbartonshire*, taken in shorthand, vol. I, Paisley, John Wallace, Lithographer, (1831). Clearly, he was already formulating a doctrine of the revelation of the nature of God through Jesus Christ. Quite possibly his interaction with Irving, until the latter died in 1834, served to shape and clarify his own thinking on the subject.

1147 *Reminiscences and Reflections*, (London: Macmillan, 1873), 132. Cf. James B. Torrance, "The Contribution of McLeod Campbell to Scottish Theology," *Scottish Journal of Theology*, vol. 26, no. 3, (1973), 295f.

1148 *Institutes*, II.x.1-2, cf. *Commentary on Jeremiah* 31:31-32, "God has never made any other covenant than that which he made formerly with Abraham." Why is this so? "God is never inconsistent with himself, nor is he unlike himself." God is ever gracious, and law comes out of his gracious heart.

Yet already in the late sixteenth century there occurred a pronounced shift in Reformed theological thinking. As B. G. Armstrong has characterized this divergence: "The strongly biblically and experientially based theology of Luther and Calvin had, it is fair to say, been overcome by the metaphysics and deductive logic of a restored Aristotelianism."[1149] Armstrong also suggests that this new scholasticism asserted "religious truth on the basis of deductive ratiocination from given assumptions or principles, thus producing a logically coherent and defensible system of belief."[1150]

Thus we meet again that which we found in Aquinas, namely, the substitution of an Aristotelian system of final causation for the centrality of God's self-revelation in Christ, and the resultant exposition of a God who is fundamentally self-determining will.[1151] Thus it was that protestant scholastics Beza and Zanchius relocated predestination under the doctrine of God, as had St. Thomas.[1152] Calvin, however, expounded predestination, not in Book I, under providence, but in Book III, in connection with "The Way in Which We Receive the Grace of Christ." Thus while predestination continues to have important--even, we have argued, unfortunate--connections with God's providential, all-determining will in Calvin, he nonetheless is expounding it in a primarily soteriological fashion[1153] in order to defend the freeness of grace.

1149 Brian G. Armstrong, *Calvinism and the Amyraut Heresy*, (Madison, Milwaukee and London: University of Wisconsin Press, 1969), 32.

1150 *Ibid.*; cf. Marvin W. Anderson, "Calvin: Biblical Preacher," *Scottish Journal of Theology*, vol. 42, (1989), 177-79.

1151 Cf. Armstrong, *op. cit.*, 32: "The distinctive scholastic Protestant position is made to rest on a speculative formulation of the will of God."

1152 Armstrong, *op. cit.*, 40.

1153 See David Neeld Wiley, "Calvin's Doctrine of Predestination: His Principal Soteriological and Polemical Doctrine," Ph.D. Dissertation, Duke University, 1971. Wiley rightly argues that for Calvin providence does not function as the primary organizing principle as it did in later Calvinist theology. It rather served to underscore the gratuitous nature of justification. However, for reasons outlined above, I cannot go so far as to agree with his view that providence even became a particular application of the doctrine of predestination. The former continues to determine the latter in important ways, although Calvin persists in maintaining that God, while decreeing all events in accordance with his will, including reprobation, is loving and gracious in his inmost life.

According to David A. Weir, it was Zacharias Ursinus who first made significant use of a prelapsarian covenant in the sixteenth century.[1154] In his Major Catechism he spoke of a

> covenant of nature, initiated in creation by God with men . . . known to men by nature . . . it requires from us perfect obedience to God, and it promises eternal life for those who keep it, and threatens eternal punishments for those who do not fulfill it.[1155]

And so began the illustrious career of Federal Theology, so designated because of the centrality of the notion of covenant or contract, translating the Latin *foedus*.[1156] The Westminster Confession, set forth by the Westminster Assembly and approved by the General Assembly of the

---

1154 David A. Weir, *The Origins of the Federal Theology in Sixteenth-Century Reformation Thought*, (Oxford: Clarendon Press, 1990), 101. Charles S. McCoy and J. Wayne Baker in their volume entitled, *Fountainhead of Federalism: Heinrich Bullinger and the Covenantal Tradition* (Louisville: Westminster/John Knox, 1991), remind us that Bullinger appears to have presented the first treatise focussed on the concept of covenant in the federal sense. Contrary to their allegation, however, James B. Torrance was well aware of Bullinger's role in expounding theology in terms of the covenant, and noted it in his article, "Covenant or Contract? A Study of the theological background of worship in the seventeenth-century Scotland," *Scottish Journal of Theology*, vol. 23, no. 1, (62). They misconstrue his statement that "federal theology, which first developed among the Puritans of England, came into Scotland about 1596," "Strengths and Weaknesses of the Westminster Theology," in *The Westminster Confession in the Church Today*, ed. A. I. C. Heron, (Edinburgh: Saint Andrew Press, 1982), 48, which means only that *in relation to Scotland* federal theology developed "first" in England. Cf. *Fountainhead of Federalism*, (8, 17-21).

1155 Zacharias Ursinus, *Volumen tractationum theologicarum*, (Neustadt, 1584), trans. Weir, *op. cit.*, 105.

1156 For further discussion of the history and doctrines of Federal Theology see, in addition to Weir, M. Charles Bell, *Calvin and Scottish Theology*, (Edinburgh: Handsel, 1985); Basil Hall's ground-breaking "Calvin Against the Calvinists," 19-37, *John Calvin*, ed. G. E. Duffield, (Appleton: Sutton Courtenay Press, 1966); Paul Helm, *Calvin and the Calvinists*, (Edinburgh: Banner of Truth, 1982); Heinrich Heppe, *Reformed Dogmatics*, trans. G. T. Thomson, (Grand Rapids: Baker Book House, 1984); R. T. Kendall, *Calvin and English Calvinism to 1649*, (Oxford: Oxford University Press, 1981); Holmes Rolston III, *John Calvin versus the Westminster Confession*, (Richmond: John Knox Press, 1972).

Church of Scotland in 1647, expounded in a subdued form this federal theology.[1157]

Chapter VII of that Confession declares that "The first covenant made with man was a covenant of works, wherein life was promised to Adam, and in him to his posterity, upon condition of perfect and personal obedience." But Adam failed, and in so doing plunged the entire human race into sin and damnation. But it pleased God to make a second covenant, the "covenant of grace."

> He freely offered unto sinners life and salvation by Jesus Christ, requiring of them faith in him that they might be saved, and promising to give unto all those that are ordained unto life his Holy Spirit, to make them willing and able to believe.[1158]

But the problem, of course, was that of assurance.[1159] How could one know whether he was one of those foreordained to truly believe? How could he be sure whether he was numbered among the chosen few? One could not simply look to what God has accomplished in Christ, as Calvin would have urged, for Christ did not die for the entire human race, according to the Westminster divines. "He purchased . . . reconciliation . . . for all those whom the Father hath given unto him."[1160] Rather, the individual was exhorted to "give all diligence to make his calling and election sure," looking to his "good works" as "fruits and evidences of a true and lively faith."[1161]

It must be said that a pastoral intent lay behind this approach. The Westminster commissioners recognized that many godly folk were tortured in mind as to their eternal destiny. They wanted to endorse Calvin's view that assurance was of the essence of faith, and yet they confronted the empirical fact that all too many persons lacked such confidence.

1157 Philip Schaff, ed., *The Creeds of Christendom*, vol. iii, (Grand Rapids: Baker, 1990), 616-617.
1158 *Ibid.*, 617.
1159 See M. Charles Bell, *Calvin and Scottish Theology*, Paul Helm, *Calvin and the Calvinists*, and R. T. Kendall, *Calvin and English Calvinism to 1649*.
1160 Westminster Confession, chapters 8 and 11, Schaff, *op. cit.*, 621, 627.
1161 *Ibid.*, chaps. xvi and xviii, Schaff, *op. cit.*, 639.

Therefore they taught that true believers "may certainly be assured that they are in a state of grace," and indeed be "infallibly" so assured. Yet such certainty would not always typify one's faith. Believers may undergo long struggles and periods of conflict before attaining it. Therefore they should strive by "evidences" of repentance to verify their election. Again, Westminster was surely right in wanting to reassure the struggler that his doubts were not an indication of divine rejection, that indeed they may often characterize the true Christian's experience.

But then, it may be argued, the Confession mistakenly directs the doubting Christian, not to God in Christ, but to his experience, his performance, his conformity to Law. Campbell would criticize a similar line of reasoning, one which seeks the knowledge that we are justified "in that way of inference from the fact that we believe combined with the doctrine that those that believe are justified." At the end of the day the strength of assurance turns upon the individual's piety, and hence proves to be the stumbling block.[1162]

The Marrow Controversy

Seventy years after the Westminster Assembly, many of the deep-seated theological issues raised in the Confession emerged full-blown to the surface again, in the so-called Marrow Controversy. Because John McLeod Campbell would later be charged with failing to heed the strictures contained in the Act of the General Assembly in 1720, it is necessary to review some of the questions raised at that time. In the course of that debate, several of the issues which were to emerge so powerfully in Row were already earnestly debated.

Back in 1720, the General Assembly of the Church of Scotland had condemned the teaching contained in the book, *The Marrow of Modern Divinity*.[1163] In that act, the Assembly charged the *Marrow* with

---

1162 *Nature*, 223.

1163 E. F., *Marrow of Modern Divinity*, third ed., (London: G. Calvert, 1645), re-published as the ninth ed., (Edinburgh: John Mosman and William Brown, 1718). It was this latter edition, reprinted in Scotland at the behest of James Hogg of Carnock, which caused such a stir in high Calvinist circles. See C. G. McCrie, ed., *The Marrow of Modern Divinity in Two Parts, 1645, 1649*, (Glasgow: David Bryce, 1902), introduction, xv-xxxi; McCrie, "Studies in Scottish Ecclesiastical Biography," *British and Foreign Evangelical Review*, xxxiii (1884), 669-719; Bell, *Calvin and Scottish Theology*, 151ff., Henry F. Henderson, *The Religious Controversies of Scotland*, (Edinburgh: T. & T. Clark, 1905), David Lachman, *The Marrow Controversy*, (Edinburgh: Rutherford House, 1988).

teaching, among other things, a universal atonement, that assurance is of the essence of faith, and that holiness is not necessary to salvation.[1164]

> On the title page, the book itself professes its intention to be touching both the Covenant of Works, and the Covenant of Grace: with their use and end . . . wherein every one may clearly see how far forth he bringeth the Law into the case of Justification, and so deserveth the name of Legalist; and how far forth he rejecteth the Law in the case of Sanctification, and so deserveth the name of Antinomist. With the middle path betwixt them both, which by Jesus Christ leadeth to eternal life.[1165]

It takes the form of an imaginary dialogue between Evangelista, a minister of the Gospel; Nomista, a legalist; Antinomista, an antinomian; and Neophytus, a young Christian.

The Marrow was a species of federal theology. It subscribed to the prelapsarian Covenant of works,[1166] expounding it as a "bargain"[1167] struck by God "with all mankind in Adam before his fall," offering eternal life upon the "condition" of Adam's perfect obedience.[1168] But Adam disobeys, breaks the covenant,[1169] thereby bringing the entire human race to ruin.[1170]

Nevertheless "there was a special covenant or mutual agreement made between God and Christ . . . that if Christ would make Himself a sacrifice for sin then He should see His seed . . ."[1171] This was, says Evangelista,

> As if God had said concerning His elect, I know that these will break, and never be able to satisfy Me; but Thou art a mighty and substantial person, able to pay

---

1164 *Acts of the General Assembly of the Church of Scotland, 1638-1842*, 534-6, cited in Bell, *op. cit.*, 152.
1165 *The Marrow of Modern Divinity*, 1645 edition, title page.
1166 *Marrow of Modern Divinity*, ed. McCrie, 17ff. Henceforth references to the *Marrow* will be to the McCrie edition.
1167 *Ibid.*, 17.
1168 *Ibid.*, 18.
1169 *Ibid.*, 23.
1170 *Ibid.*, 25.
1171 *Ibid.*, 35.

Me, therefore I will look for my debt off Thee . . . . Thus
Christ assented, and from everlasting struck hands with
God . . ."

In this way, Jesus Christ "entered into the same covenant of works
that Adam did, to deliver believers from it"[1172] by fulfilling it on their
behalf.[1173]

Clearly, therefore, the *Marrow* did not espouse a universal atonement.
Christ as the Second Adam procured righteousness for "all that are in
Him."[1174] The "bargain" Christ struck with God was on behalf of "His
seed," the "elect", the "believers" only.[1175]

What may have led the General Assembly to suspect a universal
scope in the *Marrow's* atonement was its notion that God in Christ
"moved with nothing but with His free love to mankind lost hath made
a deed of gift and grant unto them all, that whosoever of them all shall
believe in this His Son shall not perish but have eternal life." Therefore
disciples of Jesus are commanded to "go and tell every man without
exception that here are good news for him, Christ is dead for him, and if
he will take Him and accept of His righteousness he shall have Him."[1176]

What does this "deed of gift" to all mean? It may be compared to
the proclamation by a king of universal pardon to all rebels, in view of
the "suit and desert of some dear friend of theirs." For God has, on the
basis of the "obedience and desert" of Christ, "pardoned us all our sins,
and made a proclamation throughout the whole world that every one
of us may safely return to God in Jesus Christ." Therefore, concludes

1172 *Ibid.*, 36. Weir, *op. cit.*, perceptively observes that the covenant of works motif,
once inserted into the revised Reformed theology, becomes a primary shaping influence of the whole of theology: "man now becomes basically a legal creature from the
beginning--at creation . . . the covenant of works becomes, in some sense, the primary
covenant which God has made with man. The Adamic relationship of perfection in
Eden takes on greater weight than the Abrahamic relationship of grace. Grace is, as it
were, a remedy to correct creation's fall into sin." The final goal then becomes restoring humans to "the covenantal state of Eden, when the law of God will be written on
the hearts of the redeemed elect" (6-7).
1173 *Marrow*, 68.
1174 *Ibid.*, 104.
1175 Cf. David Lachman, *op. cit.*, 24.
1176 *Marrow*, 112-113.

Evangelista, quoting Hebrews 10:22, "I beseech you make no doubt of it, but 'draw near with a true heart in full assurance of faith.'"[1177]

However, the *Marrow* was rightly accused of holding that assurance is of the essence of faith. The universal proclamation and invitation of God in Christ is a warrant for any sinner to come to Christ, and to ground his faith in that universal "deed of gift." True, the atonement, in the thinking of the Marrow folk, was not truly universal. But since God has hidden the names of those foreordained to reprobation, and offers the pardon "generally", it would be sheer folly for anyone to decline God's offer on the possibility that he may not be one of the elect. Rather, it is an invitation to make one's "calling and election sure." He ought rather to say, "I do believe in Christ, and therefore I am sure I am elected."[1178]

Was the *Marrow* antinomian? Certainly Evangelista argues that Christ fully satisfied the Covenant of Works, even to the point of receiving its penalty of death which should have been exacted upon sinners. Therefore, "the law, as it is the covenant of works, hath not anything to say to true believers, for indeed they are dead to it, and it is dead to them."[1179]

But this does not mean that the Christian is not required to obey God's law. Indeed, Evangelista assures Antinomista, faith will invariably bring forth holiness. Without it, even if accompanied by an apparent peace and joy in Christ, it is not a true believing in Christ. For "true faith" grows from "faith of adherence to faith of evidence." It "produceth holiness of life." Therefore, each must heed the words of 2 Corinthians 13:5 and "Examine yourself whether ye be in the faith; prove your own self."[1180] For all true Christians are subject to Christ, and his commandments, which were already enumerated in the Decalogue and then endorsed, in so many words, in the teaching of Christ.[1181]

What was really at stake for the Marrow Brethren was the unconditional freeness of the Gospel. The *facere quod* of Rome which promises that "if a man exercise all his power and do his best to fulfill the law, then God, for Christ's sake, will pardon all his infirmities and

---

1177 *Ibid.*, 113.
1178 *Marrow*, 114.
1179 *Ibid.*, 103, cf. 106f.
1180 *Ibid.*, 95-96.
1181 *Ibid.*, 146-54.

save his soul,"[1182] is but another version of the notion found among some Protestants that God accepts one who does his best, not because it is meritorious, but for Christ's sake. But, argues Evangelista, the obedience required by God is a perfect one. Therefore, to be justified in God's sight, "you must either bring Him a perfect righteousness of your own and wholly renounce Christ, or else you must bring the perfect righteousness of Christ and wholly renounce your own."[1183]

Only the latter course will do for fallen humankind. "For we shall not find the favour of God, true innocency, righteousness, satisfaction for sin, help, comfort, life or salvation anywhere but only in Jesus Christ."[1184] Thus the *Marrow* sought resolutely to point the sinner away from his own best efforts at converting himself, whether weeping or praying or fasting or walking the path of good works, and to fix his eyes solely upon Christ.[1185]

While the covenant of works was conditioned upon human obedience, the covenant of grace was not. There, God was "party on both sides." Indeed, on the human side, "Christ paid God till He said He had enough, He was fully satisfied, fully contented . . . ." This free and gracious covenant therefore is complete. "There is not any condition or law to be performed on man's part by himself. No: there is no more room for him to do, but only to know and believe that Christ hath done all for him."[1186]

This unconditional language was meant to invite the sinner to come to Christ just as he was, but the General Assembly was concerned that it might invite a wanton disregard for God's Law. Was it not a command to "follow holiness . . . without which no man shall see the Lord"? The *Marrow*, as we have seen, recognized the need for obedience, but wanted to place it as a response to grace, rather than as a condition of it.

D. C. Lachman, in his comprehensive survey of *The Marrow Controversy* acknowledges that a central question concerned the absoluteness of the covenant of grace. Are there any preparations required of a person before he can come to Christ? Is faith an instrument or a condition to be performed? Is holiness of life a prerequisite for

---

1182 *Ibid.*, 90.
1183 *Ibid.*, 91.
1184 *Ibid.*, 92.
1185 *Ibid.*, 100.
1186 *Ibid.*, 111.

salvation or an inevitable evidence of it? He admits that Reformed divines in the seventeenth century often called the covenant conditional while others said it was absolute.[1187] He notes, for example, that David Dickson considered the Covenant of Grace to be a "contract" stipulating three conditions for those who would be in covenant with God: acknowledgement of sins, faith, and evidence of the validity of his faith by obedience to Christ's commands.[1188]

Lachman rightly reminds us that for Dickson, it is Christ who grants faith and who works conversion and guarantees their perseverance.[1189] But, it must be pointed out, this graciousness in Christ cannot be known directly by the individual, because not all are included in the atonement. It can only be known discursively, by examining the evidences in oneself, and then not absolutely. For the high Calvinist, the question is not, "Has Christ done it all?" but rather, "Have I fulfilled the conditions for receiving what Christ has done so as to prove that I have received the grace to fulfill them?"[1190]

Such an approach would seem little removed from the *facere quod* of St. Thomas in this regard, for, although it eschews the language of merit, the concept remains in the sense that there are conditions which we must fulfill in order to receive grace. It is said that these conditions are in some sense met by God. But conditional language draws our attention away from what God has done objectively in Christ and toward our own subjective appropriation of it, making our attempts at appropriation the real determinant in our salvation.

But the *Marrow*, harking back to Calvin,[1191] insisted that repentance is always consequent to faith. For repentance, consisting in humbling oneself before God, grieving over one's sins, and turning from sin to the Lord, prior to coming to Christ, is, in a word, "impossible."[1192] It must spring from, rather than precede, faith. Indeed, "No man can turn to God except he be first turned of God; and after he is turned he repents."[1193]

1187 Lachman, *op. cit.*, 36.

1188 David Dickson, *Therapeutica Sacra*, (Edinburgh: Evan Tyler, 1664), 87, cited in Lachman, *op. cit.*, 47.

1189 Lachman, *op. cit.*, 48.

1190 Cf. Bell, *op. cit.*, 92-98.

1191 However, the *Marrow* does not appeal to Calvin for support in the present context.

1192 *Marrow*, 126-27.

1193 *Ibid.*, 127.

In any case, the doctrines propounded in the book were found to be contrary to Scripture and the Westminster Confession, and the General Assembly therefore prohibited its ministers recommending the book or its contents in any way. Rather, they were "enjoined and required to Warn and Exhort their people, in whose hands the said Book is, or may come, not to read or use the same."[1194]

But the spiritual struggles addressed by the *Marrow* continued into McLeod Campbell's time. The questions raised by a limited atonement and the call to repent and by one's repentance to demonstrate his election presented themselves poignantly in the parish of Row. And so this new pastor, wanting to instruct his people in the Gospel of grace, was driven to re-examine the teaching of the Bible. Indeed, he later acknowledged that he confined himself to the study of the Scriptures in his pulpit preparations.[1195] He was always an evangelist at heart, but he soon saw that he could not hold out the Gospel to everyone under the old Federal scheme. Calvin had taught a universal atonement coupled with a universal offer of salvation, but qualified it with a restricted election.

The Marrowmen also wanted very much to expound the Gospel in such a way that each hearer could hear it with reference to himself, but Campbell knew that he could not say with confidence that "Christ died for *you*," because the Marrow brethren were one with the high Calvinist orthodoxy of his day in holding that only God knows who are included in the atonement by his prior, secret election. So McLeod Campbell saw clearly that such a doctrine, however self-consistent it might be given its own premisses, was not preachable.

What is it about the writings of a nineteenth-century theologian who was deposed from the ministry after only five years in a country pulpit,[1196] who wrote in an awkward, obscure style, that requires our attention today? We find a clue in an 1857 letter from McLeod Campbell to his brother-in-law Neil Campbell, who was seriously ill at the time.

1194 *Register of the Actings and Proceedings of the Commission of the General Assembly of the Church of Scotland, May 17, 1716-May 9th 1721*, 12, cited in Lachman, *op. cit.*, 125.

1195 *Reminiscences and Reflections*, 125.

1196 He was deposed by the General Assembly of the Church of Scotland for teaching "the doctrine of universal atonement and pardon through the death of Christ" and that "assurance is of the essence of faith and necessary for salvation." *The whole Proceedings in the Case of the Rev. John McLeod Campbell, Minister of Row*, 1.

." . . what is nearest our hearts is that you should be prepared . . . for the great change that may be . . . . To know the love of God as a love that reaches us in our sins in the blood of Christ, is the . . . path to peace in life, and in death . . . . Dear Neil, there is no other path. No other for you, no other for me, no other. Unless the forgiveness that the death of Christ for my sins shows me to be in God for me, draws me to God, and gives me confidence to trust my soul to Him, I do not understand the Gospel . . . let the love of God draw your heart to Him with cords of love. Look steadfastly at the Cross of Christ, and freely; and yield your heart to all the comfort of it and all the hope . . . . Dear Neil . . . do not be tempted to delay committing your soul to Him . . . . Fix your thoughts on *Christ dying for your sins*, and receive the teaching of the Spirit of God in your heart, enabling you to understand that blessed sight.[1197]

Here we see the pastoral heart of this young preacher, and his concern to fix our gaze on the self-sacrifice of God in Christ in such a way that the Gospel of grace comes home to us in with a powerful sense of unconditional freeness. He was convinced that good theology addresses the pastoral needs of the people. And this correlation between theology and pulpit was the hallmark of all his writings. True theological understanding begins with the fact that God has disclosed himself in these last days, fully and finally, by a Son. When the thought of the will of God is grounded in the self-revelation of God in and through his Son, the freeness of grace in all its *unmeritedness* as well as its *unrestrictedness* is maintained.

The Self-revelation of God

The burden laying so heavily upon McLeod Campbell was the conviction that Calvinist theological systems had abstracted the will of God from the nature of God as revealed in Christ. Thus the personal and relational language of the Scriptures was downplayed in favor of legal and commercial metaphors for the nature of God and the person and

---

1197 *Memorials*, vol. I, 303-5.

work of Christ. Preoccupation with God as a Lawgiver, the human race as lawbreakers and Christ as the Lawkeeper who is punished in their stead had obscured the Person of God as a loving Father and constructed artificial barriers hindering the warm fellowship which God had sought to re-establish with his orphaned children.

To be sure, humankind needed saving, God's laws must be upheld, and the Cross was the crucial culmination of Christ's reconciling activity. But he was striving for an atonement that really atones, and a reconciliation that truly reconciles. To this end, he re-interpreted the concept of the will of God in light of God's self-unveiling in the incarnation and atonement.

Campbell was convinced that in the life, death and resurrection of Jesus a true at-one-ment between estranged parties was accomplished. Therefore, to interpret the Cross as the place where the "transferred effects" of sin are somehow placed on Jesus, and then to consider justification as the action of God dealing with us "as if" we are righteous, by virtue of the "transferred merits" of Christ is to construct a system so unreal as to be almost unbelievable.

All of this, while derived from a proper desire to do justice to the biblical emphasis on the demands of Law, results in the Gospel being preached primarily in judicial rather than filial categories. And so the vibrant, personal relationship which Christians ought to have with God dies the death of a thousand legal qualifications. For there is something deadening to the spirit of sonship in being required to pause and say, 'I would cry to my father. I see His heart towards me,---the Son reveals it: but I must remember that to be justified in drawing near with confidence I must think of myself as clothed by imputation with a perfect righteousness, because the Father of my spirit must see me so clothed in order that He may be justified in receiving me to His Fatherly heart.[1198]

What has happened here? Replies Campbell, direct trust in the Father's heart has been supplanted by "trust in the judicial grounds on which the title and place of sons is granted to us."[1199]

While legal and commercial metaphors are employed in Scripture, exclusive concentration on these obscures the fact that God is primarily

---

1198 *Nature*, 221-22.
1199 *Nature*, 348.

a Father, and only consequently a lawgiver, for the Commandments, as McLeod Campbell reminds us in a sermon,[1200] are the heart of the Father coming out in the form of Law. And while Christ dies in order to fulfill the righteous requirements of the Law, God's primary concern is not that Law be satisfied, but that his fatherly heart be satisfied. For his heart's desire is that many sons be brought to glory, being re-united with their Father.

In other words, McLeod Campbell became convinced that the fundamental issue is the *doctrine of God*. High Calvinists, he argues, begin by presupposing an abstract conception of God and his attributes. But this is to fly in the face of revelation. We cannot, he insists, deduce from prior conceptions of the love of God certain views of creation, incarnation, and so on. In this way we end up "substituting our own deductions for the faith of the gospel."[1201] Some, like John Owen, even argued that God is not love in his innermost being. He only decides to be loving toward certain ones. For justice is his essential attribute, while his love is arbitrary.[1202]

Such a conception of God fits well with a limited atonement, for it is then asserted that God is related to all people according to law and the dictates of justice, but only to some on the basis of love.[1203] Campbell advances three arguments against limited atonement at this point. First, the Scriptures teach otherwise.[1204] Second, it undercuts evangelism, because it "takes away the warrant" for every person to believe that Christ "loved me and gave himself for me."[1205] Third, the doctrine of limited atonement fails to take the life of Christ as the revelation of the nature of God as love.[1206]

Those favoring a particular redemption argue that God is primarily self-determining will. We are given no other reason for a limited

---

1200 *Responsibility for the Gift of Eternal Life*, (London: Macmillan, 1873), 106. The "sermons" in this book are, the editor tells us (v), re-writes of Row sermons. The original is in Sermon XIII, *Sermons and Lectures*, vol. I, 319: "God's law is God's own heart come out in the shape of a law."
1201 *Nature*, xxix.
1202 *Nature*, 163ff, cf. James Torrance, "The Incarnation and Limited Atonement," *Evangelical Quarterly*, vol. 55, no. 3 (1983), 84-5.
1203 *Nature*, 63.
1204 *Nature*, 59-60.
1205 *Nature*, 60.
1206 *Nature*, 64.

atonement than that God "wills it because he wills it." God is not required to love everyone because love is not his essential nature. Justice is. Love is only an arbitrary, occasional act of God. But here Campbell finds the Achilles heel of the Calvinist doctrine of atonement: "an arbitrary act cannot reveal character." If the cross, as an act of love, is an arbitrary act, grounded not in the innermost being of God, then "what He has done has left us ignorant of Himself," and "He is to us an unknown God."[1207]

Self-revelation and a Point of Contact

But for McLeod Campbell, the suggestion that God is unknown is anathema. It would undermine his driving conviction that God has bared his fatherly heart to us in Jesus and bids us enter into close fellowship with himself. Moreover he shares Calvin's notion of a universal *sensus divinitatis*, an awareness of the reality of God that precedes all investigation or speculative inquiry.

> It is justly held that the faith that there is a God, has a root in us deeper than all inferential argument, a root in relation to which all inferential argument is but so to speak, complemental; owing its authority rather to that root rather than that root at all to it . . . . And surely those who deal with men who are attempting to be atheists act most wisely when they throw them back on this root of faith in God in their own inner being, instead of permitting a course of argument which allows their thoughts to run away to find without them what unless found within them will never be found at all.[1208]

But while Calvin is reluctant to attribute any positive content to this notion beyond the bare recognition that there is a God, and indeed hastens to add that fallen humans immediately pervert and distort this knowledge into sheer idolatry, Campbell even believes that the fatherhood of God is naturally known.

> That this God, in whose existence we necessarily believe, is the Father of our spirits, is to be regarded as a *further*

1207 *Nature*, 64-65; cf. Michael Jinkins, *op. cit.,* 279-80.
1208 *Nature*, 297.

> *truth*, the faith of which has a *corresponding depth of
> root in us*: and this I understand the Apostle to recognize
> in the use he makes in preaching to the Athenians, of the
> expression as used by one of their own poets, 'For we are
> also His offspring' . . . these words of the poet [were] the
> utterance of a truth that was deep in all their hearts.[1209]

Moreover, also contained within our "certain knowledge of God" is
the fact that "God is love."[1210] It was on the basis of his belief in a
universal awareness of God that he critiqued Henry Mansel's Bampton
Lectures.[1211] Mansel seems to have favored a kind of metaphysical
agnosticism influenced by Kant and Schleiermacher. Thus he averred
that our natural cognition is restricted to "things as they appear to us,"
and has no knowledge of "things in themselves."[1212] The knowledge we
have of God is not direct, but the result of reflection upon our "Religious
Consciousness" of the "Feeling of Dependence" and the "Conviction
of Moral Obligation."[1213] Therefore, concluded Mansel, we can have
no knowledge of "*what* God is in His own Absolute Being," but only,
indirect knowledge "*that* God is."[1214]

To this McLeod Campbell recoils in horror. "The *only comfort
possible after reading his book*, and seeing to what it amounts, is,
that it is not true; for he defends faith on grounds which make faith
impossible." How can we believe in a God who is "unknowable"? If we
are to love God with all our hearts and minds, we must have "*knowledge
of God as He is.*" Faith and love, argues Campbell, are always grounded
in knowledge. "The heart cannot truly bestow itself on a mere possible
loveliness." But we have a consciousness of the certain "knowledge
of God," and Campbell is as certain that God is love as he is that God
exists.[1215]

But such knowledge is not the result of abstraction from empirical
experience or any other kind of discursive reasoning. It is intuitively

---

1209 *Ibid.*
1210 *Memorials*, vol. II, 314, 316.
1211 *The Limits of Religious Thought*, fourth edition, (London: John Murray, 1859).
1212 Mansel, *op. cit.*, 81.
1213 Mansel, *op. cit.*, 72.
1214 *op. cit.*, 81.
1215 *Memorials*, vol. II, 313-317.

known by anyone who is honest with himself. And for Campbell, the notion probably springs from his missionary zeal. As a pastor he was chagrined by the want of rejoicing in God on the part of his parishioners.[1216] They were driven away from God, he thought, by excessively legal images of God. Emphasis on God as a Lawgiver whose wrath is poured out on lawbreakers aroused fear in the hearts of devout souls who knew their own failings only too well.

Their pastor wanted to woo them to the living God by a fresh exposition of a Fatherly God, who loved each of them. And he felt that in so doing he could appeal to a deeper, almost forgotten, and yet innate sense that God was really in his innermost being a caring Parent for whom their welfare was uppermost. He was fond of quoting II Corinthians 4:2, where Paul describes his evangelistic strategy as "by manifestation of the truth commending ourselves to every man's conscience in the sight of God."[1217]

He would seem to have a high estimate of the human conscience. Conscience, he tells us, "fully recognizes the truth of that revelation of ourselves which the gospel makes to us. Were it otherwise, assuredly its light would be no light to us."[1218] Conscience functions as a point of contact in the listener for the proclamation of the Gospel. Yet we must also say that "the teaching of the Spirit of God in conscience, should help our understandings most."[1219] Our conscience is not wholly reliable, for it shares in our "evil state."[1220] But there remains enough of an awareness to validate the preaching of the Gospel within.

There may be many who are content to assent to a particular formulation of the atonement which they cannot comprehend, professing it to be a mystery. But a doctrine which fails to commend itself to conscience ought at least to be questioned.[1221]

But Campbell was unwilling to go very far down the road of conscience. While it is true that "conscience testifies to the need be for an atonement," the empirical evidence suggests that historically human conscience has been misguided. Heathens sacrificed to devils rather

1216 *Reminiscences*, 176.
1217 E.g., *Nature*, xxi, 15, 20, *Reminiscences*, 125.
1218 *Nature*, 5f.
1219 *Nature*, 6.
1220 *Nature*, 5.
1221 *Nature*, 6.

than to the living God, and their offerings were calculated to "propitiate the divine favour." Whatever light they had in their conscience must be judged by a "higher light."[1222] We must look elsewhere than to "dark and blind endeavors of the heathen to propitiate an unknown god," or various "angry deities."[1223]

But for the atonement to commend itself to every man's conscience, it "must be felt to commend itself by its own internal light, and its divine fitness to accomplish the high ends of God in it."[1224] This is not to say that the exposition of the Gospel, with its word of condemnation of our sinfulness as well as its promise of mercy, is automatically welcomed by the sinner. In fact, "I am tempted to turn away, alike from the testimony of Scripture, and the testimony of conscience."[1225] However, by the operation of the Spirit of God,[1226] we are "thoroughly awakened" to hear the "voice" of conscience and thus are "forced" to own up to the truth.[1227]

By now it will be apparent that Campbell takes conscience in a sense much wider than simply an awareness of morality. And indeed, in *Fragments of Truth*, which contains several lectures given between his Row ministry and the writing of his books, he discusses in more depth his understanding of the term.[1228]

> What is conscience? We do not mean by conscience a merely natural faculty enabling us to discern right from wrong. Conscience is the meeting-place between God and man. *God expresses Himself*, so to speak, in various forms,--in Creation, in Providence, in Scripture . . . but there must be in man an ear that can hear the voice of God. *Conscience is that ear*. Conscience is the inward meeting-place between the Father of Spirits and the creatures whom He has made in His own image. *There* we feel that God is--there we recognize Him as

---

1222 *Nature*, 6-7.
1223 *Nature*, 8.
1224 *Nature*, 9.
1225 *Nature*, 11.
1226 *Nature*, 6.
1227 *Nature*, 12.
1228 *Fragments of Truth: Being expositions of Passages of Scripture chiefly from the Teaching of John McLeod Campbell, D. D.* (Edinburgh: David Douglas, 1898), Forward.

the rewarder of them that diligently seek Him--there we hold intercourse with Him . . . there is what is either right or wrong in our religion.[1229]

By conscience, therefore, Campbell means a point of contact between God and humankind, a point of spiritual receptivity and apprehension. It may seem that we have the beginnings of a kind of natural theology,[1230] but the noetic effects of sin are not overlooked. In fact, he takes full cognizance of Hebrews 9:14, "How much more shall the blood of Christ, who through the eternal Spirit offered himself without spot to God, purge your conscience from dead works to serve the living God?" McLeod Campbell takes this to mean that the conscience has become unclean, "and thus man's thought of God--his attempts to draw near to him are not holy; he comes offering dead works instead of living worship."[1231] Thus by the operation of the Holy Spirit our eyes are opened "to see the mind of the Father revealed in the death of the Son" and in that way our conscience is "purged,"[1232] or awakened.

One wonders, however, whether it really serves Campbell's purposes to posit conscience and a prior awareness of the Fatherhood of God as points of contact for the Gospel. It undermines his vigorous emphasis on the unconditional freeness of grace by suggesting that there is some capacity in our fallen human nature to receive or prepare for God by itself. What is more, it opens the possibility of other interpretations as to just what might be the content of our 'prior awareness'--perhaps, not of God's fatherliness, but of his fundamentally judicial nature, which demands certain conditions be met prior to a bestowal of grace! Has he not departed from his central conviction that God is to be known *only in Christ*? These, however, are defects which can be corrected while maintaining his basic insights concerning revelation and the nature of God.

1229 *Ibid.*, 172.
1230 Cf. *Reminiscences*, 1873, 94-106, where he laments that "natural religion" is often depreciated in the supposed interests of exalting "revealed religion", and argues that reason and revelation ought to harmonize.
1231 *Fragments of Truth*, 173.
1232 *Fragments of Truth*, 179.

Self-revelation and Atonement

For these reasons, we return to McLeod Campbell's conviction that we cannot comprehend spiritual realities apart from a Christological context. He is fond of reminding us, it was the Son's mission to declare the Father's Name. When Jesus came into the world, according to the record of Hebrews, he confessed, "Lo, I come to do thy will, O God." And that Will was not for the Son to act out an arbitrarily assigned part, but to shine as the very Light of Life, thereby showing us the Father.[1233]

Therefore we must say that God interprets *himself* to us. Our point of departure must be the "divine self-manifestation."[1234] It is not for us to begin with prior speculations or conceptions regarding the divine nature and then seek to fit the Gospel account into these. Rather than start with an "abstract question--what is an atonement for sin?" and allow our own preconceptions to determine the response, "it is surely wise to seek its answer in the study of the atonement for sin actually made."[1235] For our desperate sinfulness distorts our apprehension of God such that we could not have anticipated the course God's love would take in the history of the human race. "God himself must make it known to us."[1236]

And in these last days He has spoken to us by a Son. Therefore the incarnation must be seen as "the highest fact" in which God's interest in and purposes for all people may be seen.[1237] The significance of this is momentous. For McLeod Campbell is departing from the typical Calvinist approach of beginning with a doctrine of God whose main

---

1233 *Nature,* 129f; cf. Heb. 2:20ff; 10:5ff.
1234 *Nature,* xxix.
1235 *Nature,* 119.
1236 *Nature,* 5.
1237 *Nature,* xxv.

attribute in relation to the human race is will[1238] and whose overriding concern is that Law be fulfilled.

The Federal Calvinist believed in the incarnation, of course, but did not allow it to be determinative. In the incarnation we are only given a manifestation of the will of God toward a few. The sonship of Christ has no bearing on our understanding of God's interest in us or his innermost heart. What is important is that Christ is a subject, disclosing to us a Moral Governor or Lawgiver. Campbell saw that when Christ's life is no longer understood as at every point revealing the Father, his love is reduced to "the fulfillment for man of the law under which man was." The life of Christ becomes "the working out of a legal righteousness for man to be his by imputation." What has happened? We have been "turned away from seeing God in Christ."[1239]

But "God is light, and in his light we are given to see light."[1240] In knowing the Son we know the Father, "not merely because of identity of will and character in the Father and the Son, but because a father as such is known only in his relation to a son.[1241] For McLeod Campbell, there is no will in God that is not the will of the Father. And God the Father has given himself to be known in the Son. Therefore the Father-Son relation must be determinative for our understanding of the nature of God. The mystery of God's being as Father, Son and Holy Spirit is not a proper subject for speculative investigation as a thing in itself, independent of all finite existence. "We can only be called to the study of it *in its*

1238 As an example of this we might note Abraham Booth's book. *The Reign of Grace From its Rise to its Consummation*, published in Kilmarnock, Scotland, in 1807. He tells us that Jehovah, as an "*infinite agent* . . . before he imparted existence or time commenced, proposed and appointed an *end* worthy of Himself, in all he determined to do. This was his *own glory* . . . . His determination was, to glorify himself in the complete salvation and endless felicity of some of the apostate race; and in the righteous condemnation of others . . . . Such being the *final cause* of the creation in general, and of mankind in particular, that sovereign Being who has an *absolute right to do what he will with his own*, having determined to create man and to leave him to the freedom of his own will, foreseeing he would certainly fall; of his free, distinguishing love, chose a certain number out of the apostate race of Adam, and ordained them to a participation of grace here and to the enjoyment of glory hereafter" (22-23, emphasis mine).

1239 *Nature*, 167-68.

1240 *Nature*, xxii.

1241 *Nature*, lii.

manifestation in connexion with man."[1242] Indeed, declared McLeod Campbell in a sermon "I cannot know God, except he reveal himself; but now he *has* shown himself: in Jesus Christ God is revealed."[1243] For the Father has given himself to be known in his Son.[1244] As Norman Macleod explained his cousin's theology:

> Accordingly, in all that Jesus was, in all He did, in all He suffered, in His works of mercy, in His constant self-sacrifice while doing his Father's will, in His tears of sympathy with suffering and of sorrow for sin, in His invitation to all to come and rest, in His offers of pardon and of life--in all He recognized, not only a revelation of the mind of Christ, but also a direct revelation of the Father's heart to man; so that in seeing what the Son was towards man we see what the Father also ever has been, is, and ever will be to us.[1245]

The Fatherliness of God

So Campbell sought to allow the Father-Son relation to be the light in which he interpreted the whole of theology. God is not an abstract God, in essence a Lawgiver whose real concern is to ensure conformity to Law and punish the guilty, but the God and Father of our Lord Jesus Christ who has unconditionally bound himself to his creatures in the humanity of his Son. That is to say, God, in his innermost being a fellowship of Father and Son *is* love.[1246] Love has a "living fountain

---

1242 *Nature*, 378.

1243 *The Everlasting Gospel. Notes of a Sermon by the Rev. J. M. Campbell, Minister of Row, Dumbartonshire*. (Greenock: R. B. Lusk, 1830), 18.

1244 *Nature*, xli.

1245 Norman Macleod, "John Macleod Campbell, D. D.," *Good Words 1872*, (London: Strahan, 1872), 355.

1246 *Reminiscences,* pp. 15Sf, 183. Campbell's neglect of the person and work of the Holy Spirit in his exposition of the atonement, especially as it relates to the connection between Calvary and ourselves is unfortunate. Cf. R. C. Moberly, *Atonement and Personality*, London, John Murray, 1907, pp. 409-410; R. S. Paul, *The Atonement and the Sacraments*, London, Hodder and Stoughton, pp. 148-49. However, in his later book, *Thoughts on Revelation*, Campbell tries to supply this want: "If Christianity cannot be realized in us apart from our relation to the Father and the Son, no more can it apart from our relation to the Holy Spirit." Moreover the "life of Sonship" can only be known in the Holy Spirit, even as the Apostles knew it after Pentecost "that in the

in the heart of a living God."[1247] He creates the world in love and for love.[1248] Consequently, McLeod Campbell could tell his parishioners that "God's character is revealed in the actual work of Christ."[1249] Indeed, God's love is "shewn in the *history of the man Christ Jesus*, but it is *in the heart of God.*"[1250]

And when the human race turns away and goes off into the far country, the living God does not abandon his familial purposes. Indeed, "the love of the Creator is . . . seen as the love of the Redeemer."[1251] So he assumes the nature and becomes the brother of those who have sinned.

But there can be no dilution of the holiness of God in the supposed interests of his love. In fact, the two are harmonious aspects of his being. He is at once loving and righteous. On the one hand McLeod Campbell finds a "real righteous severity" in God.[1252] For God *is* a moral being. He is goodness in his innermost being and he correspondingly gives human creatures goodness as the law of their being.[1253] There is no moral weakness or laxity in God. He always demands that justice be rendered.[1254]

McLeod Campbell emphasizes that we must never allow God's character as Lawgiver to "sink" into his character as Father. And yet on the other hand, neither should we consider the notion of the Lawgiver as giving a more fundamental picture of God.[1255] For the Commandments, as we have already observed, are the heart of God coming out in the form of Law. Therefore we must say that "What God is in that He is love is what God wills us to be."[1256]

---

power of the Holy Ghost proceeding from the Father and the Son, they might be Sons of God in spirit and in truth" (*Thoughts on Revelation*, London, Macmillan, 1862, pp. 136-37).

1247 *Reminiscences.*, 149-50.

1248 *Ibid.*, 190f, 249, 251; *Sermons and Lectures*, vol. I, (Greenock: Lusk, 1832), Sermon I, 11.

1249 Sermon I, *Sermons and Lectures*, vol. I, 17.

1250 Sermon XIII, *Sermons and Lectures*, vol. I, 320.

1251 *Reminiscences*, 190.

1252 *Nature*, 187.

1253 *Nature*, xxivf.

1254 *Nature*, 185.

1255 *Nature*, 72.

1256 *Nature*, xxxviii.

Therefore God is primarily the Father and only consequently, derivatively, the Lawgiver. From his self-disclosure in the man Christ Jesus, we come to know God as an eternal communion of love between Father and Son. If we are wanting the "full and perfect light of the Gospel" we need look no further than Jesus Christ, for "the Son who dwells in the bosom of the Father reveals the Father."[1257] Theology finds its proper starting-point there in the self-revelation of God.

Consequently we begin, not by grafting the gospel onto an abstract God who is mainly a sovereign, moral governor promulgating laws, enforcing them by rewards and punishments, dispensing mercy when and where he arbitrarily chooses, but with a Father God who longs for a personal relationship with each person he had made.[1258] There are laws and judgments to be dealt with, but *they are not so many conditions to grace*. God does not have to be conditioned into being gracious. He is gracious, and therefore he provides a means of atonement.

> We must forbid all *direct* dealing with wrath and judgment as though these might be first disposed of, and *then* attention be turned to other considerations. We have here to do with PERSONS,--the Father of spirits and his offspring. *These are to each other more than all things and all* circumstances.[1259]

God's overriding concern is to gather his offspring in his home again as his own dear children. Everything he does and has done for us and for our salvation is determined by his fatherly nature. The righteous demands of the Law are satisfied, his wrath is dealt with, but not for the sake of Law, but for the sake of his fatherly longing.

And so McLeod Campbell declares in his *Nature of the Atonement*,

> The great and root-distinction of the view of the atonement presented in these pages is the relation in which our redemption is regarded as standing to the fatherliness of God. In that fatherliness has the atonement been now represented as originating. By that fatherliness has its end been represented to have been determined. To that

---

1257 *Reminiscences*, 234, 244.
1258 *Nature*, 188-89.
1259 *Nature*, 212, emphasis his.

fatherliness has the demand for the elements of expiation found in it been traced.[1260]

Yet there is no tension between his fatherliness and his holiness. Neither the Cross nor his very being provide any battleground for his attributes, for he is one. His holiness, grounded in his fatherly heart, "craves" our holiness. Divine justice looks at the sinner, not simply as the proper object of punishment, but with a desire that the sinner cease being unrighteous. All the divine attributes are against a person insofar as he is a sinner, and yet they all appear as intercessors for man, and crave his salvation."[1261]

With fatherliness as a central metaphor, he interprets the atonement in relational terms. God's wrath against sin is to be understood in the passive sense as the "distance" between God and alienated humans which ceases in their being reconciled to Him.[1262] Seen in its active aspect, his wrath resembles the attitude of a "judging doctor" eyeing a cancerous disease in us and wanting to root it out, that we might be saved.[1263] Even this embodies a fatherly concern.

In light of all that McLeod Campbell has expounded regarding the self-revelation of God the Father in his Son, we would expect him to say that forgiveness is not an arbitrary manifestation of the will of God, but is rather grounded in his nature. And that is exactly what we find. All profitable exploration of the atonement begins with the conviction that "there is forgiveness with God."[1264] We must reject any doctrine which teaches that the atonement was necessary in order to change God's heart toward us and make him gracious. Indeed, if God were not already gracious, no atonement could ever render him so. But the Scriptures are one in their testimony that the love of God is the cause and the atonement the effect. "For God so loved the world that he gave his only begotten Son, that whosoever believeth in him, might not perish, but have everlasting life."[1265]

1260 Nature, p. 338
1261 *Nature*, 29-30.
1262 *Nature*, 213.
1263 *Fragments of Truth*, 276.
1264 *Nature*, 18, cf. *Reminiscences*, 188ff.
1265 *Nature*, 20.

But what exactly is forgiveness? It is not a mere declaration of absolution by divine fiat, as the Socinians would have it. This overlooks God's holiness and his consequent "wrath against sin." For genuine forgiveness to be effected, God must deal with "deserts" of human sin. Forgiveness is "love to an enemy surviving his enmity, and which, notwithstanding his enmity can act towards him for his good." To be more precise, the "Father of the spirits of all flesh" is forgiving in his desire to free him from his evil condition in which he lives as an orphan, and bring him to sonship in the Father's home.[1266]

The Representative Humanity of Christ

Before we discuss Campbell's exposition of the atonement proper, we need to consider his doctrine of the representative or "vicarious" humanity of Christ.[1267] For in keeping with his insistence on the self-revelation of God, Campbell says that we can only understand the atonement in the light of the incarnation. The incarnation must be regarded as *the primary and highest fact in the history of God's relation to man, in the light of which God's interest in man and purpose for man may be truly seen.*[1268] If we wish to know God's purposes, his will for humankind, we must look to the *homoousion*, because God has disclosed himself there. And so the life of Christ sheds light upon the work of Christ, and what he has done is to be interpreted in terms of who he is. And who he is, says Campbell, is the One who represents all people in his humanity.[1269]

This may be viewed from two different perspectives. In a very real sense, "we have a common life which knits all generations together, and binds us to one another, making us members of one body, children of one family, the father of which is God."[1270] McLeod Campbell seems to take this as axiomatic, although acknowledging that it may rub against the grain of "modern individualism."[1271]

1266 *Nature*, 21ff.

1267 See James B. Torrance, "The vicarious humanity of Christ" in Thomas F. Torrance, ed., *The Incarnation*, (Edinburgh: Handsel, 1981), 127-47.

1268 *Nature*, xxv.

1269 Cf. Robert Mackintosh, *Historic Theories of Atonement*, (London: Hodder and Stoughton, 1920), 217; James Torrance, "The Contribution of McLeod Campbell to Scottish Theology," *Scottish Journal of Theology*, vol. 26, (1973): 309.

1270 *Bible Readings*, 131.

1271 *Nature*, 401ff.

This helps account for the effect one generation's errors have on a later one, and even for the effect individuals have upon each other:

> We are all mysteriously bound together, we cannot sin, neither can we suffer alone; the sins of the fathers are upon their children to the third and fourth generation . . . we are all bound together, and yet each has an individual responsibility.[1272]

This last qualification is important, because it indicates that we must always steer a course between a radical individualism on the one hand and a thoroughgoing "realism" on the other.[1273] His rejection of hyper-realism would seem to be a dismissal of a sort of platonic concept of the Ideal Man who stands behind the Many in the sensible world.[1274] Nor are we self-contained monads, who act and have our being without reference to one another. We are "persons in relation," to borrow a phrase from John Macmurray.[1275]

And yet Campbell is not here positing some prior capacity in humanity for salvation, even in the form of an antecedent bond between all people which can readily be "utilized" by the salvific work of Christ. For the tragic truth is that "we have lost sight of this common life, and are living each one for himself, a selfish, separate, ungodly life."[1276] In our sinful, selfish state, life is "solitary in all aspects of it." We are "brotherless" as well as "fatherless."[1277]

Christian Kettler detects a certain semi-Pelagianism in Campbell's reference to a "'capacity' of restoration to sonship."[1278] But that capacity is defined by Campbell as a "mute cry," which Christ comes and voices in his confession on our behalf, And that confession is one which "humanity could not have originated," but which serves as the "grounds on which God really puts his own acting in the whole history of redemption."[1279]

1272 *Bible Readings*, 128.
1273 *Nature*, 401f.
1274 Cf. James Torrance, "The Vicarious Humanity of Christ," 140, Christian Kettler, "The Vicarious Humanity of Christ and the Reality of Salvation," Ph.D. diss., Fuller Theological Seminary, (New York: University Press of America, 1991), 266.
1275 John Macmurray, *Persons in Relation*, (London: Faber and Faber, 1961).
1276 *Nature*, 132.
1277 *Nature*, 369, cf. *Bible Readings*, 133-34.
1278 He cites *Nature*, 236. See Kettler, *op. cit.*, 175, no. 83.
1279 *Nature*, 237-38.

Clearly, for Campbell, this cry is no more than an expression of a need we could not articulate or even name, because the only thing we had to offer was our destitution. The sole ground for our restoration is not in us but in Christ. Thus, he elsewhere stipulates that if we use the language of capacity to name our condition, "in truth, humanity had this capacity only relatively, that is, as dwelt in by the Son of God."[1280] The only possibility of humanity's restoration, therefore, is constituted by Christ.

But exactly what *is* the relation between his humanity and ours? McLeod Campbell expounds this in terms of a "double relation":[1281] Christ possesses a relation with us as man as well as a relation with us as God. There would be no promise for humanity in the mere fact of his own humanity, because our humanity is broken humanity; the mutual bonds between persons which constitute our humanness are torn asunder. His coming alongside us as a mere man—even as a perfect man—would not heal the damage between us. We are "brotherless" and "fatherless."[1282] But Christ comes and stands in the breach. He becomes our brother and lives a life of true sonship, and in his person and work he reconstitutes humanity in his own Person.

The way in which he does this will occupy us presently, but suffice it to observe at this point that the *will of God* is at the heart of all this, "the atonement having been accomplished by the natural working of the life of love in Christ, and having been the result of His doing the Father's will, and declaring the Father's name in humanity."[1283] The will of God is anchored in the self-revelation of God in Christ. And we perceive that will most vividly in the atoning work of Christ.

But the question which presents itself at this juncture concerns the relation between Christ's humanity and ours. Is there not a gulf? Is he not an individual separate from us, trapped in past history? Were Christ merely human, that would be true. But "there must be a relation between the Son of God and the sons of men, not according to the flesh only, but according to the spirit." As the Son of God possessing the "power of an endless life,"[1284] he has "power over all flesh to impart eternal

---

1280 *Nature*, 160, cf. 168.
1281 *Nature*, 160.
1282 *Nature*, 169.
1283 *Nature*, 154.
1284 *Nature*, 181.

life."[1285] He has so constituted things that in his humanity he "embraces all men."[1286]

Campbell does not profess to understand this, but he adds that "it is mystery in the region in which we are prepared for mystery, being, first, in the manner of being of God, and then, where the line of meeting is between God and man."[1287] He locates the mystery of "the nature of the relation of the Son of God to humanity" in the greatness of God in his fatherliness and his power to effect a real change in our humanity. The life-giving power that the Son of God puts into humans in this relation is part of "the acting of God as God, and [of] the divinity of the Son of God."[1288]

Campbell's point seems to be that the *Redeemer is the Creator*, that the One who speaks and things are, who calls and they come to be, indeed, the One who sustains in being the entire human race, is One who, through the incarnation and atonement, possesses a *restored* "universal relation" to humankind. The possibility of this "universal relation" is therefore grounded both in his life-giving divinity and in his work in the atonement.[1289] Consequently, we can speak about an "actual relation of our spirits to Christ as present in us, our true and proper life" even while we persist in sinful rejection of this reality.[1290]

This notion of the universal relation of Christ to humanity, both "according to the flesh" and "according to the spirit," is foundational to McLeod Campbell's interpretation of the atonement, because it provides a basis for a real at-one-ment between God and humankind. In this way, the air of unreality, of legal fiction, that attaches to purely forensic models is replaced by the "depth and reality of the bonds which connect the Savior and the saved."[1291] It is no longer a matter of God "imputing" Christ's righteousness to us and our sins to him. This One

---

1285 *Nature*, 160.
1286 *Nature*, 360.
1287 *Nature*, 373.
1288 *Ibid.*, John McIntyre, who prefers the language of "identification", to describe the relation of Christ to humankind, attributes this identification to the will of God: "Of his own free grace, Christ himself has elected to include us in that obedience". *On the Love of God*, (Glasgow: Collins, 1962), 210.
1289 *Nature*, 379.
1290 *Nature*, 380.
1291 *Nature*, 161.

Who has taken the nature of those who had sinned works out a real reconciliation "from the flesh."[1292]

From the flesh, Christ acts *representatively*. Tuttle rightly reminds us that Campbell employs a cluster of metaphors to describe Christ's work, including "representative,"[1293] "identification,"[1294] and "vicarious."[1295] The latter was not happy with substitutionary language, associated, as it was, with certain penal interpretations, and enunciated in such a way as, he felt, to preclude our living involvement in all that Christ accomplished. The kind of substitution he rejected was that according to which Christ was supposed to have undertaken our punishment in the form of "pain as pain,"[1296] taking the law's retribution upon himself so as to confer a "legal title" of admission into God's presence.[1297] His criticism of penal theories will occupy us presently.

In McLeod Campbell's thought, Christ assumes "our nature" and becomes "our true brother,"[1298] establishing a living relation with humankind in his own humanity. In this way, the Son of God took all humankind with him into the presence of God, representatively standing in for us and acting on our behalf before his Father. He did this throughout his life, but supremely in his death, offering up a life of true sonship to the Father. Because he offers that perfect righteousness which is true sonship, to the Father on behalf of humanity, we are accepted, are justified, in the person of Christ. Such justification Campbell hails as "a work of infinite excellence performed by Christ as the representative of men."[1299]

James Torrance shows that McLeod Campbell interprets the representative work of Christ in terms of the priesthood of Christ, representing God to humankind "in bringing God's word of forgiveness to men," while he also "represents *men to God*, and *deals with the Father on behalf of men* as our great High Priest, our Intercessor.[1300] But all this

---

1292 *Fragments of Truth*, 248.
1293 Sermon XIV, *Sermons and Lectures*, 329.
1294 *Nature*, 80, 159, 161.
1295 *Op. cit.*, 141.
1296 *Nature*, 115-18.
1297 *Nature*, 151-54.
1298 *Nature*, 139.
1299 *Nature*, 70; cf. Sermon V, *Sermons and Lectures*, vol. I, 101.
1300 James Torrance, "The Contribution of McLeod Campbell to Scottish Theology,"

must be interpreted with constant reference to the inclusive humanity of Christ, whereby Christ bears a universal relation to all humankind and represents them in all that he does.

Christ in our Place

We have at some length explored Campbell's understanding of the self-revelation of God, the fatherliness of God, and the representative humanity of Christ, because all these are crucial for an adequate grasp of his model of the atonement. A proper interpretation of this great salvation wrought by God in the flesh of his Son cannot begin with our own "sense of need," or with our prior concerns about sin and guilt. These "How questions" presuppose a certain understanding of "Who" God is, an understanding not grounded in the self-revelation of God in Christ. If we bring to the Gospel the notion that its main agenda is to deal with our sin, our law-breaking, we are thereby assuming that God is primarily a Lawgiver whose will is that sinners be brought into conformity with Law.

But only God can reveal God. He has disclosed himself fully and finally in his Son, whom he has appointed heir of all things. Therefore, we understand the atonement in light of the incarnation, the "How" in terms of the "Who." McLeod Campbell beckons us to assume the "attitude of reverently learning" from the actual course God's grace *has* taken in the history of the incarnation for our redemption.[1301]

When it is asked, Who has come and taken our place for our salvation, we can only answer, the One by whom and for Whom all people were created for sonship. Jesus Christ comes out of the bosom of the Father to fulfill "his Father's yearnings" for us.[1302] These filial purposes for humankind are not incidental or peripheral to God's will; they express his very heart.

'Will' and 'Love' are practically synonymous terms in Campbell's doctrine of God, because for McLeod Campbell, there is no will in God that is not the will of a loving Father. This is a corollary of his doctrine of revelation, since he is convinced that "the Son alone could reveal

---

309, "The Vicarious Humanity of Christ," 143-44; cf. Tuttle, *op. cit.*, 139.

1301 *Nature*, xxix.

1302 Cf. James Torrance, "The Contribution of McLeod Campbell to Scottish Theology," 304-305.

the Father."[1303] To put it more pointedly, "apart from Christ we know not our God."[1304] Foundational to his theology is the conviction that the will of God cannot be abstracted from the self-revelation of God in and through his Son. In the teaching and actions of Christ, the disciples "were contemplating the doing of the will of the Father by the Son," a will springing from his loving heart.[1305] In the Son's revealing the Father, therefore, we have to do directly with the will of God; that is to say, His will as His mind and character, —that in respect of which we say, God is love."[1306]

In this way, McLeod Campbell's theology constitutes a *Christological critique* of the "soteriological voluntarism" detected in both Aquinas and Calvin. He suggests concerning John Owen and Jonathan Edwards,[1307] both of whom taught a double decree, "it would have been well that they had used the *life* of Christ more as their light." In the light of revelation[1308] which is to say, in the light of Christ, we see that God's will is grounded in his innermost heart of love and that he expresses that love in all his works and ways. The loving God revealed in his Son is One who wills to accomplish an atonement for all humankind.[1309]

Campbell in fact believes that the "will of God, which the Son of God came to do and did, this was the essence and substance of the atonement."[1310] This is the case, not because God could simply will forgiveness and it would be so (as St. Thomas[1311] had acknowledged theoretically and Socinus had taught dogmatically).[1312] In fact, the

---

1303 *Nature*, 73, 168.
1304 *Nature*, 167.
1305 *Nature*, 72-73.
1306 *Nature*, xxxvi, xxxvii.
1307 Cf. Michael Jinkins, *op. cit.*, 1-182.
1308 *Nature*, xxix.
1309 *Nature*, 54-68.
1310 *Nature*, 124.
1311 *Summa*, 3a.46, 2 ad 3.
1312 See R. S. Franks, *The Work of Christ*, 362ff. Socinus apparently stipulated that God would sometimes decide to declare forgiveness for the repentant, which serves as another illustration of how the failure to ground the concept of the will of God (properly) in the self-revelation of God in Christ leads to the loss of the freeness of grace in its *unmeritedness*. Calvin also taught that the incarnation stemmed not from an "absolute necessity" but from "a heavenly decree." But this does not mean God could have simply declared an amnesty to sinners: it was on this decree that "men's salvation depended." Apart from the condescension of God's majesty in his inhomination,

restoration of humankind sought by the Father could *not* be accomplished through "a simple act of the divine will" exercising "infinite power." Yet in his great love God proceeded "at great cost" to embark upon a mission requiring "self-sacrifice."[1313]

Nevertheless, the will of God occupies the heart of the atonement. Hebrews 10:9 attributes to Jesus the fulfillment of the words, "Lo, I come to do thy will, O God," and says that by that will "we are sanctified, through the offering of the body of Jesus once and for all."[1314] It is worthwhile noting that McLeod Campbell does not deny that our salvation is grounded in "the offering of the body of Jesus once and for all." His concern is to probe more deeply into that offering, into the Cross, in order to understand the *nature* of the atonement. That which constituted the atoning power of the Cross was not, he believed, the conventional conception of penal-substitution (as we shall see), but rather the fact that the will of the Son accorded with the will of the Father.

What can we say about this will shared by both Father and Son? The will of God reflects "what *God is*." It is grounded in his "nature and character" as " good," "holy," "true," "just," and "love."[1315] His point about the correlation of will and atonement is here explained as the atonement being grounded in the nature and character of God. While he enumerates several attributes here, he clearly tells us elsewhere that the attributes are a unity in God. All of them are opposed to the sinner in that God's wrath is against sin, and yet even those attributes particularly associated with his holiness are on the side of the sinner:

> [T]hey, as well as mercy, appear as intercessors for man, and crave his salvation... *justice* looking at the sinner, not simply as the fit subject of punishment, but as existing in a moral condition of unrighteousness and so its own opposite must desire that the sinner should cease to be unrighteous—should become righteous: righteousness in God craving for righteousness in man.[1316]

"the situation would surely have been hopeless" (*Institutes* II.xii.1). Yet it remains troubling for Calvin to be contemplating the divine will in abstraction from Christ.

1313 *Nature*, 24-25.
1314 *Nature*, 124.
1315 *Ibid.*
1316 *Nature*, 29.

Evidently, for Campbell, Christ is the hermeneutical key to the nature of the Father, and Christ discloses a God who is fundamentally love. Therefore all the attributes are interpreted in that light. As we shall see, God is first a Father and then a Lawgiver. The Law is an expression of his fatherly heart, and all the aspects of his nature which express his concern for conformity to law are more deeply rooted in his loving desire that the sinner be forgiven and restored to his heart.

That loving desire for the restoration of the sinner, let it be repeated, is the will of God. And Christ reflects and discloses that will in all that he does. When he states, "I have declared thy name," he points us to

> *that in the work of Christ* which caused the shedding of His blood to have a virtue which was not in that of bulls and goats, which he represents as the will of God done, the mind of God manifested, the name of God declared by the Son.[1317]

Here, clearly, the "will," "mind," and "name" of God are all roughly equivalent. But in what sense is this true? Campbell goes on to explain that in doing the will of God, Christ fulfilled the two main commandments, loving the Father with all his heart and his brothers as himself.[1318] That is to say, the "will" of God, the "mind" of God and the "name" of God all connote, in the self-revelation of God in Christ, the *nature of God as love*. It was the fact that Christ shared the loving will of the Father in his death which gave his blood atoning virtue. Therefore, we must receive these words, "Lo, I have come to do thy will, O God," "as the great key-word on the subject of the atonement."[1319]

And he comes in a reconciling movement of love to draw all people into the eternal communion of love within the Being of God himself as

1317 *Nature*, 125.
1318 *Ibid.*
1319 *Nature*, 124.

Father and Son.[1320] He knows well the plight of our "orphan spirits," lost in their alienation from the Father's heart. And so he unites himself to our humanity, and as the Head of every human[1321] constitutes in his own person the "living way" back to the Father.[1322]

This is not to say that the incarnation is the whole of the Gospel. That would be "stopping short."[1323] In the Scripture, "the love of God is connected with the need of man as sinner" in the atonement. There it is that the Gospel possesses its 'remedial character'. The Apostles declare that "God commendeth His love toward us, in that, while we were yet sinners, Christ died for us," and "Herein is love, not that we loved God, but that He loved us, and sent His Son to be the propitiation for our sins." Clearly, both St. Paul and St. John "see the love of God, not in the incarnation simply, but in the incarnation as developed in the atonement."[1324]

Between the evil condition of humankind and the joyous life of sonship lies a vast gulf. On the human side we see spiritual darkness, sin, guilt, inward disorder, toward which is directed the condemnation and wrath of God. But on the other side we see the divine intentions for us: "eternal life partaken in, righteousness and holiness, the acceptance and favour of God, inward harmony . . ."[1325] Christ comes to span that gulf.

Doubtless due to Campbell's great stress on the Fatherly love of God, and on the Son's confession of his love and our sinfulness, all with the prospect of winning us to an answering love and repentance, some

---

1320 *Nature*, 172f; cf. John McLeod Campbell, *Thoughts on Revelation*, (London: Macmillan, 1862), 119, 135ff.

1321 *Nature*, 160; Sermon XIV, *Sermons and Lectures*, vol. I, 345ff; Sermon XV, *op. cit.*, 67ff.

1322 *Nature*, 100f.

1323 *Nature*, xxviii.

1324 *Nature*, xxx.

1325 *Nature*, 15f.

have characterized his interpretation of the atonement as Abelardian.[1326] For those accustomed to finding in the atonement a legal relation only between Christ and the sinner, this is understandable, because he rules out forensic notions of "imputation," "transferred merit" and the like.

Yet this can mislead us. Campbell places great emphasis on the holiness of God and the unchanging demands of his laws. When Galatians 4:4 tells us that Christ "redeemed us who were under the law", we learn that our status "under the law" had to affect the nature of the atonement.[1327] If fallen humans were to be rescued, God would have to assume their plight and take their place on the Cross, there to die and take our penalty upon himself. But for Campbell, legal categories do not exhaust the significance of the atonement. Indeed, they are not the primary means of interpretation.

God in Christ did not come merely to give us legal access into the divine courtroom, but to admit us into the divine family. That latter image is closer to the heart of God in Campbell's thought, because law comes out of Gods heart and God's deepest yearning is for our fellowship, and not our conformity to law.

When we abstract the legal righteousness of Christ from the "law of the spirit of life of sonship", we lose sight of the fundamental movement in God's provision of atonement, which is the longing of the Father's heart for our sonship. In this way we would also lose sight of the

1326 See, for example, Nicholas R. Needham, *Thomas Erskine of Linlathen: His Life and Theology 1788-1837*, (Edinburgh: Rutherford House, 1990), 332f; Andrew L. Drummond and James Bulloch, *The Scottish Church 1688-1843*, (Edinburgh: Saint Andrew Press, 1973), 209; R. S. Paul, *The Atonement and the Sacraments*, (London: Hodder and Stoughton, 1961),140-49, W. Adams Brown, "Expiation and Atonement (Christian)", in James Hastings, *Encyclopedia of Religion and Ethics*, (New York: Charles Scribner's Sons, 1912), vol. V, 650, and George Carey, *The Gate of Glory*, (London: Hodder and Stoughton, 1986), 128-30. John Stott's otherwise illuminating book, *The Cross of Christ*, (Leicester: InterVarsity, 1986), goes even further to make the surprising suggestion that Campbell's book "stands in the same general tradition" as Socinus (141-42). Apart from the fact that Campbell explicitly rejects the notion that God could or did forgive sins by fiat (*Nature*, xxx; 19-21), he has too much to say regarding the necessity of Christ in our humanity fulfilling the righteous requirements of the law, even to the point of death on a cross, to reconcile sinful humans to God, to warrant such an interpretation. Cf. Ronald Wallace, *The Atoning Death of Christ*, (Westchester: Crossway Books, 1981), 88.
1327 *Nature*, 27.

revelation of the Father by the Son, for a subject can reveal a Lawgiver, but only the Son can disclose his Father.[1328]

What Christ did in his life, death and resurrection fulfilled the righteous demands of the law, but in a deeper sense, it disclosed the mind of God the Father, a mind which looks upon us always in love, which is ready to forgive, and which bestows that forgiveness in Christ's fulfillment of the law. The Cross therefore *not only reconciles us to God, but also reveals God's very heart to us.*

Thus McLeod Campbell could preach to his listeners, that they carried deep wounds which could only be healed lightly apart from the saving Gospel. And what was that wound? "You are without God in the world—this is your wound—this is your hurt."[1329] This wound they carried despite all that God in Christ had done for them. Their basic problem lay in their "present ignorance of God's love."[1330] They had never truly heard the Gospel in such a way as to grasp its completeness and its inclusion of each of them personally. And so he tells them:

> We know that it is a faithful saying, and worthy of all acceptation, that Christ Jesus died to save sinners. We know that we are entitled to say to one and all of you confidently, He was wounded for *your* transgressions, He was bruised for *your* iniquities. We know that we are authorised to declare unto you, that God's gift *to all of you* is eternal life, and this life is in his Son . . . . We are assured that if once you understood and believed the love which God has shown to you, all doubts, fears and hesitations about drawing near him would vanish— you would immediately rejoice to approach him as your reconciled Father in Christ . . ."[1331]

Even here, the legal dimension is recognized. Because Christ was wounded for our transgressions, he constitutes in his person God's gift of life to us. But Campbell sets the legal dimension upon the foundation of God's fatherly love, so that we look past the legal to the filial, and

---

1328 *Nature,* 73-74.
1329 Sermon No. I, *Inghin An Reachdaire,* 4.
1330 *Ibid.,* 5.
1331 *Ibid.,* 13.

realize that we need not linger in the courtroom, we can (so to speak) proceed to the Father's living room.

But we must here recall Campbell's exposition of the representative humanity of Christ. For Jesus Christ embraces us in his humanity in a real way so that we have a part in his dying and rising and even in his confessing.[1332] Thus, in view of Campbell's recognition of the legal dimension as well as his emphasis on the saving humanity of Christ, an Abelardian interpretation of the atonement is completely ruled out.

It is not as if, argues McLeod Campbell, we are each to go our individualistic way and try to duplicate the work of Christ such that the real atonement happens not in him but in us. Rather, our relation to the Christ who was crucified is more like that of a branch or twig to the tree. Far from being solitary, self-reliant plants, they draw their life from the tree. So it is in our relation to Christ, for he is the vine of which we are only so many branches.[1333]

Campbell also questions whether the Cross accomplished much if it only served as a great proof of love. No one should lay down his life unless it is "necessary in order to save the life for which he yields up his own." But it *was* necessary for Christ to die for us.[1334]

Nevertheless, Robert S. Paul alleges that Campbell has left behind the 'satisfaction' theory of the atonement and its basis in "the objective fact of what God in Christ [has] *done* for our salvation," in favor of concentrating upon what "Christ is doing and *will* do to save us from sin." The facts of the Gospel are by Campbell essentially interpreted as "the supreme example of general moral and spiritual principles." Hence, Professor Paul thinks, we are here given a "variation on Abelard," whereby the believer no longer "places his ultimate reliance on what Christ has done for him," but rather in a "general spiritual principle that Christ's passion illustrates."[1335]

We have just noted Campbell's explicit rejection of exemplarist theories, but Paul's charge goes further. Has the Scottish theologian

---

1332 Cf. Christian D. Kettler, "The Vicarious Repentance of Christ in the Theology of John McLeod Campbell and R. C. Moberly," *Scottish Journal of Theology*, vol. 38, no. 4, (1985): 538-541; Kettler, *The Vicarious Humanity of Christ and the Reality of Salvation*, 190-202.

1333 *Nature*, 329f.

1334 *Nature*, 26f.

1335 Robert S. Paul, *The Atonement and the Sacraments*, 145-46.

abandoned an objective doctrine of atonement? Trevor Hart reminds us that one of Campbell's central insights is that the forgiveness of God precedes the atonement,[1336] which in the latter's mind rules out any possibility of humankind accomplishing its own peace with God.[1337] Says Hart, "this key theme of Campbell's theology disintegrates the very moment that it is conceded that that which atones for man's sin springs from man himself (albeit in response to a prior manifestation of divine love) and not wholly from God."[1338] James Denney finds in Campbell the conviction that "Christ has done something for us which we could never have done for ourselves, and enables us to do in union with Himself what we could never do alone; and if our union with Him is His work, His position as Saviour is unimpaired." Thus Denney concludes: "in the strictest sense of the term it was an objective atonement."[1339]

There exists a strong basis for such an interpretation of Campbell's doctrine of atonement as something which God has already accomplished: "The Gospel declares that the love of God has not only *desired* to bridge over this gulf [of sin between God and humankind], but *has actually bridged it over*, and the atonement is presented to us as that in which this is accomplished."[1340]

A proper understanding of the atonement derives from the nature of God. On the one hand, God's justice, his righteousness, truth, and faithfulness all "presented difficulties in the way of our salvation, which rendered for their removal an atonement necessary." But on the other, the goodness and love of God "also demanded an atonement, that our salvation might be consistent with the well-being of the moral universe" as well as meeting the needs of sinners themselves. Therefore, in Campbell's mind, "salvation otherwise than through the atonement is a

---

1336 Cf. James Torrance, "The Contribution of McLeod Campbell to Scottish Theology," 304.

1337 Trevor Hart, in an essay, "Anselm of Canterbury and John McLeod Campbell: Where Opposites Meet?" read to the Aberdeenshire Theological Club on January 16, 1989. He cites in this connection *Nature*, 18.

1338 *Ibid.*

1339 James Denney, *The Christian Doctrine of Reconciliation*, (London: Hodder and Stoughton, 1917), 119, 260. Cf. J. H. Leckie, "Books That Have Influenced our Epoch, John McLeod Campbell's 'The Nature of the Atonement,'" *Expository Times*, vol. 40 (February 1921): 201.

1340 *Nature*, 25-26, cited in Hart, *op. cit.*

contradiction."[1341]

But we must not divide the divine attributes. God is ever consistent with himself, and his laws are grounded in his fatherly heart. In one sense "all the divine attributes are against the sinner" in the outpouring of God's "wrath." But underlying that interest in justice is a concern for the sinner, and thus even the justice and righteousness and holiness of God are in accord with his mercy and "appear as intercessors for man, and crave his salvation."[1342]

McLeod Campbell's guiding principle is that the divine attributes possess a "central and essential unity,"[1343] constituted by the fact that "God is love."[1344] "Every attribute of God tells one tale," he declares, "and that is that God desires to bless him." For love is the "foundation of all" attributes. He knows this because of God's self-disclosure in and through Jesus Christ.[1345] In the light of Christ, we learn that God is a loving Father, who sent his Son to assume our nature and deal on our behalf with the condemnation of sin, so that we might be adopted as sons in his family.[1346]

Since the very nature of God demanded an atonement for the sinner, God condescended to be that atonement himself. This bold language is employed by McLeod Campbell to emphasize the oneness of Father and Son, and the basis for the atonement in the very nature of God. So he declares in a sermon, "God in your nature tasted death for you . . . you have sinned against God, but he loves you—he took your nature and died for you."[1347]

So it was that the "way opened into the holiest by the blood of Christ" was "the only way." This is the meaning of Jesus' declaration that he is the way, the truth and the life. The way to the Father must be the way of his Cross.[1348]

"Vicarious penitence" is easily misunderstood if it is considered in

---

1341 *Nature*, 29.
1342 *Nature*, 30.
1343 *Nature*, 63.
1344 *Nature*, 65.
1345 Sermon IX, *Sermons and Lectures*, vol. I, 190-91.
1346 *Nature*, 69.
1347 Sermon VII, *Inghin an Reachdaire*, 20; cf. Sermon I, "The Testimony of God Concerning His Son," *Sermons and Lectures*, 11-12.
1348 *Nature*, 294f.

isolation from the death of Christ or from his representative humanity. Then we are left with the problem of "how Christ's repentance avails for others."[1349] We cannot simply turn to his famous statement about Jesus making "a perfect Amen in humanity"[1350] to the judgment of God on the sin of man, as if it were an adequate summary of his teaching.

McLeod Campbell interprets the atonement in terms of the priesthood of Christ, which itself presupposes the representative humanity of Christ. For Christ, the One by Whom and for Whom all are created for that true worship which is sonship, assumes our humanity into union with himself and in our name and on our behalf becomes both Priest and Victim that by his blood he might fit us to partake in the worship.

Now "partake" or "participate" is a favorite term of his, because it underscores the personal dimension in the saving life and death of Christ.

> It is to our personal relation to God as the Father of our spirits that the atonement belongs; out of disorder in that relation has the need for it arisen, to bring that relation into harmony with its divine ideal is the end which it has contemplated.[1351]

And it is precisely this relational notion which underlies his understanding of the atonement as "spiritual." For he often says that the atonement was "moral and spiritual" rather than penal.

By this terminology he is not seeking to dilute the seriousness of our plight or of the divine remedy. The kind of penal atonement he was rejecting was one which in its extreme form represents the Son as by the cross "exercising an influence over the Father to make Him gracious towards us."[1352] That would contradict the essential Fatherliness and graciousness of God, making his grace conditional upon sin being punished. But God is love and grace in his innermost being, and this determines the character of all his actions toward us.

Of course most Calvinists would disclaim such an interpretation. But even then there remains an attempt to find in the atonement "a

1349 Cf. Ian Hamilton's article on Campbell in *New Dictionary of Theology*, ed. Sinclair Ferguson *et. al.*, (InterVarsity Press: Leicester, 1988), 126-27.
1350 *Nature*, 135-36.
1351 *Nature*, lii.
1352 *Nature*, 229.

ground of confidence towards God distinct from what it has revealed as the mind of God towards man."[1353] That is to say, our confidence in approaching God is not grounded in his nature, but in a work done on the cross. Hence we are not given a sense of sonship, but of legal access, and we find ourselves "pleading the merits" of Christ's atoning work, rather than confidently approaching the loving heart of the Father disclosed in the Cross.[1354]

But this error is exposed in the light of the Son's mission: "Lo, I come to do thy will, O God." And that will, is to declare his Father's Name, to disclose his heart. Our faith is therefore directed by Christ in all his works and ways to the One Whose will he came to fulfill. We can receive "true knowledge of eternal realities" from the atonement. When Christ suffered, he was not receiving the wrath of God as a personal object of divine displeasure. God was never angry with him. The cup of suffering which was Christ's was received from his loving Father's hand, and throughout he was sustained by his love. Our sins were never in some mysterious way transferred to Jesus.[1355] But he did feel the divine wrath, and he acknowledged that wrath in his confession, as we shall see presently.

This is not to disclaim a fulfilling of the law in the atonement, for there is certainly that. The atonement is "moral" as well as spiritual, and as such is grounded in the very being of God who *is* moral.[1356] While there is no conflict between the spiritual and the moral, since God's law is grounded in his love, neither is there any diminution by that fact. We must recognize "the fixedness of that moral constitution of things of which the law is the expression, and that the "root of that constitution of things is the Fatherliness of the Father of our spirits."[1357]

So Christ came not only to deal with a broken relationship, but with a relationship that had been broken in the violation of law. Law must be dealt with. Jesus did not simply come to announce that God is forgiving, that he has never been angry, and therefore all ought to return to his arms. He came to work out a costly at-one-ment in his life and in his

---

1353 *Nature*, 230.
1354 John McLeod Campbell, *Christ the Bread of Life*, (Glasgow: Maurice Ogle, 1851), 73-97.
1355 *Fragments of Truth*, 249.
1356 *Nature*, xxiv-xxv.
1357 *Nature*, 205.

death. And that meant, among other things, addressing this broken law.

The Cross in Campbell's Theology

There has been heretofore little recognition of the importance of the legal dimension in Campbell's interpretation of the Cross. C. E. Pritchard questions whether in Campbell's teaching, "that kind of importance is given to the death of Christ which it has in Holy Scriptures."[1358] John Macquarrie finds no "clear necessity" for the death of Christ; in fact, "Gethsemane rather than Calvary was, for Campbell, the climactic moment of the atonement."[1359] Paul T. Nimmo contends that, "for McLeod Campbell, the physical sufferings on the cross are evidence of nothing more than that Jesus of Nazareth had a bad day in Jerusalem and that sufficient enmity toward Him existed to effect His torture and execution."[1360] Brian Gerrish recognizes that Campbell's view of the atonement "does have reference to the vindication of God's law," but does not correlate this with the Cross as such.[1361]

Eugene Bewkes finds vestigial remains of an "outmoded biblical theology" in Campbell's references to the Cross as Christ's "tasting of death for every man"; the deeper insights are found in Campbell's exemplarist ideas.[1362] George Carey finds the Scottish theologian as promoting a "variation of the moral influence theory" such that "the real atonement takes place when, with the same attitude and response of Christ's perfection, obedience is seen in us."[1363] Sidney Cave observes that in Campbell's thought "belief in God's Fatherly love does not imply

---

1358 C. E. Pritchard, "Modern Views of the Atonement," *North British Review*, vol. 46, (June 1867), 203.

1359 John Macquarrie, "John McLeod Campbell 1800-1872," *The Expository Times*, vol. 83, no. 9, (1973): 268; cf. Macquarrie, *Jesus Christ in Modern Thought*, (London: SCM Press, 1991), 402-3. But cf. *Nature*, 299f where such a notion is explicitly denied.

1360 Paul T. Nimmo, "A Necessary Suffering? John McLeod Campbell and the Passion of Christ," *Theology in Scotland*, vol. XII, no. 2 (2005), 65.

1361 Gerrish, "The Protest of Grace: John McLeod Campbell on the Atonement," in his book, *Tradition and the Modern World. Reformed Theology in the Nineteenth Century*, (Chicago: University of Chicago Press, 1978), 88-89.

1362 Eugene Garrett Bewkes, *Legacy of a Christian Mind*, (Philadelphia: Judson Press, 1937), 212f; 240ff.

1363 Carey, *op. cit.*, 130.

that there was no necessity of Christ's redeeming act,"[1364] but does not interpret this "redeeming act" with reference to the Cross. John Macleod avers that in Campbell's exposition, "the penal, the forensic, the judicial aspect of the great transaction were spirited away."[1365] R. W. Dale thinks Campbell wholly rejects the doctrine that Christ on our behalf submitted to death as the penalty for our sins.[1366] James C. Goodloe contends that McLeod Campbell "argues that any legal, forensic or penal theory grossly misrepresents [the atonement's] nature and must be cast aside."[1367] Leanne Van Dyk avers that "The sufferings of Christ were not, Campbell insisted, substituted punishment."[1368]

Robert Mackintosh classifies Campbell's teaching as a "theory of vicarious penitence," according to which Christ had to die in order to perfect his "vision of the evil of sin," that he might repent and confess the sin and guilt of the human race in such a way as to "become the spring of repentance and of holiness in all his people."[1369] Robert S. Franks expounds Campbell as a proponent of the "vicarious confession" theory, according to which Christ atones by a "condemnation and confession of sin in humanity," his sufferings not being penal but a revelation of God's nature.[1370] Nowhere does Franks seem to acknowledge the Cross as the place where Christ fulfills the sentence of God upon human sin.

1364 Sidney Cave, *The Doctrine of the Work of Christ*, (London: University of London Press, 1947), 232.

1365 John Macleod, *Scottish Theology in Relation to Church History Since the Reformation*, (Edinburgh: Banner of Truth, 1974), 258.

1366 R. W. Dale, *The Atonement*, (London: Congregational Union of England and Wales, 1902), 424-25.

1367 James C. Goodloe, "John McLeod Campbell: The Extent and Nature of the Atonement," *Studies in Reformed Theology and History*, New Series, no. 3, 1997.

1368 Leanne Van Dyk, *The Desire of Divine Love: John McLeod Campbell's Doctrine of the Atonement* (New York: Peter Lang, 1995), 110. Van Dyk does concede that, "if the notion of penal substitution could be articulated in a way that would clearly place it under the broader framework of the love of God, perhaps Campbell would have, at least in a modified way, retained it" (*op. cit.*, p. 115). This writer is attempting to show that this is precisely what Campbell does, although, without using the phrase, "penal substitution."

1369 Robert Mackintosh, *op. cit.*, 227, 269-70.

1370 Franks, *The Work of Christ*, 665-672.

H. R. Mackintosh also classifies Campbell's doctrine as the "vicarious penitence of Christ," bearing at its heart at least the suggestion that "our Lord's atonement is the perfect acknowledgement made by Him of the righteous judgment of God as embodied in his pain." While, for Campbell, "the Cross was necessary . . . because the last step love can take in condemning sin and resisting it is to bear its malignant assault to the very end," Mackintosh wonders why the Cross was essential, when it would seem, on such a reckoning, that a "verbal acknowledgement" was enough.[1371] Andrew J. Campbell summarizes McLeod Campbell's doctrine of atonement as "Christ...making confession to God on behalf of men" and thus making "reconciliation possible."[1372] Vernon F. Storr offers a similar interpretation.[1373] Otto Pfleiderer represents Campbell as teaching that Christ, retrospectively, offered a "vicarious contrition" for the sins of humankind, condemning its sinful past as its representative, and prospectively, communicated his righteousness to humankind and revealed the divine Fatherhood.[1374] J. H. Leckie initially saw the "Amen in humanity" of Christ as embracing not only repentance, but also "His endurance of the curse and shame of death,"[1375] but eight years later appears to have retreated to nothing more than a "vicarious penitence" interpretation[1376]

Michael Jinkins thinks that Campbell's primary concern is with the revelatory aspect of Christ's work: God has come in the flesh to show

---

1371 H R. Mackintosh, *Some Aspects of Christian Belief,* (London: Hodder and Stoughton, 1923), 96-97.

1372 Andrew J. Campbell, *Two Centuries of the Church of Scotland 1707-1929,* (Paisley: Alexander Gardner, 1930), 191.

1373 Vernon F. Storr, *The Development of English Theology in the Nineteenth Century 1800-1860,* (London: Longmans, Green and Co., 1913), 426-27.

1374 Otto Pfleiderer, *The Development of Theology in Germany Since Kant and its Progress in Great Britain since 1825,* (London: Swan Sonnenschein, 1890), 383.

1375 J. H. Leckie, "John McLeod Campbell: The Development of His Thought II," *The Expositor, Eighth Series* 21 (1921): 114.

1376 Leckie, "Books That Have Influenced Our Epoch. John McLeod Campbell's 'The Nature of the Atonement," *Expository Times,* vol. 40, no. 5, (February 1929): 202.

humankind that he has already forgiven them prior to the Cross.[1377] However, James B. Torrance asserts that in Campbell's thought, Jesus Christ made on our behalf "the One True Response to the Father in his whole life of filial obedience as well as in his sufferings and death upon the Cross,"[1378] and says that in Campbell's teaching, we see Jesus "not only vicariously confessing our sin...but submitting *for* us to the verdict of guilty, in offering his life in death on the Cross."[1379] However, Torrance does not develop these points, nor does he show how the concepts of the righteous "wrath" of God against sin, the "penalty" of death, and the nature of God as a Lawgiver function together in Campbell's doctrine of atonement, but he sets us on the right track.[1380] Trevor Hart demonstrates that Campbell "speaks clearly . . . of Christ's death as a bearing of men's sins, and as bearing or dealing with the righteous wrath of God."[1381]

George M. Tuttle, explains the retrospective aspect of the latter's doctrine as involving "Christ's confession and repentance of human

---

1377 Jinkins does say that "Christ, by taking our humanity unto himself, and by absorbing the curse and death into his divine being, delivers humanity from the power of guilt and sin and the curse" (217). But he also tells us that "God's revelation of himself in Christ is God's supreme act of sharing this eternal, communal life which is essential to his being" (205); "God has come into the flesh to show humanity that all persons are forgiven, that the barrier to access is down" (219); and "God's forgiveness of sins makes possible the atonement" (231); "God became flesh to effect atonement because he had already forgiven humanity" (289). If this were Campbell's teaching, he would be open to the charge of Socinianism. See Michael Jinkins, "Atonement and the Character of God: A Comparative Study in the Theology of Atonement in Jonathan Edwards and John McLeod Campbell."

1378 James B. Torrance, "The Contribution of McLeod Campbell to Scottish Theology," 305-6.

1379 James B. Torrance, "The Vicarious Humanity of Christ," 143.

1380 Cf. this writer's 1988 essay, published as "Christ in Our Place in the Theology of John McLeod Campbell," *Christ in Our Place: The Humanity of God in Christ for the Reconciliation of the World*, ed. Trevor Hart and Daniel Thimell, (Exeter: Paternoster, 1989), 182-206, which attempts to demonstrate that for Campbell, God is a Father and, derivatively, a Lawgiver, both images yielding essential insights into the nature of God which affect the nature of the atonement. The article further argues that Campbell's doctrine of atonement is, in a qualified sense, penal, since it includes the notion that in acknowledgement of God's wrath against sin, Christ must die because death is the divinely-prescribed *penalty* for sin.

1381 See Trevor Hart's 1989 paper, "Anselm of Canterbury and John McLeod Campbell: Where Opposites Meet?" 13.

sin. Acknowledging the reality of God's wrath towards sin,[1382] Christ responds to that wrath with perfect repentance, which actually connotes a "perfect sorrow," a "perfect contrition," and a "confession" of the evil of human sins. Thus the term "repentance," which ordinarily implies a turn from sin, may be inappropriate.[1383] Tuttle goes on to observe that in Christ's confession of the sins of humankind,

> [I]t is constantly shown that in standing on God's side as it were in condemnation of their evil he did what no other person was able to do. He thus endured the suffering and death which stem from the divine judgment, and with this offering of himself God was well-pleased.[1384]

Here Tuttle has taken us to the heart of it. We are not saved by a mere verbal confession, nor by sympathy. The atonement embodied a "oneness of mind," between Father and Son, a common love of humankind and abhorrence of sin, but it was more than attitude that redeemed humankind—it took the cross, and the cross as filled with divine judgment on sin.

Unfortunately Tuttle does not elaborate this thought. It remains for us to see how Campbell develops and correlates his convictions concerning the nature of God as Lawgiver as well as Father, the place of law in God's dealings with the human race, as well as the importance of Christ's death as a submission to the "penalty" for sin. This becomes particularly significant for our investigation, since Campbell's doctrine of atonement is anchored in the will of God as manifested in his Son. Does he succeed, at this crucial point, in maintaining the freeness of grace in all its *unmeritedness* as well as its *unrestrictedness*?

For McLeod Campbell, we know God the Father through his Son, and the Father-Son relation must be determinative for our understanding of the nature of God and his actions.[1385] God's overriding concern is to gather his offspring in his home again as his own dear children.[1386] Everything he does and has done for us and for our salvation is determined by his fatherly nature. And so McLeod Campbell explains:

1382 *John McLeod Campbell on Christian Atonement: So Rich a Soil*, 94.
1383 *Ibid.*, 126-27; cf. *Nature*, 137, 139.
1384 Tuttle, *op. cit.*, 127.
1385 *Nature*, lii.
1386 *Nature*, 25.

The great and root-distinction of the view of the atonement presented in these pages is the relation in which our redemption is regarded as standing to the fatherliness of God. In that fatherliness has the atonement been now represented as originating. By that fatherliness has its end been represented to have been determined. To that fatherliness has the demand for the elements of expiation found in it been traced.[1387]

Yet we must emphasize that God is at once loving and righteous, On the one hand we see a "real righteous severity" in God.[1388] For God *is* a moral being. He is goodness in his innermost being and he consequently gives human creatures goodness as the law of their being.[1389] He always demands that justice be rendered.[1390]

Therefore, we must never collapse God's character as Lawgiver into his character as Father. Neither should we consider the notion of the Lawgiver as giving a truer picture of God.[1391] God is primarily the Father and only consequently, derivatively, the Lawgiver. The righteous demands of the Law are satisfied, his wrath is dealt with, but not for the sake of Law, but for the sake of his fatherly longing.[1392] The Scottish theologian takes with utter seriousness God's holiness and "wrath against sin," which alone expose the real "sinfulness of sin."[1393] Indeed, "it is just because [the awakened conscience realizes that] he has sinned and deserves punishment . . . that the wrath of God seems so terrible."[1394] And this wrath against human unrighteousness "was not a feeling that has passed, or could pass away: no revelation of the unchanging God could."[1395] God is not merely a congenial and indulgent grandfather

---

1387 *Nature*, 338.
1388 *Nature*, 187.
1389 *Nature*, xxxivf.
1390 *Nature*, 185.
1391 *Nature*, 72.
1392 Cf. the interpretation offered by Campbell's grandson, John McLeod Campbell, D. D., in his article, "John McLeod Campbell, 1800-1872," included in Ronald Selby Wright, ed., *Fathers of the Kirk*, (Oxford: Oxford University Press, 1960), 164-65.
1393 *Nature*, 21, 147.
1394 *Nature*, 80-81.
1395 *Nature*, 209.

figure, affirming humankind in its rebellion. In his holy nature he ever continues to oppose all that which is contrary to his holiness.

> The wrath of God against sin is a reality, however men have erred in their thoughts as to how that wrath was to be appeased. Nor is the idea that satisfaction was due to divine justice a delusion, however far men have wandered from the true conception of what would meet its righteous demand. And if so, then Christ, in dealing with God on behalf of men, must be conceived of as dealing with the righteous wrath of God against sin, and *as according to it that which was due*...[1396]

Eugene G. Bewkes thinks that Campbell wrongly tries to straddle two incompatible currents of thought. On the one hand, Campbell endeavors to find room for a genuine wrath in God and consequent need for satisfaction, but on the other he calls attention to the grieving love of God which is disclosed to sinful humankind by Christ. The latter is a "deeper concept," but surely, argues Bewkes, "the notion that the wrath has got to be assuaged or held back by a specific act or atonement which will allay the coming forth of the fury of that wrath is hardly tenable."[1397]

Campbell's deeper insight, we are told, is that God's love will be satisfied when we come to know his love in such a way that we "share his abhorrence of sin," repent of it, and "by devotional living" enter our sonship.[1398] But McLeod Campbell mistakenly imports the notion of repentance into what Christ did. In fact, "the more essential and really fundamental meaning in Campbell's mind here is that Christ does not repent *for us*, and certainly not for himself, but he has feelings of the divine mind, which when reproduced in us, *cause us to repent*."[1399] Clearly Bewkes favors an exemplarist interpretation of the atonement, which, as we have demonstrated, Campbell decisively rejects. But it is instructive that even one so earnest to find such a doctrine in Campbell has to reckon with elements which he admits are incompatible with it.

Indeed, Bewkes concedes that when the concept of wrath is permitted to shape the atonement, "it suggests an 'objective' transaction, an act

---

1396 *Nature*, 135.
1397 Bewkes, *op. cit.*, 206.
1398 *Ibid.*, 206.
1399 *Ibid.*, 213.

of atonement which somehow sustains God's justice, which Adam's Fall and its consequences have offended."[1400] But as we are seeking to demonstrate, Campbell propounds such a view while maintaining, in profound consistency, the love of God. For McLeod Campbell, love and wrath are not contraries, not attributes which must battle on Golgotha.

For the Scottish theologian, by "seeing the Father in the Son," we learn that God has his laws, which express his loving will for humankind.[1401] The "law of the Father" declares a "fixed and immutable constitution of things" that must be upheld. In fact, his law is "found to be fixed and altogether unbending, incapable of accommodation in a way of pity, or indulgence, or consideration of circumstances."[1402]

Let us be clear on this: Campbell does not begin with an abstract notion of law, the violation of which creates the need for an atonement. Rather, he begins with the life and death of Christ, believing that true knowledge of God the Father's nature is there disclosed. "Let us think of Christ as the Son who reveals the Father, that we may know the Father's heart against which we have sinned, and how sin, in making us godless, has made us orphans."[1403]

And what do we learn through Christ concerning the Father's heart? When his children rebelled, there was no easy way back. God could not simply receive us back without an atonement, for law is grounded in his loving nature. In fact, "the Father's heart did demand an atoning sacrifice . . . the shedding of blood in order to the remission of sins, because it demanded blood in which justice would be rendered to the fatherliness which had been sinned against."[1404] Nimmo seeks to undermine Campbell's seeming support here for the soteriological necessity of the Cross by arguing that "the underlying reason" for this statement of Campbell's "is spiritual and not penal:" that 'justice would be rendered against the fatherliness which had been sinned against.'"[1405]

However, there is a vivid legal aspect in Campbell's conception of the atonement. God is a God of law, of justice, who demands that his

---

1400 *Ibid.*
1401 *Nature*, xxxviii, 188.
1402 *Nature*, 188,189; cf. 190.
1403 *Nature*, 171.
1404 *Nature*, 184-5.
1405 Nimmo, *op, cit.*, 62; cf. *Nature*, 185.

justice be satisfied. We must immediately go on to acknowledge that Campbell will not permit us to detach the legal from the filial, because the latter is prior. The law of God stems from his fatherly nature. Nimmo contends that this author "unwittingly acknowledges" that Campbell "risks the law becoming divorced from the Father" by noting that "God's primary concern is not the law be satisfied but that his fatherly heart be satisfied."[1406] But Campbell stresses that the law still must be honored. "Without the shedding of the blood of Christ, the Father of Spirits could not receive back to the bosom of his love His rebellious children."[1407]

Consequently, the Son of God comes in our nature, presenting himself as a "sacrifice for sin." He did more than reveal God's displeasure with sin. He died for it. "Christ condemned sin, not only by being the opposite of sin, but by giving himself as a sin-offering to God—by submitting to feel and experience the wrath and curse of God, due to us for sin."[1408]

Clearly, we find the fundamental sense of Christ taking the righteous consequences of the law upon himself in his death in the mature expression of Campbell's thought in *Nature of the Atonement*. Christ could not go around the law to the Father's heart in his atoning work:

1406 *Ibid., pp. 69-70, n. 10, cf.* Thimell, "The Place of Christ in the Theology of McLeod Campbell, 185. Nimmo overlooks Campbell's conviction that, in the nature of God, love and law, fatherliness and law are not antinomies, but two harmonious aspects. To say that fatherliness is primary and law secondary is not to introduce an incompatibility. Nor does it mean that they are alternatives. Campbell eloquently expresses their fundamental harmony when he states, *"God's law* is God's own heart *come out in the shape of a law"* in *Responsibility for the Gift of Eternal Life* (London: Macmillan and Co., 187), p. 106, emphasis his. This really takes us to the crux of Campbell's argument. A proper doctrine of the atonement is grounded in the self-revelation of God in Christ. In Christ we see a God who is fatherly, who loves us unconditionally, even as sinners, and longs for our reconciliation. Yet also in his fatherliness he has given us law to guide our life in relation to him. When his law is broken, his fatherly heart wants to see that legal, as well as the filial breech, healed, and so he comes in Christ to bring us back through his cross. It is the very notion of an incompatibility between love and holiness, grace and law in God that leads, Campbell believes, to a conception of penal atonement embodying conditional grace and thereby destroying the filial relation God wants to have with us. He also thinks that it leads to the Calvinist doctrine of the double decree. He cites John Owen and Jonathan Edwards as teaching that justice is an "essential" attribute of God while love is "arbitrary," and thereby positing a God who is fundamentally untrammeled will, who wills law for all and redemption for a predestined few.
1407 *Nature,* 186.
1408 *Ibid.*

"In Christ's honouring of the law, the *sentence of the law* was included, *as* well as *the mind of God* which that sentence expressed."[1409]

Tuttle thinks that such passages should not be construed as pointing in the direction of a "penal" interpretation, since "Christ is not conceived to have tasted death in the same dimension as that which is due to humanity."[1410] But this is to miss Campbell's point. The latter does think that Christ experienced death with a full apprehension of its significance while sinners never fully comprehend "life as God's gift" and death as "withdrawal of that gift."

But that does not mean Christ was spared the tasting of death in the same dimension due the sinner. Quite the opposite! He tasted it in that very dimension, but to a *far greater degree*: "As our Lord alone truly tasted death, so to Him alone had death its perfect meaning as the wages of sin, for in Him alone was their full entrance into the mind of God towards sin."[1411]

In fact, Campbell even goes so far as to say that since the "penalty" which the law invokes upon sin is death, Jesus must die:

> Death having come as the wages of sin, it was not simply sin that had to be dealt with, but an existing law *with its penalty of death*, and that death as already incurred . . . . This honouring of the law . . . has, indeed, been followed out to its fullest measure, [in] that our Lord not only tasted death, but that that death was the death of the cross.[1412]

The centrality of the death of Christ in Campbell's theology of the atonement is substantiated throughout his *magnum opus*.[1413] Pardon of sins and eternal life were achieved by the Son of God through "the sacrifice of Himself by which Christ put away sin by becoming the propitiation for the sins of the whole world."[1414] But suffice it to say that the moral dimension is fully recognized.

1409 *Nature,* 303; cf. Trevor Hart, "Anselm of Canterbury and John McLeod Campbell: Where Opposites Meet?" where he argues that, for Campbell, the submission of the incarnate Son to the sentence of the law was in order to save us from sin (13).
1410 Tuttle, *op. cit.,* 121.
1411 *Nature,* 302.
1412 *Nature,* 303-4, italics mine.
1413 Cf. *Nature,* 186, 187, 193, 214.
1414 *Nature,* 23.

It will be seen therefore that his rejection of the term "penal" can be misleading. There was a certain kind of penal atonement to which he objected. The following points must be borne constantly in mind in seeking to interpret McLeod Campbell on this issue:

1. That the Father ever looked on the Son as a personal object of wrath, as a sinner, he rejected.[1415] But God does look in wrath toward sin.[1416] Thus Campbell's real concern here is with the nature of God as love. He loves the sinner while hating the sin. Both Calvin and St. Thomas would agree with him on this. Rather, Jesus assumed a penalty which should have fallen upon the human race.[1417]

2. Mainstream Calvinism was able to say that since God loves the elect, Christ suffers the penalty of the Cross.[1418] But Campbell saw that suffering a penalty as an arbitrary act of love (since not for all) does not reveal the character of God. Again his concern is for the nature of God as love.[1419] For the Cross, he believed, gives us access to the very heart of God.[1420]

3. He rejects the kind of penal interpretation which says that only if law is satisfied can there be grace.[1421] This would make Law the main objective. So again Campbell's concern regarding the nature of God as love in his innermost being comes to the fore. "God has not changed, God is not interceded with, as if God were made more kind to us in consequence of Christ's work. It is *God's own love that intercedes, when Christ intercedes*."[1422]

4. Moreover, any quantitative interpretation of the sufferings of Jesus, according to which his sufferings must be weighed in scales against the just sufferings of the damned, is rejected.[1423] This strikes Campbell as impersonal and less than loving.

5. There is no point in the Cross at which we are exposed to another, darker side of God, a God of nothing but anger toward those who

---

1415 John McLeod Campbell, "Reconciliation: the Atonement," *Fragments of Truth*, 249; *Nature*, 312-320.
1416 *Nature*, 135-7.
1417 *Nature*, 302-3.
1418 *Nature*, 134.
1419 *Nature*, 63-5; 140-1.
1420 *Nature*, 74, 141-42.
1421 *Nature*, 20, 147.
1422 Sermon XXX, *Sermons and Lectures*, vol. II, 280, emphasis his.
1423 *Nature*, 139-40.

transgress. It was "in the light of that true knowledge of the heart of the Father in which the Son responded to the Father's condemnation of our sins," so that his intercession was not one which

> contemplated effecting a change in the heart of the Father, but a confession which combined with acknowledgement of the divine wrath against sin, hope for man from that love in God which is deeper than that wrath, —*in truth, originating it in*—determining also its nature.[1424]

6. Wrath, in McLeod Campbell's theology, is also interpreted relationally in terms of "distance", a description of the alienation and estrangement between God and humankind. But this distance is overcome in our returning to the Father s heart.[1425] This we may do in the power of the Spirit since Christ has removed all barriers between us and God.[1426]

We have seen the kind of penal interpretation which Campbell rejects, but what alternative does he propose? An atonement which really atones, he believes, must include the "Christ's honouring of the law," not only in terms of its "sentence" upon sinners, but also acknowledging the "mind of God" (i.e., wrath) expressing that sentence.[1427] And that sentence is described in the Biblical warning that the "wages of sin is death."[1428] That being its "penalty," Christ must die:

> Death having come as the wages of sin, it was not simply sin that had to be dealt with, but an existing law *with its penalty of death*, and that death as already incurred . . . . This honouring of the law . . . has, indeed, been followed out to its fullest measure, [in] that our Lord not only tasted death but that that death was the death of the cross"[1429]

1424 *Nature*, 147-8.
1425 *Fragments of Truth*, 96-99; *Nature*, 213.
1426 Sermon XIV, *Sermons and Lectures*, vol. I, 333.
1427 *Nature*, 302; cf. Trevor Hart, "Anselm of Canterbury and John McLeod Campbell: Where Opposites Meet?" where he argues that, for Campbell, the submission of the incarnate Son to the sentence of the law was in order to save us from sin (13).
1428 *Nature*, 302.
1429 *Nature*, 303f, italics mine.

Were this all that Campbell was teaching, there would have been little alarm (at least in high Calvinist circles). But Campbell insisted on interpreting the atonement with constant reference to the Father-Son relation. Any constructions based on prior conceptions of a God who is absolute will, particularly in the arena of soteriology, are to be dismissed as abstractions untrue to the nature of God revealed in Christ. Consequently, he avers that "the Father's heart did demand an atoning sacrifice . . . the shedding of blood in order to the remission of sins, because it demanded blood in which justice would be rendered to the fatherliness which had been sinned against."[1430]

He stoutly insists upon the nature of God as fatherly love determining all that we understand about the nature of the atonement. Thus he discards all penal interpretations which seem to imply conditional grace, or a kind of wedge between Father and Son or an assumption that the real ends of atonement are judicial rather than filial. Trevor Hart aptly observes that at times McLeod Campbell is so vehement in his criticisms of contemporary expositions of the atonement that he "seems to be moving away" from legitimate biblical insights which he in fact retains.[1431] The ineluctable conclusion is that McLeod Campbell believed in a (properly formulated) penal understanding of the atonement.

What, then, is the place of the Cross in Campbell's theology of the atonement? What is the saving significance of the death of Christ? We recall that in his thought, "God is revealed by the atonement."[1432] The Son of God came in humanity to do the will of the Father, and in the atonement our attention is drawn to the "declaring of the Father's name which is in Christ's death."[1433] By this language we sense that Campbell is meaning more than a verbal communication. Indeed, he tells us that this declaring is an "utterance in death."[1434] The same is true of Christ's "condemnation of sin," his "Amen in humanity":

> That oneness of mind, which towards man took the
> form of condemnation of sin, would in the Son's dealing
> with the Father in relation to our sins, take the form of a

1430 *Nature*, 184-5.
1431 Cf. Trevor Hart's paper, "Anselm of Canterbury and John McLeod Campbell: Where Opposites Meet?" 14.
1432 *Nature*, 213, cf. 74.
1433 *Nature*, 301.
1434 *Ibid.*

perfect confession of our sins. This confession, as to its own nature, must have been a *perfect Amen in humanity to the judgment of God upon the sin of man.*"[1435]

What is the relation of this "Amen in humanity" to God's wrath? Christ "responds to the divine wrath against sin, saying, 'Thou art righteous, O Lord, who judgest so.'"[1436] That is to say, in his death he accepts the verdict of 'guilty' pronounced upon sinful humanity. In a sermon, McLeod Campbell explains it this way:

> Christ condemned sin not only by being the opposite of sin, but by giving Himself as a sin-offering to God. By submitting in His death to undergo the curse of God upon sin, He gave his testimony to the righteousness of God's curse upon sin.[1437]

Likewise, Campbell says that Christ "suffered and died, and thus expressed his Amen to God's righteous sentence upon sin."[1438]

Clearly, in Campbell's thought, the death of Christ was required in order to fulfill the sentence of God's law upon sin. While it is clear from this discussion that Christ died *for* our sin, the question we must put to Campbell is, in what sense did Christ *bear* our sin? We are given a moving picture of the sympathy of Christ for sinners. He felt a "holy sorrow" for the misery our sins have brought us. Christ's sufferings were not artificially imposed by the Father; rather, they arose "naturally out of what He was." They were painful in proportion to his holiness and love.[1439] There is doubtless an important truth in this. We may share his concern that the atoning element in his sufferings not lie merely in

---

1435 *Nature*, 135-6.

1436 *Nature*, 136.

1437 John McLeod Campbell, "The Teaching of God in the Cross of Christ," *Responsibility for the Gift of Eternal Life.* (London: Macmillan, 1873), 100; cf. Sermon IV, *Sermons and Lectures*, vol. I, 70.

1438 Sermon XXVII, *Sermons and Lectures*, vol. II, 238; cf. *Bible Readings*, 78: "Christ *is* God, so loving us as to die for us. We had brought death into us by our disobedience . . . He has overcome the accuser by Himself, as man, confessing sin and bearing its consequences in His own body on the tree. Thus He is the way to the Father."

1439 *Nature*, 115.

the "pain as pain."[1440] But does this exhaust the meaning of the New Testament declaration that "God made him who knew no sin to be sin for us" (2 Corinthians 5:21)? When one goes back and reads the Row Sermons, he is struck by the explicit and earnest defense of the "fallen humanity" of the Savior.[1441] We are under a "delusion," he tells us "to suppose that his human nature was superior to ours, so that his suffering was unlike our own." His human nature, "while always holy, is still proved to be under the law of death, and 'of its own substance mortal and corruptible' . . . the holiness always in Christ's human nature, was there by the Holy Ghost." The human nature of Christ was not "in itself good," not "in itself different from our nature, although always holy, by the Holy Ghost."[1442] Indeed, Christ "was sent in the *likeness of sinful flesh*, that is, he *took sinful flesh*. Christ took our *flesh just as it was, in that condition which made the law to be weak.*"[1443]

In McLeod Campbell's early thought, Christ is God come as man, taking our fallen nature upon himself, and offers himself on our behalf as a sin offering to God.[1444] At this point, it seems likely that he was influenced by his friend, Edward Irving, who taught, in a carefully formulated way,[1445] that Christ, while never personally committing sin, nevertheless assumed our sinful nature in the incarnation.

We do not know why McLeod Campbell departs from this emphasis in his later teaching. Perhaps he was more powerfully influenced by Irving during those Row years. Many of the elements of his preaching in that era are strikingly reminiscent of themes in the teaching of Irving:[1446]

1440 *Nature*, 116.

1441 Cf. Sermon I, 20ff; Sermon XIII, *Sermons and Lectures* vol. I, 300-301.

1442 Sermon XIII, *Ibid.*, 304.

1443 Sermon XIV, *Ibid.*, 341.

1444 *Ibid.*, 344.

1445 Irving, *The Orthodox and Catholic Doctrine of Our Lord's Human Nature*, (London: Baldwin and Cradock, 1830).

1446 Cf. *The Collected Writings of Edward Irving*, vol. v, 499ff, 557; Gordon Strachan, *The Pentecostal Theology of Edward Irving*, (London: Darton, Longman and Todd, 1973), 76ff; Andrew L. Drummond, *Edward Irving and His Circle*, (London: James Clarke, 1936), 134f; Mrs. Oliphant, *The Life of Edward Irving*, (London: Hurst and Blackett, 1862), 185, and David W. Dorries, *Edward Irving's Incarnational Christology*, (Fairfax, VA: Xulon, 2002), 297-469.

the fallen humanity, the manifestations of the gifts of the Spirit,[1447] the apocalyptic expectation,[1448] and chiliastic emphasis.[1449]

When the latter died in 1834, perhaps Campbell gained some critical distance from those views. By the time he pens his *Nature of the Atonement*, the doctrine drops out of sight.[1450] He came closer earlier, in *Fragments of Truth*.[1451] But without an overt emphasis on Christ's having assumed our fallen flesh, his strong insistence on God having tasted death in our nature is weakened, the reality of our sinful nature being healed in him is called into question, and the link between God and humankind through the real humanity of Jesus is undermined.[1452]

In any case, what distinguishes Campbell's view from that of his opponents is the insistence that in the Cross we see the will of God grounded in the eternal nature of God as love. But that is because there, we hear the Son of God declaring the Father's name, doing and accepting his will. In this manner the judicial requirements are honored, but only as rooted in the fundamental reality of God as fatherly.

The Calvinists were quite willing to speak of the will of God, but had detached it from the self-manifestation of God in his Son, such that God could will to be gracious to a select portion of the human race while reprobating the rest.[1453] Christ comes to obey the law and receive the wrath of God upon his (imputed) sin in a suffering equivalent to that deserved by the elect. Thus the merits of his righteousness are transferred to the elect and they, by virtue of his substitution, are permitted legal access to the presence of God.

But Campbell responds by insisting that all true apprehension of the will of God must be bounded by God's self-unveiling in and through His Son. The elements in the atonement are all grounded in the will of God which Christ came to do:

> I hold it to be a great principle that nothing is to be believed concerning the atonement which is not a following out of

1447 Sermon XVII, *Sermons and Lectures*, vol. I, 303

1448 *Inghin an Reachdaire*, Sermon VIII, 26ff.

1449 "The Everlasting Gospel," a pamphlet published by R. B. Lusk, 1830, 28ff.

1450 Cf. *Nature*, 158.

1451 *Fragments of Truth*, 239.

1452 Cf. George M. Tuttle, *John McLeod Campbell on Christian Atonement. So Rich a Soil*, 120; John Macquarrie, *Thinking About God*, 172ff.

1453 *Nature*, 64-5.

our Saviour's own words, 'Lo, I come to do thy will, O God,'—nothing which is not the manifestation of his character, as *God revealing Himself to man,* and as *man yielding himself to God.*[1454]

And what do we learn from the atonement concerning God's character? That he is love. "Love is the law of his being, and by reference to this *Love,* all questions with regard to his work are answered."[1455] This is what he means when he speaks of the death of Christ as an "Amen in humanity." Christ is saying Amen to the just judgments of God upon sin, but also to the loving heart of God who yearns to restore our orphan spirits to himself.[1456] In thus disclosing God as he himself eternally is, he constitutes the "revelation of God's love to all men."[1457]

It seems evident that McLeod Campbell saw the Cross as a window into God's heart, but also as more than a window. It was a fulfilling of the law, the one true sacrifice for sin which we were unable to offer. But it was a saving sacrifice because it was God as man, taking it all to himself, and Christ expressing the mind and heart of God in that sacrifice.

Campbell's point seems to be that nothing else would open the way into God's very heart. Either we see the heart of God throughout the life and death of Christ or we will never see it at all. "There is no one part of God's acting, from the beginning to the end, that any man can have a right apprehension of who does not know that God is love."[1458] And unless we see that loving heart, we are never able to come to God's heart as his sons and daughters.

He is not in this way denying the need for the death of Christ. Christ must die for our sins. But that in itself would be insufficient to conduct us to God's heart as his dear children. We would still be left in the distance, grateful at legal access, assuring ourselves by mental reference to the imputation of our sins to Christ, but unable to approach God personally and enjoy his presence.

1454 "Reconciliation: The Atonement," *Fragments of Truth,* 241.
1455 *Ibid.,* 242-43.
1456 *Nature,* 101, 148-49.
1457 *Nature,* 64-74.
1458 Sermon IX, *Sermons and Lectures,* vol. I, 189.

So Campbell's stress on the oneness of mind succeeds in maintaining the unconditional love of God (his love motivated the atonement; it was not calculated to change God's heart but express it), and in keeping incarnation and atonement inseparably together so that the atonement discloses God's heart, and it makes the cross itself an invitation of God to come all the way home. Nothing remains to be done prior to our coming.

Our grounds for coming are Christ's life and death in our nature. For he "did remove the barrier that was between God and man . . . did declare a peace, and put every one of the human race in this condition, that now we have free access to God."[1459] This constitutes Campbell's version of Calvin's conviction that "all parts of our salvation are comprehended in Christ."[1460]

Even our strength for responding to this unconditional invitation is constituted by "God's might, in the Spirit of Christ," for Christ has replaced that barrier with himself as the "living way" by the Spirit to the Father.[1461]

This latter point is crucial for McLeod Campbell. Christ as a sacrifice for sin is only the "first part of the message of salvation." The second part is that in Christ our Savior we have "power in him to have communion with God." For God has given us in Christ, the Holy Spirit to enable us to "come to him, to walk with him, and to delight in him."[1462] Therefore, when Christ beckons us, "Enter ye by the strait gate" (Matt. 7:13), he is saying, "I am the door, I am the way . . . approach God in me and through me." Here we must notice the

> unconditional character of the gift of Christ. No person can obey this command unless he understands it, and believes it to be addressed to him, just as he is . . . . There is no previous labor, no preparatory work, nothing at all to be done . . . . You have nothing to do to qualify you for entering in . . . . The very command . . . supposes that nothing is to be done, but just to enter in.[1463]

1459 Sermon III, *Ibid.*, 44.
1460 *Institutes*, II.xvi.19.
1461 Sermon III, *Sermons and Lectures*, vol. I, 44-45.
1462 Sermon VIII, *Inghin an Reachdaire*, 22.
1463 Sermon III, *Sermons and Lectures*, vol. 1, 46-47; cf. Sermon VI, *op. cit.*, 124; cf. Sermon VIII, *Inghin an Reachdaire* 20.

For Campbell, God's unconditional gift of Christ *is Christ*; it is God's *self-giving*[1464] that we see in his Son.[1465] If we are uncertain as to who this God is who invites us, we need not extrapolate the nature of God from the world around us: "You are not left to find out God's character by your own natural reason, but . . . you are to look to Jesus, and to see God."[1466] Our confidence in coming to God is securely anchored in "God's character, revealed in Christ,"[1467] in his life[1468] and atoning death,[1469] because "he who was crucified on Calvary is God over all."[1470]

The reason the atonement constitutes an unconditional invitation to come to God through Christ is that God's character, his innermost nature, is love. "The God who has revealed himself in Jesus Christ" is one who in Christ has bestowed his "free, unbought, unmerited love."[1471] Because there is already loving forgiveness in God, God bestows that forgiveness unconditionally through the Cross of Christ, and invites us to respond in evangelical repentance.[1472] In this way *the nature of the atonement is grounded in the nature of God as revealed in Christ*. So we see that when the will of God is grounded in the self-disclosure of God in Christ, the freedom of grace in all its *unmeritedness* is preserved.

Once again we note that for Campbell, the will of God cannot be divided from the self-disclosure of God in and through Christ. Only then will we understand the atonement as the Son of God lovingly condescending to come in our nature and in his obedient fulfillment of the will of God the Father unto death, taking our place and so accomplishing a true reconciliation between God and humankind.

But the atonement reveals the nature of God. "The cross of Christ is to be seen just as the heart of God unveiled in its feelings towards man." And what do we see in this unveiling? God loves all people and "yearns" for all to return.[1473] In fact, Campbell declares that

---

1464 Sermon VIII, *Sermons and Lectures*, vol. I, 174-75.
1465 Sermon V, *ibid.*, 101.
1466 Sermon II, *ibid.*, 37.
1467 *Ibid.*, 48.
1468 Sermon VIII, *ibid.*, 184.
1469 *Ibid.*, 177-8.
1470 Sermon II, *ibid.*, 37.
1471 Sermon XV, *ibid.*, vol. I, 382-83.
1472 Sermon VI, *ibid.*, vol. I, 126-27; 131, 136; cf. Sermon XI, *op. cit.*, 256; cf. John Calvin, *Institutes*, III.iii.1-2.
1473 Sermon XIII, *Sermons and Lectures*, vol. I, 320.

If love be of God's character—if it be of God's substance—if God *is love*, then God loves every man. Yea the person who limits the love of God to some, has actually denied that there is love in God at all, for it would not be love, but mere partiality or caprice: however beneficial to those who were the objects of that capricious choice, yet, in respect of him whose choice it was, it could be no manifestation of character.[1474]

Conclusion

Investigating Campbell's concept of the will of God in relation to his doctrine of revelation in Christ has shed light on the heart of his theology, because in his view Jesus came for the sole purpose of doing the will of God. Thus, in all his teaching and action, the Son of God leads us straight as an arrow to the will of God, which always expresses the loving heart of God.

In the Son's revealing the Father, "we have to do directly with the will of God; that is to say, His will as His mind and character,—that in respect of which we say, God is love."[1475] For McLeod Campbell, there is no will in God that is not the will of the Father, who is love. By grounding his concept of the will of God in his self-revelation in and through the Son, the freeness of grace in all its *unmeritedness* as well as its *unrestrictedness* is upheld.

For McLeod Campbell, this was no academic dispute. The very Gospel was at stake. His conviction was that by anchoring the Good News in the self-manifestation of God the Father in and through his Son, he could hold out an unconditional invitation to every sinner to return to the God who had already accomplished the whole of his salvation. As he told his auditors in one of his final sermons at Row:

My dear friends, I dare not part with you without more pointedly stating to you what it is which God commands to be preached to you, that you may cease from dwelling in the far country, and return to your father's house. It is that which is set forth in the love that met the prodigal son while he was yet afar off. It is the love of God

---

1474 Sermon XVI, *ibid.*, 386.
1475 *Nature*, xxxvi, xxxvii.

revealed in Jesus. It is in that love which is manifested in the forgiveness which you have in Jesus Christ. It is the revelation of God coming forth and taking your nature, and in your nature making atonement for your sins. It is the revelation of love and holiness on the part of your God, and of forgiveness to your own souls, which is in this. It is the revelation of your God, in the suffering, and in the risen Christ. It is the revelation of your God, in that Christ is now standing in the presence of God for you. It is the revelation of your God, that your flesh has been crucified with Christ, and that you are to regard yourselves as risen with Christ, and are called to dwell before God, as those who are alive and were dead. It is this that God commanded to be preached to you, that you may return from the far country.[1476]

1476 Sermon XXXIV, *Sermons and Lectures*, vol. II, 417.

CHAPTER 4

CONCLUDING THOUGHTS

It has been suggested, not without justification, that the Reformers did not challenge a great number of medieval doctrines; most of them were left intact. And to be sure, Thomas' teachings such as the Trinity, the Person of Christ, or Creation were not denied. Protestant theology, avers Richard Muller, rather undertook an "adjustment of a received body of doctrine and its systematic relations to the needs of Protestantism, in terms dictated by the teachings of the Reformers on Scripture, grace, justification, and the sacraments."[1477]

But this is to miss the point. For the Reformers, especially, for our purposes, Calvin, what was at stake was nothing less than the *nature of God*. When he railed against Pighius and Servetus and the schoolmen generally, the center of his concern was Who God is. This is why he maintained that God *is propitious* and therefore he provides propitiation. This, too, is why when he came to John 3:16 he said that we must affirm that God *is love* and therefore he sends his Son. But in Calvin's thought, the sole access to the knowledge of God for postlapsarian humankind is through the Son. In this way, the freeness of grace in that it is *unmerited* is preserved, for God discloses himself through Christ as one who is a gracious Father in his inmost life.

For St. Thomas, the plans and intentions of God for the human race are not known by reflection upon God's self-unveiling in his Word-made-flesh, but through deductions based upon the metaphysic of final causality. On this basis, he constructs a doctrine of providence wherein God directs all things toward an end. Predestination follows as a corollary of providence. Then Christ comes to carry out God's eternal decree of salvation.

God's being as a unity of intellect and will seems, in some sense, to be qualified in his exposition of predestination. The divine will assumes a certain primacy, in that, his will not being determined to

1477 Richard Muller, *Post-Reformation Dogmatics, volume 1:Prolegomena to Theology*, (Grand Rapids: Baker, 1987), 17.

one good only, he can and does will to show his goodness to some by predestinating them to eternal felicity, while reprobating other, equally undeserving sinners. For this reason we attribute a kind of 'soteriological voluntarism' to Thomas. The dispensation of grace is also determined by the divine will. God decides to give grace to those who cooperate well with the first grace, but grace is a gift, a God-given accidental quality of a human disposition. In this manner he expounds the Gospel of grace in the language of merit and introduces a kind of conditionality into grace. We conclude that Thomas' failure to anchor the concept of the will of God in the self-disclosure of God in Christ results in a significant loss of the freeness of grace, both in the sense of its *unmeritedness* as well as in its *unrestrictedness*.

Calvin mounts an evangelical critique of medieval theology, interpreting the Gospel in terms of *sola gratia*. But *sola gratia* is the exegesis of *solus Christus*, for grace is nothing other than God's gracious self-giving. When God became human, he so assumed our humanity into unity with his divinity that we might by mutual connection grow together. And this God does for the entire human race without exception, because God is gracious and loving in his inmost life.

Law, does not propose certain conditions for grace, for that would be to obviate its character as grace. Law does express God's unchanging intentions for the human race, but when they go astray the Son of God becomes a Son of man that they might become sons of God. In the person of Christ our salvation is already accomplished. Therefore our repentance is not, as Thomas taught, a condition of grace but a lifelong response in union with Christ by the Spirit. The Christian life becomes one of gratitude, of obeying God's law and joyfully feeding upon Christ and offering up our prayers and praise.

Yet there is a fissure in Calvin's doctrine of God, for alongside this tremendous underscoring of the inherent love of God lies another notion, concerning the absolute freedom of God. God is unbound even by his love. He always acts in accord with justice, but not necessarily in harmony with love. Indeed, the doctrine of Providence, by which we confess that God governs all the motions of his creatures, means also that among sinners equally deserving of perdition, God predestines those of his own choosing before the dawn of time and that he reprobates others directly and intentionally. The problem for Calvin is that his doctrine of the double decree makes no reference to Jesus Christ. He has thereby stepped out of his own avowed parameters, for he has repeatedly told us that there is no knowledge of God outside of his incarnation in Jesus of Nazareth. Thus we see that dividing the will of God from the self-revelation of God in Christ results in the loss of the freeness of grace in its *unrestrictedness*.

Finally, we showed how McLeod Campbell was spurred by the pastoral needs of his people to reconsider not only the notion of limited atonement (which had been imported by later Calvinists), and Calvin's twin decrees, but also the doctrine of God presupposed by them. His response was to insist on a thoroughgoing Christological critique of Calvinism, for he was convinced that Jesus Christ constitutes God the Father's self-disclosure and self-giving.

For Campbell, God is loving and merciful and fatherly in his inmost life. He brought the human race into being out of the overflow of his love, and when they fell into sin, he came in the flesh of Jesus to offer up that life of prayer and faithful obedience which we could not. As such the entire life of Jesus was one faithful Amen to the will and heart of the Father, but in his death especially, he said Amen to the judgment of God upon sin. His dying was an acceptance of the divinely-prescribed penalty for sin, but because it was God in our nature who thus tasted death, it is not proper to speak as if God the Father stood over against the Son and exacted a punishment as a condition of grace. Christ is God standing in for us, taking our desserts upon himself. Therefore Campbell shares with Calvin the conviction that grace is nothing other than God's self-offering for the human race. But there can be no double decree. In Christ we see that God's love embraces the entire world. Thus the freeness of grace in its *unrestrictedness* is maintained.

But that same love which sent the Son of God to come and make atonement on behalf of all humankind, also motivated him to accomplish everything necessary to our salvation. So he assumes our humanity, doing the Father's will, declaring his name, confessing our sin and submitting to the verdict of guilty. In his atoning acts, Christ has already removed every barrier, so that nothing remains for the sinner to do but to come home in joyful repentance. Thus, by anchoring the concept of the will of God in the self-revelation of God in and through the Son, the freeness of grace in all its *unmeritedness* is preserved.

However, Campbell's hesitancy to affirm that it was our actual (fallen) nature which Christ assumed tends to call into question the reality of the bonds which Christ establishes with the human race. In this way he is somewhat open to the charge of substituting a moral fiction for a legal fiction, for how can one detached person repent for another? Yet his insistence that Christ's relation to humanity is a real one, Christ having reconstituted a living relation between God and humanity in his own life and death, significantly qualifies this criticism.

Certainly it is no small accomplishment to succeed in maintaining the *freedom of grace* in the Gospel, in the fullest sense of its *unmeritedness* as well as its *unrestrictedness*. McLeod Campbell's writings do not constitute a systematic theology in the fullest sense of the word, but his *Nature of the Atonement*, his sermons, letters, and other works, present some trenchant criticisms of the way theology was done in the Thomist and Calvinist traditions. Moreover his central insights regarding the exclusive rights of a Christological hermeneutic are welcome indeed. In this manner, the nineteenth-century Scottish theologian provides us, not with a complete, alternative systematic theology, but with significant insights which serve to correct and strengthen Thomas' and Calvin's theologies.

BIBLIOGRAPHY

Althaus, Paul. *The Theology of Martin Luther*. Philadelphia: Fortress, 1966.

Anderson, Marvin W. "Calvin: Biblical Preacher." *Scottish Journal of Theology* vol. 42, (1989): 167-91.

Armstrong, Brian G. *Calvinism and the Amyraut Heresy*. Madison, Milwaukee and London: University of Wisconsin Press, 1969.

Athanasius. *The Orations of Athanasius Against the Arians*. The Ancient and Modern Library of Theological Literature. London: Griffith, Farran, Okeden and Welsh, n. d.

Bainton, Roland H. "The Immoralities of the Patriarchs According to the Exegesis of the Late Middle Ages and of the Reformation." *Harvard Theological Review* vol. xxiii, (January, 1930): 39-49.

Bandstra, Andrew J. "Law and Gospel in Calvin and in Paul," *Exploring the Heritage of John Calvin*, ed. David E. Holwerda, Grand Rapids: Baker, 1976, 11-39.

Bagchi, David and Steinmetz, David C. , eds., *The Cambridge Companion to Reformation Theology*. Cambridge: Cambridge University Press, 2004.

Battles, Ford Lewis. *Interpreting John Calvin*, ed. Robert Benedetto. Grand Rapids: Baker, 1996.

Bavinck, Herman. "Calvin and Common Grace." *Calvin and the Reformation*, ed. William Park Armstrong, New York: Fleming Revell, 1909, 99-130.

Beeke, Joel R. *The Quest for Full Assurance: The Legacy of Calvin and His Successors*. Edinburgh and Carlisle, Pennsylvania: Banner of Truth, 1999.

Bell, M. Charles. *Calvin and Scottish Theology. The Doctrine of Assurance*. Edinburgh: Handsel Press, 1985.

_____. "Saving Faith and Assurance of Salvation in the Teaching of John Calvin and Scottish Theology." Ph.D. thesis, Aberdeen University, 1982.

Bewkes, Eugene Garrett. *The Legacy of a Christian Mind*. Philadelphia: Judson Press, 1937.

Booth, Abraham. *The Reign of Grace from its Rise to its Consummation*. Kilmarnock: Crawford, 1807.

Blanchette, Oliva. *The Perfection of the Universe According to Aquinas*. University Park: Penn State Press, 1992.

Bouwsma, William J. *John Calvin: A Sixteenth Century Portrait*. New York: Oxford University Press, 1988.

Breen, Quirinius. *John Calvin: A Study in French Humanism*. Grand Rapids: Eerdmans, 1931.

Brown, W. Adams. "Expiation and Atonement (Christian)", in James Hastings, ed. *Encyclopedia of Religion and Ethics*. Vol. v, New York: Charles Scribner's Sons, 1912, 650.

Calvin, John. *Calvin's Calvinism*. trans. Henry Cole, London: Sovereign Grace Union, 1927.

_____. *Calvin: Institutes of the Christian Religion*, two vols, ed. John T. McNeill, trans. Ford Lewis Battles, Philadelphia: Westminster Press, 1960.

_____. *Calvin: Theological Treatises*. ed., trans. J. K. S. Reid, Philadelphia: Westminster Press, 1954.

_____. *The Catechism of the Church of Geneva, that is, a Plan for Instructing Children in the Doctrine of Christ*, in *Calvin: Theological Treatises*, ed. J. K. S. Reid, Philadelphia: Westminster, 1954.

_____. *Commentaries on the Book of the Prophet Jeremiah and Lamentations*. vol. III, trans. John Owen, Grand Rapids: Baker, 1989.

_____. *Commentaries on the Catholic Epistles*. trans. John Owen, Grand Rapids: Baker, 1989.

_____. *Commentaries on the First Book of Moses called Genesis*. vol. 1, trans. John King. Grand Rapids: Baker, 1989.

_____. *Commentaries on the Last Four Books of Moses*. vols. I, III, IV, trans. Charles William Bingham. Grand Rapids: Eerdmans, 1950.

_____. *Commentary on the Book of the Prophet Ezekiel*. vol. II, trans. Thomas Myers. Grand Rapids: Baker, 1989.

_____. *Commentary on the Book of the Prophet Isaiah*. vol. III, trans. William Pringle. Grand Rapids: Baker, 1989.

_____. *Commentary on the Book of the Prophet Jeremiah*. vol. 1, trans. John Owen. Grand Rapids: Baker, 1989.

_____. *Commentary on the Book of Psalms*. vol. IV, trans. James Anderson. Edinburgh: Calvin Translation Society, n. d., reprinted 1989, Grand Rapids: Baker.

_____. *Commentaries on the Twelve Minor Prophets*. vol. I, trans. John Owen. Grand Rapids: Eerdmans, n. d.

_____. *Concerning the Eternal Predestination of God*. trans. J. K. S. Reid. London: James Clarke, 1961.

_____. *The Epistle of Paul the Apostle to the Galatians. Ephesians, Philippians and Colossians*. trans. Parker. Grand Rapids: Eerdmans, 1974.

_____. *The Epistle of Paul the Apostle to the Hebrews and the First and Second Epistles of St Peter*. trans. William B. Johnston. Grand Rapids: Eerdmans, 1963.

_____. *The Epistle of Paul the Apostle to the Romans and to the Thessalonians*. trans. Ross Mackenzie. Grand Rapids: Eerdmans, 1973.

_____. *The First Epistle of Paul the Apostle to the Corinthians*. trans. John W. Fraser. ed. David W. Torrance and Thomas F. Torrance. Grand Rapids: Eerdmans, 1960.

_____. *The Gospel According to St. John*. 2 vols, trans. Parker. Grand Rapids: Eerdmans, 1961.

_____. *Institutes of the Christian Religion*. First ed., Basel, 1536, trans. Ford Lewis Battles. Grand Rapids: Eerdmans, 1975.

_____. *Instruction in Faith (1537)*. trans., ed. Paul T. Fuhrmann. London: Lutterworth, 1949.

_____. *John Calvin's Sermons on Timothy and Titus*. trans. L.T., (1579 Facsimile edition), Edinburgh: Banner of Truth, 1983.

_____. *Matthew. Mark and Luke*. vol. I, trans. A. W. Morrison. Edinburgh: St. Andrews, 1972.

_____. *Selected Works of John Calvin. Tracts and Letters*. vols. 1-3, ed. Henry Beveridge and Jules Bonnet. trans. Henry Beveridge. Grand Rapids: Baker, 1983.

_____. *Sermons on Deuteronomy* (facsimile of 1583 edition), trans. Arthur Golding. Edinburgh: Banner of Truth, 1987.

_____. *Sermons on The Epistle to the Ephesians*. trans. Arthur Golding, Edinburgh: Banner of Truth, 1975.

_____. *Sermons on Isaiah's Prophecy of the Death and Passion of Christ*. trans., ed. T. H. L. Parker. London: James Clarke, 1956.

_____. *Sermons from Job*. trans. Leroy Nixon. Grand Rapids: Baker, 1952.

_____. *Sermons on the Saving Work of Christ*. trans. Leroy Nixon. Hertfordshire: Evangelical Press, 1980.

_____. *Treatises Against the Anabaptists and Against the Libertines*. trans., ed. by Benjamin Wirt Farley. Grand Rapids: Baker, 1982.

Calvinus, Ioannis. *Institutio Christiane Religionis*. ed. A. Tholuck. London: D. Nutt, 1846.

Calvinus. *Novi Testamenti Commentarii*. ed. A. Tholuck. 7 vols, Berlin, 1834.

Campbell, Andrew. J. *Two Centuries of the Church of Scotland 1707-1929*. Paisley: Alexander Gardner, 1930.

Campbell, Donald, ed. *Memorials of John McLeod Campbell. D. D.*, two vols. London: Macmillan, 1877.

[Campbell, John McLeod]. *Bible Readings*. Edinburgh: Edmonston and Douglas, 1864.

Campbell, John McLeod. *Christ the Bread of Life*. Glasgow: Maurice Ogle, 1851.

_____. "The Everlasting Gospel." Notes of a Sermon by the Rev. J. M. Campbell, Minister of Row, Dumbartonshire, pamphlet published by R. B. Lusk, Greenock, 1830.

_____. *Fragments of Truth*. Fourth edition. Edinburgh: Edmonston and Douglas, 1898.

_____. *Inghin an Reachdaire*, no. 140, London: F. Collins, J. Nisbet and T. Flinn, n. d. This bound volume of sermon pamphlets not numbered consecutively is found in New College Library, Edinburgh, and catalogued under this title.

_____. *The Nature of the Atonement*. Fourth edition, London: James Clarke, 1959.

_____. *Notes of Sermons by the Rev. J. Mc. L. Campbell. Minister of Row, Dumbartonshire*, taken in shorthand, vol. I, Paisley: John Wallace, Lithographer, 1831.

_____. *Reminiscences and Reflections*. London: Macmillan, 1873.

_____. *Responsibility for the Gift of Eternal Life*. London: Macmillan, 1873.

_____. *Sermons and Lectures*. two vols, Greenock: R. B. Lusk, 1832.

_____. *Thoughts on Revelation*. London: Macmillan, 1862.

Campbell, John McLeod, D. D. [grandson of above]. "John McLeod Campbell, 1800-1872," in Ronald Selby Wright, ed., *Fathers of the Kirk*. Oxford: Oxford University Press, 1960, 155-166.

Carey, George. *The Gate of Glory*. London: Hodder and Stoughton, 1986.

Case-Winters, Anna. *God's Power*. Louisville: Westminster/John Knox, 1990.

Cave, Sidney. *The Doctrine of the Work of Christ*. London: University of London Press, 1947.

Chenu, Marie-Dominique. *Aquinas and His Role in Theology*, trans. Paul Philibert. Collegeville, Minnesota: The Liturgical Press, 2002

Chenu. *Toward Understanding St. Thomas*. trans. Albert M. Landry and Dominic Hughes. Chicago: Henry Regnery, 1964.

Copleston, F. C. *Aquinas*. Middlesex: Penguin, 1955.

Copleston. *A History of Medieval Philosophy*. London: Methuen, 1972.

Courtenay, William J. "Covenant and Causality in Pierre D'Ailly." *Speculum* vol. 46, (1971): 94-119.

_____. "The King and the Leaden Coin: The Economic Background of 'Sine Qua Non' Causality." *Traditio* vol. 28, (1972): 185-209.

Dale, R. W. *The Atonement*. London: Congregational Union of England and Wales, 1902.

Dallimore, Arnold. *The Life of Edward Irving*. Edinburgh: Banner of Truth, 1983.

D'Arcy, M. C. *St. Thomas Aquinas*. Westminster, Maryland: Newman Press, 1955.

Davies, Brian. *The Thought of Thomas Aquinas*. Oxford: Clarendon Press, 1992.

Denney, James. *The Christian Doctrine of Reconciliation*. London: Hodder and Stoughton, 1917.

Dillenberger, John. *God Hidden and Revealed*. Philadelphia: Muhlenberg Press, 1953.

Donnelly, John Patrick, S.J. "Calvinist Thomism." *Viator* vol. 7, (1976): 441-55.

Dorries, David. "Nineteenth Century British Christological Controversy Centring Upon Edward Irving's Doctrine of Christ's Human Nature." Ph.D. Thesis, Aberdeen University, 1987.

Dowey, Edward A. *The Knowledge of God in Calvin's Theology*. New York: Columbia University Press, 1959.

Drummond, Andrew L. and Bulloch, James. *The Scottish Church 1688-1843*. Edinburgh: Saint Andrew Press, 1973.

Drummond, Andrew Landale. *Edward Irving and His Circle*. London: James Clarke, n.d.

Eardley, Peter S. and Still, Carl N. *Aquinas: A Guide for the Perplexed*. London and New York: Continuum, 2010

Elders, Leo. *The Philosophical Theology of St. Thomas Aquinas*. Leiden: E. J. Brill, 1990.

Elwood, Christopher. *Calvin for Armchair Theologians*. Louisville: Westminster John Knox Press, 2002.

Ernst, Cornelius, O. P. *The Theology of Grace*. Butler: Clergy Book Service, 1974.

Erskine, Thomas. *The Brazen Serpent*. Third ed., Edinburgh: David Douglas, 1879.

_____. *Remarks on the Internal Evidence for Revealed Religion*. Edinburgh: Waugh and Innes, 1823.

Farrell, Walter, O. P. *A Companion to the Summa*. Four vols, New York: Sheed and Ward, 1941.

Farthing, John L. *Thomas Aquinas and Gabriel Biel.* Durham: Duke University Press, 1988.

Franks, Robert S. *The Work of Christ.* London: Thomas Nelson, 1962.

George, Timothy. *The Theology of the Reformers.* Nashville: Broadman, 1988.

Gerrish, Brian. *The Old Protestantism and the New.* Chicago: University of Chicago Press, 1982.

_____. *Tradition and the Modern World. Reformed Theology in the Nineteenth Century.* Chicago: University of Chicago Press, 1978.

Gilson, Etienne. *The Christian Philosophy of St. Thomas Aquinas.* London: Victor Gollancz, 1957.

_____. *The Elements of Christian Philosophy.* New York: New American Library, 1963.

_____. *History of Christian Philosophy in the Middle Ages.* London: Sheed and Ward, 1955.

_____. "The Spirit of Thomism," *A Gilson Reader.* ed. Anton C. Pegis. Garden City: Image Books, 1957, 247-276.

Goodloe, James C. "John McLeod Campbell: The Extent and Nature of the Atonement," *Studies in Reformed Theology and History*, New Series, no. 3, 1997.

Grabmann, Martin. *Thomas Aquinas: His Personality and Thought.* trans. Virgil Michel. New York: Russell and Russell, 1963.

Gunton, Colin. *Becoming and Being. The Doctrine of God in Charles Hartshorne and Karl Barth.* Oxford: Oxford University Press, 1978, reprinted 1980.

_____. *Enlightenment and Alienation. An Essay Towards a Trinitarian Theology.* Basingstoke, Marshall: Morgan and Scott, 1985.

Hall, Basil. "Calvin Against the Calvinists." *John Calvin.* ed. G. E. Duffield, Appleton: Sutton Courtenay Press, 1966, 19-37.

_____. *John Calvin: Humanist and Theologian.* London: Routledge and Kegan Paul, 1956.

Hamilton, Ian. "John McLeod Campbell." *New Dictionary of Theology.* ed. Sinclair Ferguson *et. al.*, InterVarsity Press: Leicester, 1988.

Hankey, W. J. *God in Himself. Aquinas' Doctrine of God as Expounded in the Summa Theologiae.* Oxford: Oxford University Press, 1987.

Harkness, Georgia. *John Calvin: The Man and His Ethics.* New York: Abingdon, 1958.

Hart, Charles A. *Thomist Metaphysics. An Inquiry into the Act of Existing.* Englewood Cliffs: Prentice Hall, 1959.

Hart, Trevor. "The Person and Work of Christ in the Theology of Anselm of Canterbury." Unpublished paper, 1986.

_____. "Anselm of Canterbury and John McLeod Campbell: Where Opposites Meet?" Read to the Aberdeenshire Theological Club on January 16, 1989.

Helm, Paul. *Calvin and the Calvinists.* Edinburgh: Banner of Truth, 1982.

_____. *Calvin: A Guide for the Perplexed.* London and New York: T & T Clark, 2008.

_____. *Calvin at the Centre.* Oxford and New York: Oxford University Press, 2010.

Henderson, Henry F. *The Religious Controversies of Scotland.* Edinburgh: T & T Clark, 1905.

Heppe, Heinrich. *Reformed Dogmatics.* trans. G. T. Thomson. Grand Rapids: Baker Book House, 1984.

Hesselink, I. John. "Christ, the Law and the Christian: An Unexplored Aspect of the Third Use of the Law in Calvin's Theology." *Reformatio Perennis.* ed. Brian A. Gerrish, Pittsburgh: Pickwick Press, 1981, 11-26.

Hoekema, Anthony. "The Covenant of Grace in Calvin's Teaching." *Calvin Theological Journal* vol. 2, (1967): 33-61.

Hopfl, Harro. *The Christian Polity of John Calvin.* Cambridge: Cambridge University Press, 1985.

Hunt, R. N. Carew. *Calvin.* London: Centenary Press, 1933.

Irving, Edward. *The Collected Writings of Edward Irving,* five vols, ed. G[avin] Carlyle, London: Alexander Strahan, 1865.

_____. *The Orthodox and Catholic Doctrine of Our Lord's Human Nature.* London: Baldwin and Cradock, 1830.

Jansen, James F. *Calvin's Doctrine of the Work of Christ.* London: James Clarke, 1956.

Jensen, Timothy Paul. "Calvin and Turretin: A Comparison of Their Soteriologies." Ph.D. dissertation, University of Virginia, 1988.

Jinkins, Michael. "Atonement and the Character of God. A Comparative Study in the Theology of Atonement in Jonathan Edwards and John McLeod Campbell." Ph.D. thesis, Aberdeen University, 1990.

Jinkins. *Love is of the Essence: An Introduction to the Theology of John McLeod Campbell.* Edinburgh: St. Andrews Press, 1993.

Johnson, Harry. *The Humanity of the Savior*. London: Epworth, 1962.

Keesecker, William F. "The Law in John Calvin's Ethics." *Calvin and Christian Ethics*. ed. Peter de Klerk. Grand Rapids: Calvin Studies Society, 1987, 19-50.

Kendall, R. T. *Calvin and English Calvinism to 1649*. Oxford: Oxford University Press, 1981.

Kenny, Anthony. *Aquinas.* Oxford: Oxford University Press, 1980.

Kenny. 'The Definition of Omnipotence." in Thomas V. Morris, ed., *The Concept of God*. Oxford: Oxford University Press, 1988.

Kettler, Christian. *The Vicarious Humanity of Christ and the Reality of Salvation*. Substantially revised version of his Ph.D. dissertation, below. New York: University Press of America, 1991.

Kettler, Christian Delvaux. "The Vicarious Humanity of Christ and the Reality of Salvation." Ph.D. dissertation, Fuller Theological Seminary, 1986.

Kettler, Christian D. "The Vicarious Repentence of Christ in the Theology of John McLeod Campbell and R. C. Moberly." *Scottish Journal of Theology* vol. 38, no. 4, (1985):529-543.

Kirkpatrick, Dow. "The Epistemology of Thomism: An Exposition and an Evaluation." Ph.D. dissertation, Drew Theological Seminary, 1945.

Kuiper, R. B. *For Whom Did Christ Die?* Grand Rapids: Eerdmans, 1959.

Lachman, David. *The Marrow Controversy*. Edinburgh: Rutherford House, 1988.

LaValee, Armand Aime. "Calvin's Criticism of Scholastic Theology." Ph.D. dissertation, Harvard University, 1967.

Leckie, J. H. "Books That Have Influenced our Epoch, John McLeod Campbell's 'The Nature of the Atonement'" *Expository Times* vol. 40, (February 1921): 198-204.

_____. "John McLeod Campbell: The Development of His Thought II." *The Expositor*, (February 1921): 107-20.

Lee, William Patrick. "The Natural Law and the Decalogue in St. Thomas Aquinas." Ph.D. dissertation, Marquette University, 1980.

Leith, John H. "The Doctrine of the Will in the *Institutes of the Christian Religion*," *Reformatio Perennis*, ed. Brian Gerrish, Pittsburgh: Pickwick Press, 1981, 49-66.

_____. *John Calvin's Doctrine of the Christian Life*. Originally Ph.D. dissertation, Yale University, 1949. Louisville: Westminster/ John Knox, 1989.

Lindbeck, George. "Nominalism and the Problems of Meaning as Illustrated by Pierre D'Ailly on Predestination and Justification." *Harvard Theological Review* vol. 52, (January 1959): 43-60.

Lusk, R. B., ed., *The Whole Proceedings in the Case of the Rev. John McLeod Campbell. Minister of Row*. Greenock: R. B. Lusk, 1831.

Macleod, John. *Scottish Theology in Relation to Church History*. Edinburgh: Banner of Truth, 1946.

McLeod, Norman. "John McLeod Campbell, D. D." *Good Words 1872*. London: Strahan, 1872, 353-360.

McCoy, Charles S. and Baker, J. Wayne. *Fountainhead of Federalism: Heinrich Bullinger and the Covenantal Tradition*. Louisville: Westminster/John Knox, 1991.

McCrie, C. G., ed., *The Marrow of Modern Divinity in Two Parts. 1645, 1649*. Glasgow: David Bryce, 1902.

_____. "Studies in Scottish Ecclesiastical Biography." *British and Foreign Evangelical Review* vol. xxxiii, (1884): 669-719.

McGrath, Alister E. *A Life of John Calvin*. Oxford: Basil Blackwell, 1990.

_____. *Iustitia Dei*. vol. I, Cambridge: Cambridge University Press, 1986.

Mackinnon, James. *Calvin and the Reformation*. New York: Russell and Russell, 1962.

H. R. Mackintosh. *Some Aspects of Christian Belief*. London: Hodder and Stoughton, 1923.

Mackintosh, Robert. *Historic Theories of the Atonement*. London: Hodder and Stoughton, 1920.

McIntyre, John. *On the Love of God*. Glasgow: Collins, 1962.

McNeill, John T. *The History and Character of Calvinism*. London: Oxford University Press, 1966.

_____. "Natural Law in the Teaching of the Reformers." *Journal of Religion* vol. xxvi, (1946): 168-82.

Macquarrie, John. *Jesus Christ in Modern Thought*. London: SCM Press, 1991.

_____. "John McLeod Campbell 1800-1872." *The Expository Times* vol. 83, no. 9, (1972): 263-68.

_____. *Thinking About God*. London: SCM, 1975.

McInerny, Ralph. *A First Glance at St. Thomas Aquinas*. Notre Dame: University of Notre Dame Press, 1990.

Mansel, Henry Longueville. *The Limits of Religious Thought*. fourth edition. London: John Murray, 1859.

Maritain, Jacques. *St Thomas Aquinas: Angel of the Schools*. London: Sheed and Ward, 1946.

Meyer, Hans. *The Philosophy of St. Thomas Aquinas*. trans. Rev. Frederic Eckhoff, St. Louis and London: Herder, 1946.

Milner, Benjamin Charles, Jr. *Calvin's Doctrine of the Church*. Leiden: Brill, 1970.

Moberly, R. C. *Atonement and Personality*. London: John Murray, 1907.

Moltmann, Jurgen. *The Trinity in the Kingdom of God*. London: SCM, 1981.

Mondin, Battista. *The Principle of Analogy in Protestant and Catholic Theology*. The Hague: Martinus Nijhoff, 1963.

Mozley, J. B. *A Treatise on the Augustinian Doctrine of Predestination*. Second Edition. New York: E. P. Dutton, 1878.

Mozley, J. K. *The Impassibility of God*. Cambridge: Cambridge University Press, 1926.

Mtega, Norbert. *Analogy and Theological Language in the Summa Contra Gentiles*. Frankfurt am Main: Peter Lang, 1984.

Muller, Richard A. *Christ and the Decree. Christology and Predestination in Reformed Theology from Calvin to Perkins*. Grand Rapids: Baker, 1988.

_____. *Post-Reformation Dogmatics*. vol. 1. Grand Rapids: Baker, 1987.

Murray, John. *Calvin on Scripture and Divine Sovereignty*. Grand Rapids: Baker, 1978.

Nash, Ronald H. *The Light of the Mind. St. Augustine's Theory of Knowledge*. Lexington: University Press of Kentucky, 1969.

Needham, Nicholas R. *Thomas Erskine of Linlathen. His Life and Theology 1788-1837*. Edinburgh: Rutherford House, 1990.

Niesel, Wilhelm. *Reformed Symbolics*. Edinburgh: Oliver and Boyd, 1962.

_____. *The Theology of Calvin*. trans. Harold Knight. London: Lutterworth Press, 1956.

Nixon, Leroy. *John Calvin--Expository Preacher*. Grand Rapids: Eerdmans, 1950.

Oakley, Francis. "Pierre D'Ailly and the Absolute Power of God: Another Note on the Theology of Nominalism," *Harvard Theological Review* vol. LVI, no. 1, (January 1963): 59-73.

_____. "The Theology of Nominalism." *Natural Law, Conciliarism and Consent in the Late Middle Ages*. London: Valorum Reprints, 1984, 59-73.

Oberman, Heiko. *The Dawn of the Reformation*. Edinburgh: T & T Clark, 1986.

_____. "Facientibus Quod in Se Est Deus Non Denegat Gratiam." *Harvard Theological Review* vol. LV, (1962): 317-342.

_____. *Forerunners of the Reformation*. Philadelphia: Fortress Press, 1981.

_____. "Fourteenth-Century Religious Thought: A Premature Profile." *Speculum* vol. 53, (1978): 80-93.

_____. *The Harvest of Medieval Theology. Gabriel Biel and Late Medieval Nominalism*. Durham: Labyrinth Press, 1983.

_____. "Some Notes on the Theology of Nominalism with Attention to its Relation to the Renaissance." *Harvard Theological Review* vol. LIII, (1960): 47-76.

O'Connor, D. J. *Aquinas and Natural Law*. London: Macmillan, 1967.

O'Donovan, Oliver. *Resurrection and the Moral Order*. Leicester: Inter-Varsity and Grand Rapids: Eerdmans, 1986.

Oliphant, Mrs. *The Life of Edward Irving*. two vols, London: Hurst and Blackett, 1862.

O'Meara, Thomas F., O.P., *Thomas Aquinas: Theologian*. Notre Dame: University of Notre Dame Press, 1997.

Parker, T. H. L. *The Doctrine of the Knowledge of God. A Study in the Theology of John Calvin*. Edinburgh: Oliver and Boyd, 1952.

_____. *John Calvin*. Herts: Lion, 1975.

_____. *The Oracles of God. An Introduction to the Preaching of John Calvin*. London: Lutterworth Press, 1947.

Partee, Charles. "Calvin and Determinism." *Christian Scholars Review* vol. 5, no. 2, (1975): 123-28.

_____. "Calvin and Experience." *Scottish Journal of Theology* vol. 26, no. 2, (1973): 169-81.

_____. "Calvin's Central Dogma Again." *Sixteenth Century Journal* vol. xviii, no. 2, (1987): 191-99.

_____. "Predestination in Aquinas and Calvin." *Reformed Review* vol. 39, (1978): 14-22.

_____. *The Theology of John Calvin*. Louisville and London: Westminster John Knox Press, 2008.

Paul, R. S. *The Atonement and the Sacraments*. London: Hodder and Stoughton, 1961.

Pfleiderer, Otto. *The Development of Theology in Germany Since Kant and its Progress in Great Britain since 1825*. London: Swan Sonnenschein, 1890.

Postema, Gerald J. "Calvin's Alleged Rejection of Natural Theology." *Scottish Journal of Theology* vol. 24, no. 4, (1971): 424-434.

Pritchard, C. E. "Modern Views of the Atonement." *North British Review* vol. 46, (March-June 1867): 184-204.

Quick, Oliver Chase. *The Doctrines of the Creed. Their Basis in Scripture and their Meaning To-day*. London: Nisbet and Co., 1938.

Quistorp, Heinrich. *Calvin's Doctrine of Last Things*. trans. Harold Knight, Richmond: John Knox Press, 1955.

Reardon, P. H. "Calvin on Providence: The Development of an Insight." *Scottish Journal of Theology* vol. 28, (1975): 517-534.

Reid, J. K. S. "The Office of Christ in Election." *Scottish Journal of Theology* vol. 1, no. 1, (1948): 5-18.

Reyburn, Hugh Y. *John Calvin: His Life, Letters and Work*. London: Hodder and Stoughton, 1914.

Rolston, Holmes III. *John Calvin versus the Westminster Confession*. Richmond: John Knox Press, 1972.

Rousselot, Pierre. *The Intellectualism of Saint Thomas*. trans. James E. O'Mahony. New York: Sheed and Ward, 1935.

Schaff, Philip, ed. *The Creeds of Christendom*. vol. III, Grand Rapids: Baker, 1990.

Schmidt, Albert-Marie. *John Calvin and the Calvinistic Tradition*. trans. Ronald Wallace, London: Longmans, 1960.

Smith, Ronald Gregor. *The Doctrine of God*. London: Collins, 1970.

Spykman, Gordon. "Sphere Sovereignty in Calvin and the Calvinist Tradition." *Exploring the Heritage of John Calvin*. ed. David E. Holwerda. Grand Rapids: Baker, 1982.

Steinmetz, David C. "Calvin and the Absolute Power of God." *Journal of Medieval and Renaissance Studies* vol. 18, no. 1, (Spring 1988): 65-79.

Stevenson, Peter Kenneth. *God in our Nature. The Incarnational Theology of John McLeod Campbell*. Eugene, Oregon: Wipf and Stock, 2006.

Stickelberger, Emmanuel. *John Calvin*. trans. David Georg Gelzer. Cambridge: James Clarke, 1977.

Trueman, Carl R. "Historically---Calvin and Reformed Orthodoxy." *The Calvin Handbook*, ed. Herman J. Selderhuis, trans. Henry J. Baron, *et. al.* Grand Rapids and Cambridge: William B. Eerdmans, 2009.

Storr, Vernon F. *The Development of English Theology in the Nineteenth Century 1800-1860*. London: Longmans, Green and Co., 1913.

Story, Robert Herbert. *Memoir of the Life of the Rev. Robert Story, Late Minister of Rosneath, Dunbartonshire*. Cambridge: Macmillan, 1862.

Stott, John. *The Cross of Christ*. Leicester: InterVarsity, 1986.

Strachan, Gordon. *The Pentecostal Theology of Edward Irving*. London: Darton, Longman and Todd, 1973.

Tamburello, Dennis E. *Union with Christ: John Calvin and the Mysticism of St. Bernard*. Louisville: Westminster John Knox Press, 1994.

Thimell, Daniel, "Christ in Our Place in the Theology of John McLeod Campbell." *Christ in Our Place: The Humanity of God in Christ for the Reconciliation of the World*. ed. Trevor Hart and Daniel Thimell. Exeter: Paternoster, 1989, 182-206.

Thomae Aquinatis, Divi. *Summa Theologica*. vols. 1-6, Leonine edition. Rome: Forzani, 1925.

Thomas Aquinas, St. *Basic Writings of Saint Thomas Aquinas*. two vols. trans., ed. A. C. Pegis. New York: Random House, 1945.

_____. *Commentary on St. Paul's Epistle to the Galatians*. trans. F. R. Larcher, Albany: Magi Books, 1966.

_____. *On Being and Essence*, trans. Armand Maurer, C.S.B., Toronto: Pontifical Institute of Medieval Studies, 1949, reprinted 1983.

_____. *On the Power of God*, trans. English Dominican Fathers. London: Burns, Oates and Washbourne, 1932.

_____. *On the Truth of the Catholic Faith*, [*Summa Contra Gentiles*]. six vols. trans. Anton C. Pegis, Charles J. O'Neil, Vernon J. Bourke, James F. Anderson. Garden City: Doubleday, 1955-1957.

_____. *Summa Theoloqiae.* vol. 1 (1a.1), trans., ed. Thomas Gilby O. P. London: Eyre and Spottiswoode, 1964.

_____. *Summa Theoloqiae.* vol. 2 (1a.2-11) trans., ed. Timothy McDermott O. P. London: Eyre and Spottiswoode, 1964.

_____. *Summa Theologiae.* vol. 3, (Ia. 12-14), ed. and trans. by Herbert McCabe. London: Eyre and Spottiswoode, 1964.

_____. *Summa Theoloqiae.* vol. 5, (1a.19-20), trans., ed. Thomas Gilby O. P. London and New York: Eyre and Spottiswoode, 1967.

_____. *Summa Theologiae.* vol. 8, (1a.44-49), trans., ed. Thomas Gilby O. P. London: Eyre and Spottiswoode, 1967.

_____. *Summa Theologiae.* vol. 13 (1a.12-13), trans., ed. Herbert McCabe O. P. London: Eyre and Spottiswoode, 1964.

_____. *Summa Theologiae.* vol. 16 (1a2ae, 1-5), trans. and ed. by Thomas Gilby O. P. London: Eyre and Spottiswoode, 1968.

_____. *Summa Theologiae.* vol. 26, (1a2ae.81-85), trans. T. C. O'Brien, 1966.

_____. *Summa Theologiae.* vol. 28, (1a2ae.90-97), trans., ed. Thomas Gilby O. P. London: Eyre and Spottiswoode, 1966.

_____. *Summa Theologiae.* vol. 29 (1a2ae.98-105), trans., ed. by David Bourke and Arthur Littledale. London: Eyre and Spottiswoode, 1969.

_____. *Summa Theologiae*. vol. 30 (la2ae.106-114), trans., ed. by Cornelius Ernst O. P. London: Eyre and Spottiswoode, 1969.

_____. *Summa Theologiae*. vol. 54 (3a.46-52), trans., ed. Richard T.A. Murphy O. P. London and New York: Eyre and Spottiswoode, 1965.

_____. *Summa Theologiae*. vol. 60, (3a.84-90), trans., ed. Reginald Masterson and T. C. O'Brien. London: Eyre and Spottiswoode, 1966.

_____. *Summa Theologica*. trans. Fathers of English Dominican Province. vol. 1 (1a.1-26), London: Burns, Oates and Washbourne, 1920.

_____. *Summa Theologica*. trans. Fathers of English Dominican Province. vol. 8 (1a.2ae.90-114), London: Burns, Oates and Washbourne, 1942.

_____. *Summa Theologica*. trans. Fathers of English Dominican Province. vol. 9 (2a.2ae.1-46), London: Burns Oates and Washbourne, 1916.

_____. *Summa Theologica*. trans. Fathers of English Dominican Province. vol. 15 (3a.1-26), London: Burns Oates and Washbourne, 1913.

_____. *Summa Theologica*. trans. Fathers of English Dominican Province. vol. 16 (3a.27-59), London: Burns Oates and Washbourne, 1926.

_____. *Summa Theologica*. trans. Fathers of English Dominican Province. vol. 17 (3a.60-83), London: Burns Oates and Washbourne, 1914.

_____. *Summa Theologica*. trans. Fathers of English Dominican Province. vol. 18 (3a.84-Suppl.33), London: Burns Oates and Washbourne, 1928.

_____. *Theological Texts*. ed., trans. Thomas Gilby. London: Oxford University Press, 1955.

_____. *Treatise on Happiness. (Summa Theologiae* la2ae, 1-21), trans. John A. Oesterle, Notre Dame: University of Notre Dame Press, 1983.

Thomas, Ivor Bishton. "John Calvin's Rejection of Roman Catholic Christianity." Th.D. dissertation, Union Theological Seminary, 1966.

Torrance, James B. "The Contribution of McLeod Campbell to Scottish Theology." *Scottish Journal of Theology* vol. 26, no. 3, (1973): 295-311.

_____. "The Incarnation and Limited Atonement." *Evangelical Quarterly* vol. 55, no. 3, (1983): 83-94.

_____. "The Priesthood of Christ." *Essays in Christology*. ed. T. H. L. Parker. London: Lutterworth Press, 1956, 153-74.

_____. "Strengths and Weaknesses of Westminster Theology." *The Westminster Confession in the Church Today*. ed. Alisdair I. C. Heron. Edinburgh: St. Andrews, 1982, 40-54.

_____. The Unconditional Freeness of Grace." *Theological Renewal*. no. 9, (June/July 1978): 7-14.

_____. "The Vicarious Humanity of Christ." Thomas F. Torrance. ed., *The Incarnation*. Edinburgh: Handsel, 1981, 127-47.

Torrance, T. F. *Calvin's Doctrine of Man*. London: Lutterworth Press, 1949.

_____. *The Hermeneutics of John Calvin*. Edinburgh: Scottish Academic Press, 1988.

_____. Introduction, John Calvin, *Tracts and Treatises on the Reformation of the Church*. vol. I trans. Henry Beveridge. Grand Rapids: Eerdmans, 1958, v-xli.

_____. "Scientific Hermeneutics According to St. Thomas Aquinas." *Journal of Theological Studies*, New Series, vol. XIII, pt. 2, (October 1962): 259-289.

_____. *Theology in Reconciliation*. London: Geoffrey Chapman, 1975.

_____. *Theology in Reconstruction*. London: SCM Press, 1965.

Torrell, Jean-Pierre O.P. *Aquinas' Summa: Background, Structure, and Reception*, trans. Benedict M. Guevin, O.S.B. Washington: Catholic University of America Press, 2005.

Tout, T. F. "The Place of Thomas in History." *Saint Thomas Aquinas*. Alfred Whitacre, O. P., Vincent McNabb, O. P., et. al., Oxford: Basil Blackwell, 1925.

Trinkhaus, Charles. "Erasmus and the Nominalists." *Archiv Fur Reformationsgeschicte* vol. 67, (1976): 5-32.

Tuttle, George Milledge. "The Place of John McLeod Campbell in British Thought Concerning the Atonement." Ph.D. dissertation, Victoria University of Toronto, 1961.

Tuttle. *John McLeod Campbell on Christian Atonement. So Rich a Soil*. Edinburgh: Handsel, 1986.

Van Buren, Paul. *Christ in our Place. The Substitutionary Character of Calvin's Doctrine of Reconciliation*. Edinburgh: Oliver and Boyd, 1957.

Vann, Gerald. *Saint Thomas Aquinas*. London: Hague and Gill, 1940.

Van Dyk, Leanne. *The Desire of Divine Love: John McLeod Campbell's Doctrine of the Atonement.* New York: Peter Lang, 1995.

Van Nieuwenhove, Rik and Wawrykow, Joseph, eds., *The Theology of Thomas Aquinas.* Notre Dame, University of Notre Dame Press, 2005

Velde, Rudi te. *Aquinas on God: The Divine Science of the Summa Theologiae.* Hants, England: Ashgate Publishing, 2006.

Verhy, John. "Calvin's 'Treatise Against the Libertines.'" *Calvin Theological Journal* vol. 15, no. 2, (November, 1980): 190-219.

Walker, Williston. *John Calvin, the Organizer of Reformed Protestantism.* London, 1906.

Wallace, Ronald S. *The Atoning Death of Christ.* Westchester: Crossway Books, 1981.

Wolfson, Henry Austryn. *Religious Philosophy,* Cambridge, MA: Belknapp Press, 1961.

Weber, Otto. *Foundations of Dogmatics.* vol. 1, trans. Darrell L. Guder. Grand Rapids: Eerdmans, 1981.

Weir, David A. *The Origins of the Federal Theology in Sixteenth-Century Reformation Thought.* Oxford: Clarendon Press, 1990.

Wendel, Francois. *Calvin. The Origins and Development of His Thought,* trans. Philip Mairet, London and Glasgow: Fontana, 1965.

Wiley, David Neeld. "Calvin's Doctrine of Predestination: His Principal Soteriological and Polemical Doctrine." Ph.D. dissertation, Duke University, 1971.

Williams, N. P. *The Grace of God.* London: Longmans, Green and Co., 1930.